Hanan Badr, Nahed Samour (eds.)
Arab Berlin

**Urban Studies**

*This publication is a result of the research project "Arab Perspectives on Transformation in Berlin", conducted by the Arab-German Young Academy of Sciences and Humanities (AGYA) and hosted at the Law & Society Institute, Humboldt-Universität Berlin. The project received funding from the Berlin Senate Chancellery – Higher Education and Research Berlin as a part of the broader collaborative research project "AGYA – Global Berlin in the 21st Century".*

**Hanan Badr** is a professor and chair for public spheres and inequalities at the Department of Communication, Universität Salzburg, Austria, and AGYA alumna. Her work focuses on global inequalities and communication, comparing media systems, activism and media, diversifying communication research, and how globalization and digitization transform journalism. She won awards including the Kluge Fellowship at the Library of Congress and the DAAD Scholarship Award.
**Nahed Samour** (Dr.) is a postdoctoral researcher and Core Emerging Investigator at the Integrative Research Institute Law & Society in the Faculty of Law at Humboldt University Berlin. She studied law and Islamic studies at the universities of Bonn, Birzeit/Ramallah, London (SOAS), Berlin (HU), Harvard, and Damascus. She was a doctoral fellow at the Max Planck Institute for European Legal History in Frankfurt/Main. She clerked at the Court of Appeals in Berlin, held a postdoc position at the Eric Castrén Institute of International Law and Human Rights, Helsinki University, Finland, and was an Early Career Fellow at the Lichtenberg-Kolleg, Göttingen Institute for Advance Study. She also taught as Junior Faculty at the Harvard Law School Institute for Global Law and Policy from 2014-2018. Her current work focuses on religion, race and gender in law.

Hanan Badr, Nahed Samour (eds.)

# Arab Berlin

Dynamics of Transformation

[transcript]

Disclaimer: The authors remain solely responsible for the content provided in this publication, which do not reflect the positions of AGYA or any of its funding partners.

agya
ARAB-GERMAN YOUNG ACADEMY OF SCIENCES AND HUMANITIES

SPONSORED BY THE
Federal Ministry of Education and Research

**Bibliographic information published by the Deutsche Nationalbibliothek**
The Deutsche Nationalbibliothek lists this publication in the Deutsche Nationalbibliografie; detailed bibliographic data are available in the Internet at http://dnb.d-nb.de



**First published in 2023 by transcript Verlag, Bielefeld**


Cover layout: Maria Arndt, Bielefeld
Copy-editing: Anne Hodgson, Berlin

https://doi.org/10.14361/9783839462638
Print-ISBN: 978-3-8376-6263-4
PDF-ISBN: 978-3-8394-6263-8
ISSN of series: 2747-3619
eISSN of series: 2747-3635

# Contents

## Introduction

## Part 1: Exile, Migration, and Belonging

## Part 2: Inclusion, Arts, and Activism



## Part 3: Social Life



## Part 4: Cultural Life

## Part 5: International Encounters in Education



## Part 6: Outlook

## Appendix

# List of Figures

# Introduction

# 1. Arab Berlin – Ambivalent Tales of a City

*Hanan Badr and Nahed Samour*

## Why Arab Berlin?

Is there a productive way to go beyond the omnipresent binary images of Arab Berlin? At present, many public debates engage with the binary images that come to mind: either the romanticized notions of Arab food fostered by the abundance of Arab restaurants and fast-food places dominating central neighborhoods of Berlin, or the securitized image of Arab Clans, especially in the German-language public discourses, reinforcing questionable and discriminatory policing practices and investigation methods (Özvatan, Neuhauser, Yurdakul 2023). Political party elites often push exclusionary media discourses and public debates, and the media flare up repeatedly to show that the multicultural façade has its limits. While there are vibrant dynamic communities on one side, there are also discriminatory structures on the other. This book asks whether a city with a multicultural façade offers equality for all its citizens and non-citizens. The reality says otherwise.[1] One recent prominent example is the debate about the violence on New Year's Eve of 2023. Dubbed the "Berliner Silversternacht-Krawalle", attacks targeted security forces, police, and firefighters in Neukölln, a neighborhood visibly populated by Arabs, despite ongoing gentrification. Immediately, conservative politicians and media coverage spoke of "little unintegrated pashas" living in their parallel societies and

1 For example, people with Arab and Turkish names are severely discriminated against on the German housing market. They are significantly less likely to be contacted by landlords than a German applicant. See Bayerischer Rundfunk/Der Spiegel, "No Place for Foreigners. Why Hanna is invited to view the apartment and Ismail is not" (2017), https://interaktiv.br.de/hanna-und-ismail/english/index.html. With no specific mention of Arab students, the study refers to recently immigrated school children and shows that young people with a migrant background are at a disadvantage in many respects compared to their non-migrant peers, with Berlin being particularly dire for these students. See Caritas Study (2019) Bildungssituation von jungen Menschen mit Migrationshintergrund (https://www.caritas.de) https://www.caritas.de/fuerprofis/fachthemen/kinderundjugendliche/bildungs-chancen/bildungssituation-von-jungen-menschen-mi. Similarly, see Bertelsmann Stiftung/Klemm, Klaus (ed.) (2023), Jugendliche ohne Hauptschulabschluss Demographische Verknappung und qualifikatorische Vergeudung.

violating law and order. This interpretation of the events in racist discriminatory language correlates origin and crime (Hauenstein 2023) and echoes right-wing sentiments that blame migrants for rising crime. This has been a trope since New Year's Eve 2015/16 in Cologne, when certain North African men sexually harassed women, leading to a nationwide discussion primarily directed against the migration of Arab Muslim men to Germany, stirring sentiments of "the Arab man" being sexually violent, not willing to integrate, and thus a danger to neoliberal freedoms (Dietze 2018). "Arab Berlin" picks up on these debates as they shape the lives and futures of Arabs and Germans, and Arab-Germans in Berlin. It engages with and resists a narrowing of debates that spread stereotypes and myths.

Five reasons make publishing this book of importance. First and foremost is that its core argument has not yet been made. The book covers a dire literature gap: much still needs to be said about Arab Berlin, whether in academic or public knowledge production, that goes beyond the binary Orientalist discourse trap. "Arabs in Berlin" was last comprehensively covered in 1998, when the Berlin Senate for Foreigners commissioned a study (Gesemann, Höpp and Sweis 1998). Transdisciplinary scholarship on Arab Berlin is still rare, if on the rise. The last twenty years (post 9/11) have seen literature appear on Muslims in Berlin (Spielhaus, Färber 2006; Mühe 2010), and since 2015 there has been research on Syrian refugees to Germany. "The Arab" has not been studied much as a category in the last twenty years, as "the Muslim" and "the refugee" have taken over. While these categories remain relevant, it strikes us that "the Arab" shares overlapping information with "the Muslim" and "the refugee" yet is not the same (Spielhaus 2013). Obviously, not all Arabs are Muslim, and neither are all Arabs refugees. It is essential to recognize the religious, cultural, and political diversity within the Arab communities and to take note of their different residential status.[2] The aim of this book is to capture this Arab diversity and simultaneously take note of the "figure of the Arab" that serves as foil for many political and legal dis-

2 On the diversity within the Arab community in the USA, see Moll, Yasemin (2023), Arab Americans are a much more diverse group than many of their neighbors mistakenly assume, https://theconversation.com/arab-americans-are-a-much-more-diverse-group-than-many-of-their-neighbors-mistakenly-assume-201930?fbclid=IwAR1KZgmo9kmmU3v53y_IQok8iKdeMl2dVHOtcdT3NM9hamFX36eTBLlmsEg.

cussions at the intersection of religion, race, and gender[3] as well as class and sexual orientation.[4,5]

The second argument for writing this book is to seek open engagement with the public debates around Arab Berlin through the book's kaleidoscopic and interdisciplinary approach. This means that the editors deliberately enter the conversation on "Arab Berlin" using an innovative approach by mixing different formats of publishing: articles, essays, interviews, and photos. Mixing long and short formats of knowledge production and mixing the academic with the journalistic tone is on purpose to engage with public discourse. We believe that the book produces knowledge and uses formats that are accessible and valuable to expert knowledge. This book articulates innovative forms of knowledge to challenge mainstream social theories and create newer forms of knowledge production. While using multiple formats might seem eclectic for academia, we believe it is a more inclusionary practice that offers a dynamic document full of living testimonies that often uses the journalistic account to give people a voice. The book is therefore not targeting an exclusively academic audience: it is a deliberate attempt to expand the elite language to connect with an audience beyond academia, from Berlin, Europe, and the world.

One of the reasons for developing this book is its connections to "Global Berlin in the 21st Century"[6], a multi-disciplinary project that pushed questions on where Berlin is heading in its global aspirations. The book engages with Berlin as a site of critical transformations globally situated within increasingly polarized democracies and rising tendencies towards the right. Berlin is a chiffre of the post-World War II liberal order, a place where seismic shifts can be observed at the same time in defense of provincialism and internationalism. Berlin is a location where transformation processes begin and new activities, possibilities, and lifestyles as well as experimental spaces open up.

3 On the intersection of religion, race and gender as captured in the concept of the "Gefährder", the potentially dangerous person in German security law, see Samour, Politisches Freund-Feind-Denken im Zeitalter des Terrorismus (2020), in: Andreas Kulick & Michael Goldhammer (eds.) Der Terrorist als Feind? Personalisierung im Polizei- und Völkerrecht, Mohr Siebeck, 49–66. See also the contribution in this book, Smour, The Arab in the law of Berin or: "How does it feel to be a problem?"

4 See Abdallah Iskandar "On framing and de-framing the queer Arab" in this book.

5 In 2022, Joe Biden was the first US president to recognize the Arab American Heritage Month, with some US states as well as the US State Department proclaiming April as Arab American Heritage Month. Biden celebrates April as Arab American Heritage Month | CNN.

6 'Global Berlin in the 21st Century' was carried out with renowned Berlin institutions and together with members of Arab German Young Academy of Sciences and Humanities (AGYA) members and alumni from Germany and the Arab world. The project was funded by the Senate Chancellery – Higher Education and Research of the State of Berlin.

It is one of Europe's megacities, a transforming society, and one of the "centers of Arab intellectual life in the West" (Ali, 2019). In the Arab world, Berlin is often described as an intellectual hub, a place to discuss academic and political freedoms, but also its crucial limitations (Tzuberi and Amir-Moazami 2022: Tzuberi and Samour 2022). Berlin can be perceived as a place influenced by general transformation processes, both liberal and illiberal, caused by phenomena like de/colonization, globalization, transculturality, debates on gender, religion, race and sexual orientation, media discourses, and changes through migration. The dynamics, dimensions, and effects of the transformation in Berlin are diverse and sometimes ambivalent. As a result, they are also subject to controversial debates. Berlin, in particular, seems to have developed into a center of Arab intellectual life that radiates this image and is appreciated beyond Germany's borders in the Arab world. In fact, the media also refer to Berlin as "Europe's capital of Arab culture" (Unicomb 2022). Some popular culture formats, like the Netflix movie The Swimmers, document the story of the Syrian Mardini sisters. Yet, crucial debates about Germany's memory politics, Germany's (lack of) decolonial efforts, and the Arab World as part of the Global South are not even taking place (Anonymous 2020). The intellectual life of this city is situated in its streets and civil society organizations, less so in its still largely homogenous universities and elite intellectual institutions.

Berlin seeks to strengthen its position as a city of increasing global visibility, motion, and relevance for the world and Arab migrants. The book therefore offers a resonance space to reflect its own identity and its desire to put itself on the map after the reunification in 1990s. Part of the ongoing debates about the Humboldt Forum in Berlin have shaped the debates about Berlin's commitment to restitution (Reimann and Samour 2022).

Returning the gaze is the fourth reason for writing this book. In the wake of Arab Uprisings since 2010/11, numerous academic publications focused on transformations in Arab countries from a Eurocentric, securitized epistemic perspective. Instead, the book editors shift the perspective to investigate transformations in Berlin, centering the gaze on the European context of Berlin as part of the Global North. This book employs bell hook's "oppositional gaze" by interrogating, questioning, and disrupting the power dynamics that usually rest the gaze on the Arab other, this time with a critical focus on "the Arab" as subject, object, and agent of transformations in Berlin. How did "the Arab" witness the various opportunities and challenges in a transforming Berlin? How did "the Arab" contribute to changes within Berlin's arts, media, culture, activism, in Berlin's social and cultural life, or in its educational and international encounters?

The fifth and most obvious reason for writing this book is the demographic transformation of Berlin's Arab population and its pronounced importance for Arab migrants and refugees. While the book does not claim representation of Arab voices in this book, it acknowledges the multi-layered formations of Arab presence in

Berlin and its complex evolution over the last decades, which witnessed a change in the constitution and formation of Arabs. Traditionally, starting in the 1970s, the Arab population in Berlin developed and changed in its characteristics. While until the 1980s, clear migration patterns marked the global migration flows in specific country pairs (for example Turkey-Germany, Algeria-France, etc.), since the 1980s, global migration patterns became more diverse and entangled in terms of background (Vertovec 2011). While Arabs in Berlin were largely Palestinian refugees from Lebanon in the 1970s (Ghadban 2000), in the last decade, the Syrian presence has gained strong visibility. Despite the increasing numbers of Arabs as German citizens, migrants, and refugees, they continue to be underrepresented in the official and formal administrative and legal-political structures (Bertelsmann, 2018).

## Two contradictory transformation processes

This book has one central argument: two contradictory processes are happening at the same time in Arab Berlin. The chapters capture the contrasting dynamics of transformation between the hard legal-political structure and soft dynamic culture in Arab Berlin. Outdated and illiberal structures lead to stagnation and exclusion on the one hand; innovative and fluid activities use the vibrant cultural scene through journalism, media, the arts (music, film, and others), and food to push toward a more inclusive future on the other. The imbalanced discourses on Arab Berlin show the persistent power of hegemonic frameworks, which reproduce cycles of exclusionary discourses of othering and discrimination. The contributions in this book, whether long academic articles, shorter essays and interviews, or photographic contributions, show those tensions.

Countless Arab initiatives claim cultural citizenship (Klaus and Lünenborg 2004) and enrich Berlin's cultural life through what have become prominent Arab spaces of cultural co-creation, including ALFILM, Oyoun, Khan Al-Janub, Bulbul, and many other initiatives establishing themselves in the city of Berlin. Some conservatives might label those valuable cultural spaces of self-determination as ghettoed fragmented public spheres, while other progressive voices might romanticize them as "multicultural initiatives". Instead, this book views those initiatives from a perspective that highlights Arab agency. Eman Helal, photographer and author in this book, speaks of the "Arab comfort zone" in Berlin.

While the book shows the arts and inclusion in Berlin's cultural and social life, it also shows an exclusionary side of Berlin. Academic scholarship and empirical evidence show that systematic discrimination of fundamental rights and freedoms occurs, even in Berlin, a city that has connected its identity with freedom since the Cold War. For Arab Berliners, the question of equality and anti-discrimination is central. It is at the intersection of religion and race in particular that the state views many

Arabs in this city. While recent studies center on anti-Muslim racism, of which anti-Arab racism must be seen as one dimension, racial *and* religious profiling (Samour 2020) constitute parts of their lives in their neighborhoods, schools, universities and workplaces.

In capturing those ambivalences of Berlin, we, the editors, together with the authors in this volume, argue that Berlin has both: it offers open spaces for a diverse intellectual life, yet it also restricts life through laws and practices that show that Berlin has not yet accommodated Arabs as equals in their midst.

## How this book was written

Throughout this book, the interpretations of contemporary transformations in Berlin vary depending on the areas in which they take place. This book's epistemic and critical intersectional position is on the margins (hooks, 1989). Located within the critical literature on migration in Germany, this book neither romanticizes Berlin nor serves as a tourism brochure. Therefore, the contributions do not seek to endorse the myth of "Multi-Kulti", the multiculturalism diversity discourse that neglects real power inequalities and exclusion (Eskandar 2022). By adopting a critical lens and engaging with post- and decolonial theory, we ask how the "colonial present" (Gregory 2004) can shed light on the realities of the various societal, cultural, and political transformations in Berlin and how they affect Arab Berlin individuals and communities. Paying attention to the epistemological paths of knowledge production, we examine where and how we can overcome coloniality as a concept of domination that persists in processes and in outcomes of research. By uncovering some areas of weakness or ignorance, the book counters the racialized epistemic violence in constructing the Arab, which permeates the public social constructions of Arabs in European cities (see Badr 2017). Epistemic violence rests on dynamics rooted in the modernity/coloniality project that began with Europe's colonial expansion and that reproduce persistent forms of biological and cultural racism (Brunner 2020: 39).

Arab Berlin follows a non-essentialist reductionist approach. No single intellectual work can capture the rich and multi-layered Arab presence in Berlin. On the contrary! Inspired by the critique of the Western knowledge formation that creates dichotomies in knowledge production and categorizes it into "West and the Rest" (Hall, 2012), in this book, we provocatively create the term Arab Berlin, which merges what could seem as two separate worlds. The central statement of this book would be, as Omaren and Gerlach express in their chapter, that Arabs have become a part of Berlin, too.

However, we do not want to reproduce essentialist perspectives that flatten and conflate "Arab existence" into one homogenous category. "The Arab" is applied here from a non-identitarian, non-deterministic perspective. This means the book did not narrow the contributions according to "birtherism" only giving voice to Arabs but allowed many voices working *with* and *on* Arab Berlin. We are also careful not to conflate Arabs with Muslims or negate other ethnicities, whether Kurds or Amazigh, or else. At the same time, the book cannot claim to capture entirely or offer a definition of what Arab Berlin is or should be, as there is no one 'single' Arab Berlin. Different epistemic perspectives on the city come both from insiders living in Berlin for decades and from newcomers. There are outsider perspectives, established and struggling, young and aged, and different life phases. In scouting the field, we have found many of Berlin's intellectual institutions to be sadly reluctant to engage with Arab thought going on at the community level: A case in point, while this book cannot reflect the many complex facets, it opens the discussion on selected central aspects.

Intensive emotional labor has been invested in this book: co-edited by two female POC scholars and mothers, the journey of writing this book was a roller-coaster during a globally difficult time of a pandemic, uncertainty, and global conflicts. We notice different subjective realities and a range of feelings and sentiments in this book, just as Berlin is full of emotions, sometimes extreme, at other times subtle. The feelings conveyed in the contributions range from excitement, confusion, disappointment, gratitude, love, rage, and hope. Even if the book editors critically reflect on the trope of the grateful migrant, readers will find gratitude in some chapters, and in others, they will find rejection and disillusionment. The book does not – and cannot – provide one coherent narrative for one Arab Berlin because the reality is complex. Our role as editors is not to *approve* of the contributors' articles in this book; instead, we see our role as curators who *enable* voices, positions, and portraits to speak.

## Structure of the book

This book examines the different structural, political, and cultural transformations in different fields in six parts. The wide range of contributions from different disciplines vary in tone and emotions. After this introduction that positions the book and explains its rationale, Part 1 entitled *Exile, Migration, and Belonging*, starts with an inspiring chapter by Amro Ali, "On the Need to Shape the Arab Exile Body in Berlin", echoing the multiple sentiments of Arabs in Berlin as an in/voluntary place of exile, a political laboratory, where Arab individuals and collectives dream and plan for freedom and equality, while also realizing that the "intellectual exile body" will always have to struggle for freedom and equality, including in Berlin, as subjects and objects of the Berlin "Zeitgeist".

In the third chapter, Abdolrahman Omaren and Julia Gerlach describe Amal, Berlin!, an online platform providing local news in Arabic, Dari/Farsi, and

Ukrainian. The initiative allows exiled professional journalists to produce relevant news as active participants in offering fact-checked information to the migrant communities. In the fourth chapter, Nazeeha Saeed, the award-winning journalist from Bahrain and a newcomer to Berlin, connects Berlin's past and present from a journalistic eye. Her chapter captures the contrast between the freedom the city promotes on the one side and the discrimination that Arab newcomers sometimes feel on the other, connecting the latter to what she terms the city's "collective trauma". Sonja Hegasy's chapter on "Hermeneutic Chicanery" is a contribution to the debate on migration and memory in Germany that points to ongoing debates between scholars of antisemitism, scholars of colonialism, postcolonial theorists, and scholars of comparative genocide studies. Refusing to play "Oppression Olympics", the chapter tries to enlarge our understandings and solidarities in comprehending past and present injustices. In the sixth chapter, Nahed Samour in "The Arab in the law of Berlin, or: 'How does it feel to be a problem?'" investigates how Arabs are addressed in the law of Berlin. Berlin's state law engages with Arabs as "minor citizens" or stateless subjects, as members of clans engaged in crime and therefore needing to be policed, their businesses raided. Pigeonholed as "not yet civilized", they are seen to need to be governed and taught what forms of speech and comportment are unacceptable behavior in a liberal democracy.

In Part 2 *Inclusion, Arts, and Activism* Iskandar Abdalla contributes the chapter "On framing and de-framing the queer Arab". Here he analyses the racialized existence of Arab queers in Berlin as an attempt to break with the figurative Orientalist formations of Arabness and Muslimness as identities. By doing so, he highlights ways of political subjectivity, despite Arabness as a marker on skin, body, family, trauma, and loss. In chapter eight, acclaimed photographer Mahmoud Dabdoub remembers life in East Berlin and shares fresh impressions of the early hours of the German reunification. "When I got off at Friedrichstraße, I was so happy to be back in East Berlin" is an account of an Arab Palestinian, who raises his hopes to overcome the wall and achieve reunification.

In his auto-biographic essay, "Berlin: A city of infinite dreams", Hashem El-Ghaili, a science communicator from Yemen with millions of followers worldwide, describes his first years in Berlin: "a city of infinite dreams", but also of "infinite problems". Berlin witnessed the production of his debut science fiction film, an important milestone in his career, offering valuable opportunities while showing the limits of accommodating highly skilled Arab ex-pats. The following chapter features an interview with Younes Al-Amayra, the co-founder of the German award-winning satire show *Datteltäter*. He describes how he uses satire to deconstruct radical social constructions and anti-Muslim discrimination. He perceives himself as closer to the Muslim community, which transcends the Arab category. At the same time, he shares his aspirations for more acceptance for People of Color (POC) in Berlin.

Part Three, entitled *Social Life*, focuses on dimensions of togetherness in Berlin. In an interview, Mahmoud Salem, a blogger and cybersecurity activist, compares Berlin to Cairo, as both megacities have an inescapable magnetic energy. He shares his disillusionment about living in Germany's capital, critiques the myth of the "poor and sexy" city, and reflects on enduring the Covid-19 lockdown in Berlin.

In chapter twelve, "The Tastes of Arab Berlin: Manifestations of Arab snack culture in the changing urban migration regime of Berlin," Miriam Stock explores the changing urban settings through an Arab infrastructure of restaurants, supermarkets, Shisha-bars, and cafés that navigate between the need to adapt to gentrification and respond to Orientalism.

In her essay, Abir Kopty, a Palestinian journalist and mother, writes about the challenges of parenting Arab children. Asking if her son will grow up to be sexist, she shares everyday situations that find her delicately balancing freedom and responsibility.

In their chapter, documentary photographer Eman Helal and media scholar Hanan Badr document "Biographies in Motion" in an academic-photographic cooperation that gives Arab newcomers who live in Berlin a voice and a face and lets them reflect on their own stories. The exhibition chronicles the protagonists' perspectives and experiences before coming to Germany to make their biographies count. It de-essentializes not only the images of the Arab migrants but also that of a romanticized Berlin.

Part 4 – *Cultural Life* – opens with a short critical essay by Fadi Abdulnour, "That's how you people do things round here, right?!". He questions the Orientalist stereotypes regarding what authenticity means for Arab people and critiques the assumptions about "authentic" Arab culture. Not only do such assumptions reproduce mainstream Eurocentric assumptions about the "other", but they also reduce the "Arab" to one homogenous category. In the interview with Christoph Dinkelaker, co-founder of Alsharq Travels, then explains how his specialized agency organizes political study trips for Germans to visit Arab countries to recognize the diversity within the Arab. He aims to promote awareness about colonialism, unite people and contribute to changing perceptions. In the interview, he recounts how a right-wing German participant on a trip to Lebanon gradually could see the diversity within the Arab societies. Arab Berlin is increasingly creating fragmentation but also chances for cooperation.

Seeing Berlin from the outside, philosophy scholar Mohammad Alwahaib in "Arendt's Shadow: Salam-Schalom from Berlin to the Holy Land" asks us to look beyond the separating rationale of the two-state paradigm for Palestine-Israel by using Hannah Arendt's work and by investigating the chances, and limits, of initiatives coming from the streets of Berlin, such as the Salam-Schalom initiative which counter such ideas of separation between Palestine and Israel and between racism and anti-Semitism.

In "Memories in the Nights of Despair": Jussuf Abbo in Berlin's Yiddish Literature of the 1920s, Tal Hever-Chybowski explores the artistic and intellectual contribution of sculptor and painter Yussuf Abbo (c. 1889–1953) in Berlin-Charlottenburg's avant-garde artistic and literary scene of the Weimar Republic. As a Palestinian-Arab Jew, Abbo engaged with the overlapping categories of identity regarding race, faith, language, and artistic stylization that were less restrictive in Berlin during the 1920s than today. Hever shares his astute observation that Yiddish-speaking Jews in Berlin "orientalized their Palestinian Jewish colleague Jussuf Abbo to westernize their own identity". This was a reaction to European Christian Orientalism that considered Jews and Arabs "to be '"oriental"' in character and essence".

Part 5 of this book is dedicated to the *Education & International Encounters* of Arab Berlin. In "Arabic Sciences in the Humboldtian Cosmos: Potentials for the Humboldt Forum", Detlev Quintern engages with Humboldt's appreciation of Arabic science, specifically geography and cartography, and the potentials of the Humboldtian non-Eurocentric universal history of science for the Humboldt Forum – one that opens up the cosmos for the Arab community in Berlin. In Chapter 20, scholar of Islam and Arabist, Islam Dayeh explores the academic career and influence of Ḥasan Tawfīq al-ʿAdl, the first native teacher of Arabic at the newly founded *Seminar für Orientalische Sprachen* at the Berlin Friedrich-Wilhelm University (Humboldt University today). While ʿAdl's achievements especially in Arabic literary history, have been recognized in Egypt's renowned academic institutions, they were erased from recognition in Berlin. Dayeh analyses encounters with German colonialism and scholarship and explores the erasure of the Arab academic.

Returning to the present day, Nadine Abdalla, a political scientist based at the American University in Cairo who frequently visits Berlin for academic cooperation, compares in her interview how academia works in Arab and German societies. She contrasts Berlin before and after COVID-19, describing how the pandemic changed the spirit of the otherwise accommodating city. Calling Berlin the new Arab cultural capital is an exaggeration, she says, even if the Arab presence is growing and increasingly diverse. In an interview with Florian Kohstall, head of the Global Responsibility Unit at the Center for International Cooperation of Freie Universität Berlin, he reflects on his journey from Cairo to Berlin, his motives for starting the Welcome@FU-Berlin program to support Arab refugee students, and what the intersections between the professional and personal mean for his work with the Arab region in educational encounters. Chapter 23 explores how Berlin can benefit from knowledge developed in the Arab World, Ehab El-Refaee, a neurosurgeoun between Germany and Egypt, traces back the relations in the medical field of higher education, reflecting on differences and similarities in medical training between Egypt and Germany at a time when medical staff is a global scarcity. He highlights the benefits of building a strong Cairo-Berlin connection in medical cooperation.

In the book's last part, entitled *Outlook*, Jan Claudius Völkel looks "Beyond Berlin: Why the rest of Germany also matters" and argues that other locations outside Berlin offer great transformative insights into Germany. Taking the reader on a journey to the Lusatia region, Görlitz, Hamburg, Munich, and the Rhine-Ruhr area, the author gives reasons to look for transformative potential beyond metropoles like Berlin to recognize contrasting dynamics taking place.

Finally, the book ends on a duality of hope and melancholy in the interview with Salah Yousif, a poet from Sudan who settled in Berlin in the 1970s. His is the voice of an Arab who has been here for many years, observing the joys, struggles, and meanings of being an Arab in Berlin. Looking from the past onto the future and maintaining a dialogue with the newcomers, Yousif's reflections on the migrants arriving in the city over the decades include the sad realization: "Always after a war, many people would come here."

## Conclusion

As the tour through the contributions in "*Arab Berlin: Dynamics of a Transformation*" shows: This is Berlin, with all its ambivalences and complexities! The book gives us an idea of the struggles for equality in this city, where equality as a liberal promise seems both tangible and elusive, often simultaneously. The idea of equality might not materialize for everyone in the same way, or even at all. This is why in addition to hope and the willingness to invest in the future of this city, we also read about reasons to worry over persistent structures of discrimination, hitting the old, in the fields of health, housing and workplace, as much as the young in the fields of school and education. The contributions in this book highlight the frictions, ambivalences, and spaces of light and shadow in a city that is longing for what it aspirates to become. It also highlights the potential missing to achieve what it could still become. The book is an invitation to diversify studies on the status of Arabs, Muslims, and refugees. Studying "the Arab in Berlin" is a way to dive into the rich history of Arabness as reflected and not reflected in Berlin. One book is not enough. *Arab Berlin* just starts a much-needed conversation.

Final words of acknowledgement are due: For this book to be published, we need to thank those who supported us during the process. First and most, we would like to thank Anne Hodgson, without her rigorous work, high professionalism, fascinating spirit, and fierce support and passion, this book would never see the light. We cannot thank you enough for supporting this book to get published.

We also want to thank our collaborator Dr. Beate LaSala, a member of the Arab-German Young Academy of Sciences and Humanities (AGYA), who laid the groundwork for this project.[7] We thank the Law & Society Institute at Humboldt-Universität zu Berlin for housing the project as an interdisciplinary work that engages with the normative and empirical layers of a community in Berlin.

The book was developed and realized within the framework of an AGYA project. We got to know each other through our membership in AGYA, where we mutually enriched and professionally developed ourselves through the interdisciplinary exchange, within the project and beyond. The book editors would like to thank AGYA Principal Investigator Prof. Dr. Verena Lepper, Egyptian Museum and Papyrus Collection, Germany, who had supported the publication as a part of the AGYA research project "Arab Perspectives on Transformation in Berlin". The editors wish to thank Dr. Sabine Dorpmüller and her colleagues Masetto Bonitz, Sebastian Fäth, and Ann-Cathrin Gabel of the AGYA Berlin Office who co-developed the Exhibition "Biographies in Motion", that is further described in detail in Chapter 14. The editors would deeply thank Julia Gerlach, who has not hesitated to cooperate in multiple ways, both as a contributor to the book and as a supporter of this project, who conducted the six interviews in this book, providing an important voice.

We express our gratitude to Daniel Baker, University of Cardiff, for proofreading the final manuscript. Furthermore, we thank Hannah Mauracher, Magdalena Hetz, Miriam Moderegger, and Deborah Fleischmann, student assistants at Paris Lodron University of Salzburg, who supported this book project in its various stages of production. We also would like to thank the Kluge Center at the Library of Congress for hosting the project in its final production phase.

The book editors also would like to thank Dr. Sabine Dorpmüller, AGYA Managing Director; Dr. Maria Röder-Tzellos, AGYA Deputy Managing Director; and Melanie Schreiber, Academic Coordinator at AGYA. They all supported the book project with thoughts and ideas, especially in the initial phase. Finally, the book editors would like also to thank their loving families, who have provided enormous encouragement and uplift throughout.

## References

Anonymous (2020) Palestine Between German Memory Politics and (De)Colonial Thought, Journal of Genocide Research 23(3) 1–9.

7 This publication is a result of the research project "Arab Perspectives on Transformation in Berlin," conducted by the Arab-German Young Academy of Sciences and Humanities (AGYA) and hosted at the Law & Society Institute, Humboldt-Universität Berlin. The project received funding from the Berlin Senate Chancellery – Higher Education and Research Berlin as a part of the broader collaborative research project "AGYA – Global Berlin in the 21st Century."

Badr, Hanan (2017) Framing von Terrorismus in Nahostkonflikt. Wiesbaden: Springer.

Bayerischer Rundfunk/Der Spiegel (2017) No Place for Foreigners. Why Hanna is invited to view the apartment and Ismail is not. https://interaktiv.br.de/hanna-und-ismail/english/index.html.

Bertelsmann Stiftung (2018) Kulturelle Vielfalt in Städten. (https://www.bertelsmann-stiftung.de/fileadmin/files/Projekte/Vielfalt_Leben/Studie_LW_Kulturelle_Vielfalt_in_Staedten_2018_01.pdf).

Brunner, Claudia (2020) Epistemische Gewalt: Wissen und Herrschaft in der kolonialen Moderne. Berlin: Transcript Verlag (https://www.transcript-verlag.de/978-3-8376-5131-7/epistemische-gewalt/).

Dietze, Gabriele (2018) Sexualitätsdispositiv Revisited, Die Figuration des "Arabischen Mannes", als Abwehrfigur neoliberaler Freiheit. In: Amir-Moazami, Schirin (ed.) Der inspizierte Muslim. Zur Politisierung der Islamforschung in Europa. Berlin: Transcript, 215–246.

El Bulbeisi, Sarah (2020) Tabu, Trauma und Identität. Subjektkonstruktionen von PalästinenserInnen in Deutschland und der Schweiz, 1960–2015. Berlin: Transcript.

Eskandar, Wael (2022) Ice Cream with German Police. Dis:orient, July 28 (https://www.disorient.de/magazin/ice-cream-german-police).

Gesemann, Frank; Höpp, Gerhard; Sweis, Haroun (1998) Araber in Berlin. Berlin: Die Ausländerbeauftragte des Senats.

Ghadban, Ralph (2000) Die Libanon-Flüchtlinge in Berlin. Zur Integration ethnischer Minderheiten. Berlin: Das Arabische Buch.

Gregory, Derek (2004) The Colonial Present. Maiden, MA and Oxford, UK: Blackwell Publishing.

Hall, Stuart (1992) The West and the Rest: Discourse and Power. In: Gieben, Bram; Hall, Stuart (eds.) Formations of Modernity, Oxford, 276–314.

Hauenstein, Hanno (2023) Silversternacht: Die Böller-Debatte ist rassistisch. Berliner Zeitung, January 3 (https://www.berliner-zeitung.de/mensch-metropole/silvesternacht-die-boeller-debatte-ist-rassistisch-li.303337).

hooks, bell (1989). Choosing the Margin as a space of radical openness. Framework: The Journal of Cinema and Media, 36, 15–23.

Klaus, Elisabeth; Lünenborg, Margreth (2004) Cultural Citizenship: Ein kommunikationswissenschaftliches Konzept zur Bestimmung kultureller Teilhabe in der Mediengesellschaft. Medien- und Kommunikationswissenschaft M&K 52(2) 193–213. https://www.nomos-elibrary.de/10.5771/1615-634x-2004-2-193/cultural-citizenship-ein-kommunikationswissenschaftliches-konzept-zur-bestimmung-kultureller-teilhabe-in-der-mediengesellschaft-jahrgang-52-2004-heft-2?page=1

Klemm, Klaus (ed.) (2023) Jugendliche ohne Hauptschulabschluss. Demographische Verknappung und qualifikatorische Vergeudung. Bertelsmann Stiftung.

Moll, Yasemin (2023) Arab Americans are a much more diverse group than many of their neighbors mistakenly assume. The Conversation, April 12 (https://theconversation.com/arab-americans-are-a-much-more-diverse-group-than-many-of-their-neighbors-mistakenly-assume-201930?fbclid=IwAR1KZgm09kmmU3v53y_IQok8iKdeMl2dVHOtcdT3NM9hamFX36eTBLlm).

Mühe, Nina (2010) Muslime in Berlin, At Home in Europe Project, Open Society Initiative.

Özvatan, Özgür; Neuhauser, Bastian; Yurdakul, Gökçe (2023) The 'Arab Clans' Discourse: Narrating Racialization, Kinship, and Crime in the German Media, Soc. Sci. 12(2) 104 (https://www.mdpi.com/2076-0760/12/2/104).

Reimann, Isabelle; Samour, Nahed (2022) Vom individuellen Unrechtskontext zum systematischen Umgang mit kolonialem Unrecht, Verfassungsblog. (Debate on Restitution, Colonialism and the Courts) Verfassungsblog, December 7 (https://verfassungsblog.de/vom-individuellen-unrechtskontext-zum-proaktiven-umgang-mit-kolonialem-unrecht/).

Samour, Nahed (2020) Artikel 5 f, in: Doris Angst/Emma Lantschner (eds.), Internationales Übereinkommen zur Beseitigung jeder Form von Rassendiskriminierung (ICERD), Nomos, 378–387.

Samour, Nahed (2020) Politisches Freund-Feind-Denken im Zeitalter des Terrorismus. In: Kulick, Andreas; Goldhammer, Michael (eds.), Der Terrorist als Feind? Personalisierung im Polizei- und Völkerrecht. Mohr Siebeck, 49–66.

Skornia, Anna Katharina (2019) Bildungssituation von jungen Menschen mit Migrationshintergrund. Deutscher Caritasverband e.V. Referat Migration und Integration (https://www.caritas.de/fuerprofis/fachthemen/kinderundjugendliche/bildungschancen/bildungssituation-von-jungen-menschen-mi).

Spielhaus, Riem (2013) Vom Migranten zum Muslim und wieder zurück – Die Vermengung von Integrations- und Islamthemen in Medien, Politik und Forschung. In: Halm, Dirk; Meyer, Hendryk (eds.), Islam und die deutsche Gesellschaft, Islam und Politik. Wiesbaden: Springer, 169–194.

Spielhaus, Riem; Färber, Alexa (eds.) (2006) Islamisches Gemeindeleben in Berlin, Der Beauftragte des Senats für Integration und Migration, Berlin.

Tzuberi, Hannah, Amir-Moazami, Schirin (2022) Introduction: Memory Politics and Minority Management in Europe. RePLITO, February 4 (https://replito.de/archive/archiveDetails?Id=62).

Tzuberi, Hannah; Samour, Nahed (2022) The German State and the Creation of Un/Desired Communities. University of Notre Dame: Contending Modernities, February 22 https://contendingmodernities.nd.edu/theorizing-modernities/the-german-state-and-the-creation-of-un-desired-communities/.

Unicomb, Matt (2021) Berlin: Inside Europe's capital of Arab culture. Middle East Eye, October 11 (https://www.middleeasteye.net/discover/berlin-germany-europe-capital-arab-culture).

Vertovec, Steven (2011) The Cultural Politics of Nation and Migration. Annual Review of Anthropology, Vol. 40, 241–256 (http://dx.doi.org/10.1146/annurev-anthro-081309-145837).

# Part 1: Exile, Migration, and Belonging

# 2. On the Need to Shape the Arab Exile Body in Berlin

*Amro Ali*[1]

> "These streets lose themselves in infinity [...] a countless human crowd moves in them, constantly new people with unknown aims that intersect like the linear maze of a pattern sheet." – Siegfried Kracauer on Berlin, "Screams on the Street" (1930).

Dislocating the Arab future from the grip of the political bankruptcy and moral morass in the Arab world might appear remote and relegated to the domain of quixotic dreams. But does it need to be that way? As communities are unsettled, resistances triggered, a chorus of voices fired up, waves of bodies set in motion for justice, and a range of emotions roused even when they no longer have an appetite, can the continued onslaught on reality not also reinvigorate political thought?

The procession of dislocation that materialized in 2011 has been viciously derailed since. Now, to coherently embark upon a regenerated starting point in this long journey of political redemption, a "we" is required: This feeds from new political ideas, collective practices and compelling narratives that are currently re-constructed and brought to life in a distantly safe city.

Berlin is where the newly-arrived Arab suddenly (but not always) recognizes that the frightful habit of glancing over the shoulder – painfully inherited from back home – gradually recedes. All the while, a new dawn slowly sets in among the meeting of peers in this new city: As such, Berlin is not just a city. It is a political laboratory that enforces a new type of beginning, one that turns heads in the direction of matters greater than the individual; and it generates a realization that the grey blur that nauseatingly blankets the future can actually be broken up.

Following the 2011 Arab uprisings and its innumerable tragic outcomes, Berlin was strategically and politically ripe to emerge as an exile capital. For some time now, there has been a growing and conscious Arab intellectual community, the political dimensions of which to fully crystalize is what I wish to explore further.

When the storm of history breaks out a tectonic political crisis, from revolutions to wars to outright persecution, then a designated city will consequently serve as the

1 Acknowledgment: The author published a longer version of this chapter on January 23, 2019, on dis:orient https://www.disorient.de/magazin/need-shape-arab-exile-body-berlin

gravitational center and refuge for intellectual exiles. This is, for example, what New York was for post-1930s Jewish intellectuals fleeing Europe, and what Paris became for Latin American intellectuals fleeing their country's dictatorships in the 1970s and 1980s.

Against those historical precedents, the Arab intellectual community in Berlin needs to understand itself better, moving away from an auto-pilot arrangement, and become actively engaged with political questions that face it. In effect, there is a dire necessity for this community to acquire a name, shape, form and a mandate of sorts. With a vigorous eye to a possible long-term outcome, this may include a school of thought, a political philosophy or even an ideational movement – all cross-fertilized through a deeper engagement with the Arab world.

This is certainly not about beckoning revolutions and uprisings, nor to relapse into the stale talk of institutional reforms. If anything, there needs to be a move away from these tired tropes of transformation – away from quantifiable power dynamics that do not address matters that go deeper, into the existential level that shores up the transnational Arab sphere. This is the very area where the stream of human life animates a language of awareness and the recurring initiative helps to expand the spaces of dignity for fellow beings. Yet, this area is currently ravaged in a torrent of moral misery and spiritual crisis.

## Freedom as wanderer

So here we are: Between Berlin's spirited idiosyncrasies and an Arab community maturing away from "ordinary" diasporic pathways lies the foment of the politically possible.

> "I was born in Tunisia, lived in Egypt, and gave my blood in Libya. I was beaten in Yemen, passing through Bahrain. I will grow up in the Arab World until I reach Palestine. My name is Freedom."

This popular streak, and variations of it, could be heard throughout the Arab world in February 2011 when hope for revolution was at its peak after the fall of Tunisia's Zine El Abidine Ben Ali and Egypt's Hosni Mubarak. Within it, freedom is a wanderer that carries contagions as it roams across Arab borders.

Syria was not yet in the verse. The revolutionary moment there would launch in March 2011 and it would be the Syrians that would pay the highest price of an ephemeral euphoria that evaporated into the terrestrial orbit of actual change. In its stead, wandering freedom turned into a dystopian monster as hundreds of thousands became themselves forced wanderers. The Mediterranean Sea, long celebrated for its grace and splendour, became a morbid burial ground of people fleeing for safety.

Buttressed by the refugee waves, an intellectual flow of academics, writers, poets, playwrights, artists, and activists, among others, from across the Arab world gravitated towards Berlin as sanctuary and refuge. This took place against the backdrop of a long-established Turkish presence (initiated by the 1961 Guestworker Treaty) and Chancellor Angela Merkel's 2015 refugee intake that partly shaped the post-2011 Arab transition.

A unique Arab milieu began to take form as new geographic, social, and cultural conditions necessitated a reconstruction of visions and practices. The exile body built on the embers and mediated on the ashes of a devastated Arab public left burning in the inferno of counter-revolutions, crackdowns, wars, terrorism, coups, and regional restlessness. It was that public that authoritarian regimes had worked so hard to contain and that everyday people battled courageously to reclaim. Tunisia's Mohamed Bouazizi set himself ablaze at the close of 2010 and, ever since, opened possibilities for claims and struggles.

The newcomers to Berlin were thrown under the weight of newfound political obligations to their countries of origin. They did, after all, depart with a guilt-ridden sense of unfinished business. The Arab uprisings brought about a hiatus between the "no-longer" and the "not-yet."[2] The individual transitioned from bondage to freedom that broke the chains of work and biological necessity. The result was an imagination unleashed to see humans thrive in freedom and exhibit their capacity to make a new beginning, only for the subsequent journey to be stomped upon by the weight of the jackboot and silenced by the thud of the judge's gavel hammer.

Yet in this gap of historical time, individual greatness and the passion of public freedom blossomed while a new character formed through the tear gas, streets, protests, and coffeehouses. In a marvellous transformation, they could "no longer recognize their pre-2011 self."[3] Hence, the arrival in Berlin not only came with an incomplete political consciousness, but an anxiety to resist a return to the "weightless irrelevance of their personal affairs,"[4] as German-Jewish philosopher Hannah Arendt conveys it. This denotes a pre-political spectre that rips the individual from group agency, and obliterates their biography from history. That is to say, the pre-2011 ghost still haunts the Arab community that settles in Berlin and learns to move within the terrain of hospitality and enmity.[5]

---

2 Hannah Arendt (1973) On Revolution. Harmondsworth: Penguin: 205.

3 Amro Ali (2016) The Hidden Triumph of the Egyptian Revolution. Open Democracy, January 25 (https://www.opendemocracy.net/en/north-africa-west-asia/hidden-triumph-of-egyptian-revolution).

4 Hannah Arendt (1977) Between Past and Future: Eight Exercises in Political Thought. Harmondsworth: Penguin: 4.

5 "...the foreigner...has to ask for hospitality in a language which by definition is not his own, the one imposed on him by the master of the house, the host, the king, the lord, the authorities, the nation, the State, the father, etc...That is where the question of hospitality begins: must

On the one hand, this new community navigated between the support and collaboration of German institutions, civil society, universities, cultural spaces, left-wing politics, churches, mosques, the large Turkish community, and a fluctuating German sense of responsibility to the refugee crisis.

On the other hand, the Arab community is menaced by local racism, a growing far-right movement in the form of the Alternative for Germany (AfD), Arab embassies, foreign security agencies and reactionary sections of the diaspora. Moreover, its members are thrown down and disoriented by the modern malaise of the "Inferno of the Same". This is how Berlin-based South Korean philosopher Byung-Chul Han aptly describes a world of unceasing repetition of similar experiences masquerading as novelty and renewal.

Consequently, we are seeing love – with all its earmarks of commitment, intimacy, passion, and responsibility – struggle to swell through the ranks from relationships to community-building in a world of "endless freedom of choice, the over-abundance of options, and the compulsion for perfection."[6]

Not only is fragmentation fomented by the upheaval caused by exile and transition, the individual in general struggles to flesh out a position towards a world that has become increasingly noisy and blurred. A world that has scrambled the once-relatable relationship between time and space, now under the neoliberal storm is turning responsible citizens into hyper-individual self-seeking consumers, discharging a plastic one-size fits all repetition of behaviour that precludes deeper forms of unity and a communal spirit.

Nonetheless, even with the challenges it confronts, the Arab community is unfolding in the shadow of complex socio-political ecologies and wide-ranging entanglements that are arguably unprecedented in modern history. Hitherto, most forced Arab migrations have happened on a country by country and era by era basis, such as Libyans fleeing Gaddafi's regime in the 1970s, or the Lebanese fleeing the civil war in the 1980s. Moreover, transnational Arab relocation to the Gulf was primarily spurred on by economic factors, to say nothing of their residency that hinged on the shunning of any hint of politics. In contrast, we are currently witnessing the first ever simultaneous pan-Arab exodus consisting of overlapping legitimacies – beyond culture, religion, nationality and economics – born of the Arab Spring.

This new exile marvel is brewing in a cultural flux with questions that are only beginning to be raised. Exile is meant here, as Edward Said writes, as "the unhealable rift forced between a human being and a native place, between the self and its

---

we ask the foreigner to understand us, to speak our language, in all the senses of this term, in all its possible extensions, before being able and so as to be able to welcome him into our country?" Jacques Derrida/Anne Dufourmantelle (2000) Of Hospitality. Stanford: Stanford University Press: 15.

6 Byung-Chul Han (2017a) The Agony of Eros, Untimely Meditations. Cambridge: MIT Press: 1.

true home."[7] Additionally, exile transpires irrespective of one being banished from the homeland, living in legal limbo, studying at university, or even one who recently acquired German citizenship. We are talking about exile as a mental state,[8] where even if you faced no political persecution if you chose to return to your country of origin, you would still feel alienated by a system that can no longer accommodate your innate or learned higher ideals.

For example, in late 2015, I attended the screening of a Syrian film in Kreuzberg titled True Stories of Love, Life, Death and Sometimes Revolution. During the question and answer session, a fellow country man in the audience asked the film's co-director, Nidal Hassan, "What can we Syrian artists even do now given that we are in exile?" Hassan replied entrancingly: "We were in exile even in Syria...we just have to continue to change the world through our practices."

From another angle, Dina Wahba, Egyptian doctoral researcher at Berlin's Freie Universität, evocatively pens the exile consciousness: "I get out, look around, and realize how beautiful it is. I feel guilty that I'm here, while some of my friends are in dark cells. I also feel guilty that I'm here and not enjoying all this beauty. Crippling fear has crossed the Mediterranean and taken over my mind. Fear is a strange thing. I cannot go home, but neither can I make a home here."[9]

As such, the sense of exile in Berlin is deepened by a wide-ranging emotional spectrum: From an all-consuming survivor's guilt vis-à-vis those that stayed behind down to a pleasant stroll through Tiergarten Park in which a nagging thought might arise that whispers, "if only back in Cairo we had such large free unmolested spaces to breathe in."

## Converging points into lines of meaning

Arab Berlin, since 2011, has sprang a swathe of energetic pockets of creativity and thought. Yet, there is something missing in these hyper-present moments: the dynamic spaces from theatre to academia to civil society volunteering are fragmented and rarely talk to each other, not to mention the disconnect from the wider Arab community. You cannot help but sense that the creative and intellectual efforts are

---

7 Edward W. Said (2000) Reflections on Exile and Other Essays. Cambridge: Harvard University Press: 173.

8 As Palestinian poet Mahmoud Darwish once put it: "Exile is more than a geographical concept. You can be an exile in your homeland, in your own house, in a room." See Adam Shatz (2001) A Poet's Palestine as a Metaphor. New York Times, December 22 (https://www.nytimes.com/2001/12/22/books/a-poet-s-palestine-as-a-metaphor.html).

9 Dina Wahba (2018) Diaspora Stories: Crippling Fear and Dreams of a Better Home. Mada Masr, August 16 (https://www.madamasr.com/en/2018/08/16/opinion/u/diaspora-stories-crippling-fear-and-dreams-of-a-better-home/).

hurled into a void rather than being taken up by a greater political current that can extract these experiences and marshal them towards a pre-eminent narrative.

This problem, if we can call it that, is not unfamiliar with the city's inherent contradictions. Strangely enough, it still echoes Siegfried Kracauer's 1932 essay "Repetition". The cultural critic and film theorist wrote that Berlin

"is present-day and, moreover, it makes it a point of honour of being absolutely present-day... His [the inhabitant's] existence is not like a line but a series of points... Many experience precisely this life from headline to headline as exciting; partly because they profit from the fact that their earlier existence vanishes in its moment of disappearing, partly because they believe they are living twice as much when they live purely in the present."[10]

The irony, therefore, is that the strength that makes up the Berlin tempest that unleashes the creative and intellectual Arab energies, also happens to be its dissolution as its intense present breaks with past and future. That is to say, the exile might pursue the present as a way to escape or numb the trauma or crippling melancholia haunting the past, and anxiety saturating the future. But this can often mean the self is reduced to individual interests with the exciting present acting no more than a euphoric smokescreen of collective advancement.

How does one obstruct the trap that enmeshes the Arab Berliner?

As the late sociologist David Frisby writes about Kracauer's idea, the crux is this: "This moment of presentness itself, however, never remains present. It is always on the point of vanishing. Hence the endless search for the ever-new and the permanent transformation of consciousness of time in metropolitan existence."[11]

This makes for the need to chase the next project or seek out the next donor, which is not simply driven by excitement as much as it is foisted upon today's entrepreneur of the self. As they self-exploit in their respective enterprise, the individual is made into "master and slave in one."[12]

Nonetheless, excitement is intimately tied to a never-ending present. Thus, the questions that arise: How does one interrupt this endless fluidity and "recycling" of presents? How can one address an animated present that seems somehow ruptured from building up on the past and navigating into the future? How does one obstruct

---

10 David Frisby (1985) Fragments of Modernity: Theories of Modernity in the Work of Simmel, Kracauer and Benjamin, Social and Political Theory. Cambridge: Polity: 142.

11 Ibid.: 141.

12 Byung-Chul Han (2015a) The Burnout Society. Stanford: Stanford University Press: 49. As Han notes, neoliberalism has transformed the oppressed worker into a free contractor, and class struggle has given way to internal struggle within one's inner being. This is set up so that anyone who fails to succeed has to feel shame and cannot blame anyone but themselves. Therefore, governments, institutions, society, and structural factors, are absolved of any responsibility.

the trap that enmeshes the Arab Berliner? How, that is, to alter the individual's scattered series of points that Kracauer alluded to and move towards a meaningful line that elevates the exile's relationship, not only to their life trajectory, but to an existential understanding in the body-politic that potentially pushes a narrative greater than the individual?

One way to understand this body-politic and appreciate Berlin's intervention in this novel community, as well as the attempts of its members to make meaning of their new-found roles and the political environment that shapes them, would be vis-à-vis other cities. This serves to examine the elephant in the room, however prudently: Why cannot other western cities with large Arab populations qualify as the intellectual exile hub?

## The Berlin Anomaly

Western cities like London, Paris and New York would have been the expected post-2011 intellectual hubs given the large number of Arabs present within them. Yet, they have arguably all fallen behind Berlin. This cannot simply be explained in terms of dynamic diversity and cultural production, which is certainly not lacking in either of these three cities. Rather, they all appear to have a relative absence of ingredients that lead to the blossoming of a full-fledged political exile community like we are witnessing in Berlin.

To start, there seems to be a common view among Arab and Muslim groups that London is dominated by the Muslim Brotherhood and Islamists, while Berlin offers more space for pluralism. But London's biggest hurdle, in fact, might be the high cost of living. To take a simple example: One has to think twice before buying an expensive London tube ticket. In contrast, Berlin's U-Bahn and S-Bahn are affordable, which alone speaks volumes for the necessity of mobility required in community building. The repercussions of Brexit also diminished the grand city of London in many eyes and worsened an already difficult visa entry.

Paris, while popular with Algerian, Tunisian, Moroccan, Lebanese, and Syrian intellectuals, is generally viewed as closed off and limited to the Francophone world. Also, the historical legacy of colonialism will generally taint any initiative coming out of London and Paris. While New York is clouded by US foreign policy and the current administration, the security mesh makes it burdensome to enter the country. Moreover, high living costs and distance from the Arab world also complicate its appeal.

Naturally, there are cultural trends that unfold across all these cities post-2011, which is why similar community formations should be encouraged. However, the cultural and political dynamics that materialise in Berlin, backed with intensity and creativity by wide-ranging institutional and grassroots support, summons Berlin and the Arab exile body to be assigned into a shared conversation.[13] If one listens closely, the hoofbeats of Arab history are reverberating out of Berlin more than any other western counterpart.

On this note, Istanbul is frequently touted as the Arab exile hub, and indeed it could easily rival Berlin had it not been for some conveniently overlooked factors. Arab activities are largely permitted if they correlate ideologically with, or not speak against, Erdogan's illiberal government. One might raise the question as to why would this be a problem if a gracious host is enabling an Arab community to thrive that would, in any case, only be concerned with external issues?

For a start, this selfish approach deflects from the grim reality that sees Turkish academics and journalists censored or imprisoned, a grave matter that should raise concern among Arab democratic aspirations. It is one thing, and understandable, to be grateful to a majestic Istanbul that gives one abode and freedom to flourish. But it is an unsettling hypocrisy to trumpet the city as a free intellectual hub while ignoring its own Turkish citizens who are attacked for voicing thoughts that deviate from the official line. Fundamental values that are compromised, particularly this drastically, are no longer values but more like hobbies. A draconian environment that divulges its effect on Turkish skin will inadvertently skew Arab intellectual development and ultimately make it difficult to garner a better representation of exile voices and thought processes.

In light of the brutal murder of Saudi journalist Jamal Khashoggi in the Saudi consulate in Istanbul, one wonders if Turkey's entangled relationship in the region does not furnish Istanbul with sufficient geographical and mental distance to render it beyond scrutiny. Had this gruesome act taken place in the Saudi embassy in Berlin, the consequence, one could reasonably speculate, would have come at a higher price for the Saudi crown prince. The weight of Germany and the EU might have been enough to abort or postpone a planned assassination.

This is not to rule out the immense potential of Istanbul's Arab community. After all, Khashoggi himself saw the city as a "base for a new Middle East."[14] It is just

13 A number of institutions and initiatives have been central to the German-Arab cultural exchange and collaboration. Among them: Free University, Humboldt University, Forum Transregionale Studien, the Goethe Institute (and its support of institutions such as the Arab Image Foundation); German Academic Exchange Service (DAAD) and its support of Arab artists and intellectuals (e.g. Akram Zaatari, whose films often show in the short competition of the Berlin Film Festival); Transmediale (which formerly ran the Arab Shorts Program); the Barenboim-Said Academy which is not only a site for Arab arts, intellectual exchanges and conferences but, perhaps, the largest scholarship program for Arab musicians in the world. Overall, the spectrum is wide, from the various foundations of the political parties and the Foreign Office, to the neighborhood dynamics in Neukölln along Sonnenallee street.

14 Sarah El Deeb (2018) Saudi Writer Saw Turkey as Base for a New Middle East. Associated Press News, October 21 (https://apnews.com/5643bc71beaf43249527f1e0d14dd67b).

that the current political incarnation comes with many bouts of wariness that need to be better understood, discussed, and thought through carefully. Thus, if current developments hold, we can expect in the distant future two competing Arab schools of thinking to emerge out of Berlin and Istanbul.

Yet, unlike Istanbul, London, Paris, and New York (vis-à-vis the US) which cannot claim historical "neutrality," the function of Berlin works strangely well as it is linked to a peculiar backdrop: The contemporary Arab approach towards Germany is premised on the notion that it was never a colonizer or invader of Arab lands. The 1941–43 Afrika Korps is given little attention in Arab historiography (although this should not detract from the dark ties that some Arab elites pursued with Nazi Germany).

In other words, Germany was not a colonizer like France or Great Britain, nor does it have an aggressive foreign policy like the US, let alone evokes ambivalence like Turkey does. Arab positions are then deducted from this negative admiration that is rarely questioned in the popular Arab worldview. However, this obfuscates the stealth colonial endeavour that lacks theatrics. German companies like Siemens and ThyssenKrupp have long been implicated in the "colonial dynamics of economic subjugation" that deepens, for example, Egypt's chronic underdevelopment, corruption, and even the skewed "technological conception of modernity," as Omar Robert Hamilton argues.[15] Yet, Germany walks away unscathed and gets praised as the country of organisation, discipline, efficiency, and Mercedes Benz.

The idea of Germany rarely arouses a divisiveness and antagonism that would aggravate Arab security officials or activists. The paradox of its power is that the savagery Germany committed in the first half of the twentieth century skirts around the Arab world. While German orientalism is not alien to Arab scholarship, this is not what is usually or immediately deplored in Arab scholarly circles and the Arab imaginary regarding Germany – to that country's stroke of luck.[16] Even strong Ger-

---

15 Hamilton frames his argument through the work of political scientist Franz Neumann who interestingly wrote in 1944 that "foreign trade may be a means of enriching a higher and better-organised nation at the expense of the less industrialized. This is the essence of foreign trade even under conditions of free competition... We believe that on the world market, commodities are not exchanged at their value, but that, on the contrary, a more industrialized country exchanges less labor for more. Foreign trade, under conditions of free competition, is thus the means of transferring profits." See Omar Robert Hamilton (2018) Industrial Colonialism: Egypt, Germany and the Maintenance of the Modern World. Mada Masr, July 5 (https://www.madamasr.com/en/2018/07/05/opinion/u/industrial-colonialism-egypt-germany-and-the-maintenance-of-the-modern-world/).

16 Perhaps two historical anecdotes can capture the essence of the Arab imagination's complex juxtapositioning that endorses Germany over other European powers. When Kaiser Wilhelm II visited Damascus in 1898, he approached the tomb of Saladin and stated: "Let me assure His Majesty the Sultan [Abdulhamid II] and the 300 million of Muslims who, in whatever corner of the globe they may live, revere in him their khalif, that the German Emperor will ever

man support for Israel does not elicit the same degree of Arab anger towards it as with the US and UK, partly because of the sound popular view that Germany is coerced by historical guilt. So, in a sense, Germany is conditionally, if not grudgingly, let off the hook.

## The city above all

However, this endeavor is more about Berlin than Germany. A city not only telescopes political dynamics of community building, but it will always exist timelessly as "an important crystallization of human civilization and its discontents."[17] By coming to terms with Berlin as a political, social, and cultural laboratory, it will be possible to illuminate the current Arab community that is shaped by a historical pattern of sites of sanctuary and exile agency.

The German art critic Karl Scheffler perhaps immortalized the essence of the German capital in 1910 with the words, "Berlin dazu verdammt: immerfort zu werden und niemals zu sein" (Berlin is a city condemned forever to becoming and never to being).[18] What Scheffler thought to be a disadvantage because of the city's "lack of organically developed structure" turned out to have hidden advantages.[19] As German writer Peter Schneider observes, the word werden, "becoming", encapsulates notions such as on the "cusp of becoming", "up-and-coming," "new Berlin," the impeding effort to transform itself but not quite there yet.

These themes of liminality strongly resonate with the self-perception of the growing Arab intellectual community's idea of rebuilding, transforming and becoming. Berlin's imperfection, sketchiness, and incompleteness, furnish a sense

---

be their friend." The Kaiser laid a wreath with the words "A Knight without fear or blame who often had to teach his opponents the right way to practice chivalry." The speech was soon translated into Arabic, to great fanfare. The Kaiser's speech made Saladin a political symbol in the Arab world (up until then he was seen only as an important historical figure). The Egyptian poet Ahmad Shawqi even composed an ode to the Kaiser. The perceived contrast was not lost on the Arab world when French General Henri Gouraud, reportedly, at the end of World War One, kicked the tomb of Saladin and proclaimed: "Awake, Saladin. We have returned. My presence here consecrates victory of the Cross over the Crescent." This insult later seared into the memory of the Syrian resistance against the French. See Doğan Gürpınar (2013) Ottoman/Turkish Visions of the Nation, 1860–1950. Basingstoke: Palgrave Macmillan, 87; Anthony Billingsley (2010) Political Succession in the Arab World: Constitutions, Family Loyalties, and Islam. New York: Routledge: 214.

17 Sharon M. Meagher (2008) Philosophy and the City: Classic to Contemporary Writings. Albany: State University of New York: 4.

18 Peter Schneider (2014) Berlin Now: The City after the Wall, trans. Sophie Schlondorff. New York: Macmillan: 7.

19 Ibid.

of freedom and growth which the compact beauty of London and Paris can never provide. If every space is "perfectly restored", this then can lead to exclusion and a sense that all spaces are occupied.[20] If Kracauer glorifies and mourns both the intense and disappearing "presentness" of Berlin, Scheffler inadvertently redeems it. He points to a realm of possibilities that presentness can eventually spill over into something by the simple fact that it is able to keep its thinking and creative residents within a sense of motion.

Compare this to other European cities (the cities of being?) where, for example, the element of surprise that traditionally accompanied travel is ironed out as tourism is homogenized, streamlined, securitized, and packaged into recognizable templates – English speaking locals, ease of WIFI access, TripAdvisor-determined accommodation. All this sees individual movements and curiosity follow predictable routes and rituals. Berlin is anything but immune to this, but the totalizing wave and façade is often punctured from the city's anarchist protests to anti-establishment graffiti, and most importantly, a culture of political vibrancy and pluralism.

This phenomenon helps recalibrate the senses back to modern predicaments. Whereas Prague's glistening Disneyfied streets and conventionally romantic spaces tells you reassuring lies about what the world wants to see, Berlin's grotty pockets and incompleteness electrifies you with the truth about the world as it is. While the post-war Berlin story – that saw Cold War divisions, reconstruction, and reunification – is anything but straightforward, we can come, as a result of such past tensions, to appreciate the current political and intellectual landscape of Berlin in the way it accentuates the idea of human value.

The marriage between city and thought is critical in understanding the exiled Arab body politic undergoing a collective soul-searching struggle, beyond the initial wandering of freedom, which is evident in the intellectual and everyday subtext. There will need to be a deeper gaze into maghfira (forgiveness), tasalah (reconciliation), inikas (reflection) on past mistakes, as well as the notion that the nation-state that brought many ills to the Arab world no longer makes any sense. Therefore, the concept of the city will need to spearhead the decolonization of nation-state models and replace it with more humane ways of governance. As such, the Arab community's exploration of forgiveness, reconciliation, and reflection comes with the aid of complementary themes embedded in Berlin's code.

The concept of Vergangenheitsbewältigung means working through and coping. Here, the past is incorporated into present experiences. It was once used in a positive way, describing that you had to deal with the past, but has become increasingly ambivalent. The term bewältigen means not only confronting the past, but also getting over it or getting done with it (it can also mean mastering a task or learning to do something for the first time). It has been overused but still serves as a beneficial

20 Ibid.: 8.

term. Perhaps the strongest instantiation is Aussöhnung, which means reconciliation. Connected to Biblical motifs and rarely used in everyday conversation, it can be employed to describe coping with the past by reconciling opposites or parties that have hurt each other. Berlin, therefore, is that paradigmatic backdrop and soundboard to the slowly maturing elements running through the political Arab community.

## Reassembling the political

Towards that end, Berlin will need to be actively thought of and treated as one critical hub and safe space to reconstruct alternative narratives and futures[21] – a space that will require a physical presence and minimal reliance on the digital sphere of social media and communication technologies. A physical presence should be emphasised over any other collaboration, including the much-loved Skype conferencing. We have hopefully learned the lesson of 2011: The digital can only take us so far, and the communities existing in cyberspace will never be a match for the real world of organizing and politicking. Certainly, the digital will be complementary, but never its replacement.[22] Han would argue, "it takes a soul, a common spirit, to fuse people into a crowd. The digital swarm lacks the soul or spirit of the masses. Individuals who come together as a swarm do not develop a we."[23]

To reemphasize, this is about Berlin. A gifted Syrian poet in Hamburg or a lustrous Moroccan film director in Munich are of little use unless they physically make the trip to the German capital, disclose their identities and make their presence felt. Better put, "meet, merge, emerge" as Australian author Stuart Braun pithily states in his aptly named book, City of Exiles: Berlin from the outside in.[24] No digital mechanism can ever be a viable substitute to the world of shadows. There needs to be a resistance to the levelling effect brought on by the digital topology that deceives with its pseudo-egalitarianism and smooth open spaces yet fragments responsibility. It does this by promoting arbitrariness and non-bindingness that undermine promises and trust that are required to bind the future.[25]

---

21 It was not a coincidence that Berlin-based Forum Transregionale Studien held a conference in 2018 titled "Imagining the Future: The Arab World in the Aftermath of Revolution."

22 Coming from the Arab world where the physical public sphere is repressed, social media makes much sense. However, it is quite a sight to ponder when I look at my digitally immersed (which I am not always innocent of either) Arab colleagues and the privacy-obsessed Germans.

23 Han (2017b) In the Swarm: Digital Prospects: 13.

24 Stuart Braun (2015) City of Exiles: Berlin from the Outside In. Noctua Press: 13.

25 Han 2017b: 52–53.

This stands in contrast to the real world's nooks, corners, crannies, and alleys that filter and impede the information pollution and the armies of trolls, and permit slowness, mediation, and trust processes back into the collective fold.[26] The orderly and measured disengagement from social media is one way to avoid the recurring problem of disintegration of one's efforts, scattering of thoughts, and inability to hone in on matters down to their essence. Without going all out Luddite, it is to reign back the digital swarm that leads to the exile's continued captivity between a sensationally feel-good-but-not-going-anywhere present and an open abyss that devours all efforts.

The political should thus not simply be understood as a destination where a Syrian has to wait for that momentous day to return to a post-Assad land (if the obvious needs reminding, even sinister dictators and their regimes cannot cheat mortality and the laws of history). Rather, it is to think and engage politically in the present and be tested within the society of Berlin.

For example, I remember a few years ago, a group of Syrians started a charity "giving back to Germany" which handed out food to the homeless. While charity is always to be commended, justice needs to be at the forefront of one's goals of becoming better acquainted with the political problem that not only leads to homelessness, but also to understand it in much more nuanced ways than what the political can popularly imply. To illustrate this, the German population is suffering from a loneliness scourge.[27] The communal capital stored within many Arab spaces can be unloaded (through volunteering and specially-designed outreach programs) into these German voids. Loneliness, a growing phenomenon in this hyper-individualised world (and one that is making inroads into Arab cities), has political implications from the way people view minorities to voting patterns, and therefore it needs to be treated as a political problem. From this, a problem is recognized, engaged with, new lessons learned, adding further experiences and wisdom to the Arab body-politic repository.

## A conference in perpetual motion

There is something unsettling about attending a brilliant symposium on Middle East studies in Berlin, only to leave with the predictable knowledge that it will fall into a black hole. Even if publications and podcasts were produced, it reaches only a few, and certainly not the wider Arab civic body in question. A continual dialogue with

26 Ibid.: 45.

27 The Local (2018) Two Thirds of Germans Think the Country Has a Major Loneliness Problem. The Local Germany, March 23 (https://www.thelocal.de/20180323/two-thirds-of-germans-think-the-country-has-a-major-loneliness-problem).

the public needs to be fostered. Think of it as a conference in perpetual motion: To widen the net to young Arabs to engage in political thinking without the need to enrol them in formal structures of learning; to translate complex academic theories into digestible intellectual gems, which could be as simple as rewriting or summarizing conference notes to be pinned up on a board in an Arab café in Neukölln. The intellectual exile body will need to forge an intimate relation with café staff, barbers and other occupations critically-positioned within common social spaces. The "antiquated" flyer will hold more weight than a Facebook post as the mere act of handing it to someone restores an invaluable human transaction that makes bonding and togetherness more realizable than what social media can offer.

It would be a delusion of utter proportions to think the mosque and church have no place in this endeavour. Any project to live out one's secular fantasies is doomed. There needs to be a move beyond the spaces of smoke-blowing chatter over Foucault versus Deleuze and the echo chamber it entails. This is not a matter of merely tolerating faith because it is deeply rooted in the Arab community. Rather, it implies coming to terms with the constructive role faith can play in an increasingly alienating environment and, therefore, that it needs to be better framed and understood rather than overlooked by intellectual currents.

Put differently, the frequent sound of church bells should not be read as annoying (as I often hear Germans and visitors complain), but an encouraging sign that the church, along with worker's unions, form a bulwark against neoliberal dehumanization. This is done by keeping shops closed on Sundays for leisure and holding the consumer-frenzy Black Friday and Boxing day type sales of New York and London at bay.

On a similar wave length, no Ramadan ever passes without the cynics moaning how the holy month slows down Muslim efficiency in the workforce. Apart from this generalization, we need to ask, is slowness a bad thing in this overheated world? In a system obsessed with sucking every last ounce of productivity from the workforce and running them down into complacent cogs in the hyper-capitalist machine, then along comes Ramadan throwing in a wrench and declaring: no, it is better to reach the outer limits of your humanness by reorienting attention back to the family, community, charity, sacrifice, and empathy with the poor and hungry, as all this has more depth and meaning than a cold abstract GDP. By carefully rethinking such facets and others through, we can gradually rehumanize the political.

It must be remembered that whether one identifies as intellectual, activist, dissident, artist, filmmaker, and so on, one has chosen to operate more vividly within, what Czech thinker Václav Havel describes as, the "independent life of society."[28]

28 Václav Havel/Paul R. Wilson (1992) Open Letters: Selected Writings, 1965–1990. New York: Vintage Books: 177.

This implies any expression that ranges from self-reflection about the world to setting up a civic organization with the aim of materializing the "truth" or living within the truth. Havel's line of thinking was nurtured under authoritarian rule in 1970s communist Czechoslovakia, however it has some resonance to Arab Berlin, and certainly much more resonance in the current state of the Arab world in which it is a struggle to live creatively and with thought.

## Merge the stream of evolving Arab politics with German progressive politics

The Arab barber and Arab author in Berlin may have developed from the same background that brought them various shades of pain, except the latter is disproportionately more noticeable, given a special title, and a de facto voice to speak for others. The barber's expression of truth is demoted as it is seen to fall below the boundaries of societal "respectability" and creative norms. The practice of faith might not only be his attainment of truth, but his coping mechanism. However, attaining truth can materialize in numerous other ways: If a Syrian barber is tending to a Palestinian customer, they might get into a conversation of a common struggle, evoking sympathy, empathy, and kinship. He might not let the patron pay if he sensed financial hardship. He could decide to put up a picture of Aleppo before the war as a reminder of what was lost but will someday be regained, even with its rubble. What looks like the everyday mundane is, in actuality, the desire to incrementally expand the spaces of dignity wherever one traverses.

The Arab author is simply one manifestation of the same political spectrum that produced that barber. The author just happens to be one of the most visible, most political, most clearly articulated expression of Arab grievances. Yet the author should not forget that he or she developed, consciously or not, from the same background and reservoir as the rest of society and the upheavals of the Arab Spring. This is where they draw their strength and legitimacy from; and this society has a very large reservoir of pain, unhappiness, confusion, and uncertainty. But when the intellectuals and activists not only recognize the futility of separation from that background, but also return to and engage with it, not as shewerma-buying customers but as citizens-in-exile in an ever-expanding conversation with moral obligations, the securing of a steadfast future is aided.

Arab Berlin would need to build a reciprocal relationship with Arab cities, beyond the institutional level. Currently, the two candidates most receptive to new ideas are Tunis and Beirut.

These would form the intellectual bridgehead cities to the Arab world. It should not be presumed, however, that Tunis and Beirut will be painless to engage with simply based on the appearance of liberty. The Lebanese capital is extremely volatile and is prone to be the wildcard of Arab cities. Tunisian gains of greater freedoms are betrayed by a brain-drain and inertia in Tunis as a result of endemic corruption and the inability to push deeper reforms. Nevertheless, there is a reservoir of latent possibilities in this novel relationship with these two cities that needs to be explored.

This arrangement is needed, or is perhaps a first step, until Cairo, the only Arab city that can move ideas by its sheer weight, is someday restored back onto the path of political maturity and intellectual openness. Perhaps this approach is also a modest attempt to address a deeper problem: One of the causes of the tragic downward spiral in the region was the historical shifting of the ideological Arab gravity centres to Riyadh, hauled away from Cairo, Damascus, and Baghdad. It is not that these three cities lost their cultural capital as much as their clout was reined in by the reckless vision of Gulf oil money. The ageless beauty and humility of Gulf Arab culture – one that was at the forefront of environmental care – was ripped apart as it descended upon an accelerated hyper-modernity devoid of politics, and the region keeps on paying the price in countless catastrophic ways because of the Gulf's ineptitude and irresponsible adventures.

This whole endeavor is under no illusion with regards to the obstacles faced. The cynics will assert the specter of the far-right and xenophobia will hamper the efforts of the Arab exile body. Perhaps, but rather than being spectators on the sidelines, the idea is to merge the stream of evolving Arab politics with German progressive politics, as well as to actively hold a mirror up to official German hypocrisy that preaches a human rights discourse yet sells deadly weapons to dictatorships (Egypt being the top importer of German armaments).[29] Moreover, the world's problems are interconnected more deeply than we could ever imagine and addressing this needs to be realized on a city level, as opposed to the national, which is within human grasp.

The other evident challenge is the visa regime. To avoid being consumed by the consular labyrinth, a focus should not be placed on importing more intellectuals into Berlin, but rather, to make do with who is available, who is able to move there, and who is able to visit or pass through. More crucial even is to gradually raise a generation that thinks in new political ways. In this, the greatest challenge I believe will be the absence of a global momentum – that only shows up in rare cycles – to galvanize the community. Momentum versus little of it is the difference between a packed public lecture with audiences sprawled across the stairs and floor, sacrificing thirst and inconvenience, to feel part of something big, as opposed to a dozen regular attendees subjected to the speaker's voice echoing in the room. The painfully long intervals between momentums will need to be filled with thinking, reading, writing, and gatherings, geared towards slowly building up the community. Because when

29 Sofian Philip Naceur (2017) Q&A with German MP Stefan Liebich: Revealing German arms exports to Egypt. Mada Masr, November 16 (https://www.madamasr.com/en/2017/11/16/feature/politics/qa-with-german-mp-stefan-liebich-revealing-german-arms-exports-to-egypt/).

the momentum arrives unannounced, there will be no time to finish reading a book or stay seated to the end of a theatre play.

The manipulation of identity will be another obstacle thrown by the Arab skeptics, particularly in official capacities, as well as their supporters, who might insinuate that something coming out of a western city is not as authentic as an Arab or Muslim one – despite the political currency emerging from an Arab body. Remember, we are dealing with Arab regimes that decry western human rights as not applicable to them all the while, for some "inexplicable" reason, granting exceptions for Western arms, neoliberalism, consumerism, torture methods, higher degrees and so forth.[30] The same regimes that sing tone-deaf nationalist rhetoric and loyalty to the homeland, and yet it is not unusual to see a growing number of the elite's children studying, working, and living in places like London and Rome with no intention of returning home.

The identity neurosis underpins the same mentality that accepts being vomited upon by Gulf capital that turns the thriving Arab cultural realm into vast wastelands simply because, as one of the superficial subtexts hold, the finance is coming from a Muslim country, and therefore something must be going right. As if the insertion of an air-conditioned sleek mosque in a mega mall rights the wrongs of the eviction of local communities, destruction of age-old mosques, and state appropriation of their lands under the flimsiest of pretexts to build that mall. Progress does not come off the back of cement trucks. The shredding of a political value system in the Arab world is why Arab Berlin exists in the first place. In any case, the bridgehead cities partially address this identity concern by repelling the superficial charges that will potentially unfold in the future.

## What is the contemporary Zeitgeist?

We live in an era that is mostly nameless, faceless, and spiritless – compounded by the very neoliberal forces that strip people stark naked before the monster of mutant capitalism. This monster knows no vision, no direction, no narrative, no meaning,

30 Given Egypt epitomizes this duality, I recommend reading Mohamed Naeem's translated essay: "Ever since its inception, the idea of Egyptian modernity was imagined as a choice between authenticity and modernity. In the popular consciousness, modernity had to be scrutinized by a lens of virtue and propriety. In short, we must take from the advanced West what suits us and abandon the rest – 'we' referring to the dominant classes, their interest and lifestyles. So, things like ballet, malls and American consumption patterns are marks of advancement, but democracy and gender equality are alien concepts that undermine the identity and particularity of the nation." See Mohamed Naeem (2016) Mother of the World, against the World and Outside of It, Mada Masr, June 9 (https://www.madamasr.com/en/2016/06/09/opinion/u/mother-of-the-world-against-the-world-and-outside-of-it/).

no choreography, and no conclusion.[31] It only knows addition and acceleration that operates through consumer desires, emotional manipulation, and false promises that repeatedly drag humans away from the realm of authenticity.

This beast of anti-politics has, not surprisingly, been eagerly adopted by liberal democracies and authoritarian regimes alike. Undoubtedly, much worse for the latter as the deliberate weakening of political pluralism, civil society, institutions, and freedom of speech, incapacitates the ability to hold back the deluge of socio-economic dehumanization. This is a crisis without the shrill dramatics of a crisis because it is quiet, smooth, seamless, and well internalized. But as with any crisis, only by naming it and giving it shape can we attempt to limit the formless threats that have yet to come. By determining something as a crisis, Jacques Derrida would argue, "one tames it, domesticates it, neutralizes it ... One appropriates the Thing, the unthinkable becomes the unknown to be known, one begins to give it form, one begins to inform, master, calculate, program."[32]

## A city that feeds on its nerves?

Perhaps one way to approach this is to return to an obscure article written in 1870 by Syrian intellectual Salim al-Bustani in the al-Jinan journal. Titled "Ruh al-Asr" (Spirit of the Age), it was most likely formulated as a response to the well-known German equivalent, Zeitgeist. Ruh al-Asr was a literary and philosophical theme that was constituted by a "metaphysical force in terms of its moral imperatives of liberty, freedom, equality, and justice."[33]

Like many of his Arab contemporaries, al-Bustani was clearly seduced by the "liberality" and "human progress" blowing from West, yet he implored his readers to defend local traditions and values as encroaching abstract principles would not make a tenable replacement. Specifically, he disdained Arabs selecting European customs for no other reason but simply because they are European[34] (a phenomenon that still protrudes its long arm into the post-colonial era). He grew concerned at the West's peripheral extremes of nihilist and anarchist violence, a precursor to the modern Islamist variant, that would violate the moderation and disruption of the momentum of Ruh al-Asr. As illustrated through the role of heroines in al-Bustani's stories, the

31 Byung-Chul Han (2015b) The Transparency Society. Stanford: Stanford University Press: 30–31.

32 Jacques Derrida/Elizabeth Rottenberg (2002) Negotiations: Interventions and Interviews, 1971–2001. Stanford: Stanford University Press: 71.

33 Matti Moosa (1983) The Origins of Modern Arabic Fiction. Washington DC: Three Continents Press: 170.

34 Ibid.: 167.

momentum of Ruh al-Asr largely centered on intelligence, common sense, and decency, with the aim of helping and lifting the individual through reading and learning, and refining society away from corruption.[35] Ruh al-Asr, hence, is a phrase we might need to revive and imbibe with new meaning.

This endeavor to breathe new life into Ruh al-Asr could have been better facilitated had Germany, or Berlin specifically, still had a strong altruistic Zeitgeist – a term which has regrettably been reduced, in a best-case scenario, to fashion trends and fads, and, worst-case, the purview of the far-right. I say this because a compelling Zeitgeist could ideally provide a backdrop and soundboard to its Arabic counterpart.

Zeitgeist, since the early nineteenth century's era of romanticism, has often guided some sort of enlightening or dark spirit in the German public sphere. With Berlin at the epicenter of the Cold War, Germans could identify themselves, or sympathize, with ideological markers – Marxist, anti-Soviet, pro-US – that may have clarified where they stood regarding political matters. A Zeitgeist came in various incarnations. For example, in the 1970s, the left-wing Red Army Faction (Baader Meinhof) terrorist group could, despite the violence they inflicted, draw sympathy from large sections of West German society, particularly the intellectual and student scene. But Zeitgeist could also propel the same strata of Germans into supporting peaceful measures like the anti-nuclear protests and environmentalism of the 1980s.

While viewing a 1970s documentary on Berlin long ago, the English commentator's closing words etched into my mind:

> "This is West Berlin. A city that feeds on its nerves, a town that has learned to live in isolation, to flourish under tension. In spite of Detente, still a frontier post, living in some sense from day to day. Truly a phenomenon of our times and a lesson for our generation."

That Berlin no longer exists. The welcome removal of the existential threat (however euphoric) has diluted collective forms of political spirits. A one-off massive demonstration against neo-Nazis is not a sustained political spirit as much as it is a political culture reactive against Nazi encroachment. The latter, however, should not be trivialized, as such a massive protest and discourse still puts Berlin ahead of the western pack who still struggle to build up a meaningful response to the wave of xenophobia and an angry far-right.

In a reunited Germany and in a new unipolar world where the ascendency of the US cemented free market economics upon the debris of communism, a desperate RAF – the German century's last controversial, political-turned-criminal child, disfigured by the Zeitgeist – issued a "discussion paper" in 1992 titled "We Must Search

35 Ibid.: 177–178.

for Something New."[36] But it was too late, utopia had sailed away; not only for the RAF, but it seems for other German political currents, too, in tune with the rest of post-cold war Europe, if not the world. In turn, what would be considered "big" and "new" became the monopoly of technology and markets.

Big ideas have generally receded since the reunification of Germany, a matter that can be glimpsed in the current clinical management style of Merkel. This shows how far the country has come since, for example, the dynamic leadership of Willy Brandt (West German chancellor, 1969–1974). In fairness, leaders generally respond to the international environment of their times and frame their actions accordingly. But they do set the tone for public thinking.

Ask a German with non-immigrant roots in Berlin as to what inspires or moves Germans today, and you will be surprised not at the answer, but how long it takes to get an answer. As if the question is something that has not crossed their minds before. Understandably, the hesitancy seems to be governed by historical wariness of Germans being inspired in murky directions. But it is also because many will sincerely confess that individual self-interest has assumed the helm. When a worthy response does come out, it is usually akin to battling climate change or helping refugees. Consequently, the inability to mould a coherent and compellingly humane narrative has partly thrown Zeitgeist to the mercy of a resurgent far-right.

At times you do see flickers of a beautiful human spirit. In the summer of 2015, there was an upsurge against the increasing dehumanization of refugees and many Germans came on board to support the mass refugee intake; also revealing a transitory leadership quality in Merkel who proclaimed "Wir schaffen das" (we'll get it done). Yet, this revived altruistic Zeitgeist barely lasted six months, it was ripped apart in the early hours of the new year 2016 in Cologne by drunk refugees who reportedly attacked German women. This, however, raises the hindsight point: there is something very problematic about a Zeitgeist and ideals that welcomes the refugee only to easily dismantle the whole endeavor upon being tested by one, albeit serious, incident.

Even if Arabs were to somehow reanimate Ruh al-Asr, they will still feel intellectually orphaned in a Europe that has lost its political imagination. Nevertheless, rather than being spectators, the Arab exile body needs to envision itself collectively engaged with the forces that are holding back the far-right tide. Together, they aid in reviving, however modestly, the better nature of the German imagination, contribute to battling the global depletion of political thought, and push out parallel democratic narratives against the germination of Arab authoritarian ones.

36 Jeremy Peter Varon (2004) Bringing the War Home: The Weather Underground, the Red Army Faction, and Revolutionary Violence in the Sixties and Seventies. Berkeley: University of California Press: 306.

But before all this, it needs to be ultimately asked: What is our Ruh al-Asr? There is no easy response. In the revolutionary honeymoon days of 2011 and 2012, this could have effortlessly been answered heterogeneously, but today, it is wanting. It certainly is not to accept the continued drive towards entrenched repression in the Arab world. To engage with the question, it would need to go deeper, way beyond discussions of solutions to the Palestinian problem or Egyptian authoritarianism.

It needs thinking at the existential level of our moral quagmire. Not only are our publics duped into cheering massacres or muted over the killing of a journalist in a consulate. The normalization of their lives toward biological and work processes also robs them of any higher attainment of the common good. We thus need to go back to basics and redefine every single word that permeate the lives among us: citizen, city, state, Arab, Muslim, Christian, Jew, Sunni, Shiite, exile, justice, happiness, education, Inshallah, and so on. To also ask, why do they matter? Questions need to be raised on the region's Christian, Nubian, Berber, Amazigh, and other non-Arab and non-Muslim minorities, and how they can be raised to a dignified equality.[37] It will require the ability to shed light on the refugee not simply or only as an object of sympathy, reform, or potential terror, but to elevate him or her as an intellectual producer. To understand what constitutes the better parts of our Ruh al-Asr is to delineate a new way of framing the world. To fight the freak reality of maskh (shapelessness) and be salvaged from the terror of the same.

Rather than a prescription for an Arab utopian future, it is better to consider present realities to build a new manual of thought, drawn from the lived veracities of the Arab world along with the experience of displacement, migration, movement, exile, alienation and settlement in Berlin into the narrative. But it adds one key question – where to next? It is to compose a new story in a relatively secure space by building up partially, for example, on Arendt's methodological assumption: "That thought itself arises out of incidents of living experience and must remain bound to them as the only guideposts by which to take its bearings."[38] In other words, whatever framework of thought develops should be an ongoing endeavour made responsive to our assessment and reconstruction as we confront shifting circumstances while voyaging across the treacherous terrain of memory, history, political imaginaries, narratives, and counter-narratives.

Facing similar transcendental questions of his time, al-Bustani struggled to make sense of the Arab future in the shadow of colonialism. From his 1875 short story, Bint al-Asr, "Daughter of the Age", he invokes the spectre of uncertainty following the influx of European influences: "These things are taking place at a

37 It is not lost on me that an Arab exile body is already inherent with tensions that dislodges voices who do not easily subscribe to the Arab label.

38 Hannah Arendt (1977) Between Past and Future: Eight Exercises in Political Thought. Harmondsworth: Penguin: 14.

time whose meaning, like the uncertain light of dawn, is yet unclear. Therefore, the minds of many people, too, are not clear. Even strangers (Europeans) are in the dark, like the natives. This state of affairs shows that the country is suffering under the burden of a cultural situation whose values are in an uncertain state of transition."[39]

Al-Bustani faced a different moment of truth in which he wondered and wandered, as to what will eventually come out of this confusion for his fellow Arabs. Nowadays, we face that confusion again, just as we have faced it numerous times since al-Bustani's day. For God knows what tomorrow brings, but the journey will draw from and humanize the symbolic capital that was born in 2011, as well as to reinvigorate it in novel ways that opens up new pathways. The galvanizing moments of 2011 was when desire and the imagination were given free reign until they were torpedoed by blood, remorse, despair, and exhaustion. More than ever, what is needed is to judiciously rekindle desire and imagination but, this time, to reign it in with knowledge and discipline.

We need to produce new personalities and thinkers who will further aid in tapping into the curiosity, relentlessness, inventiveness, and ingenuity of a heartbroken community; to adopt emerging texts as guides, imbibe philosophical thinking into the heart of upcoming ventures, and to produce books worthy of inheritance to the generations yet to arrive; and we need to encourage not only the learning of the German language and refining our approach to the Arabic language, but to be constantly conscious that political thinking is inescapably structured by the words we use and evade, and therefore a revitalized vocabulary is needed to question and discuss the taxonomies of power. But above all, we need to come to terms with our mortality that humbles us into the awareness that our milestones are heirlooms of past struggles, and the fruits of our efforts might only sprout beyond our lifetime. One is not expected to do everything, but nor should one relinquish their responsibility to do something worthwhile for others.

By breaking through Kracauer's words of anonymity and aimlessness at the opening of this essay, we need to find ourselves, and each other, on the streets, from human to human crowd to an animated body-politic, becoming that new people on the Berlin scene with names, aims, and voices, that intersect with what is just and good. The surge of different rhythms harmoniously complementing the other will reveal larger than life meanings, sounding off a special melody that will be worth listening to.

39 Matti Moosa (1983) The Origins of Modern Arabic Fiction. Washington DC: Three Continents Press: 166.

## References

Ali, Amro (1916) The Hidden Triumph of the Egyptian Revolution. Open Democracy, January 25 (https://www.opendemocracy.net/north-africa-west-asia/amro-ali/hidden-triumph-of-egyptian-revolution).

Arendt, Hannah (1973) On Revolution. Harmondsworth: Penguin.

Arendt, Hannah (1977) Between Past and Future: Eight Exercises in Political Thought. Harmondsworth: Penguin.

Billingsley, Anthony (2010) Political Succession in the Arab World: Constitutions, Family Loyalties, and Islam. New York: Routledge.

Braun, Stuart (2015) City of Exiles: Berlin from the Outside In. Noctua Press.

Deeb, Sarah El (2018) Saudi Writer Saw Turkey as Base for a New Middle East. Associated Press News, October 21 (https://apnews.com/5643bc71beaf43249527f1e0d14dd67b).

Derrida, Jacques/Dufourmantelle, Anne (2000) Of Hospitality. Stanford: Stanford University Press.

Derrida, Jacques/Rottenberg, Elizabeth (2001) Negotiations: Interventions and Interviews, 1971–2001. [in English translation of French interviews.] Stanford: Stanford University Press.

Frisby, David (1985) Fragments of Modernity: Theories of Modernity in the Work of Simmel, Kracauer and Benjamin. Social and Political Theory. Cambridge: Polity.

Gürpınar, Doğan (2013) Ottoman/Turkish Visions of the Nation, 1860–1950. Basingstoke: Palgrave Macmillan.

Hamilton, Omar Robert (2018) Industrial Colonialism: Egypt, Germany and the Maintenance of the Modern World. Mada Masr, July 5 (https://madamasr.com/en/2018/07/05/opinion/u/industrial-colonialism-egypt-germany-and-the-maintenance-of-the-modern-world/).

Han, Byung-Chul (2015a) The Burnout Society. Stanford: Stanford University Press.

Han, Byung-Chul (2015b) The Transparency Society. Stanford: Stanford University Press.

Han, Byung-Chul (2017a) The Agony of Eros. Untimely Meditations. Cambridge: MIT Press.

Han, Byung-Chul (2017b) In the Swarm: Digital Prospects. Translated by Erik Butler. Untimely Meditations. Cambridge: MIT Press.

Havel, Václav, and Paul R. Wilson (1992) Open Letters: Selected Writings, 1965–1990. New York: Vintage Books.

Meagher, Sharon M. (2008) Philosophy and the City: Classic to Contemporary Writings. Albany: State University of New York.

Moosa, Matti (1983) The Origins of Modern Arabic Fiction. Washington DC: Three Continents Press.

Naceur, Sofian Philip (2017) Q&A with German Mp Stefan Liebich: Revealing German Arms Exports to Egypt. Mada Masr, November 16 (https://madamasr.com/en/2017/11/16/feature/politics/qa-with-german-mp-stefan-liebich-revealing-german-arms-exports-to-egypt/).

Naeem, Mohamed (2016) Mother of the World, against the World and Outside of It. Mada Masr, June 9 (https://madamasr.com/en/2016/06/09/opinion/u/mother-of-the-world-against-the-world-and-outside-of-it/).

Said, Edward W. (2000) Reflections on Exile and Other Essays. Cambridge: Harvard University Press.

Schneider, Peter (2014) Berlin Now: The City after the Wall. Translated by Sophie Schlondorff. New York: Macmillan.

Shatz, Adam (2001) A Poet's Palestine as a Metaphor. New York Times, December 22 (https://www.nytimes.com/2001/12/22/books/a-poet-s-palestine-as-a-metaphor.html).

The Local (2018) Two Thirds of Germans Think the Country Has a Major Loneliness Problem. The Local Germany, March 23 (https://www.thelocal.de/20180323/two-thirds-of-germans-think-the-country-has-a-major-loneliness-problem).

Varon, Jeremy Peter (2004) Bringing the War Home: The Weather Underground, the Red Army Faction, and Revolutionary Violence in the Sixties and Seventies. Berkeley: University of California Press.

Wahba, Dina (2018) Diaspora Stories: Crippling Fear and Dreams of a Better Home. Mada Masr, August 16 (https://madamasr.com/en/2018/08/16/opinion/u/diaspora-stories-crippling-fear-and-dreams-of-a-better-home/

# 3. Amal, Berlin! Arab media, Berlin-style

*Fig. 3.1: Team Amal, Berlin!*

© Eman Helal

Amal, Berlin! is an online platform providing local news in Arabic, Dari/Farsi, and Ukrainian. It serves the growing community of newcomers to the city. The intention behind Amal is to help the media landscape adapt to the needs of the changing population of the German capital.

This chapter is about a new journalistic experience – which is why we have chosen to draft it in a new style. Instead of dividing the topic into two parts, each written by one of us, we've decided to compose it as a dialogue or, shall we say, a mosaic. This is our way of reflecting on how we work and see our project Amal, Berlin!

Amal, Berlin! consists of a team of journalists from the Middle East, Ukraine, and Germany. We started our work in 2016. In 2017 we then launched our local news website, amalberlin.de, and began posting our news on Facebook. Two years later, in 2019,

we founded another similar platform in Hamburg called amalhamburg.de. In 2022, when the war in Ukraine made millions of Ukrainians leave their country, we opened a new section in our Amal team. Amal in Ukraine went online in August 2022, and in January 2023, Frankfurt am Main became the third German city with an Amal newsroom. Six journalists report for the Arabic, Dari/Farsi, and Ukrainian communities in the Rhein-Main-Region. All in all, 25 journalists in exile are working for Amal, plus management and admin staff.
We are proud to be a part of this book and of Arab Berlin. Our work is as new as the Arab Berlin phenomenon. In other words, although Arab people have always lived in Berlin, it is new to celebrate such a thing. And that is what we celebrate!

Julia Gerlach and Abdolrahman Omaren are the two authors of the present chapter. Julia Gerlach (J.G.) has worked as a journalist covering the Arab World outside and inside Berlin ever since she finished her studies in Political Science and Islamic Science at the FU. She began working for ZDF TV and covered the Middle East as a correspondent for several German newspapers from 2008 to 2015. Having moved back from Cairo to Berlin in September 2015, she found Berlin much changed from the city she had left more than a decade earlier: with more Arabs living in the city and many more on their way there, especially from Syria, Berlin had turned into an Arab capital. Among the newcomers in 2015 were many journalists looking for jobs. There was an obvious need for their professional skills, as many newcomers had problems getting information and finding their way in the new country. Misinformation, rumors, and fake news were in rampant circulation.

**J.G.:** Let me start from the beginning. It was in the autumn of 2015, and my sister Conny and I were sitting at her kitchen table, talking. That was where the idea of Amal was born. We wanted to bring two needs together: to create a news platform to serve the community of newcomers, and to create jobs for the journalists in exile here. We chose Arabic and Farsi as our languages since the majority of the newcomers were from the Middle East – either from Arabic countries or from Afghanistan and Iran. Soon Oscar Tiefenthal, the director of the Evangelische Journalistenschule (EJS), was on board. He supported the idea from the beginning and was willing to host the project on the premises of the school. Our next step proved more difficult: we needed funds. But the Protestant Church (EKD) stepped in, and, by the summer of 2016, we were ready to recruit the founding members of the project. At the time there were quite a few projects for journalists in exile, so we were not alone in inviting and choosing the potential members of the team; the journalists themselves were choosing us from a variety of different offers and options. One of our colleagues told us later that he was hesitant to join Amal, as he was not sure if this would be just another project starting and closing again in no time. Luckily for us, he took his chances, and he is still with us after five years.

In September 2016, we started with a workshop. All members of the founding team had already worked as journalists in their home countries, so there was not much need to provide journalistic training. In a three-month workshop, we discussed how to work as a journalist in Berlin: Where to get information? Whom to call to get an interview with a politician? What laws to know about? How about copyright? We also worked a lot on soft skills like how, and how not, to talk with Germans, etc. And so, at the end of the initial phase, the founding team had developed the principles of the Amal project together – and so Amalberlin.de was launched in March 2017.

Abdolrahman Omaren (A.O.), the second author of this chapter, graduated from Damascus University with a BA in media communications in 2005, after which he worked for several Arab newspapers and TV channels. Since 2014, he has lived in exile in Berlin, and since 2016 has been the editor-in-chief of the Arabic pages of Amal, in charge of choosing the topics and editing the articles and news. He is the soul of the Arabic editorial board.

**A.O.:** The Amal, Berlin! platform was an opportunity for me to work as a journalist in my mother tongue, as it is for my fellow journalists on the team. This work depends mainly on language, and mastering one's language is the essence of such work. Words are our means of expression and communication with our Arab readers. Unfortunately, even if Berlin is a very big and diverse city, its press institutions have very limited diversity. Obviously, language plays a crucial role in that. It's very difficult to find a job in one of the news organizations if you are not 100 percent fluent in German, and there are not many media outlets in other languages. The Arab community in Germany has not succeeded in establishing newspapers in their own language, unlike other communities, such as the Turkish or Russian communities. I think that even if people master a language other than their mother tongue, they still need to read in their mother tongue from time to time because language conveys, not only news but also emotions.

Finding information in Arabic has always been difficult in Berlin. Moreover, the number of Arabic media outlets has been very limited. In other European capitals such as Paris and London, Arab news media have a long tradition. However, Amal, Berlin! cannot be compared to newspapers such as Al-Sharq, al-Awsat or Al-Arab, which are known for diaspora journalism. That is reporting that follows the news of the Middle East and addresses Arab readers in their home countries. By contrast, our platform addresses the Arab community in Berlin and the whole of Germany, while we do not direct our content to Arabs residing in their home countries. So, we are not an Arabic news website in Germany; instead, we are a German website that speaks Arabic.

**J.G.:** This is one of the most important principles of our work: We are a local news platform. This means that we report on what is going on in Berlin, Hamburg, Frankfurt, and Germany. This is where we are and where we can get information and make sure that what we write is correct. We leave the reporting on other places like Syria, Afghanistan, and Iran to other media agencies that have reporters there. There are quite a few websites reporting in Arabic on the Arab world and in Dari on Afghanistan, for example. Amal's unique selling point is that we are one of very few media outlets reporting in Arabic, Ukrainian, and Dari/Farsi on what is going on in our cities.

It is also important to stress that we are a journalistic news platform and not just another information outlet. We don't explain to our readers how Germany works; we report on what is going on and let the readers make up their minds about what to think of the different topics. This makes us very different from the news portals set up by the government to tell people what rules they have to follow. We don't explain what democracy is, but instead, report on a regular basis on what the federal government does and how politicians debate policies in the Bundestag. We believe that our readers are smart enough to draw their own conclusions on how democracy works and what it is about. This eye-level principle is very important for our work.

**A.O.:** Every morning, we read the local newspapers and search for topics of interest to the Arab readers residing in Germany as parts of German society; this means that our news is diverse and covers more than just migration. We report the news that matters to society as a whole. The tales of the city, the funny and the sorrowful, the strange and the rare, the serious and the surprising – everything! Recently we have obviously reported a lot about COVID-19. Our topics often involve the lives of newcomers, with their achievements or attempts to integrate into the new community. For example, one story involved Zina Al-Kurdi, a pupil who achieved the highest high-school average in Berlin and was honored by the municipality for her diligence. Another featured a bus driver, Ahmed, who found a job in his desired profession.

In terms of politics, apart from writing news, we conducted a big media campaign before the recent elections in Germany. Our objective was to prepare information for the ca. 80.000 new voters from the Middle East to help them make their own choice on election day. We produced some animated videos explaining the German political system and conducted interviews with members of all parties in the Bundestag. We talked about their political visions. Even the AfD was present in our media campaign, although it is a xenophobic party. Media neutrality in Germany allows all politicians to speak and leaves the voters to choose. An important part of the campaign was a series of discussion sessions with people who had just obtained their German citizenship and were about to vote for the first time in a German election and experts that were streamed live on Facebook.

*Fig. 3.2: A screenshot of Amal, Berlin!*

**J.G.:** We believe that it is important to know what is going on in the city in order to be able to participate and become a part of society. In this regard, we understand our work to be "journalism plus". We report the news with the objective of helping people to integrate into the new society. This is also why we get funding from civil society organizations. In the beginning, we started with funding from the church. Since 2019 our sources of funding have diversified, and we now receive money from foundations like Körber-Stiftung, Crespo-Foundation, and Schöpflin Stiftung, who see us mostly as an integration project, as well as several Landeskirchen (i.e., the regional bodies of the Protestant church). We belong to the Gemeinschaftswerk der Evangelischen Publizistik gGmbH, which is also part of the Protestant church.

My work as a correspondent reporting from Cairo was a completely different experience in terms of my relationship with readers. As a correspondent, you are very far away, and you hardly ever get feedback. If you are lucky, you might get an angry letter from one of your readers if they think that you were too harsh on one of the heads of state; or some readers may complain about your spelling. You might get one or two letters in a month. Amal is completely different. We post a story on Facebook and get feedback immediately. People tell you what they think, and we very often engage in long discussions. That's an important part of our work, and we believe that it is important that people can discuss the news and what is going on around them. Sometimes the topics are delicate – for example, news on the so-called Arab clans or everything related to the conflict in Palestine/Israel.

**A.O.:** Speaking of social media, journalistic work has become even more difficult. Journalists and professional journalistic platforms are competing with content producers without a journalistic background. The trust of the general public in the news media is declining. For us that means that we need to convince our readers again and again, that we must try our best to provide them with accurate information, and that they can trust us. The press in its traditional form faces great challenges from the creators of entertainment content. There are now dozens of Arabic-speaking people who have channels on websites such as TikTok spreading news and information extensively without any journalistic or specialized background. Unfortunately, in order to get more followers and views, they sometimes exaggerate and lie. Apart from that, they do not respect the intellectual property rights of others, and steal content and republish it on their accounts, which deprives the original content owners from reaching followers and interacting with their audience. The impact of social media on the press in general, and the Arab press in particular, should be the subject of an in-depth study. Solutions must be provided to confront piracy and false content.

**J.G.:** It might be interesting to mention that lately, we have witnessed some changes in the way people are commenting on topics related to the Israel-Palestine-Situation and anything related to antisemitism. In the summer of 2021, we had some severe and very harsh discussions about the situation in Gaza, and many people posted statements on their Facebook pages proclaiming their solidarity with the Palestinian cause. Soon the discussion changed, and comments on our page were toned down a lot. We noticed that posts on topics that might have provoked a long discussion before were now being passed over without many comments. When we noticed this change, we looked for the reasons: Was it because we were writing the posts differently, in a way that somehow wasn't provoking our readers? Were people simply tired of the heated discussions? Was this a reflection on the controversies over journalist Niema al Hassan and politician Sarah-Lee Heinrich? Niema al Hassan, a German TV and print-media journalist, had been accused of promoting antisemitism after making critical comments on the Near-East conflict. And Sarah-Lee Heinrich, a German Green party politician, had been accused of harboring homophobic views based on the social media posts she had made years ago when she was young. The internal processes in the Arabic Section of Deutsche Welle may also have played a role. For many Arab social media users, it was a shock to learn that DW as an employer was looking through the FB accounts of the employees and that some of the journalists had been fired because of posts that they had liked or shared many years back. As a consequence, it seems that people may have become more hesitant to post at all, and more cautious about what and how to comment on social media.

**A.O.:** At Amal, Berlin! we deal with topics that one does not find in the traditional Arab media. As we live in a European capital, and in a part of the world that respects human rights, it was necessary to emphasize religious tolerance in our topics and respect the freedom of people in their sexual orientation. Recently we met Christian Hermann, the homosexual imam, who told us about his spiritual journey and how he was able to align and live his sexual and religious orientations at the same time. This isn't the first time we've tackled issues related to homosexuality, though we know that many of our readers may not like it. However, it is a part of the city we live in, and we've become a part of that city too. There should be no barriers to talking with and getting to know each other. I believe that the dialogue we provide through our platform contributes in one way or another to converging viewpoints, giving an opportunity to hear other voices and see the world from multiple perspectives and in many colors.

There are dozens of pages on Facebook that publish news in Arabic, but most of them lack reliability and professional fact-checking. One never knows who runs those pages, what their publishing standards are, and whether they make sure that the information they publish is correct. By spreading rumors, intentionally or unintentionally, they may contribute to harming to some of their followers and make them afraid of integrating into their new communities. Social media has made it possible for anyone who owns a smartphone to post content with ease, regardless of whether it is true or offensive to others. Therefore, the presence of Arabic language platforms belonging to authentic and well-known institutions is very important. This protects readers from being deceived by false and harmful news. In one case, when we published news about a government decision to change the residential laws for migrants, one of the readers commented: "Now I believe the news because you published it. I read it elsewhere, but I did not believe it, we know you and trust what you publish."

**J.G.:** When we started Amal in Hamburg, we faced severe criticism from some parts of the German public. Several readers of Hamburger Abendblatt wrote letters and comments saying that Amal was a project preventing integration, as we provide people the opportunity to be informed without having to learn German. Those people would then not have the incentive to work towards their German certificates. The COVID-19 pandemic brought change into this debate: Now it seems common sense that it is important that everybody knows what is going on, even if their German is not good enough to read a German newspaper.

Many of the newcomers of 2015 are now fluent in German and about to become German citizens. We still believe that we should continue to report in their mother tongue because there will always be new people coming to Germany from Middle Eastern counties who need to know what is going on even before they are good enough in German to follow the national media.

We also think that the German media landscape is still a little too monotonous and needs some colorful sprinkles to make it more interesting. In 2015 there was a trend in German media to publish special issues in Arabic to welcome the newly arrived refugees from Syria. Diversity was celebrated. In this context, Amal, Berlin! is more than a way to get information about Berlin and news reporting on current affairs in Germany across to the new arrivals. We also would like to see Amal as a small contribution to changing the German media landscape as such. It's time to make it more like the rapidly changing society it belongs to.

# 4. The Arabs of Berlin face generations laden with guilt and trauma

*Nazeeha Saeed*[1]

## Introduction

Driven out of their countries of origin by the political and security situation in the Arab region, growing numbers of Arabs started arriving in Berlin about a decade ago. Yet, there are concerns about the authenticity of their integration into German society. The growing number of new arrivals in the past few years fleeing war, oppression, injustice, arbitrary arrest, interrogation, insecurity, and poverty shocked German society, especially the capital Berlin, where many of them settled. This reopened old wounds and reawakened German collective trauma related to immigration and associated with others, i.e., those with different features, colors, languages, and cultures.

How did Berlin receive the Arab newcomers? How did they add to a city that is cold for more than six months a year? How can Arabs adapt and integrate into a new society with decades-old traditions?

## Arabs in Berlin

> "Berlin is where the newly-arrived Arab suddenly (but not always) recognizes that the frightful habit of glancing over the shoulder – painfully inherited from back home – gradually recedes. All the while, a new dawn slowly sets in among the meeting of peers in this new city: As such, Berlin is not just a city. It is a political laboratory that enforces a new type of beginning, one that turns heads in the direction of matters greater than the individual; and it generates a realization that the grey blur that nauseatingly blankets the future can actually be broken up." (Ali 2019)

1 Translated from Arabic by Samira Jabaly.

Sociologist Amro Ali describes the city's relationship with the Arabs who arrived there after revolutions in their countries failed them. He explains:

> "Following the 2011 Arab uprising and its innumerable tragic outcomes, Berlin was strategically and politically ripe to emerge as an exile capital. For some time now, there has been a growing and conscious Arab intellectual community, the political dimensions of which to fully crystalize is what I wish to further explore." (Ali 2019)

Several reasons made Germany an attractive destination for Arab refugees. The first is that in the Arab psyche, Germany is associated, not with colonization, but with its unconditional support for Israel that stems out of its guilt towards Jews, and lack of differentiation between antisemitism and anti-Zionism (Awad & Abdelazim 2019). Second, after it emerged from the rubble of the racist and barbaric Nazi regime, Germany managed to reinvent itself as a superpower. Finally, Germany decided to open its doors and welcome refugees, especially those from Syria during the Merkel era.

The Arabs now living in Berlin come from different backgrounds and social classes. Some of them were among the elites in their countries, professionals in fields like medicine, research, journalism, trade, activism, civil society, academia, and theatre, while others work in the crafts and trades. Together they provide a solid foundation for the diaspora society in a multi-cultural city open to change and new ideas.

There are no statistics available about the exact number of Arabs living in Germany or Berlin. The available information pertains to immigrants and foreigners in general, or to Syrians only, who over the past 10 years have become the largest immigrant community in the country, and in Berlin in particular. The exact numbers can actually be inferred from other statistics, such as the number of students or credential attestations.

For example, in the German Academic Exchange Service's (DAAD's) annual report of 2018, Syrian students came in sixth among foreign students, with 8600 Syrian students in German universities, and a growth of 228 percent between 2015–2018, becoming the biggest population of Arab students in Germany. According to the German Federal Statistical Office, as cited in Al-Araby (2019), there was an increase of 20 percent in the number of foreign degrees attested for employment purposes (in the fields of medicine, nursing, pedagogy, engineering, and technical services) in 2018 compared to 2017. The number of degrees completed in 2018 was 36,000 certificates, 4800 of which were for Syrians, followed by South Americans and Africans. 61 percent of these degrees were in the health and medical fields, while the number of vocational degrees increased by 72 percent compared to 2017. These newcomers added a new atmosphere to the city, especially in the cultural and art scene. First Arabic bookstores were opened: Khan al-Janub [2] in 2018 and *Der Divan* was established with Qatari support in 2017. The British website *Middle East Eye* named Berlin the Arabs' business and cultural capital in Europe (Unicomb 2021). New markets boomed, rich immigrant families opened new businesses in Berlin and Arab journalism thrived in the city: Arab Berlin launched in 2015 and Radio Arabica in 2019 to mention a few.[3] Contrary to what is expected from a country with a sad and cruel history of dealing with differences, the presence of Arabs in Berlin became quite normal.

In an interview in 2021 with the Iraqi poet, Nada al-Khawwam, who lives in Berlin she said: "With no sea or warm hearts, this city cannot be trusted," She adds:

> "My experience in Berlin is different from any other. Even after three years of getting to know the city and living in it, I am still a stranger to it. These years would have been unbearable if it was not for the Arab-speaking communities that transformed the city with oriental charm, especially Sonnenallee, now known as the Arabs' street. There you can hear Fayrouz and Rahbani music every morning mixed with coffee brewed over hot sand. The various Arabic dialects tickle your ears; there's the smell of bread and delicious Arabic sweets; the company of friends you meet on a sidewalk in Berlin; we share the exile experience, a cup of cardamom tea, the concerns of the east and the details of the city. All of this breathes life back into the lifeless body. Often, the simple details relieve the burden of exile."

For the Arabs today, Berlin might resemble what New York used to be for Jewish intellectuals who fled Europe in the late thirties of the last century, and what Paris used to be for Latin American intellectuals, who fled their country's dictatorships in the 1970s and 1980s. Arabs found in Berlin a refuge from political crises, from revolutions, wars, and vile oppression. According to Amro Ali, the city became a magnet and a haven for exiled intellectuals. He believes that "to coherently embark upon a regenerated starting point in this long journey of political redemption, a 'we' is required: This feeds from new political ideas, collective practices, and compelling narratives that are currently re-constructed and brought to life..." In this way, he believes, Berlin allows space to unleash Arab intellectual and creative capacities seeing its present separate from its past and future. According to Ali, exile might pursue the present as a means to escape the trauma and the numbness it induces.

So, to what extent can this Arab generation 'dream', laden with multiple traumas of imprisonment, enforced disappearance, detainment, torture, destruction,

---

2 Editor's note: Chapter 15 in this book is written by Khan al-Janub's founder and owner Fadi Abdelnour.

3 Editors' note: Amal Berlin! is featured in this book. See Chapter 3 by Abdolrahman Omaren and Julia Gerlach.

and annihilation (Hein 2021, Graham-Morrison 2020), in a European city laden with its own Nazi history? To what extent can they dream of integrating and transcending pain and suffering? And on the other hand, can the city and its society transcend a past immersed in Nazism, death, and desperation, and become a home for the newcomers?

As the political scientist Vivienne Matthies-Boon analyses, protesters and political activists in Egypt in 2011 lived through profound collective experiences in their fight for human dignity, the elimination of violence in the state, judiciary, and police, and a more equitable social and economic system. These experiences had a far-reaching social and political impact. In fact, the demonstrators' plight did not come without a personal and emotional cost, as they faced oppressive state tactics, police violence (utilizing torture, rape, and humiliation) and increased economic chaos and social polarization (Matthies-Boon 2014).

Exile, as described by Edward Said, the Palestinian intellectual, is more than just a non-voluntary expulsion, it is an act of uprooting and ejection into an exodus of a specific intellectual, social, and psychological nature and with certain sensitivities and positions. Words like depression, anxiety, fear, alienation, insecurity, and sarcasm become familiar when talking about exile (Said, 1993).

## History of Arabs in Germany

It is important to clarify that the term Arabs, used to describe all people coming from West-South Asia and North Africa, is prejudiced and even condescending. This generalization obliterates the other ethnicities that live in the region, like the Amazighs, Berbers, Armenians, Kurds, Nubians, and other minorities. Yet we will use this term here because it conveys how the West sees us as 'one' (the Arabs). Western perception do not distinguish between the different origins and ethnicities, and at times, it even wrongly assumes that all people coming from that region are Muslim. There is a rich diversity in identities, religions, languages, and ethnic origins of people living or coming from the Middle East and Northern Africa. In 'Out of Place,', Edward Said (1999) in which he identified himself as a Palestinian, Arab, Christian, American with two cultures; American and Arab, and one that exists out of the place identified and stereotyped by others. Said says:

> "I was never able to grasp all these complications and entanglements. Why wasn't my mother a simple English woman? I lived with these contradictions my whole life, and I always wished that I was only an Arab, or only European or American, Orthodox Christian, Muslim or pure Egyptian etc." (Said 1999, pp. 56).

Minorities in the Arab region, like Amazighs, Armenians, Kurds, Nubians, Christians, Yezidis, and Baha'is living amidst a Muslim majority, are struggling with the authorities, demanding that their existence, identities, languages, cultures and religions are recognized under the umbrella of the Arab Muslim majority (Abwalnaja 2014).

Arabs' relationship with Berlin goes back to 956, when the first Arab arrived in Berlin coming from Spain and stayed there for a while. According to history books, Ibrahim Bin Yacoub, the messenger of al Hakam II, Caliphate of Andalusia, delivered a letter to King Otto I, King of Germany, and the Holy Roman Emperor, proposing to strengthen relationships between them. Upon his return, Bin Yacoub painted to the Caliphate a picture of Germany, which was so far unknown to Arabs (Salama 2016). The development of these relationships was documented when Abbas Basha I, (Salama 2016; Abu Latifa 2019) within his efforts to modernize Egypt and the Ottoman Empire, sent the first group of Egyptian medicine students in 1849 – 1850 to Munich university to study medicine (Heyworth-Dunne 1939).

The Weimar Republic (1918 – 1933) was a golden era for Arab political refugees who were allowed to engage in political work. Hotel Esplanade in Berlin hosted the first Arab National Congress in 1916, in which the committees for the liberation of Tunisia and Algeria from French colonialism were founded (Abu Latifa 2019). Afterwards, several Arab political, cultural, and artistic movements became active in Berlin, and consequently several Arab-German associations were established. These were allowed to publish newspapers and bulletins that covered news of political tensions in the Arab countries, especially Egypt under British occupation. Some newspapers in Berlin even assigned columns to fugitive politicians to promote their ideas and views.

The Arabs, also, played an economic role in Berlin. Abu Latifa (2019) cites records of Arab businessmen who arrived in Berlin at the end of the $19^{th}$ century. For example, Abd il Aziz Shaweesh (1876–1929) started as a cigarette vendor and eventually owned his import-export business. Rahmeen Saleem achieved great success in selling agricultural machinery in Germany. In 1922 he opened several branches in Germany and Baghdad. The most successful, however, was the Palestinian businessman George Hoori (1891 – 1965) who came to Berlin after WWI and worked in import/export business and monopolized the importation of Jaffa oranges to Germany. Assaf Al Kareem Siba'ii from Beirut also achieved a lot of success in 1933 working as a real estate agent (Salama 2016).

The generation of WWII probably still remembers the voice of Younis al Bahri, the broadcaster that started every morning with "Here is the Arab neighborhood in Berlin" over the Nazi Arabic radio that was established to promote Nazi propaganda in Arabic. The station was run by Taqi al Deen al Hilali, a Tunisian who moved to Germany to complete his doctoral dissertation in 1940. There he became close to Hitler and managed his Arabic-speaking radio service in the context of Germany's support to the Arab people against the European imperialists who were at war with Germany. The station's programs were a mixture of war reports, segment on history and literature, recitation of the Holy Quran and musical segments, but most importantly anti-British propaganda (Maskeen 2021).

The Arabs' relationship with Berlin is not recent, for throughout history war and unrest drove people to seek refuge in safer places. When Berlin became safer in the early 1960s, Germany invited thousands of Moroccans to come as "guest workers" and help in the post-war reconstruction efforts, as it was extended to workers from Turkey and Vietnam (Deutsche Welle 2013). The 1980s and early 1990s witnessed the arrival of thousands of Lebanese and Palestinian refugees who fled the war in Lebanon. Chronologically, they became the base for the Berliner Arab community (Qantara 2018). Yet, there are no official statistics about the number of Arabs who settled in Berlin throughout the different immigration waves.

## The newcomers

In September 2021, several men and women of Arab origin were elected to the German Parliament. Among them were businessmen and women of Egyptian, Moroccan, Iraqi, Yemeni, and Syrian origins who won the votes of citizens of non-German origin (Muslim and Middle Eastern origins) as well as those of German origin who believed in the candidates' platforms/political parties and the importance of ethnic and cultural diversity and the rejection of xenophobia in order to guarantee the security and safety of non-Germans, facilitate their lives, and fight discrimination.

It was the first time this number of candidates of Arab origin, the second and third generation of immigrants and refugees, were elected to Parliament. This event marked the beginning of a new phase in German history, where these communities changed from mere spectators in the political scene to policymakers by nominating German candidates (of Arab and Middle Eastern origin) able to win the constituents' votes.

In Germany, right-wing political parties and associated media outlets promote a stereotypical image of Arabs and Turks. They mainly focus on the crimes committed by Arab and Turkish individuals and portray those as the norm in these communities. The term "Arab family clans" was coined to refer to Arab (and Turkish) families who allegedly formed clans in Berlin and have exceptional influence in the neighborhoods they live and work in (Abu Muailiq 2016). These families are accused of involvement in illegal activities like trafficking drugs, prostitution, armed robbery, and tax evasion. In 2018, German politicians demanded taking stricter measures against these so-called Arab clans. Politicians also demanded the allocation of more resources in the police forces and judiciary and requested improved investigations. Stephan Harbarth, at the time a CDU member of the German Bundestag, called "for the employment of discreet tapping and surveillance methods, because these clans were isolated from society" (Deutsche Welle 2018).

Sonnenallee, informally known as the Arabs' Street in Berlin, bears witness to the history of Arab presence in the city. Previously the street was known as 'Little Beirut', named after the Lebanese shops and cafes that filled the street with their smoke and old Arabic songs (Al-Habbal 2007, see Miriam Stock in this volume). In 2015, when refugees, mostly from Syria, started to flow into the city, the street turned into one of the most vibrant streets in Berlin. Visitors cannot but notice the shop signs written in both Arabic and German – and often not even in correct German. Shisha cafes and Syrian sweets can be found along Sonnenallee and the surrounding streets, in addition to restaurants selling Arab food.

Chancellor Angela Merkel's decision in 2015 to admit more than 1 million refugees, over 80 percent of which were Syrians, revived discussions about integration-related challenges, started dialogues, and mobilized campaigns for and against the decision in the German political scene. This, as expected, incited anti-immigrant sentiments that contributed to the rise of right-wing politics, especially the Alternative for Germany party which came in third in the 2017 elections.

Once again, Berlin found itself face to face with trauma, as hundreds of thousands of immigrants started to come to Germany, especially Berlin, seeking refuge from the war, unrest, and totalitarianism that was wrecking their countries, mainly Turkey, Syria, Iran, and Afghanistan. German society found itself experiencing fear and anxiety for reasons unclear to it.

Events like the Nazi regime, the war and its aftermath, and the country's division into East and West Germany had resulted in the expulsion and removal of thousands of people from Berlin. Some of them returned after a while, while others remained in exile until their death. This history has remained problematic despite the intended transparency in dealing with it.

This awkward relationship with both immigration and exile became clear when Berlin – and other German cities – came face to face with the new refugees, or what was called at the time "the immigration wave."[4] The city was surprised to see that it was turning from a city that refugees fled from into a destination for refugees. Here, Germans had to face reality – a history that had been left undealt with for decades. But as Martin Bayly, a sociologist at the London School of Economics, has

4 Book editors' note: using the word "immigration wave" is used here verbatim. It reproduces a negatively connotated threat theme that constructs migrants as threatening force of nature. Similar terms include swarms or flood or crisis. UN Refugee Agency UNHCR as well as human rights NGOs criticize this language in politics and media. See the press release here: https://www.unhcr.org/56bb369c9.pdf. For helpful materials in German see: https://mediendienst-integration.de/ and www.glossar.neuemedienmacher.de.

said, "Forgetting the past may affect our ability to prepare for future crises."(BBC 2021).

The decades-old discussion over whether Berlin was or was not a city of refuge has become irrelevant during the most recent so-called 'immigration wave,' as it has become clear that Berlin is de facto a destination for refugees; the new reality.

The German government at the time displayed a high level of commitment toward refugees. According to media reports, the state of Berlin agreed in 2018 to allocate 1 billion euros to support refugees. These were spent on accommodation as well as German language and integration courses, in addition to financial support for job seekers. According to *Berliner Morgen Post*, the number of people who benefitted from these forms of support was around 45,000, the majority of which were refugees arriving in Germany in 2015 and 2016 (Deutsche Welle 2018). These allocations made up 3 percent of the state's total budget. In addition to accommodation expenses, 60 million euros were allocated annually to integrate refugees. Additional financial support was allocated for social and cultural projects and vocational training. Furthermore, a special budget item of 14.5 million euros was allocated to address the needs of the large number of unaccompanied underage refugees in Berlin.

According to Andreas Germershausen, commissioner of the Senate for Integration and Migration in 2018, "Germany has learned from the mistakes of the past," as the "policies are more focused now on integration. This work is based on the law that was legislated in 2005, which encourages providing courses on German language, history, and culture." (Qanatara 2018; Al-Hawwas 2021).

Germershausen believes that failing to provide comfortable conditions for the newcomers is critical. "If we made it difficult for the immigrants to join the labor market, we would be choosing to hold dynamite in our hands, and this would mean that we have not learned from the mistakes of the past." (ibid.) The number of Arabs in Germany in 2016 was 800,000 and some claim that they are living in parallel societies and refusing to integrate with their German neighbors.

If given the choice, many immigrants would choose Berlin because it provides plenty of jobs and living costs are relatively lower than other European cities. In addition, there are government programs that facilitate integration and help immigrants to enter the labor market.[5] Another factor is Germany's need for laborers, as it already suffers from a deficiency of hundreds of thousands of workers every year. Additionally, the ethnic and cultural diversity of Berlin adds to its attraction. According to the Federal Office for Migration and Refugees (Bundesamt für Migration und Flüchtlinge, BAMF) as cited in media reports, the numbers of Arab refugees in Germany continue to rise. The number of first-time asylum seekers reached 100,278 between the beginning of 2021 and the end of September of the same year. Most of the asylum seekers were from Syria, Afghanistan, and Iraq. (Deutsche Welle 2021)

---

5 Book Editors' note: see Chapter 9 by Hashem Al-Ghaili in this volume.

## Reconciling with the past

Hundreds of thousands of Arab refugees moved to Berlin during the past few years. This presented a challenge to the city and its ability to accommodate the newcomers and the residents' ability to embrace them given the historical complex of dealing with immigration and the mass trauma of war, rifts, and authoritarianism, in addition to the legacy the Nazi regime left in the social structure and its traces that can still be seen today.

On the 80th anniversary of the first Nazi deportation of Jews to the Jewish ghetto in Lodz in Poland on October 18, 1941, German President Frank Walter Steinmeier admitted that the Nazi crimes are a historical burden that Germans continue to bear (Deutsche Welle 2021). He said, "We Germans still bear a share of the guilt that perpetrators, accomplices, and supporters of the systematic murder of Europe's Jews heaped upon themselves." He added: "To this day we feel ashamed that fellow citizens were taken from the heart of society, harassed, deprived of their rights, expropriated – and finally dispatched on a journey to their death." In an interesting gesture, the German President added: "The unsettling thing is that it all happened in broad daylight. The crimes were committed in front of everyone. The segregation and deportation happened in the heart of German daily life, and this is a terrifying fact."

Yes, it all happened in broad daylight in front of everyone. The whole society witnessed the oppression, discrimination, repression, and killing committed in the form of systematic genocide against minorities, mainly Jews. However, the privileges enjoyed by those social groups on good terms with the regime prevented the interventions to stop the massive violations. Also, the fear and intimidation the Nazis planted contributed to their refrainment from interfering.

Social sciences have two opposing viewpoints on this point. Thomas Hobbes believes that people perceive "the other" as dangerous, selfish, and unworthy of trust, which explains why they are treated with caution and doubt, and assume that all that stands between us, and violent chaos is a strong state and stern leadership (Hobbes 1968). On the other hand, the Dutch historian, Rutger Bregman, argues in his book "Humankind", "When cities were bombed, the most interesting observation was the high level of cooperation and vigorousness shown by the affected communities." (Bregman 2020) Historian Bregman believes that the life of our ancestors in prehistoric times and tribal societies was not as horrific as we often imagine. These societies were actually self-organized and peaceful to a great extent. Yet, when social hierarchies, military regimes, and permanent rulers emerged, violence and inequality emerged with them. Human history does not lack stories about families who harbored neighbors and friends, took children to safety, or provided assistance. But since so few of them are considered acts of heroism celebrated by authors and filmmakers in artistic and literary works to ensure they are remembered and passed on to future generations.

Berlin, having suffered under the Nazi authoritarian regime and affected by the desolation, killing, displacement, uprooting, war, and destruction during that era, had to face the same history after 70 years. But this time it was on the other side of history; this time it was the safe, stable, supportive destination for the expelled, the exiled, and those escaping war and dictatorship.

The Nazi regime, in only six years (1933–1939), managed to introduce major social, economic and community changes that targeted minorities like non-Caucasians, non-Christians, ethnic minorities like Europe's Roma, communists, and followers of other political beliefs, the sick and impaired, especially those with disabilities and genetic disorders, homosexuals, and transgender individuals. But most of all, it targeted Jews. Nazi thought became prevalent in society during these six years, and for several reasons, the regime succeeded in recruiting many Germans into its ranks – driven mainly by fear and herd behavior (defined in psychology as the behavior of individuals within a group acting collectively without much planning or thinking), but also attracted by the privileges and advantages the Nazi regime offered them.

What is noticeable about the prevalent thought at the time, is that it not only degraded the humanity of many groups in society and, with time, turned their existence itself into a crime; it even dehumanized their pain and suffering. German President Steinmeier referred to this in his above-mentioned speech: "These atrocities happened in front of everyone, in front of society, neighbors, security officers, military personnel, health care workers, academics and others in society."

## Social Trauma

This was the beginning of a prevailing collective 'trauma' induced by war, displacement, and then the return migration of Germans who lived in neighboring countries, banished to retaliate against Nazi encroachment and the gruesome atrocities and crimes Nazis had committed there.

Nazi behavior was normalized and incorporated into a lifestyle that reflected the new regime. This was evident in the strict, controversial approach it introduced for raising children, as elaborated in *The German Mother and her First Child*, by Dr. Johanna Haarer, in 1934. The book's recommendations were incorporated into a training program for the Reich's mothers that was designed to inculcate proper child-rearing principles in all German women. The book was accorded a nearly biblical status in nursery schools and childcare centers. Haarer urged mothers to ignore the emotional needs of young children so as to raise strong soldiers and believers in Nazi teachings. She recommended that physical and emotional communication with children be kept to a minimum, even when carrying a child (Haarer 1943; Kratzer 2019).

The impact of war trauma can linger in societies for years. David Trickey, psychologist and representative of the UK Trauma Council, says: "When the way you see yourself, the way you see the world, and the way you see other people are shocked and overturned by an event – and a gap arises between your 'orienting systems' and that event simple stress cascades into trauma, often mediated through sustained and severe feelings of helplessness." (BBC 2021) Facing the impact of the trauma may require a person to revisit their beliefs and self-perception.

For two decades after the war, Germans were preoccupied with reconstruction efforts, restoring social relations, and reinstating normal activities like production, education, and agriculture. In addition to all of that, Jews were busy searching for their loved ones and trying to process and understand the atrocities that had been committed against them. They were occupied with documenting all the stories, property, and documents they could find in an effort to restore memory.

People who had survived the Nazis and the war, and the children who were born immediately after the war and the defeat of the Nazis, did not realize that they were unintentionally passing their trauma, fears, shocks, and horrifying experiences to the next generations.

Collective trauma – as defined by psychologists – happens when a large number of people experience a psychological shock as a result of an event or a series of events that occur at the same time; especially crises in which many lose their loved ones. Furthermore, people who found themselves in situations where they had to decide who lives and who dies, experienced an unprecedented moral dilemma that added to their trauma.

War is considered a cause for a collective trauma (Petbender 2017), because it impacts everyone, including those who did not take part in the battles and those who did not even know people who took part in the battles: They have been consumed with the fear of hunger, arrest, the oppressive police state, death or injury in the war, inhospitable shelters, even if they did not actually experience these shocking conditions. Horrifying stories may also instigate the same pressures and feelings that cause trauma among persons who did not experience the war.

The German psychologist, Kora Kebacca, holds the child-rearing methods that were applied in the Nazi time responsible for some psychological problems that the so-called 'war grandchildren" (Kriegsenkel, a term coined by Sabine Bode 2014) suffer from, although they have never experienced a war themselves. Kebacca calls Haarer's book *The German Mother and her First Child* and the emotionless child-rearing methods it promotes "dangerous." (Lichtenberger & Al-Mikhlafi 2013). The ramifications of trauma are both psychological and social – on a large scale. When people experience a traumatizing event, it affects their relationships, connection with the social systems, and role as citizens. Psychological traumas have social, economic, and political ramifications, and the response needed is not limited to psychological therapy. According to Metin Basoglu, a founder of the trauma studies faculty at King's College London,

> "Addressing collective trauma will also take more than psychiatry [...]. The scale of the problem means that meaning-making tools should be delivered through media channels: in writing, in booklets and videos, kids' channels, TV channels, newspapers, all avenues and channels of information, and the internet." (BBC 2021).

Berlin, like other German cities, attempts to transparently deal and reconcile with its history. Like other German and European cities, it built monuments commemorating the victims of war and Nazism. It also has several museums that serve this purpose, most importantly the Holocaust Museum, the Memorial to the Murdered Jews of Europe and the Topography of Terror Documentation Center. The city is also preparing for the opening of the Exile Museum in 2025, which is planned to document stories of exile, be they historical ones that focus on the exodus of the Jews, or contemporary ones that focus on the new refugees including Arabs. In addition, the brass plates, so-called *Stolpersteine*, affixed in front of buildings in residential neighborhoods, catch the eye. These plates commemorate the stories of Jews dragged to their miserable fate in concentration camps. The plates bear the name of the person who used to live in that address, their date of birth, and the fate that befell them.

Pain, trauma, and depression caused by these events were often the topic of literary and drama works, plays, films, and even of intellectual and academic works and papers written in the past decade. Yet, these topics were only discussed among the elites, intellectual circles, academics, writers, artists, playwrights, and directors, while the rest of traumatized society never dealt with the shock and pain they had endured, and consequently never recovered.

These official and community efforts, like telling the stories of the victims, allocating special holidays in remembrance of them, building monuments, and acknowledging the loss, suffering, and trauma contribute to the commemoration of victims in the wider context. But do these efforts of commemoration actually contribute to the recovery from collective trauma?

> "Masses can endure traumas and overcome them unless the traumatizing event is related to the identity of the society. Collective traumas can reshape society's perception of itself and the world" (BBC 2021).

Collective trauma is a catastrophic event that ruptures the social fabric. It starts with a collective shock, then turns into collective memory and then culminates into a structuring framework that allows groups to redefine themselves and their future direction. Psychologist Hirschberger argues that there are differences between the victims and perpetrators, and accordingly the meaning changes in common stories and behavioral attitudes, shared rituals, traditions, regulations, social spaces, common fate, and relationship with the 'other'. (Hirschberger 2018)

Collective traumas can have a lingering impact if they are not dealt with. When people fail to face their trauma and discuss it, unhealed scars become permeant in society. Consequently, when faced with relevant stimulants, they risk reawakening feelings of anger and hostility. In other times, they resort to passivism and carelessness to avoid experiencing these stimulants altogether. At the collective level, this means that violence and anger linger on, then followed by withdrawal (BBC 2021). This may explain why Germans were very cautious when they learned that thousands or dozens of thousands of refugees were crossing the oceans and mountains to arrive at their borders. This sudden change led some to sympathize and volunteer to offer help, while for others, the xenophobic Nazi legacy resurfaced and manifested in hate speech targeting Arab foreigners. In addition to the response of society, there were also humanitarian efforts that responded to the needs of refugees and provided the necessary means for a dignified life.

## Challenges facing the Arabs of Berlin

The stereotypical images intentionally promoted by German right-wing parties and associated media outlets equally target Arab newcomers and those who had arrived five decades earlier. Stereotypes usually emphasize traits like ignorance, polygamy, big families, and lack of proper care in raising children. Arabs are associated with terrorism and extremism, which contributes to preconceptions, prejudices, and different forms of Islamophobia.

Racism has soared in the past years, with dozens of people with migrant backgrounds falling victim to racist and violent attacks. One of the latest was the attack in Hanau (BBC 2020). As criticized by Amnesty International, German authorities have been accused of failing to address hate crimes, including attacks on shelters designated for asylum seekers. Amnesty emphasized the urgency of providing protection and launching independent investigations about possible biases inside law enforcement forces in the country (Amnesty 2016). In line with that, in Berlin in 2019, residents woke up one April morning to find posters hung across streets, metro stations, and buses bearing the Syrian flag and a hand raising the victory sign and a slogan: "Go back home, the war is over, Syria needs you."(Abwab 2019). Another poster said: "With the fall of the last ISIS stronghold, Syria will need young men and women to help in the postwar reconstruction efforts." As confirmed by German Intelligence later, the campaign was organized by the "Identity Movement," a nationalistic white supremacist movement active in Europe, North America, Australia, and New Zealand. The movement is considered "suspicious." Some of its members have been linked to right-wing parties, with some well-known activists being former members of such parties. (Deutsche Welle 2019).

The Federal Anti-discrimination Agency, established in 2006 to provide advice to those who face discrimination because of their ethnic origins, religious beliefs, sexual orientation, or age, posts figures on their homepage that prove that racism has visibly increased. The annual report for 2019 states that the number of registered discrimination cases in Germany increased by 10 percent (Posen 2020).

Berlin, as a city with a multi-ethnic population, promotes a culture of openness and tolerance and encourages foreigners to seek help and assistance through its official channels and websites. The General Act on Equal Treatment bans and prevents all forms of discrimination on the grounds of race, ethnic origins, sex, religion or belief, disability, age, or sexual orientation. Germany introduced necessary laws and procedures needed for processing refugees and asylum-seeking operations. Germany recognized the refugee's right to seek asylum and developed a complicated, bureaucratic, multi-phased process each individual must go through to be deemed a "good person" in the eyes of the German state and prove that they intend to serve the country well rather than becoming a burden to it. By opening its doors to refugees in 2015, Germany emerged as a protector of human rights; a country that introduced relatively advanced immigration laws, and one where refugees can live without fearing uncertainty and poverty compared with other countries in Europe or other continents. However, Germany failed to embrace the refugees and relate to them. Also, the tardy way discrimination incidents were handled indicates that society is still traumatized and has not dealt with the past.

So, can we say that Germany does not have a problem with the newcomers? It does. Problematic issues include the rise of right-wing politics, the increasing number of incidents connected to racism, and the bureaucratic way the country deals with the asylum-seeking process and attempts to elude the accompanying responsibilities. In addition, the failure to understand the uncertainty, loss, and fear associated with the asylum-seeking process and the bitter feeling of alienation refugees feel, is an issue. Newcomers are expected to overcome all physical and mental ordeals, to innovate, and to succeed in a new country – which many of them have actually managed to do. But this does not mean that all the majority needs is to get German identification papers as travel documents; they need a society that embraces them and helps them overcome their pain.

In an article published in the independent Arab online medium Raseef22, Fadi Abdelnour, Palestinian publisher, graphic designer, and one of the founders of Khan al-Janub, describes encounters with German cultural and institutional racism as "indirect racism enveloped with sympathy and eagerness to help." He adds: "For example, you can easily get funding to make a film about ISIS or war in Syria, but it is not easy at all to secure funding to make a film about social drama in Algeria, for example." (Yousif 2021). In the same article, the Syrian theater director, Anis Hamdoon, explains:

> "It is clear to all those working in German cultural circles that non-German cultural organizations (and here I am talking about Syrians), are confined to topics of war and destruction. We are treated as if we only know one thing, war [...] and I believe this comes out of ignorance and arrogance" (Yousif 2021).

Arabs experience how German society tends to essentialize them and puts them in boxes they are not allowed to escape from. Journalists coming from the Gulf countries are expected to write about Gulf issues; Arab women are expected to talk about women's issues; while artists are expected to talk about the turmoil in their countries, the war, and the revolution – otherwise they have no place in the cultural and arts scene. Arabs face incidents of discrimination and racism on a daily basis in white European society, as practices of racial profiling show (Knight 2020). It is enough to stand in the central station and watch policemen selectively approach people of color, specifically men, to ask for their IDs, and search them. Other acts of harassment against minorities are also common: verbal or physical discrimination by civilians also takes place. Not all such instances are reported to the police or the Federal Anti-discrimination Agency, many are only discussed among friends, dismissed altogether, or not even considered to be discrimination (Fida 2021).

The Syrian journalist and women rights activist, Yasmeen Marei, who moved to Berlin in 2016 says:

> "I found myself, just like thousands of foreigners, confronting a serious issue that touches the details of our daily life, shapes it, and defines our paths: 'integration'. I thought extensively about the term that has become associated with fear and inferiority, most importantly the fear of losing distinctive features like habits and traditions, and anything related to culture and lifestyle" (Saeed 2021).

## How to move forward?

The question here is: How can a city that has suffered so much from exile, desperation, war, and discrimination deal with the notion of refugees today? It is not easy to be a refugee or a migrant in a country that has an unfortunate history that features displacement, alienation, and exile, and one that still has in its subconscious transgenerational unhealed wounds. This society never got rid of its heavy legacy of guilt and shame. The city may be full of monuments commemorating victims of the holocaust, displacement, and exile; but the memory of the city is laden with misery and an even heavier burden as incidents of the past were swept under the carpet. Feelings of frustration, guilt, and anxiety resurfaced when refugee newcomers came from different places, reawakening a post-traumatic disorder that emerges whenever they feel threatened, anxious, or scared, even if they are in their comfort zone.

There are many ways to bridge the gap between hosts and guests. Art is one possible way; it is a tool the newcomers can use to introduce themselves to the hosting community. As journalism tries to fulfill its role by introducing the newcomers and the baggage they bring with them, integration being pushed by the state will remain lacking and one-sided. Arab and foreigner integration in German society has to be met with efforts from the German side to learn how to accept the new people with their cultures, religions, habits, and traditions.

## References


Abu Latifa,; Ibrahim, Muhannad (2019) من تاريخ الصحافة العربية في برلين قبل الحرب العالمية الثانية (الجزء الثاني) مهند إبراهيم أبو لطيفة (From the History of Arab History in Berlin Pre-WWII, Part 2), al-Bayader, May 2 (https://al-bayader.org/2019/05/264127/).

Abu Muailiq, Yasser (2016) "حقائق حول العصابات العربية في ألمانيا (Facts About Arab Clans in Berlin)", DW, April 13 (https://www.dw.com/ar/حقائق-حول-العصابات-العربيةفي-ألمانيا/a-19184724).

Abwab (2019) الأسد يناديكم... العنصرية تسوق لنفسها في صناديق إعلانات العاصمة برلين (Assad Is Calling You. Racism Is Marketing Itself in the Advertising Boxes of the Capital, Berlin), April 27 (https://www.abwab.eu/أخبار-ألمانيا/الأسد-يناديكم-العنصرية-تسوق-لنفسهافي/).

Abu Alnaja, Hadir (2014) النوبيين يطالبون بإحياء اللغة النوبية وأن يكون هناك تمثيل نوبى فى أفريقيا (Nubians Demand the Revival of the Nubian Language, and Nubi Representation in Africa). Rose al Yousif, April 2 (https://rosaelyoussef.com/85860/النوبيين-يطالبون-بإحياء-اللغة-النوبية-وأن-يكون-هناك-تمثيل-نوبىفى-أفريقيا).

Al-Habbal, Muhammad Sami (2007) زونين أليه ـ شارع العرب البرليني همزة وصل مع الثقافة الغربية (Sonnenallee – the Arab Street in Berlin, the Link with Western Culture), DW, October 9 (https://p.dw.com/p/BoNG).

Al-Araby (2019) لاجئون شباب في ألمانيا... انخراط في الجامعات وسوق العمل (Young Refugees in Germany Engagement in Universities and the Labor Market). Al-Araby, December 15 (https://www.alaraby.co.uk/لاجئون-شبابفي-ألمانيا-انخراط-في-الجامعات-وسوق-العمل).

Al-Hawwas, Ahmad (2021) Nine Arabs among the 83 immigrant MPs in the German Parliament. Who are they? How did they win? Al-Jazeera, 22 December (https://www.aljazeera.net/politics/2021/12/22/9-نائبا-من-العرب-ضمن-83-مهاجرا-في-البرلمان).

Ali, Amro (2019) On the Need to Shape the Arab Exile Body in Berlin. dis:orient, January 23 (https://www.disorient.de/magazin/need-shape-arab-exile-body-berlin).

Amnesty International (2016) ألمانيا تتقاعس عن التصدي للتزايد في جرائم الكراهية (Germany Is Failing to Address the Increase in Hate Crimes) (https://www.amnesty.org/ar/latest/press-release/2016/06/germany-failing-to-tackle-rise-in-hate-crime/).

Antidiskriminierungsstelle Deutschland (2023) مرحبا بكم لدى الهيئة الاتحادية لمكافحة التمييز (Federal Anti-Discrimination Authority) (https://www.antidiskriminierungsstelle.de/AR/homepage/homepage-node.html).

Arab Deutschland (2022) معلومات عن الشارع العربي | شارع العرب في برلين (Arab Street), Arab Deutschland, November 6 (https://arab-deutschland.com/شارع-معلوماتعن-يقع-واين-برلين-العربفي-/).

Aslan, B. [@BaharAslan] (2020) "Bitte Keine Araber" Als Antwort Auf Bewerbungsschreiben: Rassismus Im Architekturbüro ("No Arabs, please" as an answer to a letter of application: Racism in a German architect's office). Twitter, January 22 (https://twitter.com/BaharAslan_/status/1217240060011126785).

BBC (2021) فيروس كورونا: كيف نتعافى من الصدمة النفسية الجماعية الناجمة عن كوفيد-19؟ (Corona Virus: How do we recover from the Covid-19 collective trauma?). BBC Arabic, February 11 (https://www.bbc.com/arabic/vert-fut-55986585).

BBC (2020) Germany shooting: What we know about the Hanau attack. BBC News, February 20 (https://www.bbc.com/news/world-europe-51571649).

Berlin Willkommenszentrum (2013) Regeln des Zusammenlebens (Rules of living together) (https://www.berlin.de/willkommenszentrum/ankommen/regeln-des-zusammenlebens/).

Bode, Sabine (2013) Kriegsenkel: Die Erben Der Vergessenen Generation. Klett Cotta.

Bregman, Rutger (2020) Humankind: a hopeful history. Bloomsbury.

Deutsche Welle (2021a) زيادة كبيرة في طلبات اللجوء إلى ألمانيا .. أكثرهم من سوريا والعراق (Mostly from Syria and Iraq, a hike in asylum applications in Germany), October 17 (https://www.dw.com/ar/طلبات-كبيرةفي-زيادة-والعراق-سوريا-أكثرهممن-ألمانيا-إلى-اللجوء-/a-59530541).

Deutsche Welle (2021b) Germany marks 80th anniversary of first Jewish deportations, October 18 (https://www.dw.com/en/germany-marks-80th-anniversary-of-first-jewish-deportations/a-59541601).

Deutsche Welle (2019) German Intelligence classifies "The Identity Movement" as an extreme right-wing movement, November 7 (https://www.dw.com/ar/الاستخبارات-الألمانية-تصنف-حركة-الهوية-كحركة-يمينية-متطرفة/a-49554397).

Deutsche Welle (2018a) ولاية برلين تخصص حوالي مليار يورو للاجئين (The state of Berlin allocates around 1 billion euros for refugees), January 10 (https://www.dw.com/ar/ولاية-برلين-تخصص-حوالي-مليار-يورو-للاجئين/a-42092406).

Deutsche Welle (2018b) لا تساهل بعد ..بألمانيا "العصابات العربية"استراتيجية جديدة ضد اليوم(A new strategy against "Arab Clans" in Germany: No more leniency), March 4 (https://www.dw.com/ar/استراتيجية-جديدةضد-العصابات-العربية-بألمانيالا-تساهل-بعد-اليوم/a-42819800).

Deutsche Welle (2013) مغاربة ألمانيا من عمال ضيوف إلى مواطنين(German Moroccans, from guest workers to citizens), June 25 (https://www.dw.com/ar/مغاربة-ألمانيامن-عمال-ضيوف-إلى-مواطنين/av-16907990).

Fida [فِداء (@fidaazaanin] (2021) Tweet, Twitter, October 11 (https://twitter.com/fidaazaanin/status/1447567628155895819?s=21).

France 24 (2019) Anti-Zionism and Antisemitism, between conception and misconception (https://www.france24.com/ar/20190220-معاداة-الصهيونية-السامية-مفهوم-إسرائيل-فرنسا).

Graham-Harrison, Emma (2020) 'My Goal Is Justice for All Syrians': One Man's Journey from Jail to Witness for the Prosecution. The Guardian, December 12 (https://www.theguardian.com/world/2020/dec/12/my-goal-is-justice-for-all-syrians-one-mans-journey-from-jail-to-witness-for-the-prosecution).

Haarer, J. (1934) Die deutsche Mutter und ihr erstes Kind. J. F. Lehmanns.

Halab al-Yaum (2021) وقفة احتجاجية في برلين لأهالي ..في اليوم العالمي للاختفاء القسري وذوي معتقلين سوريين في سجون النظام(On the International Day of the victims of enforced disappearances. A sit-in in Berlin for the families of Syrians detained by the regime). August 30 (https://www.youtube.com/watch?v=VDNP_-7B7Ew).

Hein, Matthias von (2021) على هامش محاكمة ضابطين سوريين في ألمانيا ..لونا تحكي قصتها (Luna tells her Story. The trial of two Syrian officers). February 23 (https://p.dw.com/p/3piet?maca=ar-EMail-sharing).

Heyworth-Dunne, B.A. (1939) An introduction to the history of Education in Modern Egypt, University of London (http://www.islamicmanuscripts.info/reference/books/Heyworth-Dunne-1939-Introduction/Heyworth-Dunne-1939-Introduction-000-035.pdf).

Hirschberger, Gilad (2018) Collective Trauma and the Social Construction of Meaning. Frontiers in Psychology, Volume 9 (https://doi.org/10.3389/fpsyg.2018.01441).

Hobbes, Thomas (1968) Leviathan. Penguin Books.

Ismail, Manal (2020) قبلة جديدة لقراء العربية في برلين .."خان الجنوب"مكتبة(Khan Al-Janoub Library. A new destination for Arabic readers in Berlin). Amal, Berlin, November 10 (https://amalberlin.de/2020/10/11/مكتبة-خان-الجنوب-قبلة-جديدة-لقراء-الع/).

Knight, Ben (2020) Racial Profiling: Germany Debating Police Methods. DW, August 7 (https://www.dw.com/en/german-police-racism/a54090661)

Kratzer, Anne (2019) Harsh Nazi parenting guidelines may still affect German children of Today. Scientific American, January 4 (https://www.scientificameri

can.com/article/harsh-nazi-parenting-guidelines-may-still-affect-german-children-of-today1/).

Lichtenberger, Arne; Al-Mikhlafi, Abdo Jamil (2013) أحفاد الحرب: صدمات نفسية موروثة من حروب لم يعايشونها (Descendants of War: Psychological trauma inherited from wars they did not experience). DW, September 3 (https://www.dw.com/ar/أحفاد-الحرب-صدمات-نفسية-موروثةمن-حروبلم-يعايشونها/a-17056409).

Maskeen, Younis (2021) تقي الدين الهلالي.. مدرس الحرمين وحليف هتلر ومؤسس السلفية بالمغرب (Taqi Al Deen Al Hilali, a teacher in the two holy mosques, Hitler's ally and founder of Salafism in Morocco), al Jazeera, July 28 (https://doc.aljazeera.net/portrait/تقي-الدين-الهلالي-مدرس-الحرمين-وحليفه/).

Matthies-Boon, Vivienne (2014) The Political Is Personal: Collective and Individual Trauma in (Post) Revolutionary Egypt. SBRL Sound – Council for British Research in the London Levant, September 22 (https://soundcloud.com/cbrl_sound/arab-uprising-vivienne-matties-boon).

Mazo, Awad; Maha, Abdul Azeem (2019) معاداة الصهيونية ومعاداة السامية بين المفهوم والالتباس(Anti-Zionism and Antisemitism, between conception and misconception)." France 24, February 20 (https://www.france24.com/ar/20190220).

Petbender, Elise (2017) خبيرة ألمانية: جيل الصدمة في سوريا قد يتحول إلى حالة إكتئاب جماعية (German Expert: "The Trauma Generation" in Syria is at risk of collective depression). Interview by Janty Kvink and Arif Jabu, DW, March 10 (https://www.dw.com/ar/خبيرةألمانيةجيل الصدمةفي سورياقديتحول إلى حالةإكتئاب جماعية/a-37859584).

Posen, Ralph (2020) ألمانيا و" مشكلتها الدائمة مع التمييز العنصري"(Germany and its everlasting problem with discrimination). DW, June 09 (https://www.dw.com/ar/ألمانيا-ومشكلتها-الدائمة-مع-التمييز-العنصري/a-53749106).

Qantara (2018) صدام بين جيلي الأمس واليوم :المهاجرون العرب في ألمانيا واللاجئون السوريون (Arab immigrants in Germany and Syrian refugees: Frictions between past and current generations). Qantara, August 22 (https://ar.qantara.de/content/السوريون في-برلين-يغيّرون-طابع-شارع-العرب-المهاجرون-العربفي-ألمانيا-واللاجئون-السوريون-صدام).

Saeed, Nazeeha (2021) "Helped me heal my old wounds": Foreign women in Berlin meet over writing, Raseef 22, August 3 (https://raseef22.net/article/1083813).

Said, Edward (1999) Out of Place – a Memoir. Dar al Adab.

Said, Edward (1993) Representations of Intellectual. Dar al Nahar.

Salama, I'tidal (2016) نجاحات فنية واجتماعية وإخفاقات سياسية ..تاريخ العرب في برلين (History of Arabs in Berlin. Artistic and social successes and political failures). al-Sharq al Awsat, August 23 (https://aawsat.com/home/article/720456/تاريخ-العربفي-برلين-نجاحات-فنية-واجتماعية-وإخفاقات-سياسية).

Unicomb, Matt (2021) Berlin: Inside Europe's Capital of Arab Culture, Middle East Eye, October 11 (https://www.middleeasteye.net/discover/berlin-germany-europe-capital-arab-culture).

Willkommenszentrum Berlin (2022) Regeln des Zusammenlebens (Rules of living together) https://www.berlin.de/willkommenszentrum/ankommen/regeln-des-zusammenlebens).

Yousif, Deler (2021) Indirect and enveloped with sympathy: Stories about 'racism' in Germany, Raseef22, October 26 (https://raseef22.net/article/1084969-غير-مباشرة-ومغلفة-بالتعاطف-عن قصص-فيالعنصرية-ألمانيا).

# 5. Hermeneutic Chicanery
## A contribution to the debate on migration and memory in Germany

In memoriam Ahmed Badawi

## West German Remembrance

West Germany – and later reunified Germany[1] – has liked to see itself as a role model for dealing with the experience of dictatorship and mass murder. Decades of widely ranging governmental and non-governmental remembrance projects have brought many at home and abroad to see Germany as a "model student" of socially effective ways of dealing with genocide, persecution, and racist murder. The renowned US anthropologist Susan Slyomovics, herself the daughter of a Holocaust survivor and the author of *How to Accept German Reparations*, has called German remembrance policies the gold standard.[2] German organizations are often invited to advise wherever there are efforts to learn from past crimes and to transition from dictatorship to democracy. The Goethe-Institut and the German political foundations (with the exception of the AfD-affiliated Desiderius Erasmus Foundation, founded in 2017) have had a major share in conveying the German experience. In 2013, the Goethe-Institut devoted an issue of its arts magazine, *Art & Thought*, to dealing with the past, opening with an editorial that states: "Germans have acquired a reputation as both experts and model students in the discipline of coming to terms with the past." (*Art & Thought* 2013: 1).

1 For research on the connection between racism, anti-Semitism, and colonial crimes in the GDR from the 1950s onwards, see the lecture by Mario Keßler (ZZF) at the Einstein Forum on October 4, 2021 (https://www.youtube.com/watch?v=7KH86kiZFjw&t=6s).

2 The lecture of Susan Slyomovics at Freie Universität Berlin in 2018 on *The Afterlives of Wiedergutmachung: Algerian Jews and Palestinian Refugees* came under attack by Antideutsche (https://www.salonkolumnisten.com/eine-moralische-katastrophe/).

After the German Nazi-era "breach of civilization" (*Zivilisationsbruch*, Dan Diner; Jürgen Habermas), with its industrialized murder of neighbors and fellow citizens, remembrance was afforded a central place from the 1970s onwards as a way of coming to terms with the past to shape the future. The aphorism by Spanish philosopher George Santayana that "Those who cannot remember the past are condemned to repeat it", dating from before World War I, became a mantra in West German "remembrance work" (*Erinnerungsarbeit*, Frigga Haug). By implication, this must mean: Those who *do* remember are *not* condemned to repeat. Therefore, the exemplary forms of remembrance in Germany should be the best test case to verify the dictum "Never again!": Will German society now be immune to the recurrence of pogroms? Will it be quick next time to recognize the dehumanization of its neighbors? These questions are very much on the minds of many new arrivals and second and third-generation migrants to the country as they watch aggressive right-wing populists march through public institutions attacking Jews and Muslims, and personally experience privately held anti-Semitic and Islamophobic prejudices.

Henryk M. Broder once wrote that the Germans misunderstood Holocaust survivor Hermann Langbein's outcry, "Never again Auschwitz!" ("Nie wieder Auschwitz!"), to mean, literally: Never again must Jews be exterminated *in Auschwitz*. Broder was alluding that they were incapable of imagining that Auschwitz might reoccur somewhere else or in other manifestations, and that they would, therefore, not be able to implement "Never again!". (Broder 2012)

If remembering the Holocaust is about not repeating genocide and extermination in the future and possibly worldwide, then other genocides must be compared with the Holocaust and vice versa. Russia's attack on Ukraine on February 24, 2022, painfully updated the question of what exactly we Germans have learned from our own history. In many pro-Russian countries, the attack brought out blatant anti-Semitism, including in the figure of the "Nazi Jew" Volodymyr Zelensky. Today, making "Never again" operational is being widely discussed across German society: Did it mean "Never again war," "Never again appeasement," "Never again anti-Semitism," or "Never again dehumanization and extermination of a minority"? Linking Germany's politics of remembrance to practical norms, such as support for the state of Israel, was important, but what level of abstraction did this involve? Had society come to an understanding about this?

## Migration and change

Broad sections of West German society only began to grapple with the perpetrators and victims of National Socialism after 1979, when the US television miniseries *Holo-*

*caust* was broadcast in Germany to much controversy.[3] At that time, I was 12, the child of a German-Egyptian family, and I watched the series and read a variety of related books for young people, such as *When Hitler Stole the Pink Rabbit*, published in German in 1973, *Damals war es Friedrich* (10th edition of 1979), *Ich bin David* (4th edition of 1979), and of course, *The Diary of Anne Frank* (47th edition of 1979). Since the 1980s, most of post-war German society – along with its migrant population – has been grappling with the rise of fascism, the devaluation of human life, and the Shoah in academia, the arts, and politics.

Migrants who settle in Germany can certainly be expected to engage with German history and the Holocaust. Sensitivity to diverse educational backgrounds, appropriately coordinated educational programming, and interest in the history of the immigrants is nevertheless needed, and increasingly available. In the immigrant society, the "perspective on and from history [...] is fractured, narratives are restructured, themes are varied, new ones are added, and old ones dropped, and the kaleidoscope of historical observation becomes more colorful." (Georgi/Ohliger 2009: 7). In this context, one can well imagine that non-Europeans who see images from a Nazi concentration camp here for the first time will be frightened. This is not a disgrace or an educational gap. They may experience flashbacks that update their own experiences of violence. And they may ask themselves: What historical continuities are there in Germany? How do the NSU, AfD, Nazi marches, and everyday racism fit into this history? Could similar transgressions still be possible today? Indeed, representatives of German politics are also asking themselves these questions. What guarantees do people with a migration background from the Global South and other minorities have that history will not repeat itself? Are they just being overly sensitive as they become aware of the German past?[4]

At the beginning of the new millennium, my friend and colleague Ahmed Badawi, to whom this text is dedicated, said in private that Muslims would become the new "internal enemies" in Germany. I vehemently forbade myself to make such remarks. Today I must admit that, as an agnostic, he sensed a form of anti-Muslim racism early on. The series of murders committed by the so-called *National Socialist Underground* (NSU) against Germans with an immigrant background and a policewoman has yet to be fully solved and saw the victims themselves placed under suspicion for years.

In Hanau in 2020, another perpetrator deliberately gunned down people with a migration background in a shisha bar. The emergency exit, through which many of them could have been saved, was locked. On October 9, 2019, a heavily armed right-wing extremist attempted to break into the synagogue in Halle on Yom Kippur and kill the 51 people gathered there. When he failed to do so, he shot and killed a female

3 For the reactions, see Hammerstein 2019.

4 See also Özyürek 2018.

pedestrian who approached him outside the synagogue about the explosions. He then drove to a Turkish kebab snack bar 500 meters away, threw more explosives, and killed yet another person there. That day on *heute journal*, newscaster Claus Kleber interviewed right-wing extremism researcher Hajo Funke on the two targets – first a synagogue, then a kebab snack bar. Kleber said, "The whole thing seems random and crazy, doesn't it?"[5]

Watching TV that October 9, 2019, I didn't find it random at all; to me, it seemed crystal clear and inherently consistent. In response to Pinar Atalay's (clearly more qualified) question in the ARD *Tagesthemen* shortly thereafter, as to whether the perpetrator, after his failure at the synagogue, had chosen the Turkish snack bar at random, the terrorism expert in the studio, Georg Mascolo, replied: yes, he was probably, like many terrorists, "nothing more than a common murderer" who "simply sought out other victims at random and murdered them."[6] These experts completely ignored the ideological superstructure that has interlocked hostility toward Jews and Muslims for almost 20 years. Wolfgang Benz summarized the research findings in the 2008 *Yearbook for Research on Anti-Semitism* as follows: "[T]he phenomenon of Islamophobia [is] interesting because it is widely argued with stereotypes that are familiar from research on anti-Semitism, such as the claim that the Jewish or Islamic religions are viciously inhumane and require their adherents to behave immorally toward those of other faiths" (Benz 2008: 10). But findings about the ideological proximity of anti-Semitic and Islamophobic acts are still being ignored. Yet the German ear, trained from decades of memory work, would have to prick up at the sweeping stigmatization of a religion, its practitioners, and practices, as well as the insinuation that they are hiding their true faith, would it not? Especially since this stigmatization includes all those who are linguistically, religiously, and politically completely assimilated in Germany (but possibly still have a Muslim-sounding name). There are more and more people in Germany who are not ashamed to claim that "Islam" is a "violent" and/or "hate" religion. A Judeo-Christian tradition is invoked that deliberately leaves out the third Abrahamic religion. "This is a remarkable process," Heribert Prantl wrote in the *Süddeutsche Zeitung* in 2010, "because the common ground now invoked was the common ground of perpetrators and victims for centuries."[7]

In this climate, the solidarity of the *Central Council of Jews in Germany* for victims of Islamophobic and Arabophobic attacks and racism was, in my view, of no small significance. While in 2009 the German media initially ignored the racially moti-

5 https://www.youtube.com/watch?v=R3eprV2IVCU, min. 7:40-7:43.

6 https://www.youtube.com/watch?v=yRMX_85lf88, min. 8:44-8:55.

7 Cf. the Jahrbuch für Antisemitismusforschung 17, edited by Wolfgang Benz since 2008, as well as the Jahrbuch für Islamophobieforschung, published since 2010.

vated murder[8] of Egyptian pharmacist Marwa el-Sherbini in a Dresden courtroom – she was a witness in an appeal proceeding –, Stephan Kramer, then the Secretary General of the *Central Council of Jews*, visited Dresden in a gesture of mourning and consternation. "The act went largely unnoted in Germany. Although the case was the first to be clearly Islamophobically motivated – the NSU series of murders only became known two years later through the self-disclosure of three perpetrators of the far-right network – there was little coverage, with very few statements by German officials," the *Tagesspiegel* reported in its commemoration ten years later.[9] The city of Dresden also long struggled with official remembrance. Just a few days after the murder, Stephan Kramer wrote:

> "In view of this situation, a clarifying word is needed. I did not travel to Dresden because, as a Jew, I belong to a minority. I made the trip because, as a Jew, I know that anyone who attacks a person because of their racial, ethnic, or religious affiliation, is attacking, not only the minority, but democratic society as a whole. Therefore, the relevant question is not why a representative of the Jewish community should have expressed grief and solidarity with Elwi Ali Okaz, but why there was not a massive stream of visitors and solidarity speeches from members of the German majority. [...] It seems that German society has not recognized the significance of the attack in Dresden. They have not realized that the murder of Marwa al-Sherbini is quite obviously the result of near unfettered hate propaganda against Muslims that ranges from the extremist fringes of society to its very core." (Kramer 2009)

Never was I more grateful for a show of solidarity, which I felt even then required civil courage. These words laid the foundation for how I can envision a practical "Never again!". Jewish solidarity in Germany is what touches me particularly, gives me courage, and plays a key role in the various threatening future scenarios I sometimes picture. I know that other friends with a migratory background go through similar threat scenarios in their mind as well. Back in my school days I remember hearing taunts of "Hegasy – gas her." (Hegasy – Vergas sie.) Only a fool would not extrapolate about future developments, having the historical background and personal experience, and given new-old right-wing extremism. I don't obsess over it, but a correlating state of mind has made itself felt in my life in important decision-making situations, putting me on guard.

8 It must not be forgotten that a police officer deliberately shot the husband, rather than the assassin, in the leg, critically injuring him as he ran to help his wife. El-Sherbini was three months pregnant. She died in the courtroom in front of her son.

9 See Dernbach 2019.

## National Socialism without a history

The debate on the "(dis)continuity of colonialism and National Socialism" (Geck/Rühling) has been ongoing for 15 years,[10] though it only entered German *feuilletons* in 2020. The so-called *Historikerstreit* 2.0. is surprisingly loud and impertinent. The enormous number of interventions and facets can be garnered from Serdar Günes' blog, compiling some 200 contributions to the topic.[11] Australian genocide researcher A. Dirk Moses calls the current dispute one among journalists – rather than historians – in an attempt to point out a crisis in the freedom of expression. The problem, however, is that the journalists, and not the academics under attack, are Germany's opinion leaders. In placing the Holocaust in a historical context, scholars such as Michael Rothberg, Jürgen Zimmerer, Dirk Moses, and others now stand accused of Holocaust relativization and trivialization. This alone deserves closer examination.

Why should referring to colonial history and the experiments on humans in the colonies cast the singularity of the Holocaust into doubt? Turn it around and the shoe fits: The brutality, the brutalization, the dehumanization of people in the European-occupied territories was a step (but not the only one – Klaus Theweleit is worth reading on this) towards the dehumanization of German Jews and Jews throughout Europe. There is nothing wrong about including one's own colonial history in answering how the breach of civilization could have occurred in the 20th century. And perhaps it is, in fact, impossible to answer at all, as Maxim Biller has pitched into the debate.[12]

Historian Jürgen Zimmerer observes:

> "that there was a genocide before the genocide and a racial state before the racial state. Germany's history of violence, therefore, began long before 1933. Such a realization anchors essential features of the Third Reich – i.e., racism, anti-Semitism, genocidal politics – in the history of the Kaiser Reich." (Interview with Jürgen Zimmerer 2021: 52)

This research finding, however, clearly does not negate the singularity of the Holocaust (of which I am thoroughly convinced). But it also does not make it impossible to

10 See e.g. Zimmerer 2011b.

11 https://serdargunes.wordpress.com/2021/06/04/a-debate-german-catechism-holocaust-and-post-colonialism/

12 "And could it not be that there will never be a final, rational answer to the question of what constitutes the inexplicably inexplicable nature of the Holocaust, which as even such people as Dirk Moses and Jürgen Zimmerer will be forced to accept?" (Biller, Die neuen Relativierer, Die Zeit, September 1, 2021).

think that the concept of 'sub-human humans' had a history before 1933. Jürgen Zimmerer points to connections in Germany's enthusiasm for the overseas possessions of the *Kaiserreich*, which also found its way into the German literature of the time. Of course, continuities such as these are only one of several explanatory threads, which, incidentally, is also what Zimmerer himself, under attack, says:

> "It has been asked again and again whether there was a path from Windhoek to Auschwitz. I think there were many paths. Seen from Windhoek, the Third Reich was by no means the necessary consequence. But to stay in the picture: Of the many roads that fed into the criminal policies of National Socialism, one began in the colonies. And this one was not a remote byway." (2011: 70)

It is therefore a malicious reading that suggests that historians of colonialism and postcolonial theorists interpret the Holocaust simply as one of many colonial acts, or as no more than a continuation of colonialism – this time at home and using other means; spinning National Socialism as an act "committed in Africa" for a change. But this is precisely the interpretation currently being insinuated against researchers – including the works of descendants of Holocaust survivors.

Why are Jewish voices being vilified in the process? For example, the event series "School for Unlearning Zionism," conceived by a group of Jewish-Israeli students at the Weißensee School of Art, including Yehudit Yinhar, was deprived of state funding (vulgo: boycotted). Let me suggest a new interpretive approach: In my view, the purpose is to (consciously or unconsciously) prevent Jewish-Arab-Muslim[13] solidarity and the alliances described above. For this purpose, a competition between victims is contrived and "envy" conjured up: In his article suggestively entitled "The Holocaust was singular. This is now denied by more than just right-wing radicals", Thomas Schmid writes about Rothberg and Zimmerer:

> "In post-colonial circles, there seems to be a kind of great envy of the Jews (and Israel). They are accused of effectively staging themselves as a victim nation. [...] More than slight traces of this conviction can be found in many postcolonial authors, who see in Jews, as it were, inheritance hustlers who have usurped a singular victim status for themselves at the expense of Blacks and other colonized people. No doubt, the post-colonials have built at least close to anti-Semitism." (Schmid 2021a)

Jews as "inheritance hustlers"? Turning allegations of anti-Semitism around could not be more perfidious.

Palestinian literary scholar Edward W. Said, commonly regarded as the founder of postcolonial studies, wrote in the Arabic daily *al-Hayat* back in 1998: "We must ac-

13 In the following, I use the term 'Arab' more often to avoid having to distinguish between practicing and the often-overlooked non-practicing or cultural Muslims from the region.

knowledge the realities of the Holocaust; not as a blank check for Israelis to mistreat us, but as a sign of our humanity, our ability to understand history, our demand for mutual recognition of our sufferings." This is the birth of postcolonial studies – not competition for the status of victimhood or the idea of "Jews as inheritance creep."

The parallel with the historians' dispute of the 1980s is also contrived: A "reaction" (as claimed at the time by Ernst Nolte) is not a "preliminary stage" – it is in fact the exact opposite of a preliminary stage. To spell it out: If I say the Holocaust was (only) a reaction to the Gulag and the crimes of Stalinism, then I am qualifying the Holocaust. If I say that dehumanization by European colonialism laid foundations for the subsequent racial theories and "ancestor passes" of the Third Reich, then I am not qualifying it. Why shouldn't the Nazi murder machinery and its ideological preparation be placed in its historical context (civilizing mission, physical-anthropological measurements, skin color maps, hierarchization of language families)?

## Can intellectuals read?

In the debate outlined here, literary critics who should know better mistakenly equate the method of 'comparing' with 'equating'. In science, comparisons are made to work out both similarities and differences. Comparison can therefore also lead to the result: Nothing is the same. "The specific feature that distinguishes the Holocaust from colonial genocides is this turn against the 'internal enemy' who must be killed – and who is not to be primarily exploited like the foreign, colonially subjugated population along with their natural resources," writes Jürgen Habermas in his response to the debate and the question of whether the Holocaust is comparable to other, colonial genocides or not (Habermas 2021:11).[14] The question common to all genocides, which is also central to prevention, is that of the transformation of average citizens into mass murderers, and here research has found answers.

Are the critics of postcolonial thinking unfamiliar with the comparative method? And even more grim: why do so many of them quote out of context or completely wrong? The journalist and editor of the *Welt* publishing corporation, Thomas Schmid, reduces Jürgen Zimmerer to a quote stating that the murder of the Jews would probably not have been possible "if the ultimate breach of taboo [...] had not occurred earlier". Schmid goes on to say that Zimmerer leaves nothing to be desired in terms of clarity, "colonialism and the Holocaust do not differ in principle, they are of the same essence" (Schmidt 2021a). But what does Zimmerer say?

> "Even the murder of the Jews, which – as mentioned – stands out from other genocides in many ways, would probably not have been possible if the ultimate

14 See also the response by Dirk Moses to Jürgen Habermas in Berliner Zeitung, 2021e.

> taboo break had not happened earlier: i.e., believing that other ethnic groups can simply be annihilated, and acting upon it. And that took place in colonialism." (2011a: 69)

Jürgen Zimmerer described the usefulness of comparative genocide research as follows:

> "As one cannot simulate specific murder situations in a laboratory, the historical examples play a crucial role. They offer the advantage that it is easier to distinguish the causes and effects, the central facts from the superfluous details and the necessary from the sufficient conditions at a historical distance. Much information that was unknown to the contemporaries is accessible to the historian. The best researched example is doubtless the Holocaust. This is partly due to the high level of scientific interest and partly to the fact that the perpetrating regime in Germany collapsed completely in 1945. As a result, no subsequent regime wanted to cover anything up, so all the archives were largely made accessible" (2011b: 215).

His project (as those of many others) is that of prevention, which only works when indicators are established that allow genocide to be recognized in advance rather than ex post. Why is it necessary to accuse Jürgen Zimmerer of dishonest motives ten years later, when his intention is clearly justified in writings available to the public? It is also about the underlying motives of a debate, as Jürgen Habermas writes in his reply.

Habermas explicitly saw no problem in comparing the "Holocaust with other genocides":

> "But the purpose of the comparison varies by context. The so-called *Historikerstreit* was about whether the comparison of the Holocaust with Stalin's crimes could exonerate posthumous Germans from their political responsibility or, as Jaspers admonished, "liability" for Nazi mass crimes. For were these not, as Ernst Nolte thought at the time, "only" a reaction to the atrocities of Bolshevism? Under other auspices, today it is not a matter of exoneration from this responsibility, but of a shift in the weights" (2021: 10).

A second example of "intellectual citation skills" involves Austrian philosopher Thomas Macho accusing Dirk Moses of using the term "guilt cult" (*Schuldkult*) in his article *The Catechism of the Germans* (2021a) to refer to German memory politics. It's a term that Reichsbürger and right-wing radicals like to use, insinuating that public Holocaust remembrance is meant to stigmatize Germans as perpetrators and murderers for generations, from denazification on into the future. When challenged,

Macho apologized to Moses for this insinuation, as Moses in fact did not use this term anywhere.[15]

And a third example for misquoting: Maxim Biller also deals with Moses' *Catechism of the Germans.*[16] Biller calls Moses an "Auschwitz blasphemer and genocide watchdog" who "in his choleric *J'accuse* text, directed against the evil Holocaust priests of our day, entertains feverish dreams of 'American, British, and Jewish elites' allegedly driving the contemporary sycophantic German gas chamber cult." (2021b) Let's leave both authors their exaggerations. But, Biller misquotes Moses in a key part of the speech that raises the red flag of anti-Semitism: Moses does not speak of "Jewish elites," but of "American, British, and Israeli elites".[17] A wordsmith such as Biller ought know how to quote. Especially when it comes to a remnant of race theory of National Socialism that equates Jews with Israelis that has been very clearly problematized in Germany at least since Ignaz Bubis. In turn any Arab who says "Jews" when he means "Israelis" will be accused of anti-Semitism.

Biller himself writes how he empathized with the Tutsis in 1994, sensitized by the genocides of the Armenian and Jewish members of his family:

"Why? Because as a Jew, and also a bit as an Armenian, I saw myself intentionally-unintentionally reflected in the Tutsis; because it was all happening in my immediate present day, I suddenly turned into a kind of escapee myself, and that in turn was enough for me to empathize with the dismembered, slain, drowned Tutsis."

This empathy also exists between Jews, Israelis, and Arabs. But wherever such empathy surfaces, it is to be suppressed, and the trope of the envious People of Color (PoC), including the vicious Palestinians, enters the debate. Biller continues, "There was no victimhood rivalry between me and them [the Tutsis], not the kind of Holocaust envy one often witnesses as a Jew from the tightly knit ranks of the sanctimonious PoC faction and their Critical Whiteness allies, but only empathy and hope that they were not all dead and their people might live on like the Jews." Holocaust enviers? Inheritance hustlers? This hermeneutic chicanery confirms many accusations by colleagues that they are being muzzled in this debate. Michael Rothberg would call Maxim Biller's account here of the Tutsi genocide precisely as "multidirectional memory".

---

15 Hanloser (2021) has found more examples of misquoting, which raises the question – especially against the background of the current debate on misquotation in the political class – whether this is a pattern?

16 Per Leo (2021) suggests that it would be better to speak of "dispositive" in Foucault's sense rather than catechism to move away from the religiously charged terminology that is the focus of criticism of Moses' text.

17 Moses writes about this in a reply: "Addressing such a state need for international legitimacy is not an allusion to the anti-Semitic idea of a Jewry ("elites") supposedly directing world politics, as Friedländer insinuates – but a standard argument in the history of international relations." (July 14, 2021).

"Remembering our colonial history, repressed until recently, is an important extension," Habermas says today. With immigration to Germany, the political culture must "expand in such a way that members of other cultural ways of life can recognize themselves in it with their heritage and, if necessary, also with their history of suffering" (2021: 11) – a pedagogical appeal that has been around for some time in the teaching of history:

> "History and identity have been a defining duo for the self-description and location of German society in framing what is national over the past two centuries. The duo has become a trio: Migration complements historical experience, broadens the historical gaze, and redefines social affiliations. This applies to society as a whole, but especially to young people, whose historical images and consciousness are only beginning to develop their contours." (Georgi/Ohliger 2009: 20).

Dirk Moses hoped that Habermas' intervention would bring more objectivity and reason into the debate. If one follows the argumentation I propose here, this can hardly be expected to happen, because the target of those who accuse Zimmerer and Rothberg of Holocaust relativization is not the research in itself but the Jewish-Arab solidarization of the protagonists. This constellation became evident in the removal of the director of the Jewish Museum in Berlin, Peter Schäfer. Under his direction, the museum had seen itself as a place for multi-directional remembrance.[18] Here, the diversity of racisms and of the degradation of peoples was reflected. The 2018/19 exhibition *Welcome to Jerusalem* had shown the city as a "place desired and longed for by members of Jewish, Christian, and Muslim denominations." Benjamin Netanyahu intervened with Angela Merkel in connection with this exhibition, saying that the museum should be defunded! That Netanyahu was not concerned with a lack of attention to anti-Semitism in the wider memory culture was apparent from his simultaneous tolerance of blatantly anti-Semitic poster campaigns in Hungary.

There is another way to approach the polemic instigated by Dirk Moses, as demonstrated by historian Jacob Eder in his response to the "Catechism of the Germans" in the Swiss online magazine *Geschichte der Gegenwart* – a model for taking on deliberate misinterpretation.[19] Eder refers to the particularly complex history of the development of German Holocaust remembrance from below (68er movement, media, art) as well as from above (ministerial bureaucracy, government representatives), between national and international objectives, all without insinuating dishonest intentions. He considers "the motives behind his [Dirk Moses'] arguments comprehensible" and shares "his criticism of the lack of confrontation with racism in this country, the failures to come to terms with the history of

18 Incidentally, the Berlin Center for Research on Anti-Semitism (ZfA) has been struggling with accusations of relativizing anti-Semitism since 2008.

19 See https://geschichtedergegenwart.ch/jacob-eders-text/.

the crimes of colonialism, and Germany's lack of empathy toward the suffering of Palestinian civilians in the Middle East conflict." Eder doubts, however, that something like a "catechism" has been enforced in post-reunification Germany and whether a consensus in fact prevails today? The author rightly concludes that it was precisely "in confronting the Nazi past that the essential political, scientific, and remembrance-cultural foundations and 'instruments' were first created, on the basis of which other histories of suffering and crime are researched, discussed, and debated today" (Eder 2021).

It should not be forgotten that the topic of colonialism was introduced to German discourse over the past ten years primarily in connection with the contested construction of the Humboldt Forum on the site of the former Palace of the Republic. Credit goes to the opponents of the plans for the Humboldt Forum, including the activists, scientists, and artists of Alexandertechnik, Artefakte//anti-humboldt, and the allied campaign No Humboldt21!. The debate about colonial history and restitution was forcefully carried from the margins into the socio-political center and is responsible for colonialism being discussed in Germany today.[20]

So, Germany has been proud – and rightly so – of its culture of remembrance, hard-won over decades. It is no coincidence that the New Right wants to be rid of it. Today, the Holocaust remembrance community is almost global. This achievement means that non-German voices are a part of the conversation. Jewish interventions such as those of literary scholar Michael Rothberg or philosopher Susan Neiman are central because they stand in for voices of people often assumed to be anti-Semitic based on their historical background (i.e., simply for being born in Muslim-majority societies). Who speaks for whom from which position is of importance in all debates – and that includes those concerning the politics of memory. How are we Germans with an Arab cultural background supposed to intervene here when even renowned personalities in Germany such as Susan Neiman face accusations of anti-Semitism from German authorities?[21] The harsh "Catechism of the Germans" was not the start of a debate, but a reaction to how Jewish scholars are defamed in Germany. In retrospect, Moses writes,

> "In the summer [2021, SH] we witnessed a proverbial death of reason. Slander rather than communicative rationality marked the 'discussion'. This kind of discussion is not new. In 2019, Micha Brumlik characterized the Jewish Museum debate as a 'witch hunt' and 'McCarthyism.'"(Moses 2021e).

---

20 The arrival of these critical positions in state politics (including critical civil society positions) marks the publication of the Humboldt Forum publication Das Projekt/The Project, ed. 2009 by Thomas Flierl and Hermann Parzinger.

21 Thus Susan Neiman at the conference 'Historiker streiten' (historians debate) in Potsdam on October 4, 2021: https://einsteinforum.de/veranstaltungen/blind-spots-of-genocide-problems-in-dirk-mosess-the-problems-of-genocide/, min. 22ff.

## The Israel-Palestine Conflict

This climate causes intellectual honesty to fade. For example, commentators equate the phrase "The Palestinians are victims of the victims of the Holocaust" as heard among Palestinians – though not only from them[22] – and the ahistorical apologetics and agitation behind "The Israelis are doing to the Palestinians what the Nazis did to them". The latter is (of course) incorrect and Israel-related anti-Semitism[23], whereas the former is not anti-Semitic (unless one insinuates that the extent of crimes should be equated). It is therefore dismaying to see that an audit conducted by Sabine Leutheusser-Schnarrenberger, Ahmed Mansour and Beatrice Mansour to investigate allegations of anti-Semitism against individual employees of *Deutsche Welle's* Arabic editorial team cites precisely the former (not the latter!) sentence as an example of Israel-related anti-Semitism. After this audit, several editors at *Deutsche Welle* were dismissed or transferred.[24] Illustrating the so-called three Ds of antisemitism – double standards, demonization, delegitimization of Israel –, the authors conclude that "the understanding of the Middle East conflict as a prolonged reaction to the Holocaust (e.g., the Palestinians are the victims of the victims)" is among "the attitudes that cross the line of acceptable political positions" (Leutheusser-Schnarrenberger et al 2022: 41). On the ground, people see themselves as victims of persecution, expulsion, and genocide in Europe, for which they are in no way (co)responsible. We should think that sentence with the Palestinians – not against them.

Anyone who defines criticism of Israeli government action as anti-Semitic is, by definition, expanding the circle of those suspected of anti-Semitism – which does not mean that there are no anti-Semitic attitudes among those criticizing Israeli policy. In 2022 Robin Schmahl conveyed to me that young Jewish people in Germany fear and partly already experience in their everyday life how the wrong attribution (*Fremdzuschreibung*) of "all Jews are Israelis and Israelis are colonial settlers", as well as this supposed relativization of the Shoah in the debates about comparing geno-

22 See, for example, Andrew N. Rubin's lecture at the Barenboim-Said Academy on June 7, 2022, min. 6:59 and min. 34:00 (Rubin's Facebook page).

23 For the genesis and my critique of the International Holocaust Remembrance Alliance's (IHRA) use of the "working definition of anti-Semitism," see my article, Antisemitismus-Debatte: (Post-)migrantische Stimmen zulassen (Anti-Semitism Debate: Allowing (Post-)Migrant Voices) (Hegasy 2020).

24 Two female journalists have since won their labor lawsuits against it, see: https://rsw.beck.de/aktuell/daily/meldung/detail/arbg-berlin-kuendigung-einer-redakteurin-wegen-antisemitischer-aeusserung-unwirksam.

cides, lead to an actual relativization in society.[25] Embedding the Holocaust in European colonialism (which – again – does not go counter to the thesis of a *Zivilisationsbruch*) is thus used among parts of the German public as a vulgar hypothesis, so to speak, to update disposable anti-Semitism in a new guise. It is precisely on this point that those scholars, journalists, and politicians who place Rothberg or Neiman in the corner of relativizing the Holocaust and anti-Semitism should reflect their own attacks critically. While anti-Semitism does like to hide behind criticism of the state of Israel, Susan Neiman, Michael Rothberg, Dirk Moses, or Yehudit Yinhar can hardly be anti-Semites. Obviously, they have a political position in the conflict over Israel and Palestine; they demand empathy with the Palestinian victims, and they resist the successful attempts to delegitimize criticism of Israel's policies as anti-Semitic on principle. In an attempt to close all peaceful channels of communication to resolve the conflict between Israelis and Palestinians, these researchers are now being vilified to the maximum. Maxim Biller permits himself the liberty of calling these scholars "Holocaust deniers light" (2021b).

Again, why are descendants of Holocaust survivors misquoted and put in a corner with neo-Nazis? From my point of view, such talk aims to stifle the international solidarity already stifled in the Middle East in the past: These are, on the one hand, bonds of solidarity and empathy between Jewish, Christian, and Muslim Arabs that crisscross the Israeli border, and on the other, the historical solidarity of persecuted peoples in the Middle East who, in their distress, believed the assurances of the colonial powers. This solidarity of the persecuted existed – even during the Nazi era, both in Germany and in the region[26] – and it exists again, for example, in the 'Days of Jewish-Muslim Guiding Culture' curated by Max Czollek in 2020, featuring 40 separate events in German-speaking countries. After that event, Maxim Biller, the central protagonist in the *Historikerstreit 2.0*, denied that the curator was Jewish. I only point to the chronology here: Czollek's Jewishness was not under review beforehand.

People with a migrant background are reading along, but hardly speak out in this debate, although they certainly do not represent a small group, and might have both as their biographical basis – a German history with references to National Socialism and a migrant history. The German-Egyptian journalist Karim El-Gawhary once hung the photos of his two grandfathers in his office: wearing a Fez as headgear on one photo, and in the uniform of the Wehrmacht on the other. This simultaneity

25 Personal exchange with Robin Schmahl in June 2022. At the same time, one can see how the equation Arabs = Muslims = anti-Semites is gaining ever wider acceptance in German society, both im- and explicitly.

26 See, for example, the work of Ronen Steinke, David Motadel, Mikhal Dekel, Robert Satloff, Marc Baer, and Gerhard Höpp.

may well signify a kind of double implication that is neither mutually exclusive nor in conflict with each other but constitutes a German reality.[27]

After the controversial BDS resolution of the German Bundestag, which initiated a climate of ongoing suspicions of anti-Semitism, I wrote in 2020 – that is, before the case of Nemi el-Hassan broke –

> "[w]hat should we Germans with an Arab or Islamic cultural background do [...] without being placed under the devastating general suspicion of being anti-Semitic? [...] Colleagues from the Arab world have confirmed this fear to me in conversations. They fear being targeted and, above all: being intentionally misunderstood and discredited."

One year later, Nemi el-Hassan, a TV journalist from Bad Saarow with Palestinian parents, who liked posts on the Instagram page of the *Jewish Voice for Peace* (one of the largest Jewish peace organizations in the U.S.), was suspended by WDR from the prospective moderation of the well-known science magazine *Quarks* because of these likes.[28]

Stop for a moment and think about this: Likes by a Palestinian woman for the *Jewish Voice for Peace* (JVP), an organization founded in 1996 to find a peaceful solution for Israelis and Palestinians, put an end to her career and portray her as an alleged anti-Semite – even though former Israeli ambassador to Germany Avi Primor, together with Israeli historian Moshe Zimmermann, went on to defend Nemi el-Hassan against this campaign in a letter to the WDR Broadcasting Council. Again, it was Israeli-Palestinian solidarity ties that were being targeted – even at the cost of deriding critical Jewish voices as anti-Semitic.

To summarize, four fronts meet in the debate highlighted here that were not necessarily originally linked, either in terms of personnel or matter:

1) Debates on memory politics, whose central figures cannot or do not want to distinguish between the idea that "Hitler and the Nazis are just a 'speck of bird poop' in over 1,000 years of successful German history" (Alexander Gauland 2018 at the national congress of the AfD's junior organization, Junge Alternative). Add to this the idea that causes leading to the Holocaust can also be found, among other things, in Germany's non-European history of violence in the 19th and 20th centuries (through the study of colonial history and cultural memory). Those who turn research on the history of violence into a "longing for a better, more acceptable, even 'normal' national history", a sentiment deemed "apparently not only widespread on the right-wing fringe of German society" (viz. Andreas Wirsching 2022), are intentionally misinterpreting their colleagues.

27 Thank you to Regina Sarreiter for her comment.

28 Cf. Huber 2021.

2) An increasing Islamophobia, already anticipated with the end of the Cold War and growing exponentially since the attacks of al-Qaeda in the USA in 2001, because no distinction is made between Islamic terrorist groups, who have Muslim as well as non-Muslim victims, and the majority faith of Islam. Whether "Islam" is a "religion of violence" or not is a question that, unfortunately, even the occasional bourgeois evening round is now pondering.
3) The rise of the AfD and its new-right cultural milieu, in which anti-Semitic, but outwardly emphatically pro-Israel motives are mixed with Islamophobic motives (viz., that they are the true opponents of Israel, not oneself).
4) The growing notion that one can point a finger at Palestinians and Arabs as the alleged "real anti-Semites" to exonerate and dismiss Germans from their own history and thus – in an act of ostensible solidarity with the state of Israel – to silence "the Other".

Regarding Israel, this leaves only the *status quo*, i.e., the occupation of the West Bank and the closure of the Gaza Strip. Jewish-Arab connections are attacked for alternative thinking; compassion is prevented, and opposition to current Israeli policy is discredited. Solidarity with Israel means working for a peaceful solution to the Israel-Palestine conflict. To advocate for a peaceful solution, means to look at and speak out about the suffering on both sides. We *Mischlinge* will not be denied our solidarity with Israel.

## References

Assheuer, Thomas (2021) Verlangen nach Entlastung. Die tageszeitung, September 11 (https://taz.de/Debatte-um-Maxim-Billers-neuen-Roman/!5797037/).

Benz, Wolfgang (2008) Jahrbuch für Antisemitismusforschung 17. Berlin.

Biller, Maxim (2021a) Partisanenlieder. Die Zeit, August 11 (https://www.zeit.de/2021/33/max-czollek-judentum-linke-kommunismus-intellektueller-juedischsein).

Biller, Maxim (2021b) Die neuen Relativierer. Die Zeit, September 1 (https://www.zeit.de/2021/36/holocaust-verharmlosung-leugnung-gleichsetzung-kolonialgeschichte-erklaerung).

Dandekar, Deepra (2022) The Role of Memory and Emotions in the Long Migration Journey to Germany. In: Martin, Staci B.; Dandekar, Deepra (eds.) Global South Scholars in Western Academy. New York: Routledge, 143–154.

Dernbach, Andrea (2019) Jahrestag der islamophoben Tat in Dresden. Marwa el-Sherbini wurde ermordet, weil sie ein Kopftuch trug. Der Tagesspiegel, July 1 (https://www.tagesspiegel.de/politik/marwa-el-sherbini-wurde-ermordet-weil-sie-ein-kopftuch-trug-5024467.html).

dpa (2018) Gauland: NS-Zeit nur ein 'Vogelschiss in der Geschichte'. Die Zeit, June 2 (https://www.zeit.de/news/2018-06/02/gauland-ns-zeit-nur-ein-vogelschiss-in-der-geschichte-180601-99-549766).

Eder, Jacob (2021) Der Weg ist das Ziel. Deutsche Erinnerungspolitik und ihre Widersprüche. Geschichte der Gegenwart, June 23 (https://geschichtedergegenwart.ch/jacob-eders-text/).

Flierl, Thomas; Parzinger, Hermann (eds.) (2009) Humboldt Forum Berlin. Das Projekt. The project. Berlin Verlag Theater der Zeit.

Friedländer, Saul (2021) Ein fundamentales Verbrechen. Die Zeit, July 7. https://www.zeit.de/2021/28/holocaust-gedenken-erinnerungskultur-genozid-kolonialverbrechen.

Friedländer, Saul; Frei, Norbert et al. (2022) Ein Verbrechen ohne Namen: Anmerkung zum neuen Streit über den Holocaust. München: C. H. Beck.

Georgi, Viola B.; Ohliger, Rainer (2009) Crossover Geschichte. Historisches Bewusstsein Jugendlicher in der Einwanderungsgesellschaft. Hamburg: Bundeszentrale für politische Bildung.

Habermas, Jürgen (2021) Der neue Historikerstreit. philosophie Magazin 60, September, 10–11.

Hammerstein, Katrin (2019) Eine Fernsehserie schreibt Geschichte Reaktionen auf die Ausstrahlung von "Holocaust" vor 40 Jahren. January 10 (https://www.bpb.de/themen/deutschlandarchiv/284090/eine-fernsehserie-schreibt-geschichte/).

Hanloser, Gerhard (2021) Die Fälscherwerkstätten der Berliner Republik, Der Freitag, July 21.

Hegasy, Sonja (2020) Antisemitismus-Debatte: (Post-)migrantische Stimmen zulassen. dis:orient, July 16. (https://www.disorient.de/magazin/antisemitismus-debatte-post-migrantische-stimmen-zulassen).

Henryk M. Broder (2012) Vergesst Auschwitz! Der deutsche Erinnerungswahn und die Endlösung der Israel-Frage. Albrecht Knaus Verlag, München.

Huber, Joachim (2021) Entscheidung von WDR-Intendant Buhrow: Nemi El-Hassan wird "Quarks" nicht moderieren. Tagesspiegel, Sept. 28. (https://www.tagesspiegel.de/gesellschaft/medien/entscheidung-von-wdr-intendant-buhrow-nemi-el-hassan-wird-quarks-nicht-moderieren/27657462.html).

Kramer, Stephan J. (2009) Im Zeichen der Solidarität mit allen Muslimen. Qantara.de, July 13 (https://de.qantara.de/inhalt/stephan-j-kramer-zum-mord-an-marwa-al-sherbini-im-zeichen-der-solidaritat-mit-allen-muslimen).

Leo, Per (2021) Unser Land erwacht aus einem historischen Schlummer. philosophie Magazin 60, September, 12–13.

Leutheusser-Schnarrenberger, Sabine; Mansour, Ahmad; Mansour, Beatrice (2022) Prüfungsbericht: externe Untersuchung der Antisemitismusvorwürfe gegen einzelne Mitarbeitende der arabischen Redaktion der Deutschen Welle sowie gegenüber einzelnen Partnern. Berlin, February 6.

Ludin, Fereshta; Abed, Sandra (2015) Enthüllung der Fereshta Ludin: Die mit dem Kopftuch. Berlin.

Mendel, Meron (2021) Juden zweiter Klasse. Die Zeit, August 18 (https://www.zeit.de/kultur/2021-08/judentum-alltag-maxim-biller-max-czollek-definitionen).

Moses, A. Dirk (2021a) Der Katechismus der Deutschen. Geschichte der Gegenwart, May 23 (https://geschichtedergegenwart.ch/der-katechismus-der-deutschen/).

Moses, A. Dirk (2021b) Dialectic of Vergangenheitsbewältigung, The New Facism Syllabus, June 15 (https://www.newfascismsyllabus.com/opinions/dialectic-of-vergangenheitsbewaltigung/).

Moses, A. Dirk (2021c) Gedenkt endlich auch der Opfer kolonialer Gräueltaten! Die Zeit, July 14 (https://www.zeit.de/2021/29/holocaust-singularitaet-dirk-moses-koloniale-verbrechen-historikerstreit).

Moses, A. Dirk (2021d) Wir haben keinen neuen Historikerstreit, sondern einen neuen Illiberalismus, Berliner Zeitung, August 7 https://www.berliner-zeitung.de/wochenende/wir-haben-keinen-neuen-historikerstreit-sondern-einen-neuen-autoritarismus-li.175278).

Moses, A. Dirk (2021e) Dialektik der Normalisierung, Berliner Zeitung, October 2/3 (https://www.berliner-zeitung.de/wochenende/dirk-moses-warum-wir-die-dialektik-der-normalisierung-ergaenzen-muessen-li.184931).

Moses, A. Dirk (2022) Affective Colonization as Minority Management. RePLITO, February 4 (https://doi.org/10.21428/f4c6e600.866f046e).

Özyürek, E (2018) Rethinking empathy: Emotions triggered by the Holocaust among the Muslim-minority in Germany, Anthropological Theory, 18(4) 456–477 (https://doi.org/10.1177/1463499618782369).

Opferberatung des RAA Sachsen e.V. (2011) Tödliche Realitäten. Der rassistische Mord an Marwa El-Sherbini. Dresden.

Prantl, Heribert (2010) Der Missbrauch der Juden durch die Politik, Süddeutsche Zeitung, November 9 (https://www.sueddeutsche.de/politik/gedenktag-9-november-der-missbrauch-der-juden-durch-die-politik-1.1021220).

Rapp, Tobias (2021) Macht uns das Gedenken an den Holocaust blind für andere deutsche Verbrechen Der Spiegel, February 12 (https://www.spiegel.de/geschichte/holocaust-macht-uns-das-gedenken-blind-fuer-andere-deutsche-verbrechen-a-00000000-0002-0001-0000-000175304219).

Rothberg, Michael (2020) Vergleiche vergleichen: Vom Historikerstreit zur Causa Mbembe. Geschichte der Gegenwart, September 23 (https://geschichtedergegenwart.ch/vergleiche-vergleichen-vom-historikerstreit-zur-causa-mbembe/).

Rothberg, Michael; Zimmerer, Jürgen (2021) Enttabuisiert den Vergleich! Die Geschichtsschreibung globalisieren, das Gedenken pluralisieren: Warum sich

die deutsche Erinnerungslandschaft verändern muss. Die Zeit, March 31 (https://www.zeit.de/2021/14/erinnerungskultur-gedenken-pluralisieren-holocaust-vergleich-globalisierung-geschichte).
Rothberg, Michael (2021) Der neue Historikerstreit bedarf einer anderen Richtung. Die Zeit, July 24 (https://www.zeit.de/kultur/2021-07/umgang-mit-dem-holocaust-historikerstreit-kontroverse-voelkermord).
Said, Edward (1998) كسر الجمود : طريق ثالث (Durchbrechen der Sackgasse: ein dritter Weg). Al-Hayat, June 30, 17.
Salamander, Rachel (2022) Wenn es brennt. Statt der geplanten Rede zur Erinnerungskultur: Einige Worte zu unseren Lehren aus der Geschichte. Süddeutsche Zeitung 58, March 11 (https://www.sueddeutsche.de/kultur/putins-krieg-und-die-geschichte-europas-wenn-es-brennt-1.5545002).
Schmid, Thomas (2021a) Der Holocaust war singulär. Das bestreiten inzwischen nicht nur Rechtsradikale. Welt, February 26 (https://schmid.welt.de/2021/02/26/der-holocaust-war-singulaer-das-bestreiten-inzwischen-nicht-nur-rechtsradikale/).
Schmid, Thomas (2021b) Der Holocaust war kein Kolonialverbrechen. Die Zeit, April 7 (https://www.zeit.de/2021/15/erinnerungskultur-holocaust-kolonialismus-menschheitsverbrechen-vergleichbarkeit-michael-rothberg-juergen-zimmerer).
Shohat, Ella (2017) On the Arab-Jew, Palestine, and Other Displacements. London.
Slyomovics, Susan (2014) How to accept German Reparations. Philadelphia.
Staas, Christian (2021) Ein Haufen Zunder. Die Zeit, June 23 (https://www.zeit.de/2021/26/holocaust-erinnerungskultur-gedenken-historikerstreit-antisemitismus).
Staas, Christian/von Thadden, Elisabeth (2021) Wie gerecht ist unser Gedenken? Die Zeit, June 30 (https://www.zeit.de/2021/27/holocaust-gedenken-aufarbeitung-koloniale-verbrechen-dirk-moses).
Thadden, Elisabeth von (2021) Wir brauchen neue Wege, um über Erinnerung nachzudenken. Die Zeit, March 27 (https://www.zeit.de/kultur/2021-03/michael-rothberg-multidirektionale-erinnerung-buch-holocaust-rassismus-kolonialismus).
Weidner, Stefan (2013) Coming to Terms with the Past. Art & Thought 98.
Wessel, Thomas (2021) Judenhass metaphorisch: Ist A. Dirk Moses der neue Achille Mbembe? Ruhrbarone, June 11 (https://www.ruhrbarone.de/judenhass-metaphorisch-ist-a-dirk-moses-der-neue-achille-mbembe/199614).
Wiedemann, Charlotte (2022) Den Schmerz der Anderen begreifen. Holocaust und Weltgedächtnis. Berlin: Propyläen.
Wirsching, Andreas (2022) Ist der Tod kein Meister aus Deutschland mehr? Über die jüngsten Versuche, den Holocaust aus der deutschen Geschichte herauszuschreiben, und das Gedenken zum 8. Mai in Zeiten des Krieges. Die Zeit 19, May 5 (https://www.zeit.de/2022/19/holocaust-nationalsozialismus-krieg-ukraine).

Zimmerer, Jürgen (2011) Von Windhuk nach Auschwitz? Beiträge zum Verhältnis von Kolonialismus und Holocaust. Münster.
Zimmerer, Jürgen (2021) Europa ist tot. Interview mit Katja Maurer. Rundschreiben medico international, 03/21 (English edition: https://www.medico.de/en/europe-is-dead-18426).

# 6. The Arab in the law of Berlin, or: 'How does it feel to be a problem?'

## The figure of the Arab, or the case for Arabness

*Nahed Samour*

How do you approach the question of "Arabness" or the figure of "the Arab" in Berlin? The case of Arabness arguably shows some similarities to the case of Blackness[1] or Latinx (Latinas/os)[2] in addressing the lived experience of Arabness. Like Blacks or Latinx, Arab diversities are based on their national origins, ideological, political, and religious similarities and differences, and the racialized consequences of diverse physical appearance and cultural and religious practice. At the same time, inner-Arab commonalities are derived from shared struggles with immigration and participation – not least as Arabs meet the "German gaze" that defines and, at times, obstructs their quest for equality in Berlin. Arabness engages with the multiple internal diversities while situating Arabs, like Blacks and Latinx, in the significant debates around domestic and global arguments around the right of a dignified life, free with equal opportunities. Exploring Arabness in this contribution is an attempt to reflect on the figure of the Arab in the context of Berlin's state power. As presented in this chapter, the figure of "the Arab" emerges as a distinctly delineated subject, object, and agent of change.

This contribution discusses Arabness in relation to the law of the *Land* [the federal state of] Berlin, in as much as "the Arab" serves as a foil for the laws of Berlin, and those laws in turn impact the situation of Arabs in Berlin. The legal competences of the *Land* Berlin include public safety and order (*öffentliche Ordnung und Sicherheit*), schools and education (*Bildung und Erziehung*), as well as of culture,[3] all major stages

1 Moten, Fred (2008) The Case of Blackness, Criticism, Vol. 50 (2) Spring, 177–218.

2 Cf. LatCrit (2002) Primer, Vol. 1 (summer) (https://latcrit.org/wp-content/uploads/2020/07/lcprimeri.pdf).

3 According to article 30 of the German constitution, the Länder are primarily responsible for legislation and thus also for administration in the areas of education, science, culture as well as public safety and order. The first area includes schools, technical colleges, universities, museums, theaters, libraries, and numerous scientific institutions, while the second includes the police and prison system.

for narrating what equal freedom should look like in Berlin. The *Länder* also play a role, as they bear responsibility for executing federal laws using their own authorities, institutions, and personnel.[4] For example, the *Land* Berlin establishes its own authority to pay (federal) social housing benefits and arrange for the accommodation of asylum seekers. It is free to decide regulatory details on payments for housing, allocating social housing units, issuing identity cards, regulating residency rights and naturalization, and deporting foreigners. Crucially, these are all acute contact points for Arabs with the law as enforced by Berlin authorities, at least at some moments in their lives.

It is through the figure of the Arab that Berlin's crucial transformations in the fields of il/liberalism, secularism, racism, and coloniality are reflected. "The Arab" is literally and metaphorically a figure to highlight erasures, breaks, and denials in Germany today, most notably through a system of surveillance, censorship, and exclusion, as will be shown. The figure of the Arab has therefore become visible as an object of transformation of Germany, most notably in the fields of migration and security. As a figure, and through an epistemological lens, "the Arab" highlights and reveals the logic of a changing liberal legal order that engages with racist, religious, and Orientalist tropes, stereotypes, and stigma. This figure lends itself as a cipher of the post-World War II liberal order, where societal, political, and legal transformations in Berlin can be highlighted against the backdrop of a figure that is both domestic and global, as well as familiar and foreign. Against the backdrop of Berlin's state laws and legal policies, the figure of "the Arab" appears in various ways – categorized, criminalized, and racialized, and on a sliding scale between invisible, visible, and hypervisible.

1. The Arab is invisible as a citizen and is indeed treated as not "citizenly" enough, not fit "yet" for a liberal democracy, to the point of being treated as a non-citizen or a stateless subject not even granted the rights of a lawful foreigner. 2. The Arab is visible as an unruly, stubborn being needing to be educated and civilized to please the sentiments of Germans. This imperative emerges in debates witnessed in Berlin state schools and on public streets, where the Arab is considered to require instruction in the forms of speech and comportment considered acceptable behavior in a liberal democracy. 3. The Arab is hypervisible in several subcategories as a "problem" and "danger" originating from outside Germany and needing to be policed and

4 Article 83, German Constitution [Execution by the Länder]: "The Länder shall execute federal laws in their own right insofar as this Basic Law does not otherwise provide or permit." Article 84 German Constitution [Länder administration – Federal oversight] ([Länder administration – Federal oversight]: (1) Where the Länder execute federal laws in their own right, they shall provide for the establishment of the requisite authorities and regulate their administrative procedures. If federal laws provide otherwise, the Länder may enact derogating regulations.

surveilled. Potentially a member of a so-called "clan", the Arab is profiled as engaging in crime, and therefore needs policing, including their raiding of their business.

The Arab is thus a crucial figure for categorizing, civilizing and policing through law.

## Categorizing the Arab

Berlin's state authorities enforce regulations around residency, naturalization, and the deportation of foreigners. In Berlin, about 4.25 percent of the resident population (160,344 people) have an Arab migrant background (i.e., are documented to be from the area of the Arab League).[5] Of these, approximately 35.5 percent are German citizens, most of whom live in the districts of Mitte, Neukölln, Tempelhof-Schöneberg, and Spandau. Of the 30,673 Berliners of Lebanese (or rather Palestinian) immigration background have German citizenship, thus approximately 72.8 percent. They mainly live in Neukölln, Mitte, Tempelhof-Schöneberg, and Friedrichshain-Kreuzberg.[6] Crucially, as even the Berlin police report states, there is imprecision in the population numbers due to many persons having been entered into the records as stateless subjects with no nationality or whose nationality is considered "unclear".[7]

In their 2021 campaign, "Our voice counts" (*Unsere Stimme zählt!*), Arab residents of Berlin expressed their frustration with their lack of local rights and representation, pointing out that two-thirds of them had no local voting rights. Their manifesto states:

> "We are part of society in schools, hospitals, as social workers, self-employed people, and much more. But when we look for work or housing, we are discriminated against because of our name and religion. Few people with a migration history are in important social positions. We finally demand equal access to all parts of society."[8]

---

5 Amt für Statistik Berlin-Brandenburg (June 2021) Statistischer Bericht A I 5 – HJ 1/21 as cited by Polizei Berlin (LKA 734 ZAK BkS) (2021) Lagebild 'Clankriminalität' Berlin, 7–8. (https://www.berlin.de/sen/inneres/presse/weitere-informationen/artikel.1203440.php) (last accessed July5, 2023).

6 Ibid.

7 Polizei Berlin (LKA 734 ZAK BkS) (2021) Lagebild 'Clankriminalität' Berlin, 7–8.

8 Unsere Stimme zählt! Für Teilhabe und Antirassismus, https://unserestimmezaehlt.de/ (last accessed July 5, 2023).

Their campaign demands reflect key inadequacies in the lived experience of Arab Berlin. They call on the government to foster the Arabic language in schools[9]; to recognize Muslim religious communities; to destigmatize mosques; to build more Islamic graveyards; to include anti-colonialism as well as Arabic history and culture in the Berlin school curriculum; to respect international law and international legal courts, also with respect to Apartheid; to end the arms trade with the countries of the Middle East; and crucially, to obtain voting rights, at least at the communal level, to influence decisions in their immediate neighborhood.[10]

Instead, Arabs in Berlin even when they have Germany citizenship are treated as "minor citizens",[11] a term coined by anthropologist Sultan Doughan[12] in researching and portraying people from the Middle East, including Arabs, in Berlin, as they accommodate in post-Shoa Berlin. She explains how German citizenship does not deliver on the promise of political equality but that "German citizens of Middle Eastern descent are continuously taken to task as not being integrated enough and (who) can be denied certain constitutional rights." Doughan portrays the extent of imposed self-denial with respect to freedom of expression:

> "Middle Easterners have to learn to accommodate German sentiments, affects and expectations. [...] Instead, they are asked to work on themselves in order to resemble the Christian-secularized majority in a range of issues, and specifically with regard to the figure of the Jew. On the other, their ethnic, legal, and class backgrounds predispose them to political experiences that cannot be easily folded into the ideals of liberal democracy. As minor citizens, they learn to manage external expectations in order to gain majoritarian approval; even if that means that certain injuries inflicted onto them have to be downplayed."

The Arab turned German citizen is not granted the chance to act as a self-confident citizen but needs to manage the expectations of "the Arab" facing German society. Social citizenship is formal and conditional, just as is equality and belonging. German citizenship does not offer protection from the ongoing German gaze, the pro-

---

9 Berlin in 2022 initiated one Arabic language hour in schools with at least twelve students, cf. Senatsverwaltung für Bildung, Jugend und Familie, https://www.berlin.de/sen/bildung/unterricht/faecher-rahmenlehrplaene/sprachen/, (last checked July 5, 2023).

10 Unsere Stimme zählt! Für Teilhabe und Antirassismus, https://unserestimmezaehlt.de/ (last accessed July5, 2023).

11 Doughan, Sultan (2022) Minor Citizens? Holocaust Memory and the Un/Making of Citizenship in Germany. RePLITO Feb. 2 https://replito.pubpub.org/pub/7u2ezjx2/release/1, (last accessed July 5, 2023).

12 Doughan writes: "My use of minor citizens is inspired by Cathy Park Hong's Minor Feelings (2021), where she describes the impossibility of Asian-American equality in the US. This impossibility is managed by Asian-Americans themselves, who learn to accommodate injuries inflicted upon them by playing along within racist imaginaries of Asians."

jections of ongoing expectations towards the Arab either. Here, it might necessary to connect the fragility of social citizenship to Du Bois' concept of double consciousness as the internal conflict experienced by those subordinated in a dominant society. The concept of double consciousness originally captured the African American experience that "only lets him see himself through the revelation of the other world. It is a peculiar sensation, this double consciousness, this sense of always looking at one's self through the eyes of others, of measuring one's soul by the tape of a world that looks on in amused contempt and pity."[13] In a similar vein, Arabs in Berlin are struggling to engage in confident citizenship and to confidently shape the course of German liberal democracy without fear of "social death":

> "Voicing injury and making political demands, especially passionately, is perceived as aggressive, irrational, hateful, immature, and stemming from raw religious sentiments. But are Middle Easterners bound to remain minor citizens because uncomfortable political demands that differ from majoritarian views can only be understood as religiously rooted atavistic sentiments and therefore illegitimate?" [14]

It is in this regard that political subjecthood, often connected with questions of citizenship and demands for equality, will, in turn, be addressed as either an annoyance to be ignored or a threat to be criminalized.[15] Doughan alludes that despite the importance of formal citizenship, "moral citizenship"[16] and thus equality might not be attained.

Yet, many Arabs in Berlin live without German citizenship, and worse yet, without formal lawful residency but rather with a temporary suspension of deportation, that can lead to deportation at any time (*Duldung*). Stateless Arab subjects in Berlin thus legally belong to a separate category, one that has gone unnoticed from German discourse for very long. Meanwhile, the situation of statelessness in Germany has risen, and it largely affects people from Arab countries. In 2022, around 29,500 people without nationality (*staatenlos*) and around 97,000 people with an unclear nationality (*ungeklärt*)[17] were registered in the Central Register of Foreigners in Ger-

13 Cf. Du Bois, 10–11.

14 Cf. Doughan, Minor Citizens? 2022.

15 Tzuberi, Hannah; Samour, Nahed (2/2022) The German State and the Creation of Un/Desired Communities | Contending Modernities, Feb. 22 (https://contendingmodernities.nd.edu/theorizing-modernities/the-german-state-and-the-creation-of-un-desired-communities/).

16 On the shift in focus from formal to moral citizenship in Dutch national and local policy and the mixing of 'citizenship' with 'integration' that gives rise to a virtualization of citizenship cf. Schinkel, Willem (2010) The Virtualization of Citizenship. Critical Sociology, Vol. 36(2) 265–283.

17 According to the German Office of Statistics "The origin of the person in question is unknown and cannot be conclusively clarified. The legal situation in many European countries does

many – and the trend is rising.[18] This is because people who have already lived in other countries as stateless persons have come to Germany (e.g. Kurdish and Palestinian nationals who have previously lived in Syria, Lebanon or the Palestinian territories occupied by Israel).[19] Facing additional bureaucratic barriers to naturalization and being either stateless or having an unclear nationality means one is left societally disadvantaged and unable to exercise one's rights. Stateless people's rights, especially when they are granted only temporary suspension of deportation (*Duldung*), are limited in some contexts – such as in relation to education, healthcare, welfare benefits, and employment – contributing to prolonged poverty and other harm. Stateless people usually do not have the right to vote, hold political office, or participate fully in democratic processes.[20] The status of statelessness or unclear nationality is determined by an administrative procedure in the Foreigners' Registration Office (*Ausländerzentralregister, AZR*). So far, however, there is a lack of cohesive recognition and assessment procedures, and administrative practice is considered confusing, with varying procedures across the sixteen German *Länder*. Yet, the legal status determines the residence permit, which is then only granted for a limited period[21], and can be extended over decades without maturing into a lawful residency, leaving the person legally and socio-economically precarious over a very long time, developing into structural problems, as the following passage shows.

not allow a person with unclear citizenship to be naturalized, as it is assumed that citizenship already exists." https://www.destatis.de/DE/Themen/Gesellschaft-Umwelt/Soziales/Asylbewerberleistungen/Glossar/ungeklaerte-staatsangehoerigkeiten.html (last accessed July 5, 2023). Local authorities do not apply the term "unclear nationality" uniformly.

18 Sachverständigenrat für Integration und Migration (2023) Ein Leben ohne Pass: Staatenlose und ihre Situation in Deutschland, March (https://www.svr-migration.de/publikation/staatenlosigkeit-in-deutschland/).

19 On the situation of Palestinians as stateless or unclear status in Germany, Wissenschaftlicher Dienst Bundestag (2018) Zur Staatenlosigkeit von Palästinensern und zur Anerkennung Palästinas und zur Anerkennung Palästinas und der von seinen Behörden ausgegebenen Reisedokumente, WD 2 – 3000 – 057/18 , May 7 (https://www.bundestag.de/resource/blob/564214/ac302f4c6cadb2d7fd79bbcdbacd2841/WD-2-057-18-pdf-data.pdf).

20 On barriers to naturalization and integration for stateless people, see European Network on Statelessness (2023) Naturalization and Integration (https://www.statelessness.eu/sites/default/files/2023-01/Naturalisation%20primer%202.pdf).

21 Sachverständigenrat für Integration und Migration (2023) Ein Leben ohne Pass. Die Situation staatenloser Menschen in Deutschland. SVR-Policy Brief 2023–1, 5 (https://www.svr-migration.de/wp-content/uploads/2023/03/SVR-Policy_2023-1_Policy-Brief-Staatenlose_barrierefrei.pdf).

## Policing the Arab

According to their own account, the Berlin police apply the term "clans" and "clan criminality" only to Arabs.[22] According to the Berlin police, a focus is placed on the criminality of members of "ethnically isolated Arab structures whose ethnic roots can be traced back in particular to so-called Mhallami-Kurds, Lebanese and stateless Palestinians who immigrated to Germany from Lebanon as war refugees" (in the late 1970s/early 80s).[23] This naming policy has significant consequences. Profiling community members as belonging to a "clan", assuming clan criminality, and raiding community businesses affect Arab families, neighborhoods and communities beyond those immediately implicated. [24] To be clear (and to state the obvious), some Arabs (in their various legal statuses as German citizens, refugees or else, to which the Berlin police makes no further reference) commit crime, sometimes together with family members. Rather than disputing this fact, the question here is why Berlin authorities opted to give this criminal activity its own, ethnicizing name instead of reverting to "organized crime" as an established legal category that has been in use for long by the Berlin authorities, including the police.[25]

The Berlin police from 2019 to 2022 used this definition for "clan criminality":

> "Clan crime is the commission of criminal acts by members of ethnically segregated structures ("clans"). It is determined by kinship relations and/or a common ethnic origin and a high degree of segregation of the perpetrators, which encourages the commission of the crime or makes it more difficult to solve the crime. This goes hand in hand with their own set of values and the fundamental rejection of the German legal system. In this context, clan criminality may exhibit one or more of the following indicators:
> a strong orientation toward the mostly patriarchal-hierarchical family structure; a lack of willingness to integrate with aspects of spatial concentration; provoking

---

22 See p.1. of the introduction to Polizei Berlin (LKA 734 ZAK BkS) (2021) Lagebild Clankriminalität Berlin. https://www.berlin.de/sen/inneres/presse/weitere-informationen/artikel.1203440.php. The Berlin police in footnote 1 then refers to Arabs as persons whose ethnicity or migration background can be attributed to a state of the "Arab League": Algeria, Bahrain, Egypt, Djibouti, Iraq, Jordan, Qatar, Comoros, Kuwait, Lebanon, Libya, Morocco, Mauritania, Oman, Saudi Arabia, Somalia, Sudan, Syria, Tunisia, United Arab Emirates, Palestinian territory, Yemen.

23 Polizei Berlin (LKA 734 ZAK BkS) (2021) op.cit., 7.

24 Jaraba, Mahmoud (2021) Arabische Großfamilien und die 'Clankriminalität,' Informations-Plattform für Journalistinnen und Journalisten zu den Themen Flucht, Migration und Diskriminierung. (https://mediendienst-integration.de/artikel/arabische-grossfamilien-und-die-clankriminalitaet.html).

25 Strafverfolgungsbehörden, Staatsanwaltschaft Berlin, https://www.berlin.de/staatsanwaltschaft/aufgaben/organisierte-kriminalitaet/#abt251 (last accessed July 5, 2023).

escalations even on trivial occasions or minor violations of the law; the exploitation of group-immanent mobilization and threat potentials."[26]

This definition has met with criticism from criminologists and criminal law scholars as entailing blunt generalizations, blurring the lines of criminal and administrative laws (with respect to criminal law and administrative trade regulation law), and being in its application empirically imprecise and vastly exaggerated, as well as stirring "German Angst" – and eventually opening doors for discrimination.[27]

In July 2022, a national definition for all sixteen federal states was suggested by the newly established "federal-state initiative to combat clan crime (*Bund-Länder- Initiative zur Bekämpfung der Clankriminalität*, BLICK).[28] The definition considered and integrated suggestions from the federal states, the Federal Office of Crime (*Bundeskriminalamt*) and various research findings. The federal states had used different definitions for the reporting periods up to and including 2021. In the new two-stage definition of 2022, the term "clan" is first defined as "ethnically open, value-neutral and detached from crime". In a second step, the context of the group-related form of crime is included. The new federal definition defines "clan" as "an informal social organization determined by a common understanding of the ancestry of its members. In particular, it is characterized by a hierarchical structure, a strong sense

26 "Clankriminalität ist die Begehung von Straftaten durch Angehörige ethnisch abgeschotteter Strukturen ('Clans'). Sie ist bestimmt von verwandtschaftlichen Beziehungen und/oder einer gemeinsamen ethnischen Herkunft und einem hohen Maß an Abschottung der Täter, wodurch die Tatbegehung gefördert oder die Aufklärung der Tat erschwert wird. Dies geht einher mit einer eigenen Werteordnung und der grundsätzlichen Ablehnung der deutschen Rechtsordnung. Dabei kann Clankriminalität einen oder mehrere der folgenden Indikatoren aufweisen:eine starke Ausrichtung auf die zumeist patriarchalisch-hierarchisch geprägte Familienstruktur; eine mangelnde Integrationsbereitschaft mit Aspekten einer räumlichen Konzentration; das Provozieren von Eskalationen auch bei nichtigen Anlässen oder geringfügigen; Rechtsverstößen die Ausnutzung gruppenimmanenter Mobilisierungs- und Bedrohungspotenziale". Polizei Berlin (LKA 734 ZAK BkS) (2021) op.cit., 7 https://www.berlin.de/sen/inneres/presse/weitere-informationen/artikel.1203440.php, (last accessed July 5, 2023).

27 Feltes, Thomas; Rauls, Felix (2020) Clankriminalität und die "German Angst": Rechtspolitische und kriminologische Anmerkungen zur Beschäftigung mit sogenannter Clankriminalität. Sozial Extra 44: 372–7; Reinhardt, K. (2021) Zum Begriff der Clankriminalität – eine kritische Einschätzung. Working Paper Eberhard-Karls-Universität Tübingen. Also see articles in Hunold, Daniela; Singelnstein, Tobias (2022) (eds.) Rassismus in der Polizei.

28 Polizei Berlin (LKA 734 ZAK BkS) (2021) op.cit., 41, https://www.berlin.de/sen/inneres/presse/weitere-informationen/artikel.1203440.php, (last accessed July 5, 2023).

of belonging and a common understanding of norms and values."[29] "Clan crime" is now defined as follows:

> "Clan crime encompasses the delinquent behavior of clan members. Clan affiliation represents a unifying component that promotes the commission of the crime or impedes its clarification, whereby one's own norms and values can be placed above the legal system applicable in Germany. The deeds must be individually or collectively significant to the phenomenon."[30]

This two-step definition has been in force for the Berlin police since January 1, 2022, replacing the older definition of May 2, 2019. Despite the separate definition of clan and clan crime, and the alleged "openness" to all kinds of ethnicities, the Berlin police concede that they "continue to carry out the fight against clan crime and focus on the criminality of delinquent clans of Arab origin."[31] Ethnicizing crime, instead of reverting to the established category of "organized crime", implicating Arabs as such and entire families through their family name, remains a focal point of criticism, as it identifies established stereotypes and stigma in the work of the police. Using these categories in police work, political speech, and the media underlines surveillance as a racializing process, entailing embodied effects of surveillance. [32] This affects Arabs and everyone else visiting Arab restaurants, corner stores, and Shisha bars in areas frequented not only by Arabs but also by other people of color. It is no coincidence that the racist murder of people of color in Hanau took place in a Shisha bar, garnering much attention as a space where people of color spend their time and can thus be easily targeted, and killed. The laws on "dangerous localities" (*kriminalitätsbelastete Orte*, §§ 21, 34, 35 ASOG, Berlin law of general security and order) can thus turn into

---

29 Ibid., 41: "Clan: Ein Clan ist eine informelle soziale Organisation, die durch ein gemeinsames Abstammungsverständnis ihrer Angehörigen bestimmt ist. Sie zeichnet sich insbesondere durch eine hierarchische Struktur, ein ausgeprägtes Zugehörigkeitsgefühl und ein gemeinsames Normen- und Werteverständnis aus.",

30 "Clankriminalität umfasst das delinquente Verhalten von Clanangehörigen. Die Clanzugehörigkeit stellt dabei eine verbindende, die Tatbegehung fördernde oder die Aufklärung der Tat hindernde Komponente dar, wobei die eigenen Normen und Werte über die in Deutschland geltende Rechtsordnung gestellt werden können. Die Taten müssen im Einzelnen oder in ihrer Gesamtheit für das Phänomen von Bedeutung sein." Ibid, 41.

31 Ibid., 41.

32 Browne, Simone (2019) Dark Matters: On the Surveillance of Blackness; Jaraba, Mahmoud (2021) Arabische Großfamilien und die 'Clankriminalität,' Informations-Plattform für Journalistinnen und Journalisten zu den Themen Flucht, Migration und Diskriminierung (https://mediendienst-integration.de/artikel/arabische-grossfamilien-und-die-clankriminalitaet.html); Özvatan, Özgür; Neuhauser,Bastian; Yurdakul, Gökce (2023) The 'Arab Clans' Discourse: Narrating Racialization, Kinship, and Crime in the German Media. Social Sciences 12: 104.

"endangered localities" were fatal racial profiling attacks can, and does, occur.[33] Race and racism, especially anti-Arab racism (in its inevitable overlap with anti-Muslim racism, anti-Black racism, and anti-Roma racism), seems to be significantly heightened when public figures and media portray some ethnicities as particularly prone to crime and in offensive violation of "our values".

In fact, Berlin public authorities, next to establishing the term "clan-criminality", have used trade law (*Gewerberecht*) as a door opener[34] and trade inspections as an alibi for "clan raids", despite heightened doubts about their legality. In a concerted effort, Berlin police and district offices, tax and customs authorities, have been inspecting Arab shisha bars, cafes, restaurants, barber shops, travel agencies, and corner stores, often sensationally accompanied by large numbers of journalists, with photo ops for politicians making sweeping political statements after the spectacle.[35] Images of hundreds of police officers raiding shisha bars, Arab supermarkets, or arcades in Berlin districts such as Neukölln, Tempelhof, or Wedding regularly make headlines nationwide.[36] Police officers often arrive at these operations with a large contingent, accompanied by customs, tax, or health authorities, particularly during the COVID-19 pandemic.

At the end of 2020, the Berlin Senate Department for Economic Affairs, Energy and Public Enterprises commissioned the Berlin School of Economics and Law (*Hochschule für Wirtschaft und Recht*) to conduct a study to investigate the so-called trade surveillance (*Gewerbeüberwachung*),[37] the category assigned to the official visits to Arab stores in Berlin. Legally, trade surveillance falls under the competence of the State Office of Criminal Investigation (*Landeskriminalamt, LKA*) in Berlin and, according to their state officers, it entails monitoring those businesses authorized as commercial enterprises for consumer protection and compliance with hygiene regulations, as well as fighting illegal gambling. Reference is also made to integrating trade surveillance into the fight against clan crime.[38] The study points out severe le-

---

33 For a list of expert opinions on racial profiling and dangerous places, Berliner Kampagne: Ban! Racial Profiling – Gefährliche Orte abschaffen!, https://kop-berlin.de/beitrag/die-berliner-kampagne-ban-racial-profiling-gefahrliche-orte-abschaffen (last accessed July 5, 2023).

34 Leuschner 16.

35 E.g., Andreas Geisel, former Berlin Senator for Interior Affairs (https://andreas-geisel.de/zu-den-razzien-in-mitte-und-neukoelln/).

36 These kinds of raids also take place in other federal states such as Lower Saxony or North Rhine-Westphalia.

37 Leuschner, Vincent; Schönrock, Sabrina; Janßen, Sebastian; Görs, Philipp (2022) Struktur und Praxis der Gewerbeüberwachung im Land Berlin. Abschlussbericht zur Organisationsuntersuchung (https://www.berlin.de/sen/wirtschaft/wirtschaftsrecht/gewerberecht/gewerbeueberwachung/),

38 Ibid., 15.

gal deficits in connection with trade surveillance and fundamentally questions the alleged link to the battle against so-called clan crime.

Also, next to a legal analysis, the study includes interviews with officers who oversee trade surveillance in Berlin. Some of the employees report their dissatisfaction and skepticism about Berlin's strategy of battling the supposed "clan" structures. In the study, for example, two employees express anger at the way migrant small businesses are placed under general suspicion.[39] In the interviews, one of the anonymous employees describes the situation in connection with a travel agency that offers pilgrimages to Mecca as an example:

> "And when it suited them, because now clan structures have to be broken up – it's more of a police concern – we'd get orders: 'Oh, now go check there, they do Hajj travel!' So we were supposed to charge these travel agencies. You'd like to know what you can actually oversee in travel agencies according to 38 (§ 38 GewO, note by the author). It was all sort of crazy. Then we were allowed to take notes on what the police are now allowed to surveil in travel agencies. But they only wanted to get in [...] to get at the clans or whoever." [40]

The study is full of reports constructing excuses for what amounts to raids on barbershops, late-night shops, or takeaways – in the hope of finding something. High-ranking LKA employees are quoted as saying that they doubt that the legally significant principle of proportionality is being respected in the battle on "clan criminality":

> "It's basically the recurring idea of the Trojan horse, that you come riding up with a 'Hello, let's do a trade inspection' and, strictly speaking, act ahead of a really profound suspicion that could explain a search measure. Of course, this is a legal issue that can also be viewed critically."[41]

---

39 Ibid., 15.

40 "Und wenn es denen aber dann passte, weil jetzt müssen gerade Clanstrukturen zerschlagen werden, also eher so ein Polizeianliegen, dann kriegten wir Aufträge, 'Oh, jetzt muss man auch noch hier – gibt's Hajj-Reisen', plötzlich möchte man in Reisebüros einreiten, möchte dann da mal wissen, was kann man denn nach 38 (§ 38 GewO, Anmerk. d. V.) in Reisebüros eigentlich kontrollieren. Und es war alles irgendwie so verkehrtrum. Dann durften wir Vermerke schreiben, was darf denn jetzt die Polizei gewerbeüberwachungsmäßig in Reisebüros kontrollieren. Dann wollten sie aber nur rein, weil sie irgendwie – ist ja auch ein hehres Anliegen, weil sie den [Clans, Anonymisierung d. V.] oder wem auch immer ans Leder wollten, ja. Und das ist halt dieses und das ist ja das, weswegen die Polizei bisher auch irgendwie so [...]. Aber das ist eben das, weswegen sie so'n Interesse noch dran haben, als Türöffner dieses Gewerberecht zu haben. Und wir haben irgendwann gesagt 'Ja, und wir sitzen aber da und haben irgendwo- das darf man nicht laut sagen, es gibt aber Vollzugsprobleme im Gewerberecht, (Int1_SenWiEnBe, Pos. 108)', Leuschner et al. (2022) 16–17.

41 Ibid., 17.

In recent years, several voices have spoken out in the Berlin House of Representatives, in the districts and on the part of the tradespeople concerned, taking a legally critical view of this practice. The question arises as to why the authorities in Berlin invest so many resources in these staged operations. An insider gives a sober answer: "In the end, we achieve nothing. You have to put it that way, it's sold differently in the press."[42] In fact, only a few journalists ask about the exact reasons for and results of these "visitations". There are cases in which a quantities of unpaid duty on hookah tobacco were confiscated. Yet, the biggest legal concern remains that these operations lack proportionality. According to the study, the officers often find nothing at all during the joint operations and the entourage has to leave without results.[43] The researchers commissioned with the study are also critical of the joint operations: "The prosecution of criminal offenses must be strictly separated from the regulatory tasks in commercial matters".[44]" Accordingly, the "Trojan horse" method described is illegal, as pretended trade surveillance serves as a bridge to unsuspected prosecution. Trade law cannot be used as a door opener for the preventive control of criminal offenses. In practice, however, the Senate, LKA, and districts do not seem to adhere to this legal principle. Instead, the political leaders in the districts play a decisive role as they push their administrations to carry out field operations in large groups. A person responsible in a district office bluntly describes the intention behind this strategy: "We just try to conduct our proceedings in a way that is externally effective or in a media-effective manner. It's not that we go out and say, 'oh man, that's not so nice', and you get a fine for a smaller amount a week later. Instead, we issue a hefty fine notice as part of educational measures."[45]

Teaching Arabs a lesson, disciplining Arabs, no matter what the rule of law requires, seems to be the clear message that even the acting officers could not help but realize. Policing Arabs is considered an educational matter. It goes hand in hand with assuring the German citizen that the state is protected from Arabness, from Arabness taking over. This image of "Arabs taking over" is a recurring theme of anti-Arab and anti-Muslim racism, one that depicts violence and lack of inherent loyalty to the law as an Arab characteristic, assuming Arabs to be powerful enough to undermine German law and legal culture. Given that Arabs compromise around 160.000 people in Berlin, a city of almost four million people, it shows that the Arab take-over reflects a "German Angst" from the Oriental other, and is not grounded in reality. The task of all law enforcement authorities is to ensure that the law is respected by everyone alike, and not to stir anxieties that can subsequently be exploited by political actors for political capital.

---

42 Ibid., 17.

43 Ibid., 51.

44 Ibid., 165.

45 Ibid., 54.

By concentrating on staged "clan crime" in conjunction with the lack of personnel, other (White) businesses in the city would "not be monitored at all."[46] Policing Arab businesses also means that other businesses are being less monitored, so that the personnel and resources put into "clan criminality" benefit other sectors in the city. As a consequence, public safety in Berlin is not being shared equally. Those affected by these inspections point out that being placed under general suspicion *(Generalverdacht)* is unfair and racially motivated, even when in their annual reports, Berlin police are adamant to stress that "no 'general suspicion' against fellow citizens of Arab migration background is intended".[47]

Many of those affected have now joined together in initiatives to draw attention to their situation. State agencies encounter frustrated tradespeople who often cannot be proven to have committed a specific crime, but who are under continuous state surveillance. In an open letter, trade people, with political initiatives such as "Unsere Stimme zählt!", and those working against discrimination and unlawful police violence, have stated: "Our neighbors are unsettled by this approach, the guests stay away. We perceive this to be harassment. The findings that are made now and then, do not justify the extent or the aggressive style of these inspections."[48] The open letter also laments the public prejudice created by such spectacularized controls: The trade people understand that trade must be controlled, "but we don't want to be prejudged and presented as criminals without evidence." The businessmen would like to have a dialogue with the district and the interior administration on how inspections can be carried out "proportionately, without discrimination, and without weapons being drawn. "We are convinced that we can move forward if we talk to each other".[49]

## Civilizing the Arab

Schools are a further space of state surveillance. For students (children or youth), this can entail their personal data being transferred outside of school to other public authorities, including police and possibly intelligence. While ethnic ascription and religion can be easily conflated, it becomes apparent how religion is used to get at the students regarding political questions. One such example is the project

46 Ibid., 59.

47 Polizei Berlin (LKA 734 ZAK BkS) (2021) op.cit., 7 (https://www.berlin.de/sen/inneres/presse/weitere-informationen/artikel.1203440.php).

48 Respekt und Dialog für Neuköllner Gewerbetreibende. Eine Initiative von Neuköllner Gewerbetreibenden, unterstützt von: Kein Generalverdacht, KOP Berlin, Unsere Stimme zählt, Initiative Hermannplatz, (https://www.facebook.com/photo/?fbid=291863896389188&set=pcb.291864079722503).

49 Ibid.

"Confrontational Expression of Religion" [50] a project of the private association DeVi (Democracy and Diversity) supported by the mayor of Neukölln (Social Democratic Party). In the survey DEVI conducted with ten schools in Neukölln and presented to the district office (*Bezirksamt*) of Neukölln, the private association demands a local office that documents "confrontational religious practice", an expression that is not defined anywhere. Therefore, it remains unclear what exactly is meant by this. According to DEVI, religious conflicts are increasing in many schools, and educators are being left alone with these problems. The association would like to set up a contact point that documents such conflicts and offers help to schools; however, by transferring the personal data of school pupils to unspecified authorities outside of the school. The project has met with a wide range of criticism. Some schools are dealing with problems related to religion in school, probably because teachers are still largely homogeneously white, with few Muslim teachers, as especially until 2023 the Berlin Senate for Education was adamant in its unconstitutional perspective in preventing female Muslim teachers from wearing headscarves.[51]

To address conflicts that arise between students of different faiths, there is no need for a registry office that lists and reports Muslims and saves their personal data, but for a pedagogical approach to children and their parents. The survey lacks engagement with the children and the parents and has collected only information from selected teachers. It is problematic to frame problems as "religious" bullying or to assume signs of an Islamist conviction, especially if it has not been considered first a pubescent posturing or a cry for attention which is quite age- typical for children and youth. The attempt to officially register students' bullying behavior is problematic in that it attributes non-religious conflicts to the realm of religion. For example, the rudimentary survey on p. 13 lists the line-up in football being based on ethnic lines: "Only Arabs are allowed to play in football. Only Turks are allowed into the bushes."[52] This behavior is not uncommon for children and youth and needs to be addressed by teachers, but it is problematic to list it as a form of bullying, and obviously religion does not play a role in it, as there is no mentioning of religion or religious denominations.

---

50 DEVI, Anlauf- und Dokumentationsstelle konfrontative Religionsbekundung, (https://demokratieundvielfalt.de/wp-content/uploads/2021/12/DEVI_Broschuere_Anlauf_und_Dokumentationsstelle_konfrontative_Religionsbekundung_A4_ICv2_03c-doppelseiten.pdf).

51 Legal Tribunal Online (LTO) (2023) BVerfG zu Kopftuch: BAG-Urteil bleibt bestehen (lto.de) Feb. 2 (https://www.lto.de/recht/nachrichten/n/bverfg-1bvr1661-21-verfassungsbeschwerde-land-berlin-neutralitaetsgesetz-kopftuch-nicht-angenommen/).

52 Bestandsaufnahme Konfrontative Religionsbekundungen in Neukölln Vorabversion vorgelegt für das Bezirksamt Neukölln, Dezember 2021, https://demokratieundvielfalt.de/wp-content/uploads/2022/01/DEVI_Bestandsaufnahme-Konfrontative-Religionsbekundung-Neuk%C3%B6lln-Dez.21.pdf (last accessed July 5, 2023), p.13.

Another example mentioned is that children want to cut the map of Israel out of the atlas or paint over it.[53] This might point to the decades-long problem of Israel in its handling of Palestinians, and in particular in not granting a Palestinian state whilst insisting on only one state, Israel, to exist. The act mentioned is not religious, but if this is considered a political act and children are taken as bearers of fundamental rights, any legal consideration would need to include the freedom of expression. Instead of falling into the trap of adultism (not granting children the right to the learning process), it is a missed opportunity to discuss how to achieve a situation of dignity, freedom, and equality for all inhabitants in respective territory. This example instead could be discussed as one of universal human rights, a self-declared pillar of Germany's post World War II foreign policy. The non-defined scope of concepts such as "confrontational religious expression", their potential to undermine freedom of religion, the reporting practices that might violate data protection law and the right to informational self-determination, as well as its discriminatory effect it might have on a vulnerable group such as children and youth, [54] has not stopped the Berlin Senate of Education to consider commissioning a larger study, keeping the state's disciplining focus on Muslim, Arab and Middle Eastern children and youth in the schools of Berlin despite a consultative educational landscape of NGO's dealing with conflicts at school already in place.

## Conclusion

In this contribution, I highlighted that the Berlin state, its laws and applications are themselves engaging in producing racist laws and practices against Arabs, be they German citizens, refugees, stateless subjects, school students or else. The Arab is constructed as a figure for the Berlin state to demonstrate it is serious about law and order, to protect German values against the violent, uncivilized Arab whether or not German citizen. It is here where Arabs as "Arabs" echoes in contemporary Berlin.

---

53 Ibid.

54 Schiffauer, Werner (2022) Zur DEVI-Studie: Bestandsaufnahme Konfrontative Religionsbekundungen in Neukölln. https://rat-fuer-migration.de/2022/01/26/stellungnahme-von-werner-schiffauer-zur-devi-studie-bestandsaufnahme-konfrontative-religionsbekundungen-in-neukoelln/. See also the criticism coming from academic, civil society, teachers and politicians concerning the DEVI survey, Stellungnahme zum erneuten Vorstoß zur Einrichtung einer "Anlauf- und Dokumentationsstelle für konfrontative Religionsbekundung" – Antidiskriminierungsverband Deutschland (2022).

It is here where Du Bois famous question "How does it feel to be a problem?"[55] echoes in contemporary Berlin.[56] First, Du Bois is referring to race relations as a social problem to be solved by policymakers. Second, he refers to the inner struggle experienced by African Americans as they strive for self-awareness and an identity on their own terms. Du Bois contends that "the real problem of humanity today is the problem of the color line – the relation of the darker to the lighter races of men in Asia and Africa, in America and the islands of the sea."[57] For Du Bois, part of this "problem" was a pressing social, existential one. Aspects of the experience included such things as unstable legal residency, poor working conditions, crowded housing, and many other stressors. Writing in 1903, Du Bois called race relations the "problem" of the present and the future. In addition to the stress exerted by Berlin state laws on the figure of "the Arab", the private market adds stress to the lives of many Arabs, from getting adequate health services to finding housing or work.[58] A large-scale experiment in 2017 by Bayerischer Rundfunk and Der Spiegel showed that in 27 percent of cases, Arabs were not invited to visit apartments being offered for rent.[59] The poll showed that this discrimination was based solely on the candidate's name, rather than nationality, place of birth, language skills, level of education, or profession. Men were shown to face more discrimination than women. Berlin fared slightly better than the cities of Munich and Frankfurt, the explanation being that more housing is in public rather than private ownership.

W.E.B. Du Bois, who studied at Humboldt University Berlin from 1892–1894,[60] wrote "The Souls of Black Folk" to help people understand the nature of this very problem, the condition of the African American in the USA as a key question of in/equality. Using his approach to ask the Arab in Berlin, ""How does it feel to be a problem?" can also serve as an inspiration to understand the prevailing legal, social, and economic conditions and the emancipatory forces growing to overcome the figure of the Arab in Berlin as "a problem".

55 Du Bois, W. E. B. (1903/1994) The Souls of Black Folk. New York: Dover Thrift.

56 On the echoes of this question also with respect to Arabs and Muslim in the USA, see Bayoumi, Moustafa (2008), How Does It Feel To Be A Probliem?, Penguin Press.

57 Du Bois, W.E.B 1903, 15.

58 See also Expert*innenkommission gegen antimuslimischen Rassismus, Berlin 2022. Berlin is the first/only state to commission an expert committee on anti-Muslim racism.

59 "Hanna und Ismail" (2017) Umfrage des Datenjournalismus von BR und DER SPIEGEL (https://interaktiv.br.de/hanna-und-ismail/, Studie: Ausländischer Name mindert Chance auf Mietwohnung (migazin.de).

60 W. E. B. Du Bois, Soziologe – Bürgerrechtler – Panafrikanist, https://www.hu-berlin.de/de/ueberblick/geschichte/persoenlichkeiten/w-e-b-du-bois, (last accessed July 5, 2023).

## References


Bayoumi, Moustafa (2008), How Does It Feel To Be A Problem?, Penguin Press.

"Hanna und Ismail" (2017) Umfrage des Datenjournalismus von BR und DER SPIEGEL (https://interaktiv.br.de/hanna-und-ismail/, Studie: Ausländischer Name mindert Chance auf Mietwohnung (migazin.de).

Browne, Simone (2019) Dark Matters: On the Surveillance of Blackness

DEVI, Anlauf- und Dokumentationsstelle konfrontative Religionsbekundung, (https://demokratieundvielfalt.de/wp-content/uploads/2021/12/DEVI_Broschuere_Anlauf_und_Dokumentationsstelle_konfrontative_Religionsbekundung_A4_ICv2_03c-doppelseiten.pdf).

Doughan, Sultan (2022) Minor Citizens? Holocaust Memory and the Un/Making of Citizenship in Germany. RePLITO Feb. 2 (https://replito.pubpub.org/pub/7u2ezjx2/release/1).

Du Bois, W. E. B. (1903/1994) The Souls of Black Folk. New York: Dover Thrift.

European Network on Statelessness (2023) Naturalization and Integration (https://www.statelessness.eu/sites/default/files/2023-01/Naturalisation%20primer%202.pdf).

Expert*innenkommission gegen antimuslimischen Rassismus (2022) Berlin.

Feltes, Thomas; Rauls, Felix (2020) Clankriminalität und die "German Angst": Rechtspolitische und kriminologische Anmerkungen zur Beschäftigung mit sogenannter Clankriminalität. Sozial Extra 44, 372–7.

https://www.hu-berlin.de/de/ueberblick/geschichte/persoenlichkeiten/w-e-b-du-bois

Hunold, Daniela; Singelnstein, Tobias (2022) (eds.) Rassismus in der Polizei.

Jaraba, Mahmoud (2021) Arabische Großfamilien und die 'Clankriminalität,' Informations-Plattform für Journalistinnen und Journalisten zu den Themen Flucht, Migration und Diskriminierung. (https://mediendienst-integration.de/artikel/arabische-grossfamilien-und-die-clankriminalitaet.html).

LatCrit (2002) Primer, Vol. 1 (summer) (https://latcrit.org/wp-content/uploads/2020/07/lcprimeri.pdf).

Legal Tribunal Online (2023) BVerfG zu Kopftuch: BAG-Urteil bleibt bestehen (lto.de) Feb. 2 (https://www.lto.de/recht/nachrichten/n/bverfg-1bvr1661-21-verfassungsbeschwerde-land-berlin-neutralitaetsgesetz-kopftuch-nicht-angenommen/).

Leuschner, Vincent; Schönrock, Sabrina; Janßen, Sebastian; Görs, Philipp (2022) Struktur und Praxis der Gewerbeüberwachung im Land Berlin. Abschlussbericht zur Organisationsuntersuchung (https://www.berlin.de/sen/wirtschaft/wirtschaftsrecht/gewerberecht/gewerbeueberwachung/),

Moten, Fred (2008) The Case of Blackness, Criticism, Vol. 50 (2) Spring, 177–218.

Özvatan, Özgür; Neuhauser,Bastian; Yurdakul, Gökce (2023) The 'Arab Clans' Discourse: Narrating Racialization, Kinship, and Crime in the German Media. Social Sciences 12: 104.

Polizei Berlin (LKA 734 ZAK BkS) (2021) Lagebild Clankriminalität Berlin (https://www.berlin.de/sen/inneres/presse/weitere-informationen/artikel.1203440.php).

Reinhardt, K. (2021) Zum Begriff der Clankriminalität – eine kritische Einschätzung. Working Paper Eberhard-Karls-Universität Tübingen.

Respekt und Dialog für Neuköllner Gewerbetreibende. Eine Initiative von Neuköllner Gewerbetreibenden, unterstützt von: Kein Generalverdacht, KOP Berlin, Unsere Stimme zählt, Initiative Hermannplatz (https://www.facebook.com/photo/?fbid=291863896389188&set=pcb.291864079722503).

Sachverständigenrat für Integration und Migration (2023) Ein Leben ohne Pass: Staatenlose und ihre Situation in Deutschland, March (https://www.svr-migration.de/publikation/staatenlosigkeit-in-deutschland/).

Schiffauer, Werner (2022), Zur DEVI-Studie: Bestandsaufnahme Konfrontative Religionsbekundungen in Neukölln. https://rat-fuer-migration.de/2022/01/26/stellungnahme-von-werner-schiffauer-zur-devi-studie-bestandsaufnahme-konfrontative-religionsbekundungen-in-neukoelln/.

Schinkel, Willem (2010) The Virtualization of Citizenship. Critical Sociology, Vol. 36(2) 265–283.

Senatsverwaltung für Bildung, Jugend und Familie. Sprache Lernen (https://www.berlin.de/sen/bildung/unterricht/faecher-rahmenlehrplaene/sprachen/).

Stellungnahme zum erneuten Vorstoß zur Einrichtung einer "Anlauf- und Dokumentationsstelle für konfrontative Religionsbekundung" – Antidiskriminierungs verband Deutschland (2022).

Tzuberi, Hannah; Samour, Nahed (2022) The German State and the Creation of Un/Desired Communities | Contending Modernities (2) Feb. 22 (https://contendingmodernities.nd.edu/theorizing-modernities/the-german-state-and-the-creation-of-un-desired-communities/).

Unsere Stimme zählt. Deutsch-Arabische Wahlforderungen #unserestimme (https://unserestimmezaehlt.de/).

Wissenschaftlicher Dienst Bundestag (2018) Zur Staatenlosigkeit von Palästinensern und zur Anerkennung Palästinas und zur Anerkennung Palästinas und der von seinen Behörden ausgegebenen Reisedokumente, WD 2 – 3000 – 057/18 , May 7 (https://www.bundestag.de/resource/blob/564214/ac302f4c6cadb2d7fd79bbcdbacd2841/WD-2-057-18-pdf-data.pdf).

# Part 2: Inclusion, Arts, and Activism

# 7. On framing and de-framing the queer Arab

*Iskandar Abdalla*

## Prologue: "Hadi"

Hadi walks through the streets of the city. His steps are sluggish, and his face wears a melancholic expression and a sense of despair. In the background, we hear his aunt talking to him on the phone, scolding him in Arabic. "Get out, you whore, you sodomite, [...] Hopefully, you will die the most terrible death." But Hadi wants to live. After she hangs up, we see him arriving to buy strawberries at the weekly market on *Winterfeldtplatz*, only a few meters away from the gay heart of Berlin in Schöneberg.

This is the scene that opens the television documentary "*Allah weiß, dass ich schwul bin,*"[1] produced by the RBB, the German public broadcaster for Berlin and Brandenburg. Then filmmaker Andreas Bernhardt tells the audience about himself and his interest in filming Hadi. During his travels in North Africa, Andreas recounts, he has met many gay men who have fled "the death lists of religious fanatics" and have come to Europe. He says he was not able to convince any of them to be filmed until Hadi, a Lebanese refugee, crossed his path. Andreas and Hadi have agreed to meet at *CSD*, the annual Berlin Gay Pride Parade. The camera wanders through the festivities capturing naked brown bodies posing and dancing vivaciously. Yet Hadi does not arrive. Unlike those who have made it to the celebration, he seems stuck in his daily troubles.

In the rest of the documentary, Andreas will be the facilitator of Hadi's "safe arrival," the helper and decoder who lends him a voice, brings his story to the light, helps him to navigate the barriers of language and bureaucracy and eventually helps us, the audience, to decipher the alleged predicament of being queer[2] and Arab, or

1 Andreas Bernhardt/Armin Faust (2020) Allah weiß, dass ich schwul bin. RBB, December 12 (https://www.rbb-online.de/unserleben/reportagen/allah-weiss-dass-ich-schwul-bin.html).

2 In this chapter I am using the term "queer", not as an alternative to "LGBT", but as an umbrella term that encloses the latter term and compliments it with a perspective that recognizes the fluidity of sexual and gender identity without necessarily denying the urge of some to cohere to a stable subject. I am also using to the term to stress the political connotations attached to it through its deployment by queer theory since the 1990s to ascribe a "positionality vis-a-

being queer and Muslim: an oxymoronic[3] being for Western sensibilities. Hadi's story is staged as one of consecutive miseries: fleeing Lebanon, being rejected, threatened, beaten up by his relatives, bullied, deceived, even raped by his Arab compatriots. Hadi appears to represent an exemplary case of a larger "problem." He is the victim, the body in which the problem is enacted and manifested, without being eligible to *frame it.* He is not the one who maps the outlines of the problem and charts a way out.

Framing Hadi's problem is the mission the camera embarks on, charting its course along specific itineraries. First, Andreas confers with an "expert on Islam" who blames Hadi's agony on religious homophobia rooted in the traditions of Islam, as justified by its authoritative texts and widely practiced by its believers. Then he speaks to a sociologist who draws upon similar incidents of violence and who complicates the frame by blaming Hadi's misery on "cultural aspects" and "social backgrounds" outside of religion. Finally, he consults the law enforcement institution designated to intervene to protect Hadi's body from the violence of his family and compatriots: the police. "Are you afraid? You should not be afraid of the German Police," says Andreas to his puzzled protagonist. At the end of the journey, Hadi is asked whether – after all that has happened to him – he still believes in God. He eventually restates his faith, giving the report its catchy title.

The frame in which Hadi's story is presented to us appears to have a temporal depth: a past that haunts Hadi violently in the present, and a present he cannot yet arrive in. To bridge the divide, Hadi's "background" is illuminated by expert knowledge, while his body is placed under the oversight of state authorities entitled to guard and protect its surfaces. Only then can the present be freed from the past and Hadi's arrival become attainable.

This contribution is not about Hadi, but about the *frame* within which his body is staged and contained – as extended, by proxy, to the bodies of queer Arab migrants in general. It attends to the frame's (mis)representations; its limits and off-limits; the knowledge it assembles within its structure and the knowledge it simultaneously shuts out. My endeavor is to unshroud the power of framing, not merely by sketching out the modalities of its operation, but also by underscoring how they are resisted and subverted by Arab queer migrants via discursive procedures, which I call *outframing* and *de-framing.* My intention is evidently not to question the veracity of Hadi's experience, but to point out the occlusion of confusing the framing of an experience with what is deemed to be its truth. After illustrating what characterizes such a frame, I will proceed with the attempts to maneuver its lines by silenc-

---

vis normativity" at odds with dominant modes of thought and living. See David M. Halperin (1995) Saint Foucault. Towards A Gay Hagiography. New York: Oxford University Press: 62.

3 El-Tayeb, Fatima (2012) Gays who cannot properly be gay. Queer Muslims in the neoliberal European city. In: European Journal for Women's studies 19 (1) February: 89.

ing what it pushes to announce; to frame *out* what it urges to represent. Then I will discuss with the attempts to *de-frame* its entire structure and reclaim queerness in radical ways. In doing so, I am drawing mainly on ethnographic data I have gathered in Berlin.

## The Frame

The modes of framing mentioned above are by no means specific to Andreas' camera, nor to Hadi's body. "*Allah weiß, dass ich schwul bin*" is one of various mediums in which the frame is manifested; one of the myriad variants of configuring and replicating it. The modes of framing at work precede style and language, travel across mediums and genres, establish and validate perceptions. They also render experiences of those who are framed as truthful, but only insofar as they can be accommodated within a certain narrative that qualifies them as *reasonably true*.

The modes of framing queer migrants from Arab-speaking countries in Germany include the trope of resorting to Islam as a chief marker of their identity – the eminent domain that would instruct us most about their plight. Their struggle is usually subsumed under a binary of "Islam" versus "homosexuality", both often understood as self-evident and self-contained categories. Homophobia is often Islamized, not necessarily in the sense of regarding it as fundamentally Islamic, but as impelled and (falsely) justified by Islamic texts and traditions. In this logic, ending homophobia must claim and visibly realize the reconcilability of both Islam and homosexuality, often under the premise of first undertaking certain reforms to qualify the former in order to accept the latter. The dominance of this framework is evident in numerous media articles and reports featuring Arab queer refugees and migrants,[4] in political debates about migration, in the pedagogy of integration and programs of sexual education, and in academic symposia and conferences.[5]

It would be unsound to deny the productivity of such a framework for scholarly contributions about homosexuality in Islamic thought and historical practices,[6]

---

4 E.g. Constantin Schreiber (2018) Moscheereport: Islam und Homosexualität. In: Tagesschau, April 28 (https://www.youtube.com/watch?v=IodRCzs1hvs) Jaafar Abdul Karim (2020) ana mithli wa-ʿarabi wa muslim. DW Jaafar Talk, October 10 (https://www.youtube.com/watch?v=GKRObpRaqWM).

5 Caroline Ausserer (2016) Religion und Homosexualität – ein Vermeintlicher Wiederspruch. Heinrich-Böll-Stiftung December 20 https://www.boell.de/de/2016/12/20/too-queer-believe-religion-und-homosexualitaet-ein-vermeintlicher-widerspruch.

6 A significant contribution to this stance of scholarship is the work of Andreas Ismael Mohr in German and Scott Kugle in English. See Andreas Ismael Mohr (2020) Schwules muslimisches Nachdenken über Gotteswort und Prophetenüberlieferung. In: Lamya Kaddor (ed.) Muslimisch und liberal! Was einen zeitgemäßen Islam ausmacht. Munich: Piper: 236–246. Scott

or to revoke its potential to forge modes of identification and sense-making for many queer Muslims around the globe. My claim is rather that the persistence of this framework as the principal fulcrum of queer experience of Arab migrants in the West warrants critical inquiry. We need to scrutinize how it pre-shapes the very possibilities of speaking about Arab queerness; how it makes some aspects publicly voiced by the same conditions of ruling out others. Even when it is in the name of calling them out, of pushing them away from the burdens of their past and fostering their arrival in the present, the *interpellation* of queer migrants, refugees, and queers of color as simply "Muslims" fixes them in a predefined location that reenacts their (racial) otherness. Queer "Muslims" become queer in a sense *despite* their Islam or culture, or when they are urged to embody the ideal of reconciliation (or the moment they do so).

What might seem like an unfitting generalization cannot be separated from the larger mechanisms through which Islam is racialized, in the sense of allowing certain differences to be fixed as "Islamic" and certain bodies to be primarily identified (and recognized) in terms of the collective religious or cultural meanings they allegedly bear.[7] It should be noted, however, that reading certain queer bodies as simply Muslims is not always an unequivocal process. In the same framework, notions of "Arab culture," "traditions," or "social background" are often invoked, whether as side effects to the allegedly homophobic work of Islam, or external components that have leaked into its edifice and need to be filtered out. Such invocations alone would not topple the racialized structures ingrained in framing modalities, as long as they do not question the mechanisms of othering and stigmatization, and as long as naturalizing difference and fixing otherness remains intact under other labels. Islam, "Arab culture," and "social background" often remain entangled, if not interchangeable, in this context, insofar as they take on the same work of naturalizing difference and fixing otherness.

Although I am writing here specifically on queers who are read – or who identify in heterogeneous ways – as "Arabs", it must be clear by now that I am not suggesting simply replacing "queer Muslims" with "queer Arabs." In a German context where race is reconfigured as religion and/or culture, and whiteness is recoded as "post-racial"[8], the point is not to opt for a more accurate term to identify a collective, but rather to pay attention to what the procedure of signifying a collective does; what

Kugle (2010) Homosexuality in Islam: Critical reflections on Gay, Lesbian and Transgender Muslims. Oxford: Oneworld Publications.

7 Yasmin Shooman (2012) Das Zusammenspiel von Kultur, Religion, Ethnizität und Geschlecht im antimuslimischen Rassismus. In: Ungleichheit, Ungerechtigkeit. Aus Politik und Zeitgeschichte, Vol. 62 (https://www.bpb.de/shop/zeitschriften/apuz/130422/das-zusammenspiel-von-kultur-religion-ethnizitaet-und-geschlecht-im-antimuslimischen-rassismus/).

8 Jennifer Petzen (2012) Queer Trouble: Centering Race in Queer and Feminist Politics. In: Journal of Intercultural Studies, 33 (3) June: 291.

it undoes; and how it structures knowledge in ways permeated by racial formations and embedded in power relations. It is to regard culturalist framing with suspicion, not only for serving as an "essential tool for making 'other'"[9], as Lila Abu-Lughod notes, but also for how it effectuates otherness by isolating those identified as others from the political and historical realms that asymmetrically attach them to the self. Recalling Spivak's famous phrase of "white men saving brown women from brown men," Abu-Lughod points elsewhere to the "haunting resonance" of culturalist framings of oppression with colonial legacies.[10]

Pertinent to this is another discursive mode through which the frame operates: what has applied for brown women, increasingly applies today for brown queers and gay men. The frame under scrutiny is characterized by a temporal geography that organizes bodies into victims and saviors; vulnerable ones stuck in archaic times and violently dragged into them, versus contemporaneous others, at once liberated and liberators, urged to uncover the former from the patina of time and help them into the present. The inclusion of Arab queer migrants becomes conditioned, first, upon their embodiment of "ideal victimhood"[11] marked by a linear passage from the past into the future, from captivity to freedom, from alienation to self-realization; and second, upon the presence of those who are entitled to facilitate their temporal and cultural conversion and to protect them from possible pushbacks. The latter are mostly white women and men in whose bodies the signs of arrival become generic. They qualify as "properly gay", to rephrase Fatima El-Tayeb.[12] El-Tayeb links such a frame, not only to racial politics, but also to neoliberal modes of urban mobility; to "a spatial politics in which marginalized groups are not completely expelled from the city [...] but remain excluded and contained through their failure to achieve consumer-citizen status."[13] This resonates with another trope that features in the modes of framing under scrutiny, particularly in a city like Berlin. This city is often promoted as a cosmopolitan queer safe haven where diverse scripts of self-realization and identity-making are viable.[14] The problem with that claim lies not in its lack of empirical support; after all, for some, queer social realities unfurl in the city, while for others they do not. It lies rather in how reiterating this same claim often becomes

9 Lila Abu-Lughod (2006) Writing Against Culture. In: Anthropology in Theory: Issues in Epistemology, ed. Henrietta Moore & Todd Sanders, Oxford: Blackwell: 470.

10 Lila Abu-Lughod (2013) Do Muslim Women Need Saving? MA: Harvard University Press: 33.

11 N. Christie (1986) The Ideal Victim. In: From Crime Policy to Victim Policy, E.A Fattah, ed. Basingstoke: Macmillan: 18.

12 El-Tayeb, Fatima (2012) 'Gays who cannot properly be gay': Queer Muslims in the neoliberal European City. European Journal of Women's Studies, February 27, 19 (1): 88.

13 Ibid.: 81.

14 Cf. Jennifer Petzen (2004) Home or Home-Like. Turkish Queers Manage Space in Berlin. In: Space & Culture, 7 (1) February: 21. Ruth Preser (2017) Lost and found in Berlin: identity, ontology and the emergence of Queer Zion. In: Gender. In: Place & Culture, 24 (3): 413–425.

a tool to deny forms of homophobia[15] and to efface struggles, sufferings, experiences of fetishization, racialization, and exclusion that inculcate the relationship of many queer migrants to Berlin on daily basis.

How do queer Arab migrants engage with such modes of framing? How do their experiences of fetishization, racialization, and exclusion challenge the very grounds upon which the claims of inclusion and protection stand? How do they reprocess and challenge the frame's invocations of identities, ordering of bodies, staging of possibilities, and references to time and space? The following two sections will hopefully lead us to an answer.

## Out-framing: Mahmood's silence

Mahmood came to Berlin in his mid-twenties, not as a refugee, as many have mistaken him to be, but as a university student. Now, after finding a job he likes, he hopes this will improve his chances of securing his own rental apartment in Berlin – something he has been unable to find since moving to the city.

> "I did so many things here ... I went to many places ... I met so many people ... but every night I still go to bed with the feeling that I have no home."[16] In five years, he lived in eight different places in four neighborhoods. He doesn't even remember how many housing requests he submitted in those years that remained unanswered. "I used different nicknames. I told them that I am gay ... that I am student, not a refugee, that I don't smoke, that I drink alcohol, but only socially. I wanted them to know that I am not the kind of Arab guy they might think I am, neither the type who is too religious, nor the loser who drinks all the time."

Mahmood identifies as gay, yet never drinks alcohol. He thinks, that speaking about drinking habits in this context is much like revealing his homosexuality, a way of "polishing" his rental applications to increase his chances, as he puts it. Mahmood's attempts to "polish" his identity to gain access to the housing market reveal both his understanding that his relationship to the city is structured by his racial difference, and his awareness of possible ways to navigate such structures and racialized imaginaries.

In his quest to find a new home, Mahmood invokes his homosexuality, not to demand acceptance or to underline his legitimate right to live in an atmosphere where

15 Cf. Ahmed Awadalla (2021) From Cairo to Berlin: Architectures of Homophobia. Heinrich-Böll Stiftung, Dec 1 ( https://www.boell.de/en/2021/12/01/cairo-berlin-architectures-homophobia).

16 This section is based on two interviews conducted with Mahmood (name changed) in January 2017 and September 2021.

his sexuality must not be curtailed or confronted with hostility, but to counteract the racialized imaginaries his Arabness invokes in others: a "refugee", either "too religious", or an alcoholic "loser." It does not really matter whether he is telling the truth (identifying as gay) or a lie (drinking alcohol). What matters is that he places himself within a frame in which Arabness can be rendered desirable; or rather frames his identity in ways that contradict how Arabness is invoked and imagined, in an effort to invalidate its racial charge.

It is, however, to be noted that navigating racial structures never operates in specified directions, it is rather contingent upon unpredictable measures and can yield an outcome opposite to what was sought. "I got once a polite rejection email telling me I was one of the nicest guys among the potential flat mates, but they preferred to rent the room out to a refugee." Mahmood recalls this incident, ironically noting that he probably acted "too nice for an Arab."

Navigating racialized imaginaries is also a process that is coupled with anxieties and doubts: doubts about oneself, doubts about how truthful or righteous it might be to perform certain scripts of identity, and doubts about how to live up to one's own desires while being desirable to others. On dating apps, Mahmood fears that disclosing his Arabness might make people less interested in him. At other times, he thinks the opposite and choses "Arab" under the category of "ethnicity" included in some dating apps. He even embellishes his profile with self-descriptions like "macho" or "dominant Arab" knowing that resorting to such clichés will make him desirable to many. But sometimes, Mahmood feels remorse at "painting a self-image" that does not relate to how he sees himself, to how he understands his sexuality and desires others. "It is not that I can't play the macho... But still, it is not me. It is not how I want to be. It is tiring to feel that you are always confined to certain roles."

Mahmood concedes that Berlin has given him sexual freedoms he never dreamt of having. At the same time, the city assigns him certain roles, images, performances, and scripts upon which being recognized and granted (sexual) freedoms are contingent and become meaningful in the first place. To make the city home, to be visible and desirable it becomes incumbent upon him to act within the confines of a predefined frame. Navigating through the architecture of that frame is not just about *fitting in*, but also about defiantly *keeping out*. It means, in Mahmood's words, not only to know "what to say when and for whom" but also "what you should better keep silent about." To elaborate on this point, I will go back to my first encounter with Mahmood in Berlin.

It was Gay Pride in the summer of 2016. We met, not at the mainstream parade, but at the alternative *Kreuzberg Transgender Christopher Street Day.*[17] As members of

17 The Kreuzberger TCSD is deemed Berlin's alternative queer pride to be critical of commercialization attempts and committed to an anti-racist agenda. See Jin Haritaworn (2015) Queer Lovers and Hateful Others: Regenerating Violent Times and Places. London: Pluto Press: 1-2.

the Berlin-based interreligious initiative *Salaam-Schalom*,[18] I and our coordinator Armin Langer had been invited to give a short speech on the main stage of the parade. After the speech, Mahmood and I joined other acquaintances: Fabian, a gay teacher in his late 30s, was there with his Syrian boyfriend. Fabian expressed his admiration for the speech and the work being done by *Salaam-Schalom*, particularly in two respects. He first praised what he perceived as the initiative's focus on combining racism and homophobia, noting that "complaining about racism" was an important cause, but it became more credible by also speaking up loudly against antisemitism and homophobia, as both phenomena in his opinion were widespread among migrants in Germany. Secondly, Fabian admired that on stage we remained "apolitical." He perceived our action as an attempt to speak about the commonalities between Islam and Judaism, while keeping political conflicts in the Middle East at bay because, in his opinion, the issue of co-existence in Germany was at stake.

It was this latter point that represented a paradox for Mahmood. While for him, accepting himself as gay did not make dismissing Islam altogether inevitable, this self-acceptance for him nevertheless implied being "silent" in certain instances regarding religion and its moral dictations, which he thought we could never fully grasp.

> "I am not really religious myself," he said. "So, what obliges you here, in a free and secular country, away from your family and from religious people, to speak as a Muslim as long as you are not religious yourself? If you do not pray, if you do not fast, if you drink alcohol, what is the point in demonstrating your Muslimness on stage [...] for a dancing crowd who just want to party and have fun?"

Mahmood's suggestion to "mute" religion, or not to speak in its name in what he perceives to be a secular context of Gay Pride stirred a controversy among the conversation partners, he told me later. Fabian and his boyfriend accused him of being "politically irresponsible," of playing down the violence of religiously motivated homophobia and ignoring the fact that even in Germany, gay Muslims have difficulties coming out. Eventually, their overt irritation apparently silenced Mahmood for the rest of the evening.

The whole conversation left an aftertaste I pondered about for weeks. How come what was meant to be – or at least what I personally thought of as – a queer political intervention was celebrated for its allegedly intentional silence about politics in the name of promoting co-existence? And how, in the same context, did Mahmood's wish to be silent about Islam become an enraging and irresponsible act ignorant to

18 The Salam-Schalom initiative was founded in 2013 by Jewish and Muslim activists in Berlin to promote solidarity among coreligionists in Germany and build a common alliance against antisemitism and all forms of racism. See Elisabeth Becker (2021) Mosques in the Metropolis: Incivility, Case and Contention in Europe. Chicago: Chicago University Press: 113.

the pain of others? What makes speaking (un)political? When does the lack of politics become irresponsible and when does its presence become a threat for peace and co-existence?

Drawing on Nancy Fraser – in relation to the Israeli-Palestinian conflict, albeit in a different context – Jason Ritchie calls our attention to a mode of liberal gay activism in which politics becomes "conceivable and appropriate [...] only to the extent that it shies away from 'transformative' demands in favor of affirmative remedies for injustices" without disturbing "the framework" that underlies their social arrangement.[19] In such a model, the acceptance and visibility of racialized queer bodies becomes contingent upon their mutation of certain political claims and identity configurations.

On the stage of the *Kreuzberger TCSD*, however, muting politics, i.e., Palestine, is not the only qualification needed for queer Arabs to be placed properly within the frame. That frame incites and assembles even as it mutes and separates. Mahmood's will to mute Islam sits uncomfortably with a disposition of stimulating discourses on "Islam", or what Schirin Amir-Moazami describes as "summoning Muslims to discourse" (*Aufforderung zum Diskurs*) in the sense that Muslims are invited, and indeed also invite themselves, to speak as Muslim subjects.[20] What should not be inferred here is that the category "Muslim", a marker of identity and a signifier of certain modes of reasoning and feeling, is in itself void of any meaning prior to its invocation by others. For many queers who identify as Muslims, including Mahmood, Islam remains a substantial domain of engagement in their ways of living and in their pursuit of making sense. The point is that engagement with Islam does not take place in a discursive void. Instead, it is anchored within a whole field of invocations, perceptions of identity, conceptions of truth, even desires and sexual fantasies that translates certain configurations of power and allows them to unfold and endure. The ways in which all these relate to the individual's quest to fashion a Muslim self are complex and multidirectional. In some cases, they coexist, impelling each other in parallel or similar directions, prompting some to "come out" and raise their voices as "public Muslims"[21], even if in the same breath they "stress that they are not believers or not practicing their religion."[22] While in the case of Mahmood their relation seems to be characterized by tensions that articulate silence as a mode

19 Jason Ritchie (2010) How Do You Say, 'Come Out of the Closest' in Arabic? Queer Activism and Politics of Visibility in Israel-Palestine. In: GLQ A Journal of Lesbian and Gay Studies, 16 (4): 561.

20 Schirin Amir-Moazami (2018) Einleitung. In: Der Inspizierte Muslim: Zur Politisierung der Islamforschung in Europa, ed. Schirin Amir-Moazami, Bielefeld: transcript: 11.

21 Riem Spielhaus (2010) Media Making Muslim: The construction of a Muslim Community in Germany through media debate. In: Contemporary Islam 4 (1): 14.

22 Ibid., 16.

of disrupting pre-established settings of communication; a will of *unbecoming* utterly "Muslim," not in absolute terms or once and for all, but only in conjecture with certain enunciations of sexuality. To unbecome in this sense is to unsettle the interpellation's structure that summons Muslimness where it ought to be framed; to alter the very law that hails the Muslim subject into being so that "a creative and transformative politics of becoming" can become possible.[23] Unbecoming Muslim in this conjecture is becoming Muslim, but *outside of the frame*.

It is a "becoming undone," to use Butler's vocabulary, that undoes prior normative conceptions of Muslimness, to "inaugurate relatively newer one that has greater livability as its aim."[24] Mahmood does not want to become the gay Muslim (or the gay Arab) he is hailed to be – neither the one who circumscribes his desires, nor the one who frames him as desirable in a different context. "*Al-sukut ʿalamat al-rida*" or "silence is the sign of approval" is an Arabic say he recalls while elaborating on what he meant by silence in this context. His intention is not to say that Islam inevitably denounces homosexuality, but rather to question the claim that it inevitably advocates it. What troubles him is not that one can be at once gay and Muslin, as he himself is, but rather when one is compelled to speak as a Muslim expressing public approval for something already implied in private. Instead of viewing such a disposition as contradictory, I argue for re-attending to silence as a creative possibility to self-craft a being that is "beside oneself" and outside a framework of recognition that establishes our legitimacy but fails to do justice to what "tear us from ourselves [...] and implicates us in lives that are not our own, sometimes fatally, irreversibly."[25] "I am Muslim and Arab yes. But I am a gay Egyptian too. I took part in the revolution. I am a hobby photographer. I go to the gym. I love techno and I do not eat spinach. My flatmate wants to kick me out and I will be homeless in two weeks. Why do my Muslimness or Arabness matter more than all that followed? Can't you all just be indifferent about that?" Mahmood asks. Provoked by his question, which does not exempt my research endeavor from the culpability of reproducing the same paradigm of (mis)recognition, I ended our conversation, hoping that I had not pressed him to talk about things he would have preferred to keep silent about.

## De-framing: Queer Arab Barty

Mahmood's take on silence should not prompt us to re-frame certain modes of queerness as "authentically" prone to silence. Silence is a discursive technique to

---

23 Mary Bunch (2013) The Unbecoming subject of sex: Performativity, interpellation and the politics of queer theory. In: Feminist Theory 14 (1): 40.

24 Judith Butler (2004) Undoing Gender. New York: Routledge: 1.

25 Ibid.: 20.

constitute identity and negotiate possibilities of being within and in relation to folds of power. Silence might be the opposite of speech, but it is never the negation of discourse. Michel Foucault reminds us that "there is no binary division to be made between what one says and what one does not say."[26] Instead of presuming such a binary, we should identify the different ways of saying or not saying things; the different incitements to speak and the different inhibitions or restrictions that lock speech. As much as silence can loosen the holds of power "and provide for a relatively obscure area of tolerance," it also can be sheltering power and "anchoring its prohibitions."[27] Mahmood's appeal for a form of silence is in itself a call to discourse; an attempt to break other silences in the frame. Mahmood does so by calling upon the differentiation between realms of exposure. He negotiates the grips of discourse by maneuvers of concealment and defies framing by being willing to stand – at least partly – out of sight and longing for indifference to belonging.

Other queer Arab voices in Berlin, though willing to resist the confines of the frame, do not endorse silence and indifference or cannot afford them in the first place. In 2019, the collective *Queer Arab Barty* was founded in Berlin by a group of "queer diaspora Arabs" out of a desire for a space that would be both "pleasurable [and] relatable". What the founders longed for was not indifference, but "self-expression and acceptance," re-claiming both themselves and a city to which they "came or were brought to by [...] [their] own volition or out of necessity," as stated by Nael Ibrahim and Erkan Affan in a sort of founding manifesto for the collective.[28] While Mahmood is overwhelmed with his perceived otherness, negotiating whether to take it as an advantage or to try to loosen its grips on his body, the founders of *Queer Arab Barty* reclaim otherness for themselves and fight for visibility that can do justice to their desires and specificities, but without being ceaselessly rendered as an object of study, analysis, sensationalism, and commodification.[29]

For the collective, Arabness is marked by a common tongue, common visual references, and a scope of "various cultures and traditions." At the same time, by virtue of a shared experience of fetishization and racialization, queer Arabness remains thoroughly tied up with the struggles of other queer communities of color in the city.[30] The collective does not claim to conquer new grounds of representation but to shake the current grounds of framing Arabs with Orientalist legacies and fetishized desires. In fact, Arabs are prolifically represented, yet often subsumed in a "(fictious)

---

26 Michel Foucault (1978) The History of Sexuality. Volume I: An Introduction, trans. Robert Hurley, New York: Pantheon Books: 27.

27 Ibid.: 101.

28 Erkan Affan/Nael Ibrahim (2019) Too Arab to be Queer, and too Queer to be Arab. In: Jeem. July 7 (https://jeem.me/de/node/280).

29 Ibid.

30 Ibid.

binary of Arab versus queer'" that flattens their experience and prevents them "from feeling like (they) belong to the city."[31] As the title they chose, *Too Arab to be Queer, and too queer to be Arab*, expresses, the authors recast the binary in an attempt to subvert the paradox it entails. Subversion here is not merely about circumventing the conventional frame by blocking out certain realms from its scope, it is about *de-framing* it altogether.

In January 2020, I attended a public event organized by the collective titled *Navigating Orientalism in Contemporary Society*. The organizers invited a group of queer artists and activists from the Arab communities in Berlin to discuss "whether it is possible to subvert/reclaim racist iconographies and typologies."[32] As panel moderator and collective member Nael Ibrahim asserts, in place of the dichotomous discourse of (ir)reconcilability that posits queer as a pole opposite to Arab or Muslim, the panel deploys queerness as an attempt to break with the figurative formations of Arab and Muslim in Germany as identities that cohere through interrelated – though not necessarily homologous – perceptions: "the hyper-sexual," "the hyper-masculine," "the terrorist," "the refugee," "the homophobe," or "the victim of homophobia." Two of the panelists, Ahmed, an Egyptian author and psychosociologist, and Hassan, a Lebanese artist and drag performer, noted how they had found themselves trapped in the category of the "Arab" which emerged ubiquitously as an unambiguous reference for their identity after they had come to Germany. For Imad, a Lebanese anthropologist, visual artist, and member of the collective, Arabness might be "a problematic term," but it bears an undeniable ontology. Arabness is marked by his skin, his body, his family, his war traumas, and his unredeemable losses. In Germany, it manifests continuously in his "lack of access to certain spaces and opportunities." Arabness might be a performance, but it is an "ongoing" one that transcends the language of choice and self-autonomy without fully circumventing agency. Imad "cannot not perform" his Arab identity, he says. Nevertheless, he thinks he can choose not "to capitalize" on this performance, which means not subscribing to dominant stereotypical imaginaries of Arabness. Precisely in resisting the latter does one claim authority for one's own performance.

For Tewa, a curator and artist, "Arabness" is both an emblem for personal identity crisis and a provoking notion. Growing up in an Amazigh family in Gaddafi's Libya, she had not been aware of her ethnic difference until when she was 14. Today, she is provoked when people – Arabs and non-Arabs – insist on labeling her an Arab. She

31 Ibid.

32 Queer Arab Barty, QAB x Vorspiel: Navigating Orientalism in Contemporary Society, on Facebook, Jan 28, 2020, https://www.facebook.com/events/524124901516142?ref=newsfeed. The speakers where Imad Gebrayel, Hassan Cupcake, (members of Arab Queer Barty) Ahmed Awadalla and Tewa Barnosa, and it was moderated by Nael Ibrahim (also a member of the collective).

is also provoked by the pressure of constantly having to deliver a statement against the attempts to Arabize her.

In these reflections, Arabness becomes a site of contestations, a domain in which a sense of disparity takes shape between the intricate ways of being and feeling like oneself on the one hand, and the established modes of outer perceptions, regimes of representations and invocations of speech and visibility on the other. The panelists acknowledge this disparity in different ways. But they also underline that conceiving of it in theory cannot make up for how confounding it is in reality. One's own feelings, desires, and ways of self-perceptions never stand aloof from how one is perceived by others, or how one is urged to perform Arabness in ways that feed and shade into prevalent hegemonic representations. Imad notes that Orientalist images are encouraged by Arabs themselves as much as they are constructed by them. He calls for creative ways to reclaim or repurpose such images if we are not able to entirely refrain from reproducing them. Imad in effect tries to translate this vision in his work as a designer and visual artist. He avoids taking up identity in terms of customary visual references and tries instead to understand it in terms of the topics he chooses to produce and how these are in turn shaped by what affects him as a queer migrant and a person of color in Europe, not just by where he comes from. Along the same lines, Ahmed endorses alternative identity mapping, stressing that if identity signifies anything at all, then not what one *is*, but what one *does*. The latter is in constant motion, not confined to a space or time. He adds that being a refugee is something he strongly identifies with, noting critically that the refugee cause has been predominantly represented in Germany in ways that distorted the complexities of refugee experience, often reducing them to "victims" of their countries of origin who must feel "grateful" for those who saved them.

In a similar vein, Hassan expresses his discomfort with the way he is being pushed to deal with certain themes in his shows. He feels pressured to restate "that Arabs are not violent, that they are peaceful, that they love music" and he feels uncomfortable always being read as a "political" performer. "Yes, drag is always political," Hassan concedes, but he refuses to endorse a vision that codes his drag art as political only in conjunction with certain references to or expressions of an imagined collective identity. Hassan complicates the "political" framing of his performances by referring to his personal life, to the people he dates, or to the neighborhood he grew up in specifically, rather than to Lebanon or the Arab world in general, as sources of inspirations that qualify as political in a different sense.

In this sense, political subjectivity unfolds not only beyond those realms of action and interaction presumed as political, but in the very act of challenging the power of defining certain actions as political when assigned to certain spaces and articulated in a certain vocabulary. In calling the personal and the particular into play as core references for being political, queer Arabs infringe the boundaries that outline their actions and the structures that hold together racialized configurations of their identity. The personal and the particular as domains of politics, the diasporic here and now with all its contingencies as a realm of identification in opposition to assumed origins, concepts of identity that dwell on the multiplicity of deeds, words, and dispositions instead of the embeddedness into a culture, an ethnicity, or a religion, all of these can be read as subversive strategies to *de-frame* hegemonic images and perceptions about queer Arabs.

Yet, despite their empowering potential, such strategies remain indebted to the contextual relations that bring them forth, marked by doubt and ambivalence. Even when one consciously intervenes in the narrative "to show what is happening from our shores, not from their shores," as Tewa puts it, there are these moments of conflict: "Is that my voice now? Am I [still] giving them what they are expecting? Or am I voicing my own traumas and giving myself the chance to overcome them through [...] [uncovering] what is happening there in reality?"

The panel did not promise to deliver any answers to the questions it raised. But Ahmed's closing words offer us insights into how to handle the frame queerly; how to speak in a voice that can do justice to one's own experiences and struggles, regardless of the puzzling question of how one's "true" voice might sound. For that, he resorts to Edward Said's notion of "speaking truth to power."[33] He propels us to "engage in troubles," to "cause fraction," to "rub against things" in the sense of creating tensions that question power, that unsettle the framing of otherness and the paradigms of debating race, religion, and culture in Germany.

## Epilogue: Bad Queers

Framing is a reasoning narrative; a way of organizing experiences in a manner that smoothly channels them into pre-established modes of sight and cognition. The frame directs sight and locates bodies within a field of vision as the only ground where their recognition becomes feasible. The frame is an episteme in which representation becomes, not merely a doorway to or an illustration of reality, but an order that aims to substitute reality by what it condenses and compresses from within a set of imagined outlines, reasoned as common sense, for whose coherence contingencies must be overlooked. Political theorist Timothy Mitchell speaks of "enframing" as "a method of dividing up and containing;"[34] an endeavor to reorganize the world so that it can resemble the very images and concepts through which it is envisioned and cognized. Following this line of thought, the frame can be understood in both senses; as a material interface, affixing bodies in a posture that

33 Edward Said (1994) Speaking Truth to Power. In: Representations of the Intellectual. London: Vintage: 73.

34 Timothy Mitchell (1988) Colonizing Egypt, London: Cambridge University Press: 44.

reproduces them as representations, images, and narratives, and as a scheme that re-organizes human experiences into clear-cut itineraries endowed with temporal dimensions and marked by totalizing concepts like religion and culture. Framing is also the process through which the conditions of recognition are set, and identity is assumed. The frame seizes and materializes how, in the Althusserian sense,[35] subjects are hailed into being and constituted as such in the very act of labeling them. To speak as a recognized subject is to respond to an authority that hails you as what you are; or rather as what you are assumed to be.

The current contribution tried to uncover how dominant patterns of framing the experience of queer Arab migrants in Germany sustain hierarchies and racialize difference. The problem with the (ir)reconcilability narrative that holds sway over their representation is not just a problem of rehabilitating binarity and essentializing identities. It also concerns the modes of control and regulation the narrative enables but never recognizes. It animates and masks particular styles of knowledge production as indispensable and unbiased despite being embedded in particular histories and configurations of power. It fails to reckon with diverse modes of desire, different ideas about love, justice, and concepts of the self that queer Arabs cherish and embrace, and the obfuscated forms of violence they are susceptible to in Berlin. The cases of Mahmood and the *Queer Arab Barty* collective were presented to demonstrate how queer Arabs migrants creatively engage with the workings of the frame and the firmness of its boundaries. They do acknowledge being complicit in maintaining its authority by responding to the hailing call as the price for social recognition;[36] it is the price they pay to become the free queer subject they are promised to be. At the same time, they master tacit maneuvers to keep themselves at distance from the discourse that bestows identity on them. They disrupt the structure of interpellation by refusing to respond to the hailing call – as in the case of Mahmood's silence about his Muslimness in conjecture with his homosexuality – or by hailing back and speaking truth to power, as Ahmed puts it. For Althusser, such provoking acts of dissonance would qualify its agents as "bad subjects", in contrast to a subordinate majority of "good" ones.[37] But "badness" in the face of normative authority is a precisely queer hallmark. "Badness"– like "strangeness"– is a quality the English word "queer" has semantically signified since the 16$^{th}$ century.[38] Today, the "bad" queer is the "shadow [that comes] in mind" when the image of the "good gay" is invoked, to use Michael

---

35 Louis Althusser (2014) On Ideology. In: On the Reproduction of Capitalism. Ideology and Ideological State Apparatus, Louis Althusser, author, trans. G. M. Goshgarian. London: Verso: 189–190.

36 Judith Butler (1997) The Psychic Life of Power. Theories in Subjection. Stanford: Stanford University Press: 112.

37 Althusser (2014) On Ideology: 269.

38 Philip Durkin (2009) The Oxford Guide to Etymology. Oxford: Oxford University Press: 216f.

Warner's phrasing, without necessarily sticking to what that implies for him.[39] Being "bad" here is namely not only about knocking back from the attempts to institutionalize gay love through marriage and "building a way of life with other queers that ordinary folk do not understand or control."[40] What is at stake here is more about refusing to place oneself smoothly in a framework that claims to represent, liberate, and include without pointing to the conditions it decrees for its claims to resonate, and without attending to the hierarchies and forms of exclusion it deploys. "Bad" queers here are those who cannot arrive; those racialized subjects who cannot be "folded back into life,"[41] or "properly be gay."[42] But "badness" can be queerly reclaimed by a will to cause fraction, to "rub against things"- as Ahmed puts it – even against one's own body. Arabness might be marked on one's own body, but it still can be *queered* by questioning how it is framed, by whom, for whom, and under what conditions. It can even be undone, not out of endorsement for anti-identity politics, but for the sake of envisioning and enacting new possibilities of being and identifying as queer and Arab, outside of authoritative frames – since a critique of authority will only fully unfold when "the one who offers [it] is willing to be undone by the critique that he or she performs."[43]

## References

Abdul Karim, Jaafar (2020) Ana mithli wa-ʿarabi wa muslim. DW Jaafar Talk, October 10 (https://www.youtube.com/watch?v=GKRObpRaqWM).

Abu-Lughod, Lila (2006) Writing against Culture. In: Moore, Henrietta; Sanders, Todd (eds.) Anthropology in Theory: Issues in Epistemology, Oxford: Blackwell, 466–479.

Abu-Lughod, Lila (2012) Do Muslim Women Need Saving? Massachusetts, Harvard University Press.

Affan, Erkan/Ibrahim, Nael (2019) Too Arab to be Queer, and too Queer to be Arab. Jeem, July 7 (https://jeem.me/de/node/280).

Althusser, Louis (2014) On Ideology. In: On the Reproduction of Capitalism. Ideology and Ideological State Apparatus, transl. G. M. Goshgarian. London: Verso, 189–190.

39 Michael Warner (1999) The Trouble with Normal. Sex, Politics, and the Ethics of Queer Life. Cambridge, Massachusetts: Harvard University Press: 114.

40 Ibid.

41 Jasbir. K Puar (2007) Terrorist Assemblages. Homonationalism in queer times. Durham: Duke University Press: 35.

42 El-Tayeb (2012) Gays who cannot properly be gay: 89.

43 Judith Butler (2004) Undoing Gender: 8.

Amir-Moazami, Schirin (2018) Einleitung. In: Amir-Moazami, S. (ed.) Der Inspizierte Muslim: Zur Politisierung der Islamforschung in Europa. Bielefeld: Transcript, 9–34.

Ausserer, Carolin (2016) Religion und Homosexualität – ein Vermeintlicher Wiederspruch. Heinrich-Böll-Stiftung, December 20 (https://www.boell.de/de/2016/12/20/too-queer-believe-religion-und-homosexualitaet-ein-vermeintlicher-widerspruch).

Awadalla, Ahmed (2021) From Cairo to Berlin: Architectures of Homophobia. Heinrich-Böll Stiftung, Dec. 1 (https://www.boell.de/en/2021/12/01/cairo-berlin-architectures-homophobia).

Becker Elisabeth (2021) Mosques in the Metropolis: Incivility, Case and Contention in Europe Chicago: Chicago University Press.

Bernhardt Andreas/Faust, Armin (2020) Allah weiß, dass ich schwul bin. RBB, December 12, 29:04 min. (https://www.rbb-online.de/unserleben/reportagen/allah-weiss-dass-ich-schwul-bin.html).

Bunch, Mary (2013) The Unbecoming subject of sex: Performativity, interpellation and the politics of queer theory. Feminist Theory 14(1) 39–55.

Butler, Judith (1997) *The Psychic Life of Power. Theories in Subjection*. Stanford: Stanford University Press.

Butler, Judith (2004) *Undoing Gender*, New York: Routledge.

Christie, N. (1986) The Ideal Victim. In: From Crime Policy to Victim Policy. In: Fattah, E.A. (ed.) Basingstoke: Macmillan, 17–30.

Durkin, Philip (2009) *The Oxford Guide to Etymology*, Oxford: Oxford University Press.

El-Tayeb, Fatima (2012) 'Gays who cannot properly be gay': Queer Muslims in the neoliberal European City. European Journal of Women's Studies, February 27, 19(1) 79–95.

Foucault, Michel (1978) The History of Sexuality. Volume I: An Introduction, trans. Robert Hurley, New York: Pantheon Books.

Halperin, David M. (1995) Saint Foucault. Towards A Gay Hagiography, New York: Oxford University Press.

Haritaworn, Jin (2015) Queer Lovers and Hateful Others: Regenerating Violent Times and Places, London: Pluto Press.

Kugle, Scott (2010) Homosexuality in Islam: Critical reflections on Gay, Lesbian and Transgender Muslims. Oxford: Oneworld Publications.

Mitchell, Timothy (1988) Colonizing Egypt, London: Cambridge University Press.

Mohr, Andreas Ismael. (2020) Schwules muslimisches Nachdenken über Gotteswort und Prophetenüberlieferung. In: Kaddor , Lamya (ed.) Muslimisch und liberal! Was einen zeitgemäßen Islam ausmacht, Munich: Piper.

Petzen, Jennifer (2004) Home or Home-Like. Turkish Queers Manage Space in Berlin. Space & Culture 7(1) February, 20–32.

Petzen, Jennifer (2012) Queer Trouble: Centring Race in Queer and Feminist Politics. Journal of Intercultural Studies 33(3) June, 289–302.

Preser, Ruth (2017) Lost and found in Berlin: identity, ontology and the emergence of Queer Zion. Gender, Place & Culture 24(3) October, 413–425.

Puar, Jasbir. K. (2007) Terrorist Assemblages. Homonationalism in queer times. Durham: Duke University Press.

Queer Arab Barty (2020) QAB x Vorspiel: Navigating Orientalism in Contemporary Society. Facebook, Jan. 28 (https://www.facebook.com/events/524124901516142?ref=newsfeed).

Ritchie, Jason (2010) How Do You Say, 'Come Out of the Closet' in Arabic? Queer Activism and Politics of Visibility in Israel-Palestine. GLQ A Journal of Lesbian and Gay Studies, 16(4), 557–576.

Schreiber, Constantin (2018) Moscheereport: Islam und Homosexualität. Tagesschau, April 28 (https://www.youtube.com/watch?v=IodRCzs1hvs).

Sherwan, Ahmed (2018) "Allah ist schwul": Für Solidarität mit muslimischen LGBTI auf den CSD. Siegsäule, July 26 (https://www.siegessaeule.de/magazin/3961-allah-ist-schwul-f%C3%BCr-solidarit%C3%A4t-mit-muslimischen-lgbti-auf-den-csd/).

Shooman, Yasmin (2012) Das Zusammenspiel von Kultur, Religion, Ethnizität und Geschlecht im antimuslimischen Rassismus. In: Ungleichheit, Ungerechtigkeit. Aus Politik und Zeitgeschichte, Vol. 62 (https://www.bpb.de/shop/zeitschriften/apuz/130422/das-zusammenspiel-von-kultur-religion-ethnizitaet-und-geschlecht-im-antimuslimischen-rassismus/).

Spielhaus, Riem (2010) Media Making Muslim: The construction of a Muslim Community in Germany through media debate. Contemporary Islam, 4(1) 11–27.

Warner, Michael (1999) The Trouble with Normal. Sex, Politics, and the Ethics of Queer Life. Cambridge, Massachusetts: Harvard University Press.

# 8. "When I got off at Friedrichstraße, I was so happy to be back in East Berlin!"

*Mahmood Dabdoub*

My life as a photographer has been strongly influenced by several countries: Palestine, Lebanon, East Germany, and now the Federal Republic of Germany. All these places have enormously impacted my understanding of culture, politics, and the everyday lives of people living there. Both East Berlin and West Berlin became important places in my student life. I could visit both as a foreigner. In the GDR, I felt understood as a Palestinian because people understood when I talked about the separation of my people. As a Palestinian in Lebanon, I was already used to not really belonging. It was a bit like that in the GDR. In Lebanon, I was a second or even third-class citizen. It wasn't quite like that in the GDR, but I was still exotic for many people at first.

I was born in Baalbek, Lebanon, in 1958, ten years after my family was expelled from Palestine. Far from home, I attended school in a refugee camp. As a child, I often devoted myself to mentally escaping into different worlds and scenarios that I constructed far from the prevailing desolation and shortcomings. My favorite escape was to paint imagined worlds of houses with tiled roofs, waterfalls, and stone bridges. In addition, at school, I was often given the task of painting illustrative panels on various subjects for several classes. This gave me a lot of courage. With the moral support of my teachers, I painted even more passionately.

After graduating from high school in Beirut, I lived in West Germany for a few months starting in 1978, searching for a place to study before returning to Beirut. There I took up a job at the Palestinian cultural office in Beirut, hoping to become a painter under Ismail Shammout. Along the way, I took photographs with a *Praktika*, an East German camera, which I would carry with me as I wandered through the alleys of the refugee camp to capture the people there, going about their daily lives. My colleagues in the cultural office liked these works very much.

The famous Palestinian painter Ismail Shammout, with whom I was allowed to study and work, then said: "Mahmoud, I don't want you to stay in Beirut. I don't want to see you handling a Kalashnikov one day. I want you to go and study, and I will help you."

With the help of a scholarship from the Artists' Association of the GDR, which was available to the Palestinian Artists' Association, I came to Leipzig in September 1981. There I learned German at the Herder Institute. At the same time, I took part in a photography workshop. After an exhibition of my photos from Beirut and the workshop results, the head of the department at the Herder Institute encouraged me to study photography. She made an appointment with the then-head of the photography department, Professor Peter Pachnicke, who, to my surprise, offered me a place at the university after an admissions interview. It was a great pleasure for me to be allowed to study at this university. However, I had to work very hard and learn a lot to progress in my development and keep up with my fellow students, who often had much more professional experience and opportunities than I did.

In Leipzig, the Hochschule für Grafik und Buchkunst (HGB) offered the only opportunity in the entire Eastern Bloc to earn a diploma in artistic photography. The best-known teachers were Evelyn Richter, Arno Fischer, and Helfried Strauß. At the same time, it was possible to do more than simply illustrate political targets. The school gave me a lot: first and foremost, the best opportunity to become something.

I began my studies in 1982 under Helfried Strauß and would travel back to Lebanon regularly, always packing my camera and numerous films. My teacher remembered that I would bring mountains of contact prints back with me, which we would review together at a leisurely pace, armed with a strong NIKON magnifier. For me, taking pictures was primarily a means of self-help because to really "arrive", I needed to get to know this unfamiliar society thoroughly.

Leipzig was a place of peace for me. I had no worries. I felt safe in the GDR; it became my new home. At that time, I took hundreds of photos in various cities, but they were never meant for the public. It was more like a seminar assignment at the university. I always went out and photographed what I saw. I came into contact with people quite easily.

Berlin was my second most visited city. Some friends there studied German with me at the Herder Institute. Berlin was a nice change. There I also had the chance to experience many tourists, and mostly they became the "target" of my camera – including the purchases they made – mostly teddy bears! I found especially many motifs at Alexanderplatz, a popular meeting place for us Arab Palestinians and others, including the Germans themselves. In addition, I would go out to the art college in Weißensee, where my friend was studying, or to Schönhauser Allee, a very busy area. Along the avenue and at the S-Bahn station were very different motifs: people, streetcars, merchants, etc. Even in our popular Viennese café, many interesting motifs would present themselves.

At that time, I was fortunately allowed to visit my brothers in West Berlin once a permit from the Foreigners Authority had been issued. After just a few days there, I came back. When I got off at the Friedrichstraße station, I was really happy to be back in East Berlin! There I felt free. I felt at home because nobody was asking for a visa as they did in West Berlin, where I'd had a bad experience when I'd said that West Berlin is an international zone, and you didn't need a visa.

In 1989, when the demonstrations in Leipzig, Dresden, and Berlin were in full swing, I watched them on TV. I was in the FRG in Cologne "legally" at the time, participating in an exhibition. Then my friend in North Rhine-Westphalia persuaded me to extend my visa to see our other friends, which was made possible, and so I traveled around West Germany to visited German and Arab friends.

As a photographer, I did well most of the time in the GDR. People were quite open to me. But there were also situations where the police prevented me from photographing events. The first time this happened to me was during a demonstration on May 1, 1986, or maybe in 1987. Later, when the big protests started in Leipzig at the fall of the Wall, I was very scared. It all felt like a crazy movie. I didn't dare photograph it, my fear of being caught and deported was too great. That's what happened to many photographers.

On the big day, November 9, 1989, I returned to the GDR to Berlin accompanied by a fellow photographer. We arrived in West Berlin by car in the evening, crossing at Checkpoint-Charlie. But I was not allowed through by car, as a non-German! Ok, I thought, and drove over to Friedrichstraße to wait for my colleague, who picked me up half an hour later. We then drove on to Schönhauser Allee, to her niece's place. She had already told me at the FRG/GDR border that she had a funny feeling. She told me, "You know, I travel to the East from time to time, but it's completely different this time," and she burst into tears. As I found out later, she had had the right feeling,

At her niece's home, we had supper and tea while we watched the news, *Die Aktuelle Kamera*, on TV. Suddenly the announcer interrupted the news to hand it over to Günther Schabowski, who spoke the famous sentence, "To my knowledge, that means... immediately, without delay." Uttering these words about the new GDR travel regulations, Politburo spokesman Günther Schabowski involuntarily heralded the end of the German division at 6:53 p.m. on November 9, 1989 and brought down the Wall.

We got ready to set off again to make our way to the border. The first gate was Bornholmer Straße. Luckily, I had three films with me. I took photos of the happy, jubilant people from the East and West, and was very taken and moved throughout that night of freedom. I had goosebumps and tears in my eyes as I accompanied this event. I was there on Bornholmer Strasse and crossed the bridge with all these people. We were all crying and so happy. And I wondered when this would happen to us Palestinians: when would we be allowed to open doors and cross bridges? It was indescribable. But I couldn't photograph any of it because I felt paralyzed. Even today I'm ashamed that I didn't capture it with my camera.

The crowds headed to the Ku'damm in the center of Berlin-West, and we were on the streets for hours until the early morning. Exhausted, I went to my brother's without fear of the police.

But then our situation began to change. We were uncertain what would await us scholarship holders of the GDR in the coming days. For the most part, many people moved to the Federal Republic to shape their future since the "new states" situation was very precarious. Fortunately, the authorities, who had known me over the years, recognized my residence permit without any problems and exchanged it for a "Federal Republic" one.

Looking back, I feel my student years were some of the best times I have experienced. They shaped me and made me the citizen of Leipzig I am today. I live in Leipzig with my wife and my three daughters, who are studying. They have learned Arabic and a lot about our original culture from us. In 2000 I became a German citizen. I see myself as a bridge builder between the Orient and the Occident. My illustrated books, the titles of which translate as "How far is Palestine?"[1], "New home Leipzig"[2], and "Land of the wounded cedars"[3], are proof of my being anchored in both worlds.

I want to show in my work that I am connected to and appreciate both worlds, because both have their justification despite the stark differences. Humanity is what connects us, and that's my motto.

As a freelance photographer, I am very busy documenting, among other things, the transformation of my city, Leipzig.

---

1 Dabdoub, Mahmond; Latchinian, Sarkis; Latchinian, Adelheid; Karasholi, Adel (2003) Wie fern ist Palästina? Fotos aus palästinensischen Flüchtlingslagern. Passage-Verlag, Leipzig.

2 Dabdoub, Mahmond (2003) Alltag in der DDR. Fotos aus den 80er Jahren. Mit Texten von Gunter Böhnke und Bernd Lindner, Passage–Verlag, Leipzig.

3 Dabdoub, Mahmond; Shalha, Ahmad (2007) Land der verletzten Zedern, Dokumente eines Krieges. Ein Fototagebuch aus dem Libanon, Passage–Verlag, Leipzig.

*Fig. 8.1: Reichstag and the Wall of Berlin*

©Mahmoud Dabdoub

*Fig. 8.2: U-Bahnhof Dimitroffstrasse, today U-Bahnhof Eberswalder Straße*

©Mahmoud Dabdoub

*Fig. 8.3: The Marx and Engels Forum, against the backdrop of the (now demolished) Palast der Republik, the former seat of parliament for the German Democratic Republic (GDR).*

©Mahmoud Dabdoub

*Fig. 8.4: "In Space and on Earth"*

© Mahmoud Dabdoub

*Fig. 8.5: "280 Leistungsverträge. Wissenschaft-Produktion"*

© Mahmood Dabdoub

*Fig. 8.6: Bornholmer Straße, East-Berlin, 9th November 1989*

© Mahmoud Dabdoub

# 9. Berlin: A City of Indefinite Dreams?

*Hashem Al-Ghaili*

## The move to Berlin

When I lived in Bremen between 2013 and 2016, I knew that although it was beautiful and quiet, it was too small for me. I was in the midst of switching careers from academic life to science communication. By then, I had switched from academic science research to science communication, where I produced science communication videos on social media where science is explained in the most straightforward and attractive way possible.[1] My work as a science communicator, filmmaker, and author has attracted a global audience, regardless of geography and education. As long as they understand English, the ubiquitous language, I can interact with them. My audience is mainly US and European, with a large base in India and the Philippines. It has a 50% equal gender balance.

But I knew I needed a push in my career, which required me to move to a bigger city. My first choice was Berlin. The incentives were great! I had always heard about how receptive Berlin was and learned it's rich in diversity and like-minded people. Indeed, I found it a living, breathing city that loves art and awards creative minds. It's a central hub for science, technology, and innovation. And I have come to feel that no matter the country you come from or your educational background, Berlin will always have a place for you.

My success on social media provided me with more exposure, so people around the world started inviting me to speak about science, technology, innovation, and social media. and I have traveled extensively to deliver talks about topics that interest me and the public. I enjoy giving public talks and my natural audience are people all over the globe who speak English. I have delivered TEDx talks, in Rome (Italy), Cluj (Romania) and Zagreb (Croatia). I also participated in a session at the European Parliament in Belgium, which was a chance to engage with policymakers.

1 You can view my work by joining me across social media: https://app.muse.io/hashemalghaili.

Berlin has always facilitated easy travel for me, with direct flights my priority. From the German capital, you have direct flights to many destinations.

I made the decision to move to Berlin end of 2016, and officially moved here on December 31st of that year, just in time for New Year's Eve. That night, I was invited to join some friends at a party, which was fun to attend. There were people from different countries and backgrounds. Everyone was in a festive mood and having a good time. When the clock struck 12 AM, we were all outside watching fireworks declaring the beginning of the new year, 2017. The celebrations were much bigger than what I was used to in Bremen. After all, I was in the capital of Germany with a population of over 3.5 million. While I enjoy fireworks and my opinion became more nuanced: they are fun and enjoyable, but the accidents associated with it made me realize they also need more responsibility.

My dreams for the new year were as big as the city – or even bigger. I *really* wanted to advance in my career and make a difference in this world, and I felt that this city might *just* be my ticket to a better tomorrow.

## Encounters with authorities

The first step in Berlin was registering as a resident, which didn't take as long as I thought it would. Every district in Berlin has its own registration offices, and this makes it easier to register large groups of people to avoid waiting for a long time to get an appointment. You just show up in the morning, grab a number from the machine, and wait for your turn.

The next step was applying for a freelance residence permit in Berlin. I had a blue card issued in Bremen but had decided to become self-employed after quitting my previous job, which required me to apply for a freelance visa. After collecting a huge number of documents, I showed up for the appointment, and initially, I received feedback that – as a freelancer – I am not eligible to get a Blue Card after all. But from there on, it took a year without a response, and yet I was already working, earning money, and paying taxes which led to frustration. Finally, when I received a response about my application, it wasn't positive: they just asked for more documents. In the end, I had to involve an immigration lawyer. Once I had a lawyer, I got the permit within 4 days. It's something I wish I had done sooner. This encounter revealed the inequality in administrative processes: people with access to and knowledge of legal services would enjoy a different, faster treatment if they can afford it. It also reveals the human factor: the outcome of some processes depends on the tolerance level of the person who handles your file.

While waiting for the work permit, I wanted to meet like-minded people in the creative industry in Berlin, so I signed up for a co-working space called Factory. I would go there and work in video production and script writing. It was a wonderful experience working with like-minded people, discussing different ideas, and sharing thoughts on different subjects. I made many friends there whom I'm still in contact with, which made me love Berlin even more. The city is rich, not only in diversity but also in talented people. At the time, I hoped to collaborate with some of them on future projects, but most were already busy working on their own projects, coming up with innovative ideas and on the verge of making the world a better place. In the meantime, some of them have built their own startups.

Working as a freelancer and signing up for a co-working space was a good way to drive away the isolation of working from home. My goal was to expand my network, meet more and more like-minded people, and collaborate with them on future projects. At first, I collaborated with a few people on smaller projects that would not justify moving to Berlin. But then, two years later, my career really took off. I was producing more video content and hiring freelancers occasionally to do some of my work. My Facebook page was gaining millions of followers and billions of video views. In 2018, the BBC featured my work and called me "The Man with 16 million fans" (Shehabib 2018). While Berlin contributed to this success, where I used its location to network and collaborate with the creative industry, I wanted to move on to something bigger. Instead of just simplifying scientific content and publishing it on social media in video format, I wanted to expand my activity to science fiction and filmmaking. I love movies, and making my own movie would be a great learning experience and enable me to push people to ask thought-provoking questions. Berlin was the perfect place for that – a hub for cinematographers, screenplay writers, film editors, visual effects companies, cinemas, and filmmaking equipment – in short, for all things connected to the craft.

## Filmmaking in Berlin – a new station

In 2018, I wrote and directed a Sci-Fi movie called *Simulation*, the product of my imagination and enthusiasm for science. Its builds on my first novel with the same title. The plot revolves around an advanced alien civilization which builds a simulated reality where infinite creatures, including humans, are imprisoned. *Simulation* was filmed in just three days, all of them in Berlin. The first day of filming was in my apartment using a green screen. I had hired a professional Berlin-based crew to take care of this under my direction. The cast and crew arrived in a massive van with amazing, high-end equipment. As a hub for filmmakers, Berlin makes renting such tools accessible. We then placed massive lamps outside the windows of my apartment to light the scene in the best way possible.

But the large van and the lighting equipment drew my neighbors' attention – and not in a good way. As we began filming the scene, they knocked on my door and asked us to stop filming. One of them argued that I was using a lot of electricity, to which I responded, "Don't worry. I'll pay for any energy costs". They then insisted that we couldn't film on the property, although I had informed my landlord months in advance. The neighbors had even threatened to call the police. My crew convinced them that we would only be filming for half a day and that everything would be removed from the property by evening. At that, they left us alone – only to return later, this time in an even larger group. They yelled at us and even claimed that we were making a lot of noise, even though we were, in fact, filming silent scenes. When we told them we were almost finished, and filming would only take half an hour more, they finally changed their tune. Ultimately, they were impressed by the equipment and even decided to ask what the film was about.

So, in the end, we could shoot the needed scenes for that day. But the pressure of being under threat to shut down production was immense. I kept telling myself, "This doesn't make any sense. I've worked so hard to get everyone on board and to come here on the same day. Shutting down production would lead to a loss of resources, time, and effort, and I'm not going to let that happen" One of the most challenging steps in the filmmaking process is making sure that everyone shows up on time on the same day, given their different schedules and plans, so I found what my neighbors did very distressing and annoying.

As the production was not as smooth as expected, it made me realize the intercultural and inter-generational frictions in Berlin. Dealing with neighbors in Berlin has its ups and downs, especially when you live in an area with a considerable age gap. Most people who live in Alt-Moabit are elderly, so they like it to be quiet. By contrast, in Kreuzberg, you will find more young people. When friends in Kreuzberg invited me to parties, I would be amazed at how loud these parties could get without hearing complaints from the neighbors, as they are more or less the same age. Living in a quiet and elderly neighborhood, I could not bring many people to organize a social gathering. Some areas in Berlin are livelier than others, which I hadn't considered when I moved here.

Finding a suitable place to rent in Berlin is a major challenge for newcomers. Flat hunting can linger for months or even years, which forces one to settle on an apartment just as a transition.

The good thing is, over time, I built good relations with some of my neighbors who were open to building connections with foreigners. We now exchange food, talk about personal things, and always greet each other with smiles. In fact, if I decided to film new scenes in my apartment, some of those who objected the previous time would defend me this time. So I have learned that the sooner you establish connections with them, the sooner you win their hearts.

The second day of filming was mainly outdoors. One of the things that I love the most about Berlin is how rich it is in locations suitable for filming literally any scene. The third day of filming was at the Berliner Union Film, a famous studio known for major productions. I had selected it for its huge green screen, something not available in other studios, let alone smaller towns. The nature of the scenes in my movie required such a big, well-equipped studio, and I felt that moving to Berlin had been the right choice, providing me direct access to such a high-end location, along with a professional cast and crew.

## Producing Science Fiction Content in Berlin

Berlin is an interconnected city that feels like a small world. When I did the casting for my movie *Simulation*, finding experienced actors and actresses wasn't difficult. So many casting agencies can help you connect with their members, but most importantly, you can easily find people on Facebook. There are several groups for filmmakers in Berlin, which makes accessing literally any talent in the business possible. In those Facebook groups, you can easily find Berlin-based editors, cinematographers, videographers, sound designers, visual effects artists, color grading artists, concept artists, and actors. As soon as you post a casting announcement or a call to join your film, you receive dozens of messages from talented people expressing interest in joining your project. If you strike a deal, you can meet face-to-face and discuss everything. I don't have to travel elsewhere to meet talented people in Berlin because they're just right around the corner. Networking here is excellent. Just one contact will connect you to their circle of talented friends, so you know you will never be short-staffed. The cinematographer will know actors, who know sound designers, who know visual effects artists, and everyone will recommend their friends or people they have worked with. This simplifies the process of assembling a crew for any project.

Science fiction movies require a lot of visual effects, otherwise known as VFX. My movie was no different. Seeking VFX professionals for my movie, I looked for a Berlin-based company in this field. And sure enough, I found lots, some of which had worked on Hollywood blockbuster movies. I ended up making a deal with MovieBrats Studios. We worked together to create VFX shots for the movie and integrate computer-generated images into existing scenes. I would visit them frequently to monitor their progress and provide art direction. As a perfectionist, I have always believed that the best art direction can be given in person. Had I lived in another city, traveling to Berlin to meet the VFX team regularly would have been a challenge.

In 2019, the movie was finally ready. I wanted to share my excitement about it with the rest of the world, but first, I wanted to share it in Berlin, the city that had made it possible. So, I organized a film screening at CineStar at Sony Center, one of the most popular cinemas in Berlin. The team there was very welcoming and happy to organize my screening. On the screening date, over 300 people showed up to enjoy watching the film together. Seeing people watch my movie was the highlight of my stay in Berlin. This great feeling made me appreciate the city even more. And it really motivated me to repeat the experience again.

*Simulation* went on to win several awards at international film festivals across the globe, including the Award of Excellence and Best Visual Effects from the Los Angeles-based international awards competition Global Shorts. Other awards included best director, short film, sound design, and original music score. Most of these aspects of the film were possible because the film was made in Berlin, so I feel that Berlin also won these awards. The film was also selected for screening in two Berlin-based film festivals, namely Berlin Independent Film Festival and Berlin Sci-fi Filmfest. So throughout, I have been aware of how Berlin has contributed significantly to my success. In the end, moving to Berlin promoted my growth. But still, I ask myself, was it just the city, or would I have been able to replicate this success elsewhere?

During my stay in Berlin and while working on the film, I worked on smaller projects that took just a few weeks, like the Sky Cruise, a futuristic Flying Hotel, and EctoLife, the World's First Artificial Womb. My most recent project, the sci-fi movie Last Stand, employed AI to explore its possibilities in filmmaking. Using so-called deep fake technology, it used AI-generated audio-visual materials featuring world leaders like Biden and Putin. The synopsis revolved around the world's reactions to contact with aliens in 2023, with strong parallels to the current global political situation.

## Challenges as an Arab expat

Focusing mainly on my work, as a highly skilled expat, I remember encountering a few instances that made me feel the invisible barriers for Arab newcomers. Once when I was walking with a friend, a middle-aged woman heard us speaking English and shouted at us, "Go back to your home. This is Germany! Speak German." Another incident involved a passerby mocking a friend and me speaking Arabic by imitating us and making ape-like sounds. Again, the language you speak is a marker of who you are. Those incidents made me realize that racists reveal themselves when they have the opportunity.

These situations make me feel how Arabs are boxed into the frame of incompetent foreigners while my reality is far from that: I am a highly skilled tax-paying expat.

One's migration background does not expire, and one keeps being treated as an Arab, even when one gets German citizenship. A prominent example is the systematic and frequent racial profiling at airports, being vetted more frequently than others and being checked and delayed for one's last name or appearance while boarding a plane. However, I hope the old mentality might fade out as new generations come in and are more open-minded.

## Living through the pandemic in Berlin

After the COVID-19 pandemic hit the world hard in 2020, I decided to stay home. I isolated myself from the rest of the world. I would only leave my apartment once a week to buy groceries. The rest of the time I spent reading about COVID-19 and sharing this content with the public on social media. Staying at home and not doing what I love to do out there made Berlin feel different, like an ordinary city, not at all like the very special place I had experienced it to be. Once again, I felt isolated, working from home. I needed to reignite my excitement when I first came to Berlin. I needed to make Berlin feel more useful again, so I wrote a new science fiction movie. Unlike the first one, which was short, the new one was a feature film over 1 hour long. This time question was, could I pull it off on my own?

Like the first movie, I hired a Berlin-based cast and crew, and the film was shot in two days. Preproduction took a while, but filming went smoothly. There was only one issue. On the second day of filming, I was supposed to be at the studio at 9 AM on a Sunday. The cast and crew were waiting for me, but I was delayed due to the morning marathon. All roads were blocked, and there was no way for my taxi to get me to the studio on time. I definitely did not see that coming. As a newcomer to Berlin, I did not know the marathon was happening. Otherwise, I would have rescheduled the filming for another day. The good thing is that Berlin has one of the world's best public transport systems, which allowed me to reach the studio before it was too late. So, in the end, while we began filming a bit late, we managed to complete our mission.

During my COVID-19 quarantine and self-isolation in my apartment in Berlin, I took several online courses and learned basic VFX. Instead of hiring a VFX company, which had been expensive, I decided this time to do all the VFX myself. Things were looking good: I was finally able to handle this on my own. But I asked myself, so what do I need Berlin for now? I've finished filming the movie and it's all about post-production now, which I can do from anywhere in the world. Essentially, I can always live in another city, plan to film my movies in Berlin, come here to film my movie, get the footage, and return home for post-production. However, Berlin isn't just a place, it's a factory for inspiring ideas. If I hadn't visited MovieBrats Studio in Berlin and had a first-hand look into what they do, I wouldn't have had the curiosity to learn how to do VFX. So, again, Berlin has indirectly contributed to my learning a new skill.

During self-isolation, I wrote my first novel, an extension of my first movie, turning the 24-minute movie into a 466-page-long novel. It's called *Simulation: The Great Escape*. Although it's still being edited and has yet to be published, I will be proud to say that my first book was written in Berlin.

The COVID-19 pandemic showed me that some of the things that I chose Berlin for can be done online now. And still, my love for Berlin continues. Some of my plans have yet to be fulfilled. For instance, I have always wanted to expand my online activities on social media into offline activities. Instead of just publishing educational video content, I also want to organize events and deliver public talks about science in front of hundreds, if not thousands, of attendees. For that, I'll need to live in a community that speaks English and is willing to attend such events. So far, I haven't managed to pull this off in Berlin. The logistics of organizing events here are very tedious, and more often, the response rate is not satisfactory. If you try to organize such events, don't expect many people to attend your educational public talks if you're planning to speak in English. Even though I consider my German language skills good, I'm not fluent enough to talk about scientific content in languages other than English and Arabic, a limiting factor when communicating science offline.

## Epilogue

Berlin is a wonderful city that I love and enjoy living in. It has offered me great opportunities to push my career forward and allowed me to work freely in an environment filled with creative and ambitious minds. However, some things still remain unfinished. If Berlin can't provide them, perhaps another city will. It is not only a city of infinite dreams but also infinite problems. Berlin is now one station on my journey. It has helped me achieve some of my goals in life. But every station stop has a start and an end. My next stop is Dubai! My career plans are to engage in more filmmaking. Dubai is a young booming multicultural city where public speaking in English would not be a problem. It is entirely different from Berlin. So far, I have spent five productive years living in Berlin. There have been ups and downs, but my accomplishments will always be tied to this place. I leave behind beautiful memories that will make me remember Berlin for as long as I live. If I ever retire, I can always return to Berlin to enjoy the winters – my favorite season.

## References

Shehabib, Ibrahim (2018) The man with 18 million fans. BBC Worklife, February 22 (https://www.bbc.com/worklife/article/20180222-the-man-with-16-million-fans).

Al-Ghaili, Hashem (2023) Last Stand. Sci-Fi Short Film Made with Artificial Intelligence. YouTube (https://www.youtube.com/watch?v=6dtSqhYhcrs).

# 10. "We want to deconstruct the radical discourses in society"

*Julia Gerlach with Younes Al-Amayra*

**Julia Gerlach:** Dear Younes, for many young Muslims and young Arabs in Berlin, you are a star. They follow your comedy show on YouTube. Would you please introduce yourself? Who are you?

**Younes Al-Amayra:** My name is Younes Al-Amayra. I have a degree in Islamic Sciences from the University of Kiel, and today I run the *Datteltäter* project with several colleagues. We started in 2015, and since 2016, we have been part of the FUNK content network program run by the ARD and ZDF. We are a YouTube channel and publish comedy videos every week. That's my main job at the moment. Before that, I worked on a project with young people dedicated to the deradicalization of extremism based on religious extremism. Some of these young people had IS experience or had just returned from Syria and other areas of conflict. I even worked as a primary school teacher at some point and have been involved in various other projects, as well. But in brief, that's what I do.

**J.G.:** One of these other projects is the Datteltäter Academy, right?

**Y.A.:** Exactly. We started in 2020. The idea behind it is to give young talented POC all they need to get their own creative projects started. These are primarily in digital formats. We offer everything that we ourselves might have needed when we started the *Datteltäter* channel. That ranges from training them to get the lighting just right to developing marketing and social media management skills. We provide sessions on how to develop ideas, how to write scripts, and how to create After Effects in animation. Most importantly, we offer a network and want to help this new generation of influencers make their voice heard.

**J.G.:** Who are the participants?

**Y.A.:** Most of them define themselves as Muslims. All of them are POC. We have some who already have experience in digital formats. Some have even been quite successful already. Others are just starting out in their careers.

**J.G.:** As for your own videos, it seems your topics have changed quite a bit in the last few years, right? When you started, you were famous for your jokes about Jihadists. Now you talk more about racism and other more general topics. Was that a conscious decision?

**Y.A.:** Yes and no: Our objective is to look at topics relevant to young people in our communities and to create comedy focusing on these issues. When we started on the whole topic of radicalization, IS played a significant role in the discussion. The other big topic was talking about refugees. Through comedy, we wanted to deconstruct the radical discourse and raise awareness and sympathy for the fate of the refugees. So, we created a large number of videos on these topics. As the discourse in society has changed, we have also shifted our focus to other areas. I think we have actually told all of the relevant stories we wanted to tell in the fields of radical thought and IS. And we find other topics more interesting now.

**J.G.:** Talking to some Imams and theologians, even those of Salafist orientation, it seems they are observing the same shift. Radical Islam is not trendy anymore.

**Y.A.:** We never tackled those topics from a theological perspective. That's not our role. We are not Imams – even if we sometimes dress up like imams. We're interested in the everyday experience of young Muslims and young POC. That's our angle. We look at relationships and conflicts in families, explore the problems of young people in school and with their peers, and so on. We initially started featuring topics on Muslims – that's true. In the beginning, it was essential to have a specific profile. People watch you because they want to see that particular thing. But now we have shifted more and more to topics on migrants in general, and we have more and more topics that are not at all related to Islam or Muslims. This is because the general discourse in society has shifted, and we have more and more viewers from various parts of society.

**J.G.:** So, do you make fun of racism now instead of Islamism?

**Y.A.:** No, we would never make fun of racism, and I wouldn't use the term Islamism in this context. What we do is use comedy as a way to raise awareness for these topics and deconstruct social discourses. Racism is a big topic in society and for our target group. That discussion started a long time ago, but since the death of George Floyd, it has been getting more critical for broader sections of society. It becomes apparent in the way the media, in general, reports incidents. At the same time, anti-Muslim discrimination still plays a role in people's everyday lives. Just think of the whole issue of women wearing headscarves. When individuals are targeted, that can be very tough. Media attention has shifted away from the focus on IS, but just look at how they are now reporting on Arab clans. It's not better than what was before – it's just different.

**J.G.:** In 2016, you became a part of Funk, the social media content network run by the public service broadcasters ARD and ZDF. That was a big step.

**Y.A.:** Yes, we are very happy that we can reach many viewers outside our community. Even though we get a lot of criticism, some people believe that we have become part of mainstream media or even belong to the establishment.

**J.G.:** That wouldn't be the worst thing to achieve, I would say. – You grew up in an Arab family in Berlin. How has the Arabic landscape of Berlin changed since then?

**Y.A.:** I grew up in Pankow, and we spoke Arabic at home. Or let's say they spoke Arabic, and I would answer in German. Back then, there were not many Arabic goods or shops in this part of the city. My father often took us to Turmstrasse to buy meat, and we sometimes went shopping for Arabic food in Neukölln or Wedding. Now you can find Arab-owned shops in many parts of the city, and the variety is much more extensive. In recent years, the arrival of many people from Syria also added to the cultural scene. I must admit that I am not involved in this Arabic community. I belong more closely to the Muslim community, and my work is mostly online. So, I can't really comment on new Arab cultural experiences in Berlin.

**J.G.:** As a last question, I want to return to this book's title, Arab Berlin. Being an Arab in Berlin, what is your dream for the future? What would you like to achieve?

**Y.A.:** I would like the image of being an Arab to change. Just imagine, in some primary schools, students are still not allowed to speak Arabic or Turkish, not even during the breaks. Only slowly and only very few schools are teaching Arabic as a language. Being an Arab is widely viewed as something negative. That's a pity, especially considering our rich Arab culture and literature, our fantastic poetry. Think of cities like Aleppo in Syria. This is the city where our global civilization began, but nobody talks about it because the public is busy talking about violence, crime, clans, and other problems. To put it briefly: It's not always a lot of fun to be an Arab in Berlin. We need to work on it. How? We need education, documentaries – and perhaps TV series because this is how you might *really* change something in society. We need something *positive*. I don't want to be stuck with stories about Arab clans for the rest of my life! I would like people to see Arab Berlin as controversial, perhaps, but mostly attractive – something they want to learn more about and will find very tasty!

# Part 3: Social Life

# 11. "Berlin has that same inescapable magnetic energy of Cairo!"

*Julia Gerlach with Mahmoud Salem*

**Julia Gerlach:** First, let me ask you a very simple question. Who are you? Could you introduce yourself to people who don't know you?

**Mahmoud Salem:** That's an impossible question to answer currently because a big part of any answer will be a reflection on someone I once was. The past and the future are two things I'm trying to separate currently. History comes with a lot of loss. And the only way to manage that kind of loss is to move forward, killing off the parts of you that no longer have a place in your future. So it becomes very hard to say who you are, based on who you were, and even more so if you were long a known entity to many people.

Let me put it this way: I'm an early adopter of social media when it was called the Blogosphere. A blogger who started blogging when blogging was not cool. Someone who became accidentally famous for all kinds of views that I probably would not subscribe to anymore. Today, I guess, I became part of the "cosmopolitan professional class" that is nomadic due the fact that the world is going to shit. Occasionally I write, I do creative direction, I work in cybersecurity, I write movie concepts – and that's it, basically. And I jump between countries, trying to find a new home. I'm currently working on starting a non-profit foundation for a project I'm not at liberty to discuss.

**J.G.:** The last time I met you, you were still Sandmonkey. Is there any Sandmonkey left in you?

**M.S.:** That depends on where. Do I still occasionally topple the government and brag about being the voice of dissent? Why should I do any of those things? I am tired.

**J.G.:** Tired of politics?

**M.S.:** Well, it's slightly worse than just political fatigue. Believing in human rights and democracy and all that good stuff, this is how I grew up. It became interesting and disheartening to notice that – when push comes to shove – it is all more or less Western propaganda. Western countries don't really believe in what they wanted to teach us. You've seen these values crumble before your eyes for the past six or seven years.

**J.G.:** So, did they crumble here or there?

**M.S.:** Here. And elsewhere. And we started seeing the reality of it, especially regarding their relationship with Sisi's Egypt. So there is extreme disappointment in the so-called "White Saviourship" – in the disciples of democracy. The whole thing we grew up on was based on nothing more than empty gestures, you know? By talking about democracy and human rights, we are maintaining a façade, but the world has lost interest in it. The Egyptian revolution was a test: does democracy work in the Middle East? The answer for them was: no. Now they say it wouldn't work, and they do not want to support it if it does.

**J.G.:** You mentioned your new project but with little detail. As I understand it, it is a foundation that will work on misinformation. Sounds interesting. What are you planning?

**M.S.:** I can't really tell you much about the project itself, but I can tell you about its *raison d'être*. Misinformation – nothing more than propaganda using algorithms – is the big problem of our time, especially given how distrustful we have become of the media. Whom do you trust in terms of media reporting? Looking at Egypt, the state now controls everything. I'm not saying we didn't have misinformation and disinformation back in 2012–2014. But we still had some people left, some independent channels. They have all been bought up or co-opted. So who is there to stop misinformation? We are dealing with either state-run campaigns against us, transnational movements and campaigns against us, or foreign state campaigns against us. And of course, as you can imagine, lots of Russian propaganda goes through the Middle East first.

Who is going to tell you the truth then? Social media, like in the days of 2011? Look at the new generation. It's mostly TikTok. There is nothing against TikTok, but we need to have some institution, some compass, to help people differentiate between what is real and what is fake. That's what we are planning.

**J.G.:** And this foundation is going to be based in Berlin?

**M.S.:** Yes. What better place? But I am only the person bringing it all together. I will not even be president. We are a team of people from everywhere, I mean, all of them are from the Middle East. It's mostly about Arab fusion media. We will hopefully have foundations supporting us financially. Fingers crossed.

**J.G.:** So, this is your project for the future. What was your project in the past couple of years?

**M.S.:** I worked as a senior Middle East cyber intelligence analyst with the German cybersecurity organization. I left there last year and spent the year revenge traveling because of COVID-19. Being locked down in 2020 in Germany was not good for my mental health, unlike most friends in other countries where lockdowns were more suggestions than law. I went to many of those places last year. What can I say? I thrive in murky environments.

**J.G.:** But how do you survive in Berlin then?

**M.S.:** What do you mean? There is a lot to do here!

**J.G.:** I mean, it's pretty organized and...

**M.S.:** Wait, are we under the impression that the Germans are efficient? I'm not. No, no, no. Berlin is a chaotic place with constant survival crises. I think maybe that's why Berlin kind of works for me. Do you know the old First World, Second World, Third World thing? I would say Berlin is kind of Second World. That's why we – from Third World countries – feel comfortable in this city. Berlin feels more and more like downtown Cairo every day. Everybody is here now. As a Palestinian friend told me once, if you want to go and see your friends from Egypt, you go to Berlin.

**J.G.:** Berlin was an Arab City until this spring. Now it's all about the Ukrainians.

**M.S.:** You mean that many people believe that now, nobody cares about us Arabs or Muslims anymore? Personally, I don't see it as a competition, to be honest. I am not crying over our lost victimhood status. But what has changed is the perception of who is the enemy. It turns out we were just a rebound enemy after the Cold War was over, and now the white people went back to their old enemy: each other. They always hated the Russians more than us. We were like the partner you get during a trial separation from your significant other, only to be dumped when they decide they want you back.

**J.G.:** Not being the focus of attention and not being the enemy also has lots of advantages. Like, you can do whatever you want without anybody watching.

**M.S.:** Yes and no. You're still getting lots of attention, just not from the German side. Berlin is still a hotspot for Arab intelligence. If you look at academics who end up being stopped in Egypt when visiting or returning, 99% are from European universities. It's impossible to monitor the US. It's much easier here. There are only 5 or 6 universities here versus 300 in the US. The truth is that Berlin is a city of spies. If the Germans are not watching you, the other states are. There is no more freedom if you define freedom as nobody watching you. It just means we just lose our protection and our priority. Who cares about what Sisi is doing to our people in Egypt or Bashar to Syrians when Russia is literally next door?

**J.G.:** Some people say that Berlin is the cultural capital of the Middle East now. Would you agree?

**M.S.:** No, London is definitely the first choice for such a dubious claim! I don't mean this to be offensive to Berlin, I hate London. I hate it so much that I was for Brexit; the harder, the better. But regarding established artists or financial opportunities, it's more like the choice between the UAE and Qatar for professionals: Whoever goes to Qatar couldn't make it in the UAE, or they got a really, really good job offer. The same goes for Berlin. You go to Berlin because you can't make it in London or get a really, really good job offer.

**J.G.:** You mean it's not about Berlin being a cool city? I thought that's why it's attractive to come here.

**M.S.:** No. It's attractive because it's easier. It's easier to immigrate to Berlin. What comes afterward is much harder: Integrating is much more difficult. There is the language and the bureaucracy. The same applies to artists: It's easy to start here; if you want visibility; if you want a place to showcase. Everybody can be an artist here. It's not so much about quality. On the other hand, money and stardom are not to be found here. You can be an artist and hit the stage, but you will not earn much.

So, yes, you have the freedom, sure. But everything else is harder. Berlin makes you get used to living poor. A lot depends on the connections you have. It's all very cliquey. I'm going to focus on something much simpler.

**J.G.:** And this simpler thing is your foundation?

**M.S.:** When I was still working in cybersecurity, I started noticing how big the topic of misinformation had become. Egypt is such a test bed for misinformation. Many of the tactics we have seen in practice were created and tested in 2011 and 2015.

**J.G.:** So, you feel stranded in Berlin?

**M.S.:** First of all, we all feel stranded when we're forced to leave our homes. It doesn't matter. Does it become home eventually, though? You spend four years in a place, and whether you like it or not, it becomes home.

**J.G.:** Yeah, and I think it's a bit like Cairo, you either love it in the first two days, or you will always hate it.

**M.S.:** No. No matter who you are, you will hate Berlin in your first six months. Because that's when you are dealing with your *Anmeldung*, getting your rental, and sorting out the apartment. And, mind you, I went through that in 2019.

**J.G.:** When it was still very easy to find an apartment.

**M.S.:** Yes, but it was very difficult to do anything else. You couldn't even pay for the gym with your credit card back then; you had to have a German IBAN. If it hadn't been for COVID-19 and the need to digitalize payments, we would still be in the early 2000s here.

So I don't feel stranded in Berlin. It comes from the nature of the city itself. Every city has anxiety. In Cairo, the energy is there, and it's not the relaxing kind. It was always, like, who am I going to fight, who's going to f*ck with me? It comes from what happens to us all on the city streets. Inside your house, you're fine. But if you have to go from point A to point B in Cairo, it is endlessly stressful. New York's anxiety is different. There it's The Machine that will grind you and spew you out, even if you are just sitting at home. You always have to be doing something, you always have to be earning money.

Berlin's anxiety is knowing that it's where everything is supposed to work, but it doesn't: The heaven that's so imperfect that it's actually hell. Everything is imprecise. You're always running around, solving some bureaucratic BS, and you will never ever truly save money. Because Germany is a scam when it comes to salary. They have somehow managed to convince their people that it's cool to be poor. Many white Germans will never question living on 1,800 euros a month in a country this rich. And many will live and die without making much more.

**J.G.:** Ok, well, you're destroying the Berlin dream. Deconstructing the "poor but sexy" mentality.

**M.S.:** Yes, but have you seen the rents lately? Poor it is not. But there is something I want to say. I might be very critical, but you know what? That's only because I am adapting. Everybody here constantly complains about the weather, legality, and lack of opportunities. But at the end of the day, I am not sure any of us are serious about moving anywhere else. Berlin seems to have the same inescapable magnetic energy

Cairo has – that thing that keeps people in places where they are not necessarily happy and that they think about leaving all the time. Berlin has replaced Cairo as the place we wish to escape from, but for some reason, we don't do anything about it. After all, we may not all be refugees here in the legal sense, but we are in every other way that counts.

# 12. The tastes of Arab Berlin

## Manifestations of Arab snack culture in the changing urban migration regime of Berlin

*Miriam Stock*

### A new taste for Berlin?

On Sonnenallee in Berlin in the summer of 2016, customers crowded into long lines before a newly opened restaurant called "Al Dimashqi" (The Damascene). They would wait up to an hour to get a shawarma sandwich. Judging by the dialect, many were of Syrian origin, though other patrons also found their way to Al Dimashqi.

At first, the success of Al Dimashqi may seem obvious. Berlin is a major destination for Syrians fleeing to Germany since 2011 and in increasing numbers since 2015 (Statista Research Department 2022). Moreover, Al Dimashqi chose a strategic location at the entrance to Sonnenallee, a street now internationally known as "Arab Street" (Stock 2019: 2).

However, a closer look is warranted to determine what made "Al Dimasqi" in particular so novel. After all, it was not the only restaurant on Sonnenallee, which had established itself as a commercial street over the years, with its Arab infrastructure of shisha cafés, chicken restaurants, and supermarkets. Sonnenallee was already home to two chicken restaurants, "Ris A" (opened in 2004)[1] and "City Chicken" (opened in 1996).[2] In addition, shawarma is available not only in Neukölln, but in many places in Berlin. Since the 1980s, a shawarma and falafel culture has developed, with Berlin's trendy neighborhoods now home to nearly a hundred such shops with Arabic connotations selling falafel and shawarma (Stock 2013: 79 ff).

What is new about Al Dimashqi, however, is its flavors. For example, a chicken shawarma has previously been served in Berlin's trendy neighborhoods with a mix of mango, sesame, and hot sauce seasoning, accompanied by salad and raw vegetables, appealing predominantly to young, white, middle-class people (ibid., 82). At Al

1 See tageszeitung 2004, Fundgrube Sonnenallee. Süßes Leben in arabischer Einkaufsmeile: 36 (https://taz.de/Suesses-Leben-in-arabischer-Einkaufsmeile/!677657/).

2 Interview with the owner of City Chicken, Aug. 2010.

Dimashqi, however, the same sandwich is filled exclusively with meat and "toum," a garlic paste – a version that is also common in Lebanon and Syria. Interior decoration also differs a lot upon closer inspection. While falafel snack bars in trendy neighborhoods often feature retro-chic and Oriental elements, and the established chicken fast food restaurants on Sonnenallee tend to lean on the McDonalds style, new snack bars such as Al Dimasqi are now opting to look cosmopolitan-modern, while still featuring clear references to Damascus and other Arab metropolises (cf. Stock 2019: 7–10).

Based on this observation, this chapter examines various forms of taste and presentation and thus manifestations of Arab snack bar culture in Berlin.[3] Different manifestations are characterized by three determinants to be examined here in more detail. First, they reflect different social backgrounds of the Arab migrants who have opened snack bars, addressing different groups of customers. Here, it is worth taking a closer look at immigration movements from Arab countries as well as socio-spatial localizations within Berlin's urban landscape. In addition, the various manifestations of Arab snack bar culture are embedded in urban neoliberal restructuring processes in Berlin that were closely interwoven with migration and have led to a range of urban phenomena. Finally, the question of what representation of "Arabness" is possible and marketable depends on the symbolic position assigned to Arab migrants in Berlin. Thus, immigration policies and discourses set an important framework for possible spaces of representation, and these have changed in the Berlin migration regime over the last fifty years. In the following, these aspects will be examined in more detail based on three typical manifestations of Arab snack bars.

To accomplish this, the following section first provides a brief theoretical context for ethnic food, urban transformation, and the role of migration regimes, before discussing the background of Arab migration and related migration policies, as well as shifting immigration discourses and their urban manifestations. Following this, three types of Arab snack bar culture in Berlin are presented: Two of them represent relatively standard manifestations before 2011, viz. gentrified and Orientalized falafel snack bars on the one hand, and chicken restaurants and men's cafés on the stigmatized Sonnenallee on the other. The third type has emerged since 2011. It can be witnessed in the new Syrian snack bar culture and the reinterpretation of the now internationally famous Sonnenallee, marketed by merchants to both Arabic-speaking consumers and a wider international audience as "Arab Street".

3 This chapter builds on a German publication in the periodical "Kuckuck – Notizen der Alltagskultur" (Stock 2017: 50–55) that looks at the changing landscape of Arab-owned restaurants in Berlin. This chapter has been updated and extended in terms of evidence and theoretical argumentation.

This chapter is based on ethnographic research conducted between 2009 and 2012 as part of my doctoral thesis on Arabic snack bars in Berlin, which included interviews with vendors, consumers, mapping, and observations, published by transcript Verlag under the title "Der Geschmack der Gentrifzierung" (cf. Stock 2013). With the reopening of Syrian eateries, the empirical material is being updated and expanded from August 2016 based on ethnographic observations and secondary analyses.

## Ethnic commodification, taste, and the role of migration regimes

Turning ethnic culture into a commodity plays a major role today in how ethnicities are represented (Comaroff/Comaroff 2009). A few examples include festivals, clothing, tourism, music concerts, and restaurants (cf. Lu/Fine 1995: 535). Commodification is also reflected in the urban context, where ethnic marketing has become an integral part of consumer landscapes. This is true for the diverse ethnic restaurants found in city centers, where they attract a broad audience – especially the mobile, highly educated middle class and tourists that major cities compete for (cf. Rekers and van Kempen 2000: 63). Berlin's urban policy has therefore also recognized ethnicity as a key resource in city branding (Lanz 2007; Schmiz 2017).

The success of ethnic commodification is based on far-reaching socioeconomic transformations in late capitalism, with culture moving to the center of economic exploitation since the late 1970s. Jeremy Rifkin (2000, 19) therefore also speaks of "cultural capitalism" where culture and economy increasingly converge. At the center of this process is staged authenticity as an urban consumer experience (cf. Zukin 2010). Ethnicity as a mark of authenticity has thus become a central resource for late capitalist surplus-value accumulation (Jain 2003: 264).

At the same time, on closer inspection, not every form of ethnic commodification is equally successful, at least not among the highly educated middle class. Ethnic marketing is socially anchored in different ways and serves different tastes. According to Pierre Bourdieu, the tastes of a social group reflect its social position. This position is determined by the degree of endowment with various capitals (cf. Bourdieu 1987), first and foremost economic and cultural capital, leading to distinct sets of tastes and social spaces (cf. Bourdieu 1983). Cultural capital in particular takes on a special function in the current late capitalist transformation. This has turned the cultural and creative industries into central drivers of urban economies (Lange 2011). The development of social space plays into the gentrification of inner-city neighborhoods, where culture is transformed into economic added-value, and authentic productions are turned into commodities in both residential and commercial sectors (cf. Zukin 2010). This begs the question of how providers and consumers manifest their cultural and economic capital in the urban environment they meet in.

Symbolic capital plays an important role in the context of migrant-owned business. It expresses the extent to which a social group is socially valued in society and determines whether a social group's cultural and economic capitals are considered legitimate or are held in disregard (Bourdieu 2001: 311). Immigration policies and associated discourses have a significant influence on the symbolic capital of migrant entrepreneurs running ethnic restaurants, because they define the spaces where representation and marketing are possible. As ethnologist and migration specialist Péter Niedermüller has shown, it is the majority in society and its dominant groups that prescribe these spaces of possibility (Niedermüller 1998: 293).

Ethnic commodifications are always embedded in an urban "migration regime" – i.e., a system of migration regulations with complex outcome of actions carried out by a multitude of actors (states, EU policy, local actors, NGOs, media, migrants), all of whom are connected through hierarchical and vertical power relations (Mecheril, Karakayali 2018, 227f). As Schwenken (2018: 214–215) suggests, migration regimes shape not only institutional arrangements, but also the immigration discourses that accompany related policies. Moreover, they create subjectivations, which means certain ideas of being a successful migrant entrepreneur, which is closely related to migration policies. Finally, this chapter explores how immigration discourses affect representational practices and the positioning of Arab migrant entrepreneurs. Let us begin with some background on Arab migration.

## Arab Migration in Berlin's Migration Regime

Even before the Arab revolutions and upheavals following 2011, about 30,000 people of different nationalities and origins (in the case of stateless Palestinians) lived in Berlin. Larger influxes of Arab migrants have increasingly come to (West) Berlin, especially since the 1970s. Before that, there were only a few Arab students or guest workers in Berlin, for example from Morocco. Among the largest immigration groups between then and 2011 were Palestinians (2008: 11,839), Lebanese (2008: 7,553), and Iraqis (2008: 2,025) (Stock 2013, 62). After the founding of the Israeli state in 1947/48 and their expulsion (*nakba*), Palestinians initially fled to Lebanon and lived in refugee camps. They continued to flee from there to East Berlin during the Lebanese civil war, which lasted from 1975 to 1990, and the Israeli invasion of Lebanon. Among the Lebanese migrants, it was mainly the rural Shiite underclass and minority groups, such as Lebanese Kurds, who came to Berlin as refugees of war. All of these groups found access to Europe via a GDR transit visa, which they would otherwise have been denied due to their diminished status including the lack of financial resources and contacts. From East Berlin, they crossed the border on foot or by public transportation such as S-Bahn to West Berlin, where they remained after their arrival, as few were granted asylum in West Germany. However, due to the unstable situation in Lebanon, their lack of citizenship and passports, they could not be sent back, so they lived for decades under a Tolerated Stay Permit – not infrequently also banned from working. Despite these precarious conditions, this influx of refugees resulted in chain migrations and family reunifications. The populations then established themselves in Berlin, primarily in the districts of Neukölln, Wedding, and Moabit (Stock 2013: 262).

The exiled Iraqis who later migrated to Berlin, fleeing the Saddam regime and the Gulf wars, often had a higher educational background than their counterparts. Moreover, most of them were granted asylum. Unlike Lebanese and Palestinian refugees, however, this group did not become concentrated in Berlin; most Iraqi migrants now live in Bavaria (Shooman 2007).

Since 2011, Syrians have made up the largest group among Arab migrants. In 2020, 40,480 Syrian nationals lived in Berlin (Statista Research Department 2022). Most of these migrants came from the middle and upper classes because they had the necessary networks, financial resources for the escape route or other access to visas (Stock 2021: 22). Berlin is popular among newcomers because of personal networks, the existing Arab commercial infrastructure, and ultimately its reputation as a "subculture metropolis" (cf. Lanz 2008, 88). The latter in particular has attracted a scene of female artists in exile establishing themselves in Berlin (cf. Bank 2018). The conditions of residence and opportunities for refugees have improved, at least temporarily, compared to that for Palestinians described above. During the tolerant asylum policies in 2015, 95.8% of Syrian asylum seekers were granted refugee status, German language courses, and access to the labor market. With the tightening of the asylum package in 2016, the admission situation became more tense and uncertain, especially with regard to family reunification and long-term prospects in Germany (ProAsyl 2016). However, the majority of Syrian immigrants received a residence permit. However, not only migration policies changed, so did the discourses about refugees and migrants.

## Immigration Discourses and Urban Transformations in Berlin

Before 2011, "Arab" migrants received little attention in the public media, and if so, only under the keyword "Muslims". For example, there was little knowledge among the German public that Germany was home to the largest Palestinian diaspora in Europe (Shiblak 2005, 13), and there has been little scholarly research on their backgrounds and living situations in Germany (see El Bulbeisi 2020). One reason for this is their comparatively small numbers compared to Turkish migrants in Berlin. Even more important, however, is the increasing Muslimization that began in the 1970s (Schiffauer 2007: 117), i.e., the blanket attribution of a Muslim cultural identity that shaped how immigrants from the Middle East and North Africa were viewed.

In the 1960s and 1970s, public perception of immigrants in Germany was still strongly influenced by the recruitment contracts for "guest workers" (*Gastarbeiter*) from the Mediterranean region, and a dichotomous division into "natives" and non-native "foreigners" (*Ausländer*) prevailed, affecting all migrants from the Mediterranean region in the same way. With the recruitment stop in 1973 and the more restrictive immigration policies that followed, the discourse changed, moving "from the category of 'foreigners' under state law to an 'ethnological view' of the 'strange other' (*Fremde*)" (Radtke 1996, 337). This was accompanied by a culturalization of migration groups, which were divided into acceptable "strangers" (*Fremde*) and all-too-strange others (*Allzufremde*), according to imagined distances and in correspondence with EC policies (Radtke 1996, 339). While immigrants from southern EC countries were identified as relatively close "culturally," migrants from the Middle East were considered particularly "alien".

This culturalization – namely to only perceive the other through a cultural lens – led to two dominant and seemingly contradictory strands of discourse typically expressed in late capitalist urban transformations: the dramatization of cultural diversity on the one hand, and the positive exaltation of cultural diversity on the other (cf. Rodatz 2012).

Dramatization involved warnings of "ghettoization," alienation, and Islamization. In the 1990s, for example, the district of Berlin-Neukölln was already referred to as a "ghetto" (Lanz 2007, 69,256). Stigmatizing the district accompanied urban neoliberal policies that saw the state withdraw its social welfare assurances as Neukölln went through de-industrialization without a social net. The district's social decline was culturalized, as migrant women became scapegoats (Soederberg 2017). This was accompanied by other migration policy measures, such as putting a temporary stop to Turkish migrants moving to Berlin-Kreuzberg in the 1980s, which caused many families to move into Neukölln (Lanz 2007, 71).

On the other hand, cultural diversity was exalted, and multiculturalism propagated, especially in left-wing circles, which celebrated the coexistence of diverse minorities in the urban environment as enriching, giving rise to the catchword of "*Multi-Kulti*" (Lanz„ 2007 81). This found its consumerist, everyday practical expression in the demand for ethnic eateries as well as in the construction of multi-cultural Kreuzberg. Both strands of discourse are, of course, two sides of the same coin, as they build on a reductionist notion of cultures as determining identity.

Since 2015, the perception of Arab migrants has shifted to focus on the "refugee," focusing on the plight and flight of these specific migrants (see Grittmann 2017). Conversely, German society can be reassured to encompass a humanistic and paternalistic "welcome culture." But since New Year's Eve in Cologne in 2015/2016 at the latest, culturalized stereotypes of "Arab men" perceived as threatening have again become dominant in discussions, following on the traditional stigmatization of Muslims and Arabs (see Schmidbauer 2017; Dietze 2016).

The same time period, however, saw the revaluation of Sonnenallee, now marketed in German mass media (cf. e.g., Küpper 2016). And in neoliberal urbanism, diversity was increasingly discovered as an urban resource for cities to compete on the global market (Yildiz 2011).

These discourses of immigration have a direct impact on the representational opportunities of Arab gastronomies in Berlin. Indeed, two reactions to the two strands of the culturalization discourse can be found before 2015, i.e., falafel snack shops in Berlin's trendier neighborhoods and the stigmatization of Sonnenallee. The media attention enjoyed by Syrian refugees since 2015 has, in fact, created space for new, self-confident representational concepts in gastronomy – developments we will now explore.

## Gentrification and Orientalization – Falafel in Berlin

When the Iraqi owner of the later snack bar "Baharat" sold falafel in Kreuzberg pubs and later at weekly markets in the early 1980s, he did not yet know that he would play a decisive role in shaping a new trend. In 1993, the *taz* described the trendy snack as "cult balls made of chickpeas" (Arns 1998: 21), and in 2010 *Spiegel-Online* even referred to Kreuzberg as the "Falafelkiez", and thus designating it a quarter or 'hood'. Since then, falafel has been sold in Berlin mainly in restaurants connoted as Arabic, along with dishes such as shawarma, halloumi, and hummus.

Entrepreneurs like the owner of Baharat aimed their offerings less at an Arab community than at trendy young, predominantly white middle class that has made inner city neighborhoods their own over the past thirty years – starting with Kreuzberg and Schöneberg, moving on to Mitte, Prenzlauer Berg and Friedrichshain after the fall of the Wall, and more recently beginning to occupy Neukölln. Falafel snack bars helped shape this everyday variant of gentrification over the past 30 years by offering food staged as vegetarian and vegan (Stock 2013: 77). In 2010, there were 100 such snack bars in Berlin's inner-city neighborhoods. Their geographical distribution underlines how closely aligned they are to gentrification. In 2010, there were 24 snack bars in Kreuzberg, 18 in Prenzlauer Berg, and only 11 in Neukölln, which at the time was still considered less gentrified, but housed by far the largest number of Arab migrants.

Many of the initial operators were Iraqi migrants, often with an academic background. 1998, for example, saw the "Dada-Imbiss" open in Berlin-Mitte. Its Iraqi owner had a background in the theater arts and claimed to have "brought life to the neighborhood" ( Stock 2013: 107) by opening his shop. Consequently, not only consumers but also entrepreneurs possessed a high level of cultural capital, which they knew how to stage in their snack bars. Their new eateries were among the much-noted "creative milieus" seen to drive early gentrification. However, due to their culturalization as "Arabs," they were hardly perceived as active agents of gentrification. Their cultural capital was thus symbolically misunderstood (Stock 2013: 105).

Paradoxically, it was precisely this culturalization that assured falafel shops such success in the course of gentrification, because entrepreneurs were able to stage their falafel snacks as "authentic", just like other ethnic restaurants (cf. Stock, Schmiz 2019), thus serving the demand of a middle-class intent on maintaining cultural hegemony.

*Fig. 12.1: Rissani, Kreuzberg*

© Miriam Stock, 2019

*Fig. 12.2: Zweistrom, Penzlauer Berg*

© Miriam Stock, 2019

> "I don't really like those gentrified bars. Those hip Prenzlauer Berg cafés don't do much for me. I'd rather have something more down-to-earth, you know, more traditional. Even with Arabic snack bars, I just like the ones that feel more traditional." (Stock, Schmiz 2019: 197)

With his preference for culture, Florian situated himself outside of gentrification, but at the same time, as an immigrant with a middle-class background and cultural capital, he belonged precisely to the early group of gentrifiers. The supposedly Orientalized decoration was then also based on retro style elements typical of Berlin neighborhoods undergoing gentrification, such as worn walls and handwritten blackboards. This also applied to the food, which the entrepreneurs had adapted to the health and food preferences of the Berlin milieus, which is why a falafel or shawarma sandwich was served with rich salads and a range of sauces.

This demand for cultural stereotypes in turn limited the snack bar owners in their possibilities of representation. This was evident in snack bars that did not follow the Oriental design logic, or only to a limited extent, such as the "Zweistrom" snack bar in Prenzlauer Berg, which chose a modern, minimalist presentation. This was perceived by Florian and other consumers as too acculturated and German to still be appropriate for "Arab" culture. For example, Ben, a 24-year-old student, said when he saw the photo of Zweistrom (Fig. 12.2)[4]:

> "Hm, I find the name funny. It's too German for me. So, with Arabic, I associate more tradition and old culture. And this is so very modern and compelling." (Stock 201, 168)

However, the snack bar owner of Zweistrom in particular found more room for differentiated representations instead of oriental stereotypes in Prenzlauer Berg, which had been gentrified and was no longer considered particularly "authentic" (Stock 2003: 13ff). It remains to be noted that even if the operators of Arab-owned snack bars actively shaped Berlin's gentrification, culturalization led to their clear symbolic subordination in the process, as the operators repeatedly culturalized themselves to achieve success. Nevertheless, falafel snack bars helped shape commercial gentrification, especially in the 1980s, 1990s, and 2000s in Berlin. Neukölln, on the other hand, was long considered marginalized.

## Men's cafés and chicken restaurants on the stigmatized Sonnenallee before 2015

Even before 2015, the district of Neukölln was home to by far the largest number of Arab migrants in Berlin. Lebanese and Palestinian refugees had moved here in the 1980s and 1990s because the rents were cheap. Neukölln, with its industries and then later deindustrialization, was long a predominantly lower-class district. Only since the early 2000s has the district experienced rapid gentrification and thus a significant change in population structure (Huning, Schuster 2015).

Seen from the outside, the district had a very bad reputation, especially in the 1990s and early 2000s, and was regarded throughout Germany as a prime example of "ghettoization," which seemed characterized by criminalization, radicalization, and the development of a Muslim "parallel society." Reducing the ghetto discourse

4 During the consumer interviews conducted for the dissertation, respondents were presented with photographs of falafel snacks. These helped to classify their taste (Stock 2013: 32).

to focus on "Muslims," made it possible to distract attention at the same time from grievances and failures in urban and migration-related policies (Lanz 2007: 245).

People who suffered from this stigmatization found a variety of ways to react to the bad reputation of Neukölln. For example, the rapper Massiv, whose parents had fled to Berlin from Palestine, staged ghetto discourses in his songs in the style of other gangsta rappers (cf. Janitzi 2012). In the documentary "Neukölln Unlimited", the main protagonist, belonging to a Lebanese family who still lived under toleration status, wore a T-shirt saying, "I am Muslim – don't panic".[5] And Samira, from a German-Palestinian family, for a while sold handbags bearing the imprint "Islam.ist.in"[6], thus creating a logotype to react to the incessant stereotype of Islamic threats (Stock 2013: 52).

In everyday consumer life, the presence of Arab migrants in Neukölln became increasingly apparent on Sonnenallee. Since the nineties, it has seen an economic service economy of Arab-owned stores emerge, including supermarkets, cell phone stores, travel agencies, bridal wear, butcher stores, and Arab restaurants. This new infrastructure closed the gap resulting from the district's poor image (cf. Bergmann 2011).

Shisha cafés and chicken restaurants were the most formative Arab-owned gastronomies for Sonnenallee. The shisha cafés were predominantly frequented by men, which is why they were also perceived from the outside as "men's cafés". An example is the "Umm Kulthum", named after the famous Egyptian singer. It is a large coffee house with simple seating, Oriental-style wall decorations, and fluorescent lighting typical of such shisha cafés (Färber/Gdaniec 2006: 116).[7] Thus, shisha cafés followed a culturalized self-representation that served as nostalgic staging for first-generation immigrants.

5 Cf. http://www.neukoelln-unlimited.de/ (Update March 15, 2017)

6 "Islam.ist.in" has two connotations. First it means, "Islam is in" and then it reads "Islamistin" meaning a female Islamist.

7 This is just one form of shisha café in Berlin. In this case, too, there are upgraded lounge-like cafés, as Alexa Färber describes. However, these no longer have a clear Arab connotation.

*Fig. 12.3: City Chicken*

© Miriam Stock, 2019

The chicken restaurants, on the other hand, have demonstrated the representational strategies of a second generation of Arab migrants located in Neukölln, consciously breaking with Oriental projections. An example is the highly successful "City Chicken," a restaurant that opened in 1996 and is run by three brothers from a Lebanese family who grew up in Germany. The menu consists primarily of chicken halves with fries, hummus, salad, and garlic paste. Falafel is not on the menu. The owners consciously decided not to go for an Oriental staging when they set up the restaurant: "We didn't want that either. Because there's so much of that everywhere. Falafel and stuff, really everywhere." By contrast, their design leans – as the English name suggests – toward McDonalds-style neon signs with photo boards depicting the food they serve: "We always focus on modernization".[8]

8 Interview with one of the owners of City Chicken, Aug. .2010.

Turkish kebab bars had previously also followed this representation strategy, which gave their premises a McDonalds-style makeover to escape the trap of being pigeonholed as folkloristic and to be taken seriously as modern entrepreneurs in Germany. This can be seen as a strategy to increase their symbolic capital (cf. Çağlar 1995). Moreover, the modernized forms of presentation appealed to their own tastes.

On the other hand, the predominantly "white" middle-class consumers who enjoyed dining in Orientalized falafel snack bars strongly rejected this McDonalds-like presentation, finding the photo boards "commercial" to the point of being "desperate" when shown them during interviews (Stock 2013: 263). Even if they were not aware of it, they considered the meat-centered chicken restaurants to be lower-class eateries.

## "Arab Street": New Syrian-marketed gastronomy on Sonnenallee

Sonnenallee was marginalized and stigmatized in the public media for a very long time. Only in 2010 did word begin to spread that this was an "inside tip" as the surrounding neighborhood gentrification gradually began to extend to Sonnenallee. In 2014, for example, an organic market opened across from City Chicken. The increasing gentrification of Neukölln, with more economically affluent stores, gradually became evident on Sonnenallee as the trendy pubs, bars, organic food stores, and falafel shops so typical of Berlin's gentrification began to open. This was accompanied by "urban renewal programs" in Neukölln, where redevelopment was also intended to attract residents and entrepreneurs with purchasing power (Steigemann 2020: 95).

The symbolic revaluation was also helped by the rapidly increasing Syrian presence since 2015, which led to a rapid increase in demand for Arabic food and gastronomy. This initially had an impact on existing Arab-owned snack bars. Previously marginalized stores and eateries that marketed themselves as Arabic saw a significant increase in sales, with numerous stores offering the typical breakfast dishes foul (a broad bean dish), hummus (chickpea puree), fatteh (a yogurt dish with chickpeas), as well as Lebanese and Syrian pizzas, so-called manaquish.

At the same time, an astonishing number of new Syrian stores and eateries emerged on Sonnenallee starting in 2015 (Steigemann 2020: 97), including Al Dimashqi in 2016, Yasmin Al Sham (The Jasmine of Damascus) in 2017, and Bab al Sham (The Gate of Damascus) in 2018. What these new Syrian entrepreneurs have in common is that they confidently promote "Syrian cuisine", bringing new dishes and serving styles to Berlin, and model their presentation on cosmopolitan Damascene snack stores by, among other things, combining Syrian photographs with modern stylistic elements (Stock 2019: 8). This is shown by the name "Damascus" alone, which appears again and again, even if the entrepreneurs do not all originally come from Damascus (cf. Fig. 12.4).

*Fig. 12.4: Al Dimashqi*

© Miriam Stock, 2023

The most common snack on offer here is shawarma, in its Syrian variant: Chicken and garlic sauce are rolled into an Arabic flatbread and fried in the fat of the meat skewer. In addition, the "Arabian plate" known in Syria has made its way to Berlin, where the rolled shawarma is cut into pieces and served with French fries, garlic, and pickled vegetables. In addition, other grilled dishes are also on offer. Beyond this, however, the new reputation of Sonnenallee has also revealed an increasing diversification of offerings, which on the one hand, has followed the diversification of residents and visitors in Neukölln (cf. Monroe Santillan,Martinez, Mouritz, Ayoub 2018), while also responding to new urban discourses on marketing diversity (Steigemann 2020). In this context, Arabic snack foods alone are shown to have very different representational strategies, depending on the consumer group addressed. Thus, Orientalized falafel snack bars, modernized McDonaldized chicken restaurants, and the new Syrian gastronomy are often found side by side and with different customer structures. At the same time, many restaurants on Sonnenallee are also turning into chain stores and opening second outlets in other locations. For example, the chicken restaurant Ris A, which has become very popular with diverse consumers, is located in both Wedding and Prenzlauer Berg. Meanwhile, Al Dimashqi has also opened in Wedding.

## Conclusion

As the examples illustrate, the representational strategies of Arab snack bars remained relatively stable from the 1990s to 2015, responding to the two forms of culturalization that characterized Berlin's immigration discourses: on the one hand, providing positive valorization and, on the other, increasing the fear of alienation. This also manifested itself in urban space, with "gentrification" of neighborhoods on the one hand and "ghettoization" on the other, as assessed by the public. The Orientalized variation of falafel snack shops took and continues to take center stage in Berlin's gentrification process, adapting to the local tastes of the Berlin scene. Different representational strategies were possible, especially in gentrified neighborhoods such as Prenzlauer Berg, as shown by the example of Zweistrom, which relied on symbols with Arabic connotations (in the form of black-and-white photos or the name's reference to Mesopotamia) while breaking with classic Orientalized, down-to-earth decor. In general, falafel snack shop owners have contributed to everyday gentrification in Berlin through their cultural capital, even if they were often misjudged by the public as creative actors and remained subordinate to other entrepreneurs (e.g., bars or cafés) in gentrification.

On the other hand, the Arab Sonnenallee began establishing itself in the late nineties as a shopping lane for the local Arab community, where shisha cafés and McDonalds-like Arab chicken restaurants, among others, dominated the image and tended to be avoided by other milieus in Berlin. Therefore, the providers chose McDonald-like presentations to enhance their snack bars, present them as modern, and resist symbolic stigmatization, stepping outside of culturalization. Especially by consumers of a new white middle class, however, this presentation was described as unfavorable, as it was perceived as commercial and did not reflect their own cultural capital.

Since 2015, the perception and manifestation of Arab gastronomy in Berlin have changed, predominantly on Sonnenallee, which has been experiencing an international revaluation, where many new stores presented themselves as modern, but also consciously chose a reference to Damascus and other large cities and thus staged themselves as both origin-oriented and cosmopolitan. These were initially aimed at a newly immigrated Syrian public, but Sonnenallee, with its diverse stores and restaurants, is now also being marketed in the international media as "Arab street"[9] to attract tourists. Reflecting changes in immigration discourse about Arab immigrants, a new urban focus is apparent here, with entrepreneurs consciously choosing new presentation practices. Their self-confidence derives from both their cultural capital and the attention received from the German public. Recent years have seen a diversification of Arab snack cultures in Berlin, reflecting the different backgrounds of entrepreneurs and consumers and building on the new urban policy framework of staging diversity. How will snack culture develop in the coming years? And how will Arab snack shops continue to shape Berlin's inner-city neighborhoods?

## References

Arns, Christian (1993) Kultkugeln aus Kichererbsen. In: *die tageszeitung* (taz) July 28, 21.

Bank, Charlotte (2008) Remaking the World: Recently displaced artists from Syria in Berlin. In: Mobile Culture Studies, the Journal Vol 4, 171–182.

Bergmann, Malte (2011) Die Sonnenallee in Berlin als Raum grenzüberschreitender Ökonomien. In: Malte Bergmann, Bastian Lange (ed.) *Eigensinnige Geographien. Städtische Raumaneignungen als Ausdruck gesellschaftlicher Teilhabe*. Wiesbaden: Springer, 45–70.

Bourdieu, Pierre (1983) Ökonomisches Kapital, kulturelles Kapital, soziales Kapital. In: Reinhard Kreckel (ed.) Soziale Ungleichheiten (= Soziale Welt, Sonderband 2). Göttingen: Schwarz, 183–198.

Bourdieu, Pierre (1987) Die feinen Unterschiede. Kritik der gesellschaftlichen Urteilskraft. Frankfurt am Main: Suhrkamp.

Bourdieu, Pierre (2001) Meditationen. Zur Kritik der scholastischen Vernunft. Frankfurt am Main: Suhrkamp.

Çağlar, Ayse (1995) McDöner. Döner Kebap and the Social Positioning Struggle of German Turks. In: Janeen Arnold Costa, Gary J. Bamossy (ed.) *Marketing in a Multicultural World. Ethnicity, Nationalism and Cultural Identity*. Thousand Oaks, Sage, 209–230.

---

9 See for example https://www.middleeasteye.net/features/berlins-arab-street-melting-pot-where-hipsters-flock-and-falafel-flourishes;
https://theculturetrip.com/germany/articles/how-berlins-arab-street-became-a-foodie-paradise/

Comaroff, John L./Comaroff Jean (2009) Ethnicity, Inc. Chicago: University Press of Chicago.

Die tageszeitung (2004) Fundgrube Sonnenallee. Süßes Leben in arabischer Einkaufsmeile, 36 (https://taz.de/Suesses-Leben-in-arabischer-Einkaufsmeile/!677657/).

Dietze, Gabriele (2016) Das 'Ereignis Köln'. In: femina politica 1, 93–102.

El Bulbeisi, Sara (2020) Tabu, Trauma und Identität. Subjektkonstruktionen von PalästinenserInnen in Deutschland und der Schweiz, 1960–2015. Bielefeld: transcript Verlag.

Färber, Alexa/Gdaniec, Cordula (2006) Shopping Malls und Shishas. Urban Spaces and Material Cultural as Approaches to Transformation in Berlin and Moscow. In: Arvaton, Gösta; Butler, Tim (ed.) Multicultures and Cities, Lund: Museum Tusculanum Press, 113–128.

Jain, Anil K. (2003) Differenzen der Differenz: Umbrüche in der Landschaft der Alterität. In: Steyerl, Hito; Guiterrez-Rodriguez, Encarnación (ed.) Spricht die Subalterne Deutsch? Migration und postkoloniale Kritik. Münster, 259–269.

Janitzki, Lena (2012) Sozialraumkonzeptionen im Berliner Gangsta-Rap. Eine stadtsoziologische Perspektive. In: Dietrich, Marc; Seeliger, Martin (ed.) *Deutscher Gangsta-Rap. Sozial- und kulturwissenschaftlich Beiträge in einem Pop-Phänomen*. Bielefeld, 285–308.

Küpper, Mechthild (2016) Die arabische Straße. In: Faz.net. (https://www.faz.net/aktuell/politik/inland/sonnenallee-die-arabische-strasse-14382811.html)

Lange, Bastian (2011) Re-scaling governance in Berlin's creative economy. In: Culture Unbound Journal of Cultural Research 3(2) 187–208.

Lanz, Stephan (2007) Berlin aufgemischt. Abendländisch – multikulturell – kosmopolitisch? Die politische Konstruktion einer Einwanderstadt. Bielefeld: transcript.

Lu, Shun/Fine, Gary A. (1995) The Presentation of Ethnic Authenticity: Chinese Food as a Social Accomplishment. In: The Sociological Quarterly, 36(3) 535–553.

Mecheril, Paul/Karakayali, Juliane (2018) Umkämpfte Krisen: Migrationsregime als Analyseperspektive migrationsgesellschaftlicher Gegenwart, In: Naika Foroutan/Juliane Karakayali/Riem Spielhaus (ed.) Postmigrantische Perspektiven. Ordnungssysteme, Repräsentationen, Kritik. Frankfurt a. M.: Campus, 225–237.

Monroy Santillan, Caroline/Martinez, Claudia/Mouritz, Tom/Ayoub, Venus (2018) Behind the Curtains of Sonnenallee. In: TU Habitat Unit (ed.) 'New Diversities' and 'urban arrival Infrastructures'? The socio-spatial appropriation and footprints of refugees in Berlin-Neukölln, 54–70.

Niedermüller, Peter (1998) Stadt, Kultur(en) und Macht. Zu einigen Aspekten "spätmoderner" Stadtethnologie. In: Österreichische Zeitschrift für Volkskunde, LII/101(3) 279–301.

Pro Asyl (2016) BAMF-Entscheidungspraxis geändert: Für immer mehr SyrerInnen wird der Familiennachzug ausgesetzt. Rechtspolitisches Papier auf Pro Aysl.de (https://www.proasyl.de/wp-content/uploads/2015/12/Rechtspolitisches-Papier_Familiennachzug_aktuell_final.pdf).

Radtke, Frank-Olaf (1996) Fremde und Allzufremde. Zur Ausbreitung des ethnologischen Blicks in der Einwanderungsgesellschaft. In: Hans-Rudolph Wicker et al. (ed.) Das Fremde in der Gesellschaft: Migration, Ethnizität und Staat. Zürich: Seismo, 333–352.

Rekers, Ans/van Kempen, Roland (2000) Location matters: Ethnic entrepreneurs and the spatial context. In J. Rath (ed.), Immigrant businesses: The economic, political and social environment. London: Palgrave Macmillan, 54–69.

Rifkin, Jeremy (2000) The Age of Access, Washington: Penguin Putnam.

Rodatz, Matthias (2012) Produktive Stadtgesellschaften: Migration und Ordnung in der (neoliberalen) "Stadt der Vielfalt". In: BEHEMOTH, A Journal on Civilization, Vol 5(1) 70–103.

Schiffauer, Werner (2007) Der unheimliche Muslim – Staatsbürgerschaft und zivilgesellschaftliche Ängste. In: Wohlrab-Sahr, Monika; Tezcan, Levent (eds.) *Konfliktfeld Islam in Europa*. Baden-Baden: Nomos, 111–134.

Schmidbaur, Julia (2017) The construction of refugees and asylum seekers in German print media: a critical discourse analysis of the "refugee crisis" in Germany from 2015–2017 (http://hdl.handle.net/10230/33254).

Schmiz, Antonie (2017) Staging a 'Chinatown' in Berlin: The role of city branding in the urban governance of ethnic diversity. In: European Urban and Regional Studies, 24, 290–303.

Schwenken, Helen (2018) Intersectional Migration Regime Analysis: Explaining Gender Selective Labor Emigration Regulations. In: Pott, Andreas; Raas, Christoph; Wolf, Frank (eds.) Was ist ein Migrationsregime? What Is a Migration Regime? Wiesbaden: Springer, 207–224.

Shiblak, Abbas (2005) Reflections on the Palestinian Diaspora in Europe. In: Shiblak, Abbas (ed.) *The Palestinian Diaspora in Europe. Challenges of Dual Identity and Adoption* (Refugee and Diaspora Studies No. 2), Paris: Palestinian Refugee and Diaspora Center and the Institute of Jerusalem Studies, 7–18.

Soederberg, Soederberg (2017) Governing stigmatised space: the case of the 'slums' of Berlin-Neukölln. In: New Political Economy, 22(5) 478–495 (https://doi.org/10.1080/13563467.2017.1240671).

Spiegel Online (2017) Kreuzberg: Frittenalarm im Falafelkiez, May 18 (http://www.spiegel.de/politik/deutschland/kreuzberg-frittenalarm-im-falafelkiez-a-483535.html).

Statista Research Department (2022) Anzahl der Ausländer in Berlin nach Staatsangehörigkeit im Jahr 2020 (https://de.statista.com/statistik/daten/studie/1094889/umfrage/anzahl-der-auslaender-in-berlin-nach-staatsangehoerigkeit/).

Steigemann, Anna (2020) 'Multi-culti' vs. Another cell phone store': – Changing ethnic, social and commercial diversities in Berlin-Neukölln. In: Cosmopolitan Civil Societies: an interdisciplinary journal, 12(1) 83–105.

Stock, Miriam (2017) Falafeltrend – Männercafés – Willkommenskultur? Berliner arabische Gastronomien im Wandel. In: Kuckuck, Notizen zur Alltagskultur Vol 1, 50–55.

Stock, Miriam (2019) Die Sonnenallee in Berlin-Neukölln. Zwischen sozialer Benachteiligung, Szenekiez und Ankunftsstadtteil. Expertise für den Mediendienst Integration (https://mediendienst-integration.de/fileadmin/Dateien/Expertise_Sonnenallee_Stock_Mediendienst.pdf).

Stock, Miriam (2021) *Verbindliche Männlichkeiten in Zeiten der Krise. Junge Männer aus Syrien in transnationalen Familien.* In: Zeitschrift für Flucht- und Flüchtlingsforschung (Themenheft Männlichkeiten und Flucht), 5(1) 13–43.

Stock, Miriam; Schmiz, Antonie (2019) Catering authenticities. Ethnic food entrepreneurs as agents in Berlin's gentrification. City, Culture and Society Vol 18 (https://doi.org/10.1016/j.ccs.2019.05.001).

Yildiz, Erol (2011) Migration und Diversität als urbane Ressource. In: Hermann, Heike et al. (eds.) Die Besonderheit des Städtischen. Entwicklungslinien der Stadt(soziologie), Wiesbaden: Springer, 125–144.

Zukin, Sharon (2010) Naked City. The Death and Life of Authentic Urban Places. New York: Oxford University Press.

# 13. Will my son grow up to be sexist?[1]

*Abir Kopty*

I'm not a perfect mother, nor do I aspire to be one. Perfection is not absolute, anyway. Everywhere has its own "perfect mother," and everywhere has people who reject that particular cookie-cutter ideal. I don't want to be like anyone else at all. Nor do I want to bend over backwards to live up to the list of regulations and standards that society has decided should be my measuring stick. My measuring stick is not straight and fixed. It is broken, full of fissures and holes. It may have been produced by society once, but I have since deconstructed and reconstructed it time and again using my own awareness, experiences, knowledge, issues, and my critical thought.

The day my child was born, I started on an ever-changing and ever-lasting journey to ask questions and look for answers I don't always find.

My child is a boy. A beautiful and innocent boy born in Berlin, a long way from our families. Most of what he knows about the world comes from his father and me. Although raising a child here is difficult and challenging, I hoped to protect him from the contradictions of our approach to parenting and that of our families. Wherever you live, however, you will still find contradicting norms, that is unless you decide to go with whatever others are doing.

One day I went to pick him up from the kindergarten and found him wearing a dress. At the time, he was obsessed with dressing up in costumes of all kinds. I laughed and told him I loved his new outfit. The same thing happened the next day, this time with his father, who reacted the same way I had. We communicate a lot about his upbringing and that meant we were prepared for the challenge. Many more situations will come to challenge us in the future, some that we won't be prepared for, and that we might fail.

It turned out that three-year-old Mina had heard a very different response from another parent: "Dresses are for girls." This one stuck in his mind. We told him it

1 Acknowledgment: The article was originally published online at (https://jeem.me/en/society/abir-kopty/will-my-son-grow-be-sexist) on 13 July 2020 by Jeem, "a feminist media organization that envisions a world where the dominant narratives in the Arabic-speaking region and its diaspora are inclusive, and defy patriarchal norms." The original contains the original Arabic audio message to the author's son. The article is reprinted here in its translation by Katharine Halls from the original in Arabic by permission of the organization.

wasn't true, and that he could wear whatever he felt like. We raised the issue at the kindergarten and with his teachers. They assured us that they agreed with us and already spoke to the father in question. The next day they pinned an article titled Boys Can Wear Dresses Too up on the wall to make sure all the parents got the message.

To be honest, and the more we think about it, the more we realize that we may have been less than honest with him. In our society and the vast majority of others as well, dresses are considered to be for girls. I wear dresses, but his father does not. In the street, he sees women in dresses, but not men. He might realize one day that we lied to him. Or maybe he'll grow up and come to the conclusion that things are neither black nor white—a far greater lesson learned to be honest.

I also lied about my commitment to challenging the stereotype of pink for girls and blue for boys. I hate pink. I cannot remember ever consciously wearing it. I refuse to dress my son in pink for the same reason. I dress him in blue, green, yellow, red, etc. but never in pink. I have thought long and hard about this stereotype and came to the realization that the issue goes deeper than the decision to dress in a certain color. It is an issue of what is permitted for boys but forbidden to girls. So, I may have not lied after all. With time, Mina will become more aware and conscious of social codes of conduct. It will become more and more difficult to protect him from the weight of stereotypes of how boys and girls are allowed to behave, including everything from games, toys and clothes to life choices like friendships, staying up late, traveling, living independently, acquiring skills, finding a job, one's relationship with their body, love, sex, sexual pleasure, and so much more.

When Mina became familiar with the concept of boys and girls, he realized that he was a boy, I am a girl, and his father was a boy. What's the difference? "Penises and vaginas" is the blunt, straightforward answer we have always given him. But when he gets older, that will no longer be the main difference. "Penises and vaginas" was the simplest answer I can think of for a three-year-old. As he gets older, we will need better knowledge and tools to help him understand that sexual organs are not how to define a person's gender or sexual identity. I still don't have all the answers and I feel ill-prepared at the moment.

I use the most basic terms possible because of his age, telling myself that he needs time to get ready for more complexity. I remember once meeting a sex education specialist in the course of my work as a journalist, and one of the most important pieces of advice she gave was that when children ask questions, they need answers that are simplified and appropriate to their age. The simplicity and rationality of these words brings me comfort when in doubt.

## Mina has never heard the word 'ayb in our house.

The word ʿayb, a reprimand used when something is shameful or inappropriate, embodies so many repressive rules that generally apply to girls and not to boys. Although my son enjoys the privileges of being male, to bring a child up with the word is to anchor that privilege deeply within the man he will one day be—the same privilege we women are constantly fighting against. So, he will grow up without that word.

Mina doesn't see conventional roles played out in the house. Cooking is mainly my responsibility, while cleaning is my partner's, and we share the other tasks. This division of labour came about over time without us ever talking about it. It just made the most sense, because I love cooking and he hates it, while he's fanatical about tidiness and order and I'm chaos itself when left to my own devices.

I also regularly change the words of the stories I read or songs I sing to Mina when they contain conventional gender roles or sexist messages. As he grows, he will no longer depend on me for songs and stories. Then, he might discover the artificial nature of the utopia I made up for him. He may be shocked to discover reality as it is. He may even feel alienated in the same way we grow more and more alienated as our critical thinking develops in adulthood. Then again, I could simply be excessively anxious about the future and the challenges it will inevitably throw our way. All I know is that I'll talk to Mina about all of this.

Our decision to raise our child without traditional assumptions and stereotypes is an ongoing process that demands constant and conscious appraisal of how we behave. For example, we recently moved houses and bought some furniture to assemble at home. That was definitely not going to be my task—not just because I didn't know how, but because I was brought up in a way that taught me that I could not and should not be good at it. Without giving the matter much thought, I let my partner do it. He finished the first item and said: "You should do the next one, so Mina doesn't think that it's always my job to do it." Oh! I had overlooked that detail. I eventually managed, with my son's help, to put together the bathroom cabinet. Mina helps us with all the household chores, and even though he has a tendency to be lazy, we involve him in cleaning, tidying, arranging, and cooking. He will not be raised as a Si Sayed[2], as most men in our societies are.

---

2 "Si El-Sayed, the authoritarian father figure of Egyptian novelist and Nobel Prize laureate-Naguib Mahfouz's most famous work, "The Cairo Trilogy", has become an Arabic synonym for monstrous male chauvinism" (Naguib Mahfouz, 2006), as written in "Fictitious Characters in the Classroom: Using Literary Characters in Teaching English Language" by Ibrahim Mohamed Alfaki (p. 37); A fictional character in Naguib Mahfouz's 'Cairo Trilogy', which acquired the (common) meaning of "a controlling and demanding husband," the distinctive traits of 'Mr. Sayed' in the trilogy. This name has also come to be used in everyday life as a common

It would have been impossible to raise a non-sexist boy if his father was one. Yet the dynamic of our relationship remains complicated, subtle, and, at times, problematic. Who decides what? Who is responsible for what? Who is emotional and who is tough? Who gets riled up and who reacts calmly? Who is firm and who is "weak" in resisting tears? Who can control their reactions—when, for example, our son falls over—and who cannot? Who knows how to do certain things and who does not? Who asks for and pays the bill in restaurants, and who never gets involved? And so many other questions besides. It is an ongoing, dialectical relationship between two people trying to free themselves from conventions and received wisdoms they reject, and ever more of its complex inner workings are revealed when it becomes a shared journey through parenthood.

I remember that as a teenager, whenever I asked my father for permission to do some activity, he would always tell me to ask my mother. My mother would then tell me to ask my father. Eventually, I would get sick of the back and forth and give up on the activity all together. If they hesitated to take any clear decision, it was because they knew nothing but a world of taboos. Taboos frightened them so much they avoided any responsibility in me being allowed to do things like going to a party with school friends, sleeping over at a girlfriend's house, or taking part in outings with friends that weren't organized by the school, etc. Even if I eventually snatched a permission to do something, the ordeal slowly ingrained in me the conviction that some requests were difficult and prickly, and that I should just avoid making them. And so, their relationship dynamic spelled out unspoken rules for me to live with. When I got older and they grew to trust me, the boundaries of what was permitted changed, and they gave me a lot of space and freedom, but that too took place quietly, and was never clearly or directly spoken.

If boundaries must be set, then these are not the kind of boundaries I want for my son. If I could go back in time and be in my parents' shoes, I would want to answer my daughter differently, for example: "Let's talk about it," "Here's what I think," or maybe "I can't make such a decision by myself, I probably need to talk to your mother/father about it first." Later, I would get back to her and say: "That's what we think, but we want to hear what you think, let us have a conversation."

That's how I wish it was when I was young. I acknowledge that this utopia I strive for cannot exist while we all live in repressed societies that are restricted in what could or could not be said. It is an impossible utopia for societies which, deprived of the means for self-determination or transformation, will turn around and seek to impose tyrannical control against the freedoms of their members. How can parents allow their children a freedom of expression they do not enjoy? If there's one

---

noun describing a man with similar traits." as written in "Lexical Issues of UNL: Universal Networking Language 2012 Panel", edited by Ronaldo Martins.

thing we can do, it is to not burden our children with our pain and to stop using our helplessness as an excuse to take out on our children.

Having a child made me realize that the way we are raised, whether we liked it or not, is the main reference on how to parent. I do not resent my parents for the way they raised me, nor do I love them any less, but I am critical. I have seen different experiences and learned a lot. I have also met many who were less fortunate than I was, and learned from them.

I took the decision to never shy away from a conversation with my son. I will encourage him to ask any question that occurs to him, be it about a certain type of dinosaur or the reason someone stole Baba's bicycle. He will be allowed to talk about as many dinosaurs he would like.

He will certainly be allowed to talk about the fearsome dinosaur of emotions. What will I do when he needs to cry? In theory, I believe tears are nothing to be ashamed of, all feelings are legitimate. However, I had to remind myself, more than once, to not fall in the trap of "boys don't cry." But I also struggled with my image of myself, that of a mother who does not want her son to be weak and cry over anything and everything. I am still looking for the balance between validating his emotions, on the one hand, and encouraging him to talk about them rather than cry on the other. When he falls over and gets hurt, he will cry and that is ok. I will cuddle him, show him love, and let him cry. But if another child steals his toy, crying will do him nothing, and he will need to articulate why he is upset and demand his toy be returned. Regardless of the situation, I will always teach him that there's nothing weak or shameful in expressing how he feels. I will do everything I can to create a supportive, respectful environment in which there is space for his feelings.

The outside world still exists, not just the Arab world, and it will jeopardize all our plans. And yet, I want him to go out and learn from his own experience, as I once did. I know I will sometimes trip and make all kinds of mistakes. I also know that he might grow up to rebel and dislike the way we raised him. That battle is one I'm not ready for yet.

With all these challenges in mind, there are things I want for Mina when he grows up. I want him:

- To never accept stereotypes and conventions, but to be critical of the habits and values of any society he lives in.
- To never shy away from, or be embarrassed by his feelings; for example he should never be ashamed to cry.
- To freely explore his gender and sexual identity for himself and to be proud of his identity and decisions.
- To be an equal partner in his romantic relationships, be they with men or women, and neither dominate or be dominated.

- To take responsibility for himself, to undertake tasks that have always been assigned to women, and above all, to see that as normal.
- To be strong and confident of who he is, and not to give in to the temptation of society's version of masculinity.
- To never allow himself to be domineering, superior, or oppressive, especially towards people less fortunate in life than himself.
- To possess a strong sense of justice and to stand up against oppression, whether it happens around him or far away.

When Israa Ghrayeb, a young Palestinian woman, was killed by her family, many people, both in Palestine and beyond, were deeply shaken, including myself. I wrote and recorded a message to Mina which he may one day read, hoping that this crime could open up a conversation about how we may one day create a masculinity aware of the social burden upon its shoulders and the role that men should play in confronting that oppression.

You can listen my message to Mina here[3]:

### Translation of the audio recording

*My dearest son,*

*You're still small, but soon, when you're a bit older, you will realize monsters exist. Those monsters may have once been oppressed, abused, and living under occupation, they also oppressed those weaker than them. One day, you will all this yourself.*

*Never think that you are entitled to ever be a monster just because you were born a boy. Don't think that having a penis gives you privileges and power over girls. When you get older, people will try to tell you that boys are better than girls, and that they can tell girls what to do. When you get older, they will try to fill your head with strange words like "shame," "honour," and "sin." When you hear these things, don't just accept them, talk back, ask questions, and disagree.*

*If one day you have a sister, people will try to tell you that you are better than her, and that you are allowed to do what she is forbidden. If one day you decide to share your life with a woman, they will tell you that you are the man of the house and that she and her body are yours. If you have children, and one of them is a girl, they will tell you that her virginity and her hymen are your lifelong obsession, that no matter how much you love her, you can never trust her or her decisions, and that the small talk of monsters outside matters more than her life.*

3 Listen to the embedded sound recording online https://jeem.me/en/society/abir-kopty/will-my-son-grow-be-sexist).

> *My dear son, we may never be able to free our homelands or our societies, but we – your father and I – vow to do everything we can to keep you free of the monster that people will try to plant inside you.*

I know that parenthood is an enormous responsibility. I know that such a responsibility becomes even more important when we live in an unjust world that oppresses our daughters and sons, even more so because we decided to be open-minded and live according to our standards rather than those forced upon us. I also realize that the decision my partner and I tmade to raise our son in a way that will ultimately free him – to some extent at least – from the constraints imposed upon him and the privileges granted to him as a boy, will be a relentless and exhausting undertaking that will require us to resist the forms of domination which exist in our own relationship, and to be creative in both the way we treat him and the way we protect him from the society around him. We must find freedom for ourselves before we can make it our gift to him.

# 14. Biographies in Motion
## An academic-artistic photo exhibition gives voice to Arab newcomers to Berlin

*Eman Helal, Hanan Badr*

### In their own voice

In the aftermath of the Arab Uprisings, the massive first wave of protests in 2010/11, many Arab intellectuals, novelists, artists, journalists, and researchers were specifically targeted and forced to migrate. This led to a notable growth of diasporic communities in European cities, particularly in Berlin.

This portrait series features faces of the Arab diasporic community in Berlin, especially those who left their countries right after the Arab Uprisings of 2010/11. It intentionally focuses on the so-called newcomers to Berlin. Instead of labeling the portraits in dry language, we chose to bring them to life by sharing the words of those portrayed as they took stock of topics like migration, education, arts, language, and identities in Berlin. The more than 40 people interviewed and photographed are from many fields: fine arts, music, literature, handicrafts, entrepreneurship, culture, and tourism, to name just a few.

This exhibition de-essentializes misconstructions about Arabs and lets new migrants speak for themselves. The project critically reflects on the non-political consequences of the Arab Uprisings beyond the liberation euphoria by retracing the fates of people who voluntarily or involuntarily left their home countries.

The exhibition started as a collaboration between an academic and a photographer, both co-authors for this chapter. An accompanying special issue 'Ten Years after the Arab Uprisings' was published in the high-ranking journal *Media and Communication,* in a project that was funded by the Arab-German Young Academy of Sciences and Humanities (AGYA).[1]

1 The exhibition, which was funded by the Arab-German Young Academy of Sciences and Humanities (AGYA), features 12 portraits out of 40 photographed individuals and cultural initiatives of Arab newcomers to Berlin. It is part of the tandem project "Arab Uprisings – Beyond Media and Liberation: Publication & Exhibition" by AGYA member Lena-Maria Möller and AGYA alumna Hanan Badr with portraits by the Egyptian documentary photographer Eman

Letting the newcomers speak and share their stories means questioning whether Berlin is truly the city of indefinite dreams for all 2: not all featured people have had brilliant new starts. Their struggles with and thoughts about uncertainty and new personal transformation also resemble the personal struggles of the co-authors, who left their home country Egypt after the massive closure of the public spheres for academia and journalism there.

When one of the co-authors (Eman Helal) left her county in 2019 to seek professional opportunities in Germany and continue her career in photography, she was unfortunately confronted with a lack of acknowledgement of her expertise. Many treated her like a novice who had just started taking pictures yesterday. Some potential employers didn't even care to check on her previous projects in Egypt and elsewhere. It felt as if her 15 years of experience simply did not count.

In a different world, that of academia, the other co-author (Hanan Badr) felt the very same subtle and invisible lines of exclusion. The journals and academic venues where she had built her reputation in the Arab region were not well known or understood, rendering her expertise invisible.

This was where the two authors connected, and their urge to make the voices of the Arab intellectuals who live in Berlin heard seeded an exhibition. The exhibition would witness their perspectives and previous experiences before coming to Germany and make their biographies count.

Working on the photographic expression of the project "Ten years after the Arab Uprisings" gave Eman Helal a chance to remember and reflect on what she had already achieved in her career. She didn't want to forget where she and her co-author came from, or what she had experienced while she was documenting the Egyptian revolution in 2011. It became important to her to raise awareness for this shared history. Therefore, working on the project became a resonance space to reflect on their experiences and cultivate the neglected feelings that had arisen but had been ignored during the co-authors' journeys in Germany.

## In and Out of Berlin: Changing perspectives

Eman Helal was living elsewhere when this project started, and the documentary exhibition focus on Berlin aligned with her original wish to move to and live in Berlin.

---

Helal. The published special issue featured eight peer-reviewed articles scrutinizing the role of media in the transformation period after 2011. The issue attracted contributions from a broad spectrum of different countries and disciplinary perspectives: media and communication studies, linguistics, political sciences, area studies, Islamic studies, and urban studies. The special issue is available Open Access here: https://www.cogitatiopress.com/mediaandcommunication/issue/view/275

From her outsider perspective, first living in Hannover and then later in Hamburg, Berlin shone like a cosmopolitan city embracing its vibrant and diverse Arab community. During her frequent visits for photoshoots and interviews, the commuting photographer realized that living in Berlin could be very hectic. She understood that the city could easily lure Arab newcomers into a comfort zone, surrounded by Arabs, eating Arabic food, and hanging out with Arab friends in their favorite spots all the time. Moving from one neighborhood to another to meet with the subjects of the photographs offered her a chance to discover how big and diverse Berlin is in terms of its architecture, its cuisines, and even the appearance of its people. These were good reasons to fall in love with and return again and again to Berlin.

Berlin is the favored location for any Arab artist or concert today. The city has gained an international standing, like Paris or London, and has become the center of Arab intellectual life. This can cause envy for Arabs who live elsewhere and have to handle logistics and financial costs when they want to connect with their culture.

One recent example: In early 2023, for example, Bassem Youssef, the Egyptian comedian and host of the most popular show Albernameg who had to leave Egypt recently, gave two consecutive sold-out shows at Tempodrom in Berlin. Another example: At the end of 2022, Eman's favorite band Cairokee performed in Berlin at Huxley's Neue Welt at Hermannplatz during their European tour. Crossing the street at the traffic light meant being surrounded by people speaking with an Egyptian accent. A long line of young people who had come from different cities and even from outside Germany to enjoy the concert waited outside and excitedly shared stories with strangers. You could even hear one of the band's songs playing from the kiosk around the corner. The sense of warmth and belonging was unparalleled.

But on another occasion in 2022 she asked an Egyptian friend based in Berlin whether he would like to go to the Al Berlin Music Festival. To her surprise, he replied that he had stopped going to those concerts because it bored him to see the same faces every time he went out.

So, after finishing the project, Eman finally reconsidered and decided not to move to Berlin after all. She has found that keeping a distance from the city, yet still traveling back and forth to attend concerts or visit friends, is her best option. That does not mean she lacks affection for the city, but she has recognized that she needs to keep her distance to miss the city.

Berlin has acquired the image of Germany's capital for Arab communities, attracting many intellectuals from outside Germany. It has a powerful attraction, not only for new residents[2], but also for Arab tourists who want to visit major cultural attractions like the Berlinale Film Festival or Arab intellectual initiatives like AlFILM

2 Book Editors' note: Chapters written by newcomers to Berlin like the Bahraini journalist Nazeeha Saeed and the Yemeni science communicator Hashem Al-Ghaili echo this sentiment. See also chapter by Amro Ali in this volume.

and ALFESTIVAL. The city has become powerfully linked in the collective Arab imagination to a life in freedom and prosperity. But a central message in the exhibition project has been to de-essentialize the Arab image of Germany and Berlin as overly positive and romanticized. The ambivalence between the dream and the reality can be reflected in popular culture.

In their song "Better than Berlin", a title that alludes to their hometown of Haifa, Faraj Suleiman and Majd Kayyal lament the anonymity of Berlin despite its crowds. They see Berlin as an enigmatic but ultimately replaceable European city:

"Berlin is mentioned because of two reasons: it's the face of a generation that travels and tries new places, lots of young people immigrate there. It's a place that's very artistic, cheap, they speak English, it's easy for people to try [to be] themselves thereBut Berlin is also recalled in the album by chance; but it's not just Berlin, it's Haifa. We just believe that Haifa is nicer" (Nabil 2022).

Similarly, in the course of this project, through her camera lens, Eman started seeing Berlin with different eyes and realized that her relationship with the city had changed. She no longer wanted to live there because she found it too hectic. Today she sees it as an excellent spot for short vacations and culture-related activities but not for long-term stays.

## Moving encounters with personal stories

Back to the exhibition: Opening in May 2022 for the *Salon Sophie Charlotte* as hosted by the Berlin-Brandenburg Academy of Sciences and Humanities (BBAW), the photo exhibition "Biographies in Motion – The Arab Intellectual Community in Berlin" brought faces in the Arab communities in Berlin out of the shadows of exile and into the center of Berlin life at Gendarmenmarkt. Why the title "Biographies in Motion"? Because the Arab Berlin stories illustrate the rise and fall, the hope and courage, but also the loss and despair inherent in new beginnings.

An exhibition space was created in the famous historic Paternoster in the BBAW building for powerful impact. The idea to use the vintage elevator with its open circling cabins was developed with Dr. Sabine Dorpmüller and her colleagues Masetto Bonitz, Sebastian Fäth, and Ann-Cathrin Gabel of the AGYA Berlin Office, who also conceptualized and curated the installation as well as the opening program. Installing the photographs with captions in the circling cabins of the Paternoster brought motion both literally and figuratively into the lives of the Arab diaspora in Berlin. The installation concept presented moving stories, giving life to each photograph and inviting each subject to tell their story as they passed from floor to floor. The audience would follow the speaker from the first to the fifth floor. Following the movement of the Paternoster upwards, visitors were invited to listen and engage with the Arab Berliners portrayed, looking back at the Arab Uprisings more than ten years ago and the reasons these people had come to Berlin and how they had carved out a new existence for themselves.

The subjects – intellectuals, artists, journalists, musicians, entrepreneurs, and cultural mediators – come from Bahrain, Egypt, Iraq, Lebanon, Palestine, Sudan, Syria, and Tunisia. They represent the diversity of the Arab diaspora in Berlin. Only 8 pictures were selected for this book to reflect diverse geographic origins and fields and to ensure gender balance. But 40 other stories from the exhibition cannot be told here. In the following, we show selected portraits with quotations from the subjects along with two pictures documenting the exhibition.

*Fig. 14.1: Kheder Abdulkarim – from Syria, 55 years*

"I am a Syrian Kurdish painter. I was persecuted as a political activist. Art allows me to process my experiences in prison in Syria as well as my new exile life in Berlin."

*Fig. 14.2: Abir Kopty – from Palestine, 46 years*

"I am an Arab mum, journalist and PhD student in Berlin. A part of my heart is still in Palestine, and while I'm grateful for the diversity Berlin offers, I think it's equally important to stay connected with the Arab World."
© AGYA/Eman Helal

*Fig. 14.3: Adham Elsaid – from Egypt, 56 years*

"Leaving my celebrity life as a professional singer, I am confined to the niche of Arabic music in Berlin. Through sports, I could make new friends beyond the Arab diaspora."
© AGYA/Eman Helal

*Fig. 14.4: Ahmed Isam Aldin – from Sudan, 31 years*

"I am a visual artist and designer. I believe our artistic work needs to reflect on social changes in Europe from Arab perspectives."
© AGYA/Eman Helal

*Fig. 14.5: Amal, Berlin![3]*

"As newcomer journalists in Berlin, we produce local news for migrant publics. We cross language barriers and encourage participation in community life." Amal, Berlin! means Hope, Berlin!
© AGYA/Eman Helal

3 Editors' note: See chapter 3 written by Abdolrahman Omaren and Julia Gerlach about Amal, Berlin!.

*Fig. 14.6: Fekra Berlin*

"We teach Arab kids who grew up here in Berlin. We select Arabic language books reflecting the children's surroundings in Europe." Fekra in Arabic means Idea.

*Fig. 14.7: Hayder Alhawani – from Iraq, 33 years*

"I am an Iraqi journalist and TV reporter. After receiving death threats, I had to flee my country. In Berlin, I had to give up journalism to earn a living."
© AGYA/Eman Helal

*Fig. 14.8: Nazeeha Saeed – from Bahrain, 39 years*[4]

"After covering the Arab Uprisings in Bahrain as a journalist for Western Media, I lost my accreditation. Moving to Europe meant losing a network of support, comfort, and wealth."
© AGYA/Eman Helal

4 Editors' note: See Chapter 4 written by journalist Nazeeha Saeed.

*Fig. 14.9: Baynatna*

"We created a home for ourselves in Berlin through the public library that we share with others. We offer a safe space for the exile community to meet and interact." Baynatna in Arabic means Between us.
© AGYA/Eman Helal

*Fig. 14.10: Wassim Muqdad – from Syria, 36 years*

"As a professional Oud player, I had to protect my hands from torture. My instrument was my most precious possession when I had to flee from Syria."
© AGYA/Eman Helal

*Fig. 14.11: Biographies in Motion Exhibition Opening*

From left to right: Eman Helal, Dr. Hanan Badr (Exhibition curators and chapter authors) and Dr. Sabine Dorpmüller (Managing director of Arab-German Young Academy of Sciences and Humanities), at the exhibition opening at Salon Sophie Charlotte, Berlin-Brandenburg Akademie der Wissenschaften in May 2022.
© Philipp Spalek

*Fig. 14.12: Dr. Julia Hauser (AGYA alumna and historian at University of Kassel) and Dina Abdelhafez (featured in the exhibition) discuss migration and higher education.*

© Philipp Spalek

*Fig. 14.13: Eman Helaland Dr. Hanan Badr at the exhibition opening*

"In this exhibition, we want to give Arab newcomers to Berlin a voice to be heard beyond the stereotypical images."


## References

Nabil, Laila (2022) 'Better Than Berlin': A Conversation with Faraj Suleiman and Majd Kayyal. Institute for Palestine Studies blog, March 24 (https://www.palestine-studies.org/en/node/1652699).

# Part 4: Cultural Life

# 15. That's how you people do things around here, right?!

*Fig. 15.1: "The Federal Republic of Germany wishes you a pleasant temporary stay."*

©subtype.studio

A while ago, I was invited to a symposium on diversity and cultural education. That evening the plan was to go out for dinner, as usual. A gentleman I had previously sat with on a panel approached me. "Fadi, you live here. Won't you take us to a good Oriental restaurant?" We were a group of six or seven people.

"I love Arab food, whether it's Moroccan or Afghan. It's simply magical," he explained to me. Now, I'm not generally comfortable doing this kind of thing. You can never please everyone and are quickly blamed for the smallest details. And in this case, I didn't know where to start. Was I to explain to him that Afghanistan is not an Arab country? I had only eaten Afghan food once – and yet to him, I was the expert.

When I eat out in Berlin, my first choice is not always "Arabic" or a place "Arabs" are expected to frequent. Berlin offers so many different global cuisines at affordable prices that I personally – as a real Arab – also like to go out for Vietnamese, Korean, or Peruvian food, or even simply for burgers or pizza. I was hungry myself. So, I then led the group to one of my favorite Arabic restaurants. The restaurant was decorated in a simple and culturally neutral style. It had a 60s DDR Sputnik-style chandelier and an angular, streamlined glass and wood counter.

*Fig. 15.2: The Arabic restaurant with the GDR decoration – Photo 1*

Copyright @taktiek

Arriving at the restaurant (see Fig. 15.2.), my fellow panelist was disappointed. "This is not authentic," he declared. That made me curious. I asked him which restaurants he felt were actually authentic. He then gave me a long lecture about where he had eaten which dishes and which ones had been truly "authentic". The restaurants he named were predominantly ones furnished in exotic Oriental style. I then asked whether he had ever been to an Arab country – from Morocco to Afghanistan. No, he said, he hadn't.

This story has stayed with me for some time. Of course, I am familiar with Orientalist patterns, but it surprised me that even enlightened young people in my peer group should apply such patterns, including people who – I presumed – have dealt with colonialist and post-colonialist perspectives. I especially did not expect this among people who belong to the arts and cultural scene.

*Fig. 15.3: The Arabic restaurant with the GDR decoration – Photo 2*

Copyright @taktiek

When it comes to decorating an Arab restaurant in Berlin, many owners fill it with reprints of Orientalist paintings from the 18th and 19th centuries as an expression of their cultural identity. It is not surprising to see works by Jean-Léon Gérôme, Georg Macco, Leopold Carl Müller, or Francesco Ballesio in a falafel or shawarma snack bar. Ballesio, like many other Orientalist painters, never traveled to the original locations himself before creating images of the Orient that were nevertheless widely accepted as "authentic".

Such colonialist and imperialist perspectives have been applied not only to Arab or Islamic societies. As we all know, as a rule, every people and every society is pigeonholed, including Germany and the Germans. But the global structures of power and representation affect the extent to which cultures are reduced to clichés – so the impact is felt less by the colonial powers than by those who were colonized. This disbalance extends, not only to Arabs or Muslims, but also to Africans, Latin Americans, Asians, and to some extent, to Southern and Eastern Europeans.

Usually, distorted or prejudiced perspectives catch my attention. I often wish they wouldn't. As a student, I was always asked to "create something 'Arabic'". I was not exactly enthusiastic about that. Above all, I didn't know what this "Arabic" should look like. And I didn't think anyone else would, either.

But I was wrong. Many people simply applied their own definitions and criteria and assumed the ability and prerogative to pass judgment. In the end, it was an older, experienced lecturer, a certain Professor Veit, who finally persuaded me to create an "Arabic" design in his basic fundamentals of communication design course. The task was to visualize a music genre of our choice. I thought it would be a good exercise to visualize Classical Arabic music, a genre broad enough to defy narrow definition.

But in the end, my designs were never "Arabic" enough for the professor. He made suggestion after suggestion that seemed absurd to me. One was that I should apply gold glitter, sprinkling it onto the drying ink – a technique I imagine a student might have used years ago to illustrate a fairy tale from the Orient, but certainly not something connected in any way with my understanding.

Veit then told me about a former student of his from Vietnam, a man who had always wanted to create "American" designs. That student, Veit said, considered "American" to be synonymous with "Western" or "modern".

Then one day, the student was asked to design something "Vietnamese". When he presented the first drafts, they were met with criticism. "But that's how people design in Vietnam," he answered. "No, no, no," Veit had said. "You're doing it all wrong if you create Vietnamese design as *you* think it should look. You should do it the way *we* think it should look."

Veit did not mince words. That statement is deeply prejudiced and, as it demeans the Vietnamese perspective compared to the Western one, one could even consider it racist. A younger professor might use different words. But in graphic design, primarily meant to serve communication purposes, Veit's stance might well be considered normal or standard: After all, in communication, it's always important to take the viewer's visual habits into account.

For example, I wouldn't go into a store with dark wood paneling and furniture, small green lamps, and a Guinness logo on the window if I were looking for a delicious falafel. I wouldn't walk into a restaurant, decorated with Asian elements and red wooden furniture if I got a craving for burgers on the road. And no matter what kind of food Abdullah offers, honestly, I would be very skeptical of him.

Our visual habits, like our habits in general, influence both our behavior and our attitudes. By consuming certain images and motifs – be they in the media, in art, or on Facebook – we form our opinions and positions. That's nothing new! And like the paintings and images of the Orient from over 100 years ago, the depictions and stereotypes of today serve certain political and cultural purposes.

Hollywood has inherited and advanced myths about the Orient shaped in Europe through painting and literature. In his book *Reel Bad Arabs*, Jack G. Shaheen[1] documents 100 American films that, over many years, have portrayed Arabs and Muslims as evildoers, money-hungry sheikhs, religious fanatics, faceless masses in black, harem maidens, and even subhuman individuals. Shaheen explains that while Hollywood no longer maligns other races to this degree, it still perpetuates myths and gross exaggerations about race and religion when it comes to Arabs.

---

1 Jack G. Shaheen (2001; 3rd revised edition 2009) Reel Bad Arabs. How Hollywood Vilifies a People. Interlink Books.

No doubt that American film productions had a huge cultural impact on the whole Western world including Germany, where viewers nowadays are certainly more conscious of stereotypes. People tend to be more capable of identifying and classifying primitive Hollywood stereotypes as such. But what about the motifs of the past 10 to 20 years? They are motifs of war and displacement victims; injured or dead people in Palestine, Syria, Iraq, or Afghanistan; people on the run, especially children in wet clothes and orange life jackets; or the dead bodies of others who have not survived the escape journey. The most prominent one is the Syrian toddler, Alan Kurdi. The motif of his dead body lying on the beach was reproduced again and again over months and even years in the media – and indeed in art, including by Ai Weiwei, posing as the dead boy in a photograph as a notable addition to countless works of art, literature, and films about these tragic events and their outcome.

*Fig. 15.4: "So why do we never see such motifs?"*

©subtype.studio

What do these motifs, and what do such images and representations do to us – especially given repeated and incessant exposure? One may argue that they are necessary to generate attention and sympathy for the victims. But is that really what they do? After all, who among us can remember the last time in the past 30 or 40 years she or he saw a picture of a dead western european or north american white person? Did we see the dead victims of mass shooter rampages in the U.S. or the attack on Charlie Hebdo in France, or bodies of the teenagers killed at that summer camp in

Norway? I certainly have not seen any such images – no photos, paintings, statues, or installations that depict and immortalize these victims in their victim status. Aren't these victims worthy of our attention and sympathy as well? This is a rather striking and peculiar contrast!

So why do we never see such motifs?

In my search for answers, I came across Susan Sontag's essay "Regarding the Pain of Others."[2] I found two of her arguments very insightful. First, it doesn't really matter with what intentions one produces, reproduces, or disseminates images and depictions of horrors. Their sheer volume dulls our feelings. Just as the health warnings on cigarette packages hardly deter anyone from smoking. Second, motifs of violence occurring only in foreign lands and happening only to "others" create a disconnect between the subject and the viewer. They suggest that tragedy is inevitable and unavoidable – and thus more acceptable – as long as it is experienced by strangers, and they create the sense that violence happens elsewhere and to others. When I arrived in Berlin, I was frankly disconcerted that whenever I noticed cultural references to the Arab region, they were always laden with violence, war, women's oppression, religion, or, ideally, a mixture of all of these.

I kept asking myself: Why is the apparent interest in such content often more important than the aesthetic quality of the work itself? And why do we hardly see works that deal with other themes – an abstract sculpture, a love poem, a family drama, a comedy, on stage or on screen? Do such works exist at all? If so, why are they not here?

The interaction between the seller and the buyer has shaped markets for thousands of years. It is habits and buying patterns that shape markets and products. And the richer the buyer, the more the maker and seller will adapt to the buyer's preferences.

On the international art markets, it is unfortunately no different. If both the public and the cultural stakeholders in Berlin and in other Western metropolises are most interested in art that deals with the suffering of others, that is simply what will be produced most. And when criteria such as quality and authenticity are aligned with Western notions and expectations of the ethnic and geographic identity of artists and artworks, the repeated and exclusive exposure to other people's tragedies will continue to dull empathy, and at the same time build a sense that other people's problems do not affect us: "We are safe here".

Some time ago, Ai Weiwei decided, very publicly, to leave Berlin. He said Germany is self-centered and was not open to dissenting voices. I was intrigued by his

2 Sonntag, Susan (2003) Regarding the Pain of Others. Picador New York (https://monoskop.org/images/a/a6/Sontag_Susan_2003_Regarding_the_Pain_of_Others.pdf).

case. A reporter immediately interviewed him for *Die Welt*,[3] ironically enough, was less concerned about Weiwei's perception of Germany and more concerned about the artist's stance on Hong Kong, China, and the evil influence of China on the *Berlinale*, which was not showing his films.

I can't judge whether his films were not shown because the Chinese government wanted it that way. What I can judge is this: If a world-renowned artist like AI Weiwei, whose works were widely recognized and celebrated – especially in Germany, finds Germany to be self-centered and not open to dissenting voices, what must younger or "less prominent" artists experience – artists more dependent on funding and commissions? Western democratic countries like Germany are said not to practice censorship. But what role do self-censorship and the limits of what can be said play concerning the published forms of expression and themes in art and culture?

And isn't paying attention to diversity actually quite trendy right now – especially in cultural venues and institutions? In a city with flourishing old and new migrant societies, the topic is widely discussed and debated. In my opinion, when cultural stakeholders talk about diversity, they are primarily concerned with the diversity of the audience. The resounding dilemma is: How to interest the migrants and their children and grandchildren in the cultural asset of the German *Leitkultur,* and how to educate them culturally as an audience? The contents are hardly questioned, nor are the structures and the representation of people of color within these structures given much consideration. And only very rarely do they appear as active players in the art scene.

As a student, I was taught by Veit that what really mattered was not authenticity as an objective criterion but that subjective expectations were met. What does that mean, then, for Berliner people of color, to whom the culture industry only concedes the role of passive spectator or else to whom it dictates which authenticity they must represent?

## References

Rodek, Hans-Georg (2019) Ai Weiwei. Warum ich Berlin und Deutschland verlasse. Eine Abrechnung." August 8 (https://www.welt.de/kultur/kino/plus198185345/Ai-Weiwei-Warum-ich-Berlin-und-Deutschland-verlasse-Eine-Abrechnung.html).

3 Rodek, Hans-Georg (2019) Ai Weiwei. Warum ich Berlin und Deutschland verlasse. Eine Abrechnung. August 8 (https://www.welt.de/kultur/kino/plus198185345/Ai-Weiwei-Warum-ich-Berlin-und-Deutschland-verlasse-Eine-Abrechnung.html).

Shaheen, Jack G. (2001; 3rd revised edition 2009) Reel Bad Arabs. How Hollywood Vilifies a People. Interlink Books.

Sonntag, Susan (2003) Regarding the Pain of Others. Picador New York (https://monoskop.org/images/a/a6/Sontag_Susan_2003_Regarding_the_Pain_of_Others.pdf).

# 16. "Traveling for a better world with Alsharq Travels"

*Julia Gerlach with Christoph Dinkelaker*[1]

**Julia Gerlach:** Christoph, you're one of the few Germans included in this book on Arab Berlin. Who are you?

**Christoph Dinkelaker:** I studied Islamic and political sciences and history in Berlin and Beirut, and in the last years of university, I founded Alsharq with two university friends. At the time, we felt that there was a lot missing in the media reporting on Western Asia and Northern Africa, and we wanted to change that. Many of the interesting developments, voices, and opinions were not being heard in Germany. We started to translate and publish articles from exciting people in the MENA-Region. We also felt that news from the Middle East was often looked at from a very Eurocentric point of view: What does it mean for our security? The three of us had witnessed the so-called "Cedar Revolution" in Lebanon. Labeling the movements as Pro-Western, Radical Islamic, etc., had little to do with what was happening. More and more, we concluded that writing and publishing about the Middle East wasn't enough to bring actual change to people's mindsets. So we started to organize trips to the region for people in Germany. Our objective is to bring people in contact with people from the Middle East and to offer them real experiences to connect with the region. That's what I've been doing, for the most part, for the past 11 years.

**J.G.:** How did you start being interested in the Middle East?

**C.D.:** I spent one year in Beirut doing my civil service at an orphanage. It was a very interesting experience and probably the year of my life that changed me the most. Later, I decided that I wanted to understand better what was going on in Lebanon and the region. I spent some time in Jerusalem working for the Friedrich Ebert Stiftung and for the Willy Brandt Center on a project on Palestinian-Israeli dialogue. I also spent many months in Damascus. Since then, I've been traveling to the region from Berlin regularly. For example, this October, I spent a month in Iraq organizing several trips, and just this week I came back from Oman.

1 Interview translated from German by Julia Gerlach.

**J.G.:** What fascinates you about the Middle East and keeps you traveling there all the time?

**C.D.:** I like to go back to the same places and connect to the same people to see how their lives have changed. For example, to see how people living under authoritarian rule organize their daily life. How many things are still possible, even under difficult political circumstances? I like the more relaxed and laid-back way of life, despite omnipresent hardships. This is very different from the restless atmosphere in Berlin. Berlin is a place where I never get to relax completely.

There are also some quite egoistic reasons to travel there: I've become used to spending several months every winter in Oman – the calmest, friendliest, most relaxed place I know. Oman is the opposite of all the conflict-related stereotypes people in Germany envision when they think of "the Arab world". That's also why I try to bring as many people as possible to Oman to share this experience.

**J.G.:** I guess you get many questions from people there about why you travel so much to Arab countries. How do people react?

**C.D.:** The interaction is often friendlier and more personal. I find it easier to connect with people I meet. In my first year in Beirut, I met people who gave me the chance to feel at home and who let me become part of their life. I got very interested in the political and social questions there, something I was never as involved in back in Germany.

In Bilad al-Sham in general I have this feeling of belonging and of feeling at home. I guess it would still be like that now, even though I'm not sure that I would find any friends or any people I know in Damascus.

**J.G.:** Because they are all in Berlin now?

**C.D.:** Yes, in Berlin or other counties – or dead.

**J.G.:** I'm sure you also get questions from people who are sure that you must be working for the Secret Service simply because they can't believe that anyone might be interested enough in Arab culture to take on the hardship of learning Arabic.

**C.D.:** Yes, sometimes I get these questions, but I don't take them seriously anymore. Many people also can't believe working with war-torn countries like Iraq and Afghanistan makes sense. They don't believe we can make money from what we are doing. So, I very often get the question of why I didn't take the opportunity to choose a more "serious" profession like becoming an engineer in Germany.

**J.G.:** Traveling through interesting countries alone, experiencing what you were describing for yourself – I understand this is fascinating. Going there with groups of tourists is something else. What makes you do that?

**C.D.:** My objective is to bring people together. That's why I take people to these countries. We might organize a hiking trip for guests from Germany with local guides. Sure, the group from Germany is still more privileged and it's never an interaction among peers. But still, it's possible to form a connection and also part of our trips to discuss these privileges and what they mean to us in such a situation. We also meet with politicians, members of civil society, and so on. The main focus is on reducing prejudices and changing the perception of the region and its people. In many cases, people make friends; in some cases, they even find love; and most people take home something that might affect their life or how they see the Middle East in some way. They take this home and share it with those around them in Germany, which is what we want to achieve.

**J.G.:** So, basically, you do what Western NGOs do when they provide political education in countries like Iraq, just the other way around? Instead of teaching the people in the Middle East, you teach Germans?

**C.D.:** That's a very nice way of describing it. Yes, I think we want to work in both directions, but we're much more able to address the audience in Germany. It's where we can change perceptions and ways of thinking. In many cases, the trips have actually changed a lot. Some people have switched jobs, others have moved to Middle Eastern countries, or as mentioned, they've even found love.

**J.G.:** But it might also go wrong. I can imagine that people might quite often reconfirm their prejudices. They might go home and say: This confirms what I've always thought about the Arabs. No wonder the countries have so many problems. There is this saying: "What's the difference between tourism and racism? Two weeks." What do you think of that?

**C.D.:** I actually haven't had many experiences like that. In one case, we had an AfD-voter on one of our trips. I think it was to Lebanon, and I guess his objective was to learn more about why the Arabs are the way they are. We did our best; at least he discovered that reality is much more diverse than he thought. He got to know many different people and perspectives. I can't imagine that it didn't change his way of thinking.

**J.G.:** I know quite a few people who came to visit me in Egypt while I was living there who felt uncomfortable and decided not to go out anymore. One friend even said, "I think I am afraid of Islam. I will stay indoors." What can you do to avoid this?

**C.D.:** It's important to let people feel at ease right from the beginning. We might organize a night out with some young people in a hipster location like Sulaymaniyah in Kurdish Iraq. That can be a good icebreaker. It's very rare for people to absolutely not get along. I remember one case of a woman who decided she couldn't cope with wearing a Hijab in Iran and the gender roles there, so she asked me to book her an early flight home.

**J.G.:** In the last decades, there's been a long discussion on the most effective ways of bridging the gap between the Arab world and the so-called West. Media reporting, NGO-work, or a different political approach by the governments have all been mentioned, but many experts and activists have come to the same conclusion as you, and say: Personal experience is the best way. The only problem is that it requires a lot of resources and traveling. It isn't feasible to connect every person with a counterpart from the other side of the Mediterranean.

**C.D.:** Yes, that's right. We can only address people who can afford our trips. That means that many are excluded. Talking about privilege is important to us. We often start the discussions at the beginning of our trips with an introduction to colonialism and talk about the hierarchies that people might observe in these countries.

**J.G.:** Do you offer trips to Syria?

**C.D.:** No, even though it's possible to go to Syria now and other agencies are offering touristic trips to Damascus, I refuse to do so for political reasons. However, we offer digital trips to Syria and to other places that are out of reach for tourism, like Afghanistan. We came up with these formats as a response to the pandemic, but they're such a success that I think we'll keep them in our program even after COVID-19. The digital trip to Syria is always booked out and is a big success. It's a two-day trip with many interesting people who tell their stories and discuss issues with the audience. We can even offer a live visit to the old city of Damascus. People see a degree of normal life going on, but at the same time, they see the many soldiers and security personnel.

By the way, on all our trips – online and offline – we have more and more people with family connections to the region. It's typical to find people in our groups who came to Germany as children. One of them told me, "I wanted to visit 'my' country, and if I had traveled there the 'normal' way, I would have spent the whole time visiting my aunts and uncles and would not have seen anything of the country."

**J.G.:** Let's change the perspective. You mentioned that you've been observing what is changing in the Middle East. I'm sure you're also observing what is changing in Berlin. What comes to mind when you think of Arab Berlin?

**C.D.:** Berlin has changed a lot. It is much more Arabic. Just think of all the goods available now: Food, clothing, and many cultural events: Music, theater, and discussions. Looking at the Arab spaces in Berlin, you realize there's a new attitude. The Arab community is much more confident. Especially since 2015, there has been a big change. We have many more migrant, post-migrant, and exile organizations working on the situation in the countries in the Middle East and who are involved in setting the agenda. They want to influence the Middle East's perception in Germany and Europe. German-founded organizations are increasingly seen as allies. They might work with an organization like ours because we're experienced in certain things, such as digital events. They also might work with us to form a better connection to the German media and to mainstream audiences. But nevertheless, it's clear: These new organizations – like Nawara, for example, an organization founded by young academics from Egypt and other countries – have their own idea of how they want the Middle East to be perceived in the Western media and society.

I also think that the spheres are divided more. I remember a few years ago there were more organizations where people of Middle Eastern and German origin would work together. Now I think the organizations are more divided. Still, there's a lot of cooperation.

**J.G.:** One of your objectives in founding Alsharq in 2005 was to change how the media reports on the Middle East. How do you see changes in this field?

**C.D.:** I think many things have changed. Even though the newsrooms are still very white-dominated, the type of reporting has changed. It's not as Eurocentric anymore, and more voices from the Middle East are present in the mainstream media. But still, we see that many voices and perspectives from the region are not being heard or paid attention to in Germany. It's a pity! There's a lot missing from German discourse. We lack translators and cultural transmitters to bring these voices into the mainstream.

**J.G.:** I'd say that the perspective has narrowed a lot. Look at how many papers have reduced the number of correspondents in the region. The horizon of a typical newspaper reader was much broader just a couple of years back. COVID-19 has narrowed it even more: We focus on the number of daily injections, and apart from that, don't look at what is happening in Cairo, Damascus, or Sulaymanyah. The German audience is not as curious about other perspectives these days. On the other hand, I know quite a few people from the Middle East living in Berlin who are perfectly happy with the feeling of belonging to the city without having any connection to the German part of the city.

**C.D.:** I think this is a problematic development, and my answer to this is the same as the answer to prejudice from the other side: The only way to overcome it is to connect people with each other. I like initiatives like "Hometown Hannover", where people interact and meet to do things together. We need more of this, connecting people to their neighbors, to the people in their *kiez*.

**J.G.:** If I booked a trip to Arab Berlin, where would you take me?

**C.D.:** We actually have a trip for that in our program. Mohammad Ali Chahrour guides groups through Neukölln and tells his story of growing up with "*Kettenduldungen*" (chain exceptional leave to remain), about going to the *Rüttli-Schule*, and he takes the group to *Sonnenallee*.

**J.G.:** Thank you. That sounds great! Now let me ask you the questions every taxi driver in Cairo and Amman would ask: Are you married? Is your wife Arab?

**C.D.:** No.

**C.D.:** That's a good one. No, I don't have kids. I'm 38, by the way, in case that was your next question. – One more thing: We didn't discuss our name, Alsharq. We chose it way back when we started in 2005. Later, we found it highly problematic because of its Orientalist connotation. That's why we chose the name dis:orient for our journalistic work. Alsharq had already become a known brand for the travel agency, so we didn't want to change it. Talking about the name is always part of our introduction when we get to know a new travel group. That's why I still think it's a good name: It's a perfect starting point for discussion and reflection.

# 17. Arendt's Shadow

## Salam-Schalom from Berlin to the Holy Land

*Mohammad Alwahaib*

Hannah Arendt, for those unfamiliar with her biography, traveled intellectually between many 'islands' of thought. She began her life with purely philosophical concerns, which is not surprising when we look at her academic background: in fact, she inherited the tradition of German philosophy through her education in German universities. She was a distinguished student and lover of Martin Heidegger in Marburg and later in Heidelberg, a pupil, and a lifetime friend of Karl Jaspers. It is under the supervision of Jaspers that she wrote her first doctoral dissertation, *The Concept of Love in St. Augustine*. For most of the time she spent in universities, Arendt was not interested in political matters. However, when the Nazis rose to power in Germany, Arendt tells us, it was the occasion that made it possible for her to face the fact of her 'Jewishness' – the vehicle that escorted her into politics. The hostility of the Nazis towards Jews, as well as other minorities, turned Arendt's attention towards politics and 'action'. Later, she was intensely engaged in Jewish politics and Zionism as a passionately active member. In the middle of all these events, Arendt declared her divorce from all forms of traditional philosophizing: "I left Germany [escaping from the Nazis] dominated by the idea... Never again! I shall never again get involved in any kind of intellectual business. I want nothing to do with that lot."[1] This period of time that she spent involved in Jewish politics is marked by a number of articles on the so-called Jewish Question[2] and parts of her famous work, *The Origins of Totalitarianism* and in these articles, we find an explicit, harsh critique of the Zionist ideology, which we are going to discuss in the subsequent remarks.

These early writings on the Jewish Question and Zionism which began in 1937 and lasted for almost a decade are the focus of this chapter as some of these ideas were manifested in Berlin's, Salam Shalom Initiative. Arendt's critique of the Zionist ideology in fact took many directions, and I will only focus on a few in this context,

1 "What Remains? The Language Remains." A Conversation with Günter Gaus. In: Baehr, Peter (2000) The Portable Hannah Arendt. New York, NY: Penguin Books, pp. 3–22.

2 This collection of articles re-appeared in a volume that bears the same title, The Jewish Writings, edited by Jerome Kohn and Ron Feldman (2007) Schocken Books: New York.

namely, her analysis of the actual presence of Arabs in the territory of Palestine, as well as the absence of any serious discussion of Arabs in the Zionist vision ideology.

## Critique of Zionism

Arendt's criticism of the Zionist vision of the nation-state is well-known. She actually viewed Zionism as an outdated form of a nation-state. In fact, as we are going to see, she stood firm against those who embraced Zionism, i.e. those who commit themselves to the creation of a Jewish/ethnic national state. Against this national vision, Arendt proposed the establishment of an Arab-Jewish Confederation in Palestine, based on the recognition of the plurality of individuals and the guarantee of their equal rights.

Thinking of a "Jewish state" from a Zionist perspective was, for Arendt, a wrong reaction to anti-Semitism in Europe, as that Jewish state would exercise the same hostility that Jewish people had suffered, but against the Arabs this time. Arendt recognized that such a state could only be established through force, and rightly so, since no people could accept the stealing of their land, or to become stateless overnight, or at best, second-class citizens. Imposing a Jewish nation-state in that way, in her opinion, would only lead to continued violence. Arendt predicted that even "if the Jews were to win the war", they would "degenerate into one of those small warrior tribes about whose possibilities and importance history has amply informed us since the days of Sparta... Thus, it becomes plain that at this moment and under present circumstances a Jewish state can only be erected at the price of the Jewish homeland".[3]"

Arendt advocated a vision of a Jewish homeland where two national identities who inhabit the land, Jews, and Arabs, could live together side by side. She did not advocate, however, a Jewish state which was supposed to take the form of an ethnic political entity that rejected the Palestinian right to a homeland. Arendt's predictions were proven to be correct: Israel since its inception entered a race with itself in terms of armament and military power and this apparent increase in military spending – which is taking over the Israeli budget – was a clear indication of how the country was turning gradually into a security state. Any Israeli government that came to power was haunted first and foremost by the question of security. The subject to be discussed and analyzed remains the same: how can such unilateral security measures affect the peaceful common future of two peoples living together in such a small territory? The Jewish state and society, with its heavy militarization and enormous military budget, as the only state in the region with nuclear armaments and

---

3 Hannah Arendt (2007) The Jewish Writings, Schocken Books: New York, p. 397.

producing high-end military technology, is very much living proof of Arendt's predictions.

Arendt stood firm in the face of Zionist claims calling for establishing a Jewish state on the territory of Palestine, and because of the denial of the rights of those indigenous people she called for a binational state. The idea of a binational state is not new, of course, as it was preceded by some Jewish intellectuals such as Judha Leon Magnes, Gershom Scholem, Martin Buber, and others, in addition to some associations such as *Bret Shalom* (covenant of peace).[4] This idea, binationalism, meant for Arendt that the state should be separated from religion and national identity. Politically, this binational solution necessarily involved Israelis losing their dream of a national state exclusive to Jews only, and Palestinians losing their dream of independent national statehood.

The frightening reality of today in light of the contradictory claims of both Palestinians and Israelis, at least since the Oslo Accords of 1993, might prompt us to think a little "outside the box"; and despite the difficulties facing the one-binational state project, I believe, it deserves some reconsideration, precisely because of the uniqueness of this conflict: as the conflict between the Palestinians and the Israelis intensifies – a conflict that is almost seventy years old –both parties are aware implicitly that it is impossible for one of them to annihilate the other, and both parties *know* really well that eventually, they *must* come up with an agreement.

In September 2022, Palestinian President Mahmoud Abbas delivered the coup de grace to the moribund so-called peace process which had begun almost 30 years ago: "Israel has decided not to be our partner in the peace process," Abbas announced, stating: "Israel is the side that destroyed the Oslo Accords it signed with the Palestine Liberation Organisation."[5] This was an official de facto collapse of the negotiations between the Palestinians and the Israelis. At times like this, we will probably find an echo for Hannah Arendt's call for a new discourse and a new solution, or in her own words: a new beginning.[6] After 30 years of fruitless peace negotiations, many scholars have turned their attention to her early writings in the 1940s, and more specifically, to her critique of Zionism and its push towards the creation of a Jewish state.[7]

---

4 For more on these influential figures in developing the idea of binationalism cf. Zohar Maor (2013) Moderation from Right to Left: The Hidden Roots of Brit Shalom, Jewish Social Studies 19 (2) Winter, pp. 79–108.

5 Mahmud Abbas delivered this statement to world leaders during the UN General Assembly on September 23rd 2022. (https://www.middleeastmonitor.com/20220924-abbas-israel-decided-not-to-be-our-partner-in-peace-process/).

6 For those who are familiar with Arendt, "new beginning" is a common theme in her major works such as The Human Condition and On Revolution.

7 The list is too long, but it might be useful to point out to a few examples: Amnon Raz-Krakotzkin (2011) Jewish Peoplehood, "Jewish Politics," and Political Responsibility: Arendt on

There is a problem concerning the difficulty of imagining this one binational-state solution. The main reason behind this is recent Palestinian and Israeli rhetoric reaching a level of contradiction that makes it hard to speak of reconciliation or compromise. This is probably a logical conclusion to the Zionist premises: the Zionists were blinded to other partners on the same land and never considered them their equals. Arendt explained this through historical events: the Zionist program in 1942, issued in Biltmore, called for establishing a Jewish commonwealth in Palestine, and the Atlantic City program that followed referred to a free Jewish Commonwealth covering the entire territory of Palestine without division. In the first program, minority rights were given to the Arab majority; in the second program, Arabs were not mentioned at all! This disregard for the Palestinians, she believed, was due to the increasingly ideological tone of Zionism which went hand in hand with its detachment from commonsense and reality.[8]

But the problem seems to be deeper than just Palestinian and Zionist claims; the problem is one of land to which each of the parties to the conflict claims its right. We know well that one of the parties lost the war, but the conflict continues until today. The truth is that, after nearly seventy years of conflict, this land or the independent state of Jews has not been fully free of fear, and it still finds itself, day after day, in an intense, violent relationship with the non-Jews it governs. The problem of land is linked to a more complex problem of identity: Palestinians want to retain their Arab identity, given the Arab-Muslim region that they want to see themselves as part of, and Jews want a Jewish state as envisioned in the Zionist ideology.

The central question for Arendt, I believe, as an alternative to the two-state solution, is the need to think along the lines of a binational state, to think of the possibility of peaceful coexistence between Zionist Jews and Arabs in a partnership that is based on equal rights. I believe that she really wanted to present a challenging alternative to us, an alternative that is based on the impossibility of getting rid of the other, one that looks at democratic institution-building, transitional justice, and a new constitution. The fact that one cannot get rid of the other is, by the way, becoming an increasing conviction among Palestinians and Israelis each day.

Some scholars believe that this Arendtian vision is detached from reality, not more than a cultural contribution or a dreamy idea. However, I believe that these opinions are a bit hasty. In fact, many factors need to be considered before coming to such a conclusion. First, there are many Israeli and Arab intellectuals and activists today who resent the strong influence of orthodox, radical parties in Israeli and Arab politics, and this belief has persuaded them to rally around the idea of a truly secular

---

Zionism and Partitions; Gil Rubin (2015) From Federalism to Binationalism: Hannah Arendt's Shifting Zionism; Eric Jacobson (2013) Why did Hannah Arendt Reject the Partition of Palestine? Idith Zertal (2007) A State on Trial: Hannah Arendt vs. the State of Israel,

8 Arendt, Hannah (1978) The Jew as Pariah. New York, NY: Grove Press Inc. pp. 131–132.

Israeli society in which citizenship rights are given to all on equal footing.[9] Second, a new opinion poll (November 2021) conducted by the Jerusalem Media and Communication Centre (JMCC) showed Palestinians in the West Bank favor one binational state over a two-state solution.[10] Third, there seems to be a revival of the Brit Shalom ideals by some Israelis who speak and write about the importance of de-colonizing Jewish identity and entering the phase of "post-Zionism"; after nearly 70 years of Israeli history, traditional Zionism has secured neither a solution for Palestinians nor an independent existence for Israelis: "Today the two-state idea is in crisis. Most people understand that it's no longer possible. In addition, Jewish existence itself is in crisis. There's a sense that our society has become a walled ghetto, armed with nuclear weapons, constantly experiencing a sense of catastrophe. We must find ourselves a vision".[11] Amnon Raz-krakotzkin, an expert on Jewish History at the University of Ben-Gurion, was certainly clear in his conviction that "the idea of separation is unrealistic; it simply doesn't work... talk of separation creates antagonism. It highlights the differences rather than the commonalities."[12]

## From Arendt to the Salam-Schalom Initiative

Echoing this Arendtian spirit, Edward Said wrote:

> "I see no other way than to begin now to speak about sharing the land that has thrust us together, sharing it in a truly democratic way, with equal rights for each citizen. There can be no reconciliation unless both peoples, two communities of suffering, resolve that their existence is a secular fact, and that it has to be dealt with as such."[13]

The practical echo to Arendt's writing, however, came from the streets of Berlin through the Salaam-Schalom initiative. Although it is no longer operating, it stands as a model. As described in its official website, The Salaam-Schalom initiative was "an intercultural activist initiative". Established in December 2013 by people

9 The list of intellectuals, leaders, and activists who are in favor of the one state solution are many. To name a few from both sides: Ali Abunimah, Abdalhadi Alijla, Jamal Dajani, Jeff Halper, Gideon Levy, etc.

10 Middle East Monitor, November 26, 2021 (https://www.middleeastmonitor.com/20211126-palestinians-favour-a-one-state-over-a-two-state-solution-poll-finds/.

11 Elhanan Miller (2012) What would Buber, Sholem and Arendt say today? The Times of Israel July 17 (https://www.timesofisrael.com/what-would-buber-scholem-and-arendt-say-today/).

12 Ibid.

13 Said, Edward (1999) The One State Solution. The New York Times Magazine January 10 (https://www.nytimes.com/1999/01/10/magazine/the-one-state-solution.html).

in Neukölln and then joined by others throughout Berlin, it stood for a peaceful co-existence and solidarity and promoted those aims "by implementing various interventions and projects which raise awareness to social and institutional exclusions in mainstream German society".[14]"

The initiative began as a response to public statements made by a rabbi marking Neukölln as a 'no-go area' for Jews due to the high rate of Muslim population in the area. Rabbi Daniel Alter, the Berlin Jewish Community's anti-Semitism officer, was open in his statement that Neukölln is a no-go-area for Jews[15], and it seemed that the activists in this movement were unable to ignore that. Salaam-Schalom was co-founded by a group of Muslim, Jewish and many other Neuköllners to counter "racialization and stigmatization that perpetuate distrust and tension along racial lines... and to promote Neukölln and indeed Berlin as a no-go area for racism and ethnic hatred." They asserted that the name "Salaam-Schalom" did not represent "a reconciliation between members of two groups; it is a sign that coexistence already exists on an everyday level." The movement was very active on social media and appealed to a wider audience. Under the motto "Muslims and Jews are not enemies", the movement organized numerous open roundtables, workshops, flash mobs, film screenings, and parties in community centers, synagogues, mosques, sometimes in apartments or parks, with hundreds of people attending these events.

At the time, Adi Liraz, an Israeli-born and Berlin-based member, wrote: "Our goal is to create dialogue... Not a dialogue that is behind closed doors but rather an open, public dialogue, to show the German society that such a dialogue is possible, that it exists, that it also makes sense."[16] The movement did not take the natural enmity between Jews and Muslims portrayed every day in the narrative of mainstream media for granted, endeavoring instead to dismantle such dogmas and stereotypes through *personal encounters*. However, the major test of the movement came during the Gaza War of 2014. In the words of the founder of the movement, Armin Langer:

> "The Israeli air force bombed Gaza, anti-Semitic riots took place on German streets and the media reproduced anti-Muslim agitation. Several Jewish-Muslim groups disintegrated that summer. Without further ado, the Salaam-Schalom-Initiative invited to a flash mob in the middle of an event of the Palestinian

---

14 Description by A. Langer at betterplace.org (https://www.betterplace.org/en/organisations/18152-salaam-schalom-initiative).

15 His statement was widely reported, e.g., Rabbiner Alter warnt vor immer mehr No-go-Areas. In: BZ Sept. 7, 2012 (https://www.bz-berlin.de/archiv-artikel/rabbiner-alter-warnt-vor-immer-mehr-no-go-areas/). This statement came after Alter himself and his seven years daughter were attacked, it is said by four suspected Arab youths because of his identity. There were no witnesses, and the case remains unresolved.

16 Yerni Brenner (2014) In Berlin, Jews and Muslims Fight for Each Other. In: Forward, December 1 (https://forward.com/opinion/210127/in-berlin-jews-and-muslims-fight-for-each-other/).

community in Berlin. It was not about peace in the Middle East, but against the anti-Muslim and anti-Semitic agitation in our home country Germany."

Mr. Langer, emphasizing the role of human connectedness in crushing such abstract enmities, had bigger ambitions: "If we already have the problems in Germany solved, we will also look at the problems of the Middle East."[17]"

The Salam-Schalom initiative, unfortunately, has been inactive for a long time. I do not intend to look into the reasons behind its inactivity, since for a young and independent initiative such as this, many practical obstacles and challenges are to be expected. In fact, this is the fate of many other initiatives that focused on the same goal, i.e., coexistence and peacebuilding, either in the Holy Land or outside of it. What is important, however, for our present purposes is to realize that although many of these initiatives may gradually disappear and eventually die, many others will come to life at the same time.

Ruth Marks Eglash writes for the Jewish Insider on a joint online fundraising campaign by "more than a dozen Israeli and Palestinian nonprofit organizations active in various aspects of peacebuilding",[18] enabling them to sustain their effort and work. This is a significant number of grassroots initiatives working against the backdrop of stabbing, shooting, and violence from both sides. The works of Arendt and her support of a binational state paved the way, I believe, for a deeper understanding of coexistence between two different identities, providing a radical alternative to the homogenous nation-state model promoted by traditional Zionism. The Salam-Schalom initiative was Berlin's echo to Arendt's call for a humanist approach to reconciliation, and a confrontation with the pathological mindset of some groups in the Holy Land, Berlin, and elsewhere in the world.

A two-state solution is destructive for geography and human togetherness since it separates people and turns this small region into Swiss cheese, or to use the words of the Israeli historian cited above: "talk of separation creates antagonism… highlights the differences rather than the commonalities".[19] This is the underlying assumption in the works of Arendt and the Salaam-Schalom initiative. The alternative is unpleasantly simple: If a way out is not based on peace and equality, as in South

---

17 Armin Langer (2016) Die Salaam-Schalom-Initiative: Ein Bündnis von Juden und Muslimen. In: PaRDeS, Zeitschrift der Vereinigung für Jüdische Studien e.V. 22, Universitätsverlag Potsdam, pp. 195–198, (https://publishup.uni-potsdam.de/opus4-ubp/frontdoor/deliver/index/docId/9976/file/pardes22_195-198.pdf).

18 Ruth Marks Eglash (2021) Israeli and Palestinian peace-building NGOs launch joint fundraising drive, Jewish Insider, December 21 (https://ejewishphilanthropy.com/israeli-and-palestinian-peace-building-ngos-launch-joint-fundraising-drive/).

19 Amnon Raz-Krakotzkin, quoted in Elhanan Miller (2012) What would Buber, Sholem and Arendt say today? The Times of Israel July 17 (https://www.timesofisrael.com/what-would-buber-scholem-and-arendt-say-today/).

Africa after apartheid, the war will continue. Peace must be actively sought, despite the many obstacles. Once we take for granted that Palestinians and Israelis are there to stay, the decent conclusion must be the need for peaceful coexistence and genuine reconciliation.

## References

Arendt, Hannah (1978) The Jew as Pariah. New York, NY: Grove Press Inc.

Arendt, Hannah (2000) The Portable Hannah Arendt, ed. by Peter Baehr. New York, NY: Penguin Books.

Arendt, Hannah (2007) The Jewish Writings, ed. by Jerome Kohn and Ron Feldman, NY: Schocken Books.

Maor, Zohar (2013) Moderation from Right to Left: The Hidden Roots of Brit Shalom, Jewish Social Studies 19 (2) Winter, pp. 79–108.

Miller, Elhanan (2012) What would Buber, Sholem and Arendt say today? The Times of Israel July 17 (https://www.timesofisrael.com/what-would-buber-scholem-and-arendt-say-today/).

Said, Edward (1999) The One State Solution. The New York Times Magazine January 10 (https://www.nytimes.com/1999/01/10/magazine/the-one-state-solution.html).

# 18. "Memories in the Nights of Despair"
## Jussuf Abbo in Berlin's Yiddish Literature of the 1920s

*Tal Hever-Chybowski*

In Berlin's avant-garde artistic and literary scene during the Weimar Republic, the sculptor and painter Jussuf Abbo (c. 1889–1953) embodied a number of interconnected and often overlapping categories of identity, culture, race, faith, language and artistic stylization: Oriental, Arabic, Jewish, Semitic, Muslim, Hebrew, Ottoman, Yiddish, Palestinian, Egyptian etc. Although these categories were as exoticizing and essentializing a century ago as they are today, they were perhaps more fluid and less restrictive in Berlin during the 1920s than in the post-war West.

Born in Ottoman Safed around 1888–1890, Jussuf (Yosef) Abbo traveled to Berlin probably in 1911 (Schöne 2019a: 14) and began studying sculpture in 1913 at the Royal Academy of Fine Arts in Charlottenburg, an affluent and vibrant city that became part of Greater Berlin in 1920. During the 1920s, he achieved great success as an artist, exhibiting his work in solo and prestigious group exhibitions in Germany, the Soviet Union, and the United States (Schöne 2019a: 203–205). Abbo was a close friend of the German poet Else Lasker-Schüler and Yiddish writer Moyshe Kulbak, and he was part of the Jewish literary and artistic milieu that centered around the Romanisches Café near Kurfürstendamm in Berlin-Charlottenburg. When the Nazis came to power in Germany, Abbo's newly wedded wife, Ruth Schulz, received threats for marrying a non-Aryan. The couple emigrated to London in 1935, but Abbo failed to maintain his status as a sought-after artist. Poverty, poor health, and despair marked the last period of his life before his death in 1953. Later his name fell into oblivion.

Recent solo exhibitions in Beirut, Berlin, and Hannover have sparked renewed interest in Abbo's work and contributed to the reconstruction of his biography and its diverse intersections with other artists and curators. A closer examination of Abbo's place in Berlin's Yiddish cultural scene of the 1920s could shed further light on his fluid artistic and literary persona in the writings of his peers.

## I

In the European Christian imagination, both Jews and Arabs were considered for centuries to be "oriental" in character and essence to varying degrees. Orientalism, a philological field rooted in the humanist tradition of the Renaissance, was entrenched in the study of Hebrew and Arabic, both of which were declared Semitic. Orientalists repeatedly depicted these languages, peoples, races, and cultures as primitive and primordial, authentic but corrupt, spiritually exalted, yet base, cunning, and false. Christian culture depicted the Semitic Oriental figure, whether an Arab or a Jew, as representing the past while simultaneously being unfaithful to its origins. Thus, this figure was both admired and detested, looked up to and looked down upon.

Recently, Aischa Ahmed has used Jussuf Abbo as a case study of "Arabic presences" in Germany around 1900. Her proposed concept encompasses both "the presence of Arab people in Germany and the prefigured images, ideas, and demarcations to the Other," (Ahmed 2020: 11) which existed well before Arabs had arrived in Germany in any numbers. Rather than focusing solely on the orientalist representations of Arabs in Germany, Ahmed proposes studying Arab people "in their historical presence and agency" (ibid.: 12). Ahmed's intervention is pertinent not only when discussing Abbo's physical presence in Berlin, but also when considering his presence as a literary figure, fictionalized and immortalized by Berlin's Yiddish writers between the two world wars. However, Jussuf Abbo's first appearance as a literary persona in Berlin was not in Yiddish but rather in German. In 1923 Else Lasker-Schüler published a poem entitled "Jussuff Abbu," in which she offered a poetic description of her artist friend, using particularly orientalist imagery (Lasker-Schüler 1923).

It is possible that Lasker-Schüler was inspired by Jussuf Abbo when she created the literary character Prinz Jussuf, which became her pseudonym. In any case, Lasker-Schüler's use of her Palestinian friend to enhance her own orientalist image was consistent with her relationships with other artists, such as the Yiddish poet Abraham Nahum Stencl, whom she decided to style as "Hamid" (Valencia 1995: 84). Stencl settled in Berlin in 1921 and was also a regular at the Romanisches Café and an acquaintance of Abbo (Valencia 1995: 112). However, one should not underestimate Abbo's role and agency in his own orientalization in Berlin's artistic scene at the time. Even before Lasker-Schüler adopted the persona Prinz Jussuf, Abbo had already Arabized his Hebrew name from Yosef to Jussuf (Faerber 1982), thus styling his oriental image. There is no reason to assume that this was a superficial posture rather than a genuine gesture of identity. Abbo considered himself an Arab, as evidenced by his decision to name his second child Hussein (the baby was born in London in 1935 after the family was exiled from Germany) (Schöne 2019b: 47).

## II

Before the formation of the Christian orientalist gaze, medieval Muslim and Jewish grammarians had already subjected Arabic and Hebrew to philologically purist and binary judgments. They distinguished between the classical, pure, and authentic languages of ancient times and the supposedly corrupt post-scriptural vernaculars, which were intertwined with layers of Aramaic, Greek, Latin, Persian, and other languages.

The desire to make categories such as 'the Arab,' 'the Hebrew,' 'the Oriental,' or 'the Semitic' faithful to their alleged origins and to restore the supposedly forsaken expression of their pure classical language was shared, with some variations, by several disparate groups, including the Arabic and Hebrew grammarians of the Middle Ages, the Christian humanist school of the Renaissance, the Christian Reformation, the Jewish Enlightenment movement, and modern Orientalists.

However, the impulse to purify, classify, and distinguish has always been challenged by the diasporic hybridity and conceptual fluidity of people's lived experiences. As European crusaders rushed to conquer the Holy Land from the Muslims in the 11th century, massacring Jewish communities on the Rhine along their way, a new language began to emerge from the ruins: Yiddish, a Jewish-Germanic vernacular that centuries later became the first language of the overwhelming majority of Jews worldwide until the Nazi Genocide.

In Yiddish, the word "Yiddish" also means "Jewish." Similarly, the term "Hebrew" can also mean "Jewish" in many different languages, including Hebrew itself. Yiddish is replete with Hebrew words and influenced by its morphology. Conversely, several varieties of European Hebrew, such as Rabbinic, Hasidic, Maskilic, and Modern, are all heavily influenced by Yiddish, as demonstrated in the works of Lily Kahn. The linguistic situation of Yiddish and Hebrew in Europe has been so complex that scholars of Judaism, even Jewish ones, often denied that Yiddish ever existed as a language in its own right. Instead, they called it a corrupt dialect of German or a 'jargon,' as Moses Mendelssohn did in the 18th century when referring to his own mother tongue.

Max Weinreich, a 20th-century Yiddish linguist and historian, is often cited as saying that "a language is a dialect with an army and navy." Yiddish never had an army or a navy, but it does have many dialects and varieties, including Old Yiddish, Western Yiddish, Lithuanian Yiddish, Polish Yiddish, Ukrainian Yiddish, Hasidic Yiddish, American Yiddish, and even Palestinian Yiddish. As Mordecai Kosover showed in his groundbreaking work, Palestinian Yiddish – spoken in Palestine since the 19th century – is a Yiddish dialect rich in Arabic words and structures. Nevertheless, in the 19th and 20th centuries, the term Yiddish came to be almost exclusively understood as referring to Oriental Yiddish, the Yiddish of Eastern European Jewry. Accordingly, Yiddish-speaking Jews from Eastern Europe were doubly orientalized when they migrated westward: first, for being Jews, and secondly, for being "Eastern Jews": Ostjuden in German, or "Mizrahiyim" in Hebrew. This occurred many decades before the term "Mizrahim" came to designate Jews of Arabic descent in the State of Israel.

Beginning in the late 19th-century, a large group of Yiddish-speaking Jewish emigrants from Eastern Europe settled in Berlin, mostly in today's Mitte. They were deemed primitive, backward, and obscurantist by German Jews and non-Jews alike, who nevertheless saw them as the authentic carriers of Jewish tradition. While some German Jews, such as Martin Buber, were enthralled and inspired by their arrival from Eastern Europe, others who tended forcefully toward assimilation sought to distance themselves from the newly arrived "Ostjuden".

In the 1920s, Berlin saw a new wave of Jewish emigration from Eastern Europe, including refugees from war-devastated Poland and the Ukrainian civil war, who were escaping pogroms of unprecedented scale. Among them were writers, artists, and intellectuals, settling mostly in the new district of Charlottenburg. Joining German Jewish writers such as Alfred Döblin, Else Lasker-Schüler, and Franz Werfel, the newly arrived Ostjuden created a vibrant literary scene in Yiddish, Hebrew, Russian, and German. They founded publishing houses, literary magazines, and flocked to the city's literary cafés. For this diverse polyglot milieu, Hebrew, Muslim, Jewish, Yiddish, Oriental, Arabic, and Semitic were creative artistic concepts, which they reappropriated, subverted, and played with in their works. Lasker-Schüller's poetic persona, for example, featured extravagant orientalism, including her extraordinary claim that her German poems were actually Hebrew poems.

When the new Yiddish literary scene was being established in Berlin-Charlottenburg, Jussuf Abbo had already been living there for a decade. Abbo was a Jewish immigrant who was fluent in both Hebrew and German. He quickly found a common language – both literal and artistic – with the Yiddish writers and became a part of their literary scene. Eventually, Abbo was even incorporated into their works.

## III

On his train ride from the 1937 World Yiddish Cultural Congress in Paris back to Warsaw, Yiddish editor and critic Nakhmen Mayzel passed through Berlin. Just a decade earlier, the city had been home to the Yiddish avant-garde in literature and art, and was the site of dozens of modernist Yiddish publishing houses, cultural institutions, and literary cafés. However, it had now become the capital of National Socialism. Mayzel wrote a short memoir essay presented in the form of a travelogue entitled "Mir forn farbay Berlin" ("We Travel Through Berlin"), in which he tried to encapsulate the short-lived glories of Yiddish Berlin of the 1920s. The essay was published in the weekly Literarishe bleter, Europe's leading Yiddish literary publication, which

Mayzel coedited in Warsaw. In one part of the text, Mayzel recalled a conversation he had with Dovid Bergelson, the president of Berlin's Yiddish writers' club and the most dominant author in the city's Yiddish literary scene at the time:

> Once, I was traveling with Dovid Bergelson on a double-decker bus in Berlin. We launched into a long, hearty, and moving conversation on Berlin's role in our work. With a trembling voice and tears in his eyes, Bergelson told me about a novel he envisioned, in which the main protagonist would be Berlin itself, to which he then felt such attachment and closeness; almost an intimacy (Mayzel 1937: 689).

The figure of Jussuf Abbo entered Yiddish literature in the context of this desire to encapsulate Berlin's Yiddish literary scene of the 1920s in a literary work. While Bergelson's short stories set in Berlin provide rich insight into that ephemeral world, he never wrote the novel he envisioned. However, Bergelson was not the only Yiddish author who dreamed of writing such a work. Perhaps the most famous attempt to provide a Yiddish literary depiction of that period is Moyshe Kulbak's satirical epic Yiddish poem, Disner Tshayld Harold, a title referencing Lord Byron's Childe Harold's Pilgrimage. In Kulbak's poem, which was published in the Soviet Union in 1931, the semi-autobiographical protagonist spends his nights in Berlin's Charlottenburg district together with Jussuf Abbo:

> Abbo is a dreamy Arab,
> A tender sculptor with moonlit hands,
> A short fellow with curly hair,
> Who yearns with clay for the Orient.
> (Kulbak 1979: 180).

Abbo appears in several episodes in the poem and is depicted as a close friend of the protagonist. There is evidence that Jussuf Abbo and Moyshe Kulbak, who moved to Berlin from Vilnius in 1920, were indeed close in real life. In 1921, Kulbak wrote a two-page introduction in German to an exhibition of Abbo's work in Hannover (Kulbak 1921). The orientalizing tone of that text, which states that "Abbo is a son of the Orient" (Ibid.: 3), is consistent with Kulbak's depiction of Abbo in Disner Tshayld Harold.

In one of his Berlin stories, "Mit eyn nakht veyniker" ("One Night Less"), Dovid Bergelson parodies the desire he himself shared with many other Yiddish writers to encapsulate Berlin in Yiddish literature. In the story, a graphomaniac poet named Max Ventsl (perhaps a parody of Abraham Nahum Stencl's name) wishes to write an epic poem about the German capital but fails to do so. The protagonist has a close friend who is referred to repeatedly as "the hairy painter Babo." In the story, "the hairy painter Babo, like Ventsl, remains unrecognized by his painter peers and critics. He never exhibited or sold anything." (Bergelson 1929: 196).

Delphine Bechtel has highlighted the striking resemblance between Babo, the friend of Ventsel in Bergelson's story from 1927, and Abbo, the friend of the protagonist in Kulbak's poem from 1931. In both stories there is also a third friend: the critic Meer in Bergelson's story and the philosopher Erich Dörn in Kulbak's poem. Although Bechtel is correct in identifying the intertextual relationship between the two works, the chronology of publication is misleading, and it leads her to the erroneous conclusion that the trio in Bergelson's story served as a model for the trio in Kulbak's poem. Instead, it must have been the opposite: the artistically forgiving and mutually beneficial relationship between Ventsl, Babo and Meer in Bergelson's story was a parody of Kulbak's and Abbo's real-life friendship.

Bergelson wrote his story in 1927, while Kulbak, who had already left Berlin by 1923, only published Disner Tshayld Harold in 1931. Therefore, it can be assumed that Bergelson had access to an earlier draft of Kulbak's poem (or parts of it). The Yiddish author Daniel Charney described the Romanisches Café in the 1920s as a literary laboratory in which writers tested their works on other writers (Charney 1947: 36). Such cafés were precisely the sites where drafts and early versions of literary works circulated, both in writing and orally, among the regular patrons. It is possible that Bergelson read or heard an early version of Disner Tshayld Harold before 1923. The fact that Kulbak's poem remained unfinished and unpublished until 1931 may even be the basis for Bergelson's characterization of Ventsl as a poet who fails to complete his great poem about Berlin.

If Jussuf Abbo is already highly orientalized in Kulbak's poem, then Bergelson's parodic transformation of him into "the hairy painter Babo" was a further reduction of his artistic persona to racial features. While Lasker-Schüler's poem "Jussuf Abbo" openly adopts an oriental literary posture, Kulbak's and Bergelson's depictions of Abbo can be seen as an attempt to distance themselves from the oriental label while reaffirming its validity. Just as German Jews labeled Jewish immigrants from Eastern Europe as Ostjuden to mitigate their own orientalized characterization within German society, Kulbak and Bergelson also orientalized their Palestinian Jewish colleague Jussuf Abbo in order to westernize their own identity. This shift of the oriental marker from Ostjude to the Arab-Jew foreshadowed the later redefinition of the term "mizrahi" in the future State of Israel, in which Yiddish-speaking Jews of Eastern European descent obtained cultural hegemony partly by negating their own oriental status through such means as suppressing their mother tongue (Yiddish) and reapplying the oriental label to Arab-Jewish immigrants in Palestine.

## IV

The Yiddish literary canon immortalized Abbo, yet he remains objectified and orientalized within it. To rediscover his presence, agency, and voice, one must turn to his own work.

A drawing from 1929 in the recent Jussuf Abbo exhibition at the Spengler Museum in Hannover (Orchard 2019: 63 [Kat.-Nr 57]) showcases two of his most typical motifs: a large, naked female figure seated in the center and a smaller, abstract figure reclining at the bottom left. While most of Abbo's recumbent figures are women, this one lacks any feminine traits. Next to this figure is an abstract object, perhaps a sketchbook or a small drawing stand. The figure's slightly raised posture, as well as the position of its arm and its concentrated gaze, suggest it is drawing the larger figure. The smaller figure thus seems to be the artist, perhaps drawing himself from a mirror behind the seated model.

The drawing has two brief inscriptions in Abbo's handwriting (See Fig. 18.1.). The bottom inscription provides the exact date of the work: "J. Abbo. 11.12.1929." The upper inscription, however, surprisingly left unmentioned in the catalog, is the title of the piece: "Zikhronot be'leylot ha'yeush," Hebrew for "Memories in the Nights of Despair". Whether the title was given in 1929 in reference to memories of an earlier period in Berlin or added later while recalling the period in which it was drawn, the temporality it creates corresponds to that of Kulbak and Bergelson: Berlin of the 1920s is being remembered by the artist during a period of despair. The title's use of Hebrew (instead of German, for example) may be seen as an intimate gesture towards the group of Yiddish writers, all fluent in Hebrew as well, who were part of Abbo's milieu during that short-lived period.

Today, Berlin once again accommodates a literary, cultural, and political scene in which concepts such as Hebrew, Muslim, Jewish, Yiddish, Oriental, Arabic, and Semitic await new meanings, connotations, and associations. The ways that these concepts intersected and interacted with one another in the past – in Berlin and elsewhere – remains to be rediscovered, reinterpreted, and reappropriated in order to question binary oppositions and subvert hegemonic discourses of division and conquest. The hybrid, fluid, and non-binary potential of these concepts remains to be explored.

*Fig. 18.1: A drawing by Yussuf Abbo*

Source: Spengler Museum in Hannover

## References

Abbo, Sebastian (2019): "Foreword". In: Dorothe Schöne (ed.), Jussuf Abbo. Kunsthaus Dahlem, Berlin. 8. November 2019 – 20. Januar 2020, Köln: Wienand, p. 6.

Ahmed, Aischa (2020): Arabische Präsenzen in Deutschland um 1900 : biografische Interventionen in die deutsche Geschichte, Bielefeld: transcript.

Bechtel, Delphine (2001): La Renaissance culturelle juive en Europe centrale et orientale 1897–1930: langue, littérature et construction nationale, Paris: Éditions Belin.

Bergelson, Dovid (1929): "Mit eyn nakht veyniker". In: Geklibene verk, Vilnius: Vilner Farlag, pp. 189–202.

Charney, Daniel (1947): Afn shvel fun yener velt, New York.

Dogramaci, Burcu (2015): "Jussufs Gedicht für Jussuf Abbo". In: Hajo Jahn (ed.), Der Blaue Reiter ist gefallen. Else-Lasker-Schüler-Jubiläumsalmanach, Wuppertal: Hammer, pp. 275–77.

Faerber, Meir (1982): "Ein unbekanntes Gedicht Else Lasker-Schülers". In: Literatur und Kritik 167/168 (Salzburg), pp. 84–85.

Hever-Chybowski, Tal (2020): "Orientals in Berlin". In: Stadtsprachen Magazin 16 (December 2020, Berlin).

Kulbak, Moyshe (1921): "Jussuf Abbo". In: Jussuf Abbo: Plastik, Zeichnungen, Radierungen, Hannover: Galerie von Gravens, pp. 3–4.

Kulbak, Moyshe (1979 [1931]): "Disner tshayld harold". In: Gut iz der mentsh: Geklibene lider un poemes, Moscow: Sovetski Pisatel, pp. 174–207.

Lasker-Schüler, Else (1923). "Jussuf Abbo". In: Plastik – Aquarelle – Farbige Zeichnungen – Zeichnungen. Graphisches Kabinett Georg Maulhardt Hamburg. Ausstellung 15. Juli bis 15. August 1923. – Lyrik.

Mayzel, Nakhmen (1937): "Mir forn farbay Berlin". In: Literarishe bleter (Warsaw) 43 (702), October 22nd, pp. 689–690.

Orchard, Karin (2019): Jussuf Abbo. Skulpturen, Zeichnungen, Druckgrafik. Verzeichnis der Bestände der Sprengel Museum Hannover. 4. Dezember 2019 – 29. März 2020, Hannover: Sprengel Museum Hannover.

Pinsker, Shachar M. (2018), A Rich Brew: How Cafés Created Modern Jewish Culture, New York: New York University Press.

Said, Edward W. (1979): Orientalism, New York: Vintage, 1979.

Schöne, Dorothe (2019a), ed.: Jussuf Abbo. Kunsthaus Dahlem, Berlin. 8. November 2019 – 20. Januar 2020, Köln: Wienand.

Schöne, Dorothe (2019b): "Jussuf Abbo – A Biography". In: Schöne 2019a, pp. 40–51.

Valencia, Heather (1995): Else Lasker-Schüler und Abraham Nochem Stenzel. Eine unbekannte Freundschaft, Frankfurt & New York: Campus Verlag.

# Part 5: International Encounters in Education

# 19. Arabic Sciences in the Humboldtian Cosmos
## Potentials for the Humboldt Forum

*Detlev Quintern*

### Alexander von Humboldt and the history of science

Alexander von Humboldt has been little studied as a historian of science. This holds especially true for his intensive studies on Arabic sciences and their impact on the genesis of modern sciences in Europe. For centuries, from the late 8th to the 16th century, Arabic was the lingua franca of science, medicine, and philosophy around the Mediterranean and beyond, in Central Asia, parts of the Indian subcontinent, and Africa, including regions south of the Sahara. Humboldt was aware of this. Accordingly, in his works on the history of science, he paid great attention to Arabic contributions and the development of universal sciences. It is surprising that the Humboldt Forum only marginally covers the life, research, and oeuvre of its eponym. There would be no shortage of museum objects, let alone archival materials.

The Humboldtian "Zeitgeist" also calls for discussing its imperial-colonial context. Humboldt was forward-looking, foreseeing the downfall of the old colonial powers, which he deemed inevitable, as they were based on slavery. He criticized the enslavement of Africans in Cuba but refrained from criticizing slave-holder U.S. President Jefferson, whom he met in 1804. Humboldt himself should be discussed anew in post-and decolonial contexts – an inspiring task that would match the mission of a contemporary Humboldt Forum.

Given Humboldt's work as a historian of sciences and discoveries, what scientific conditions enabled European 'discoveries', especially in the Americas? Historic Arabic sciences were of outstanding importance. Humboldt found that Arabic sciences, mainly in their Latin translation, had contributed to the ability of Spaniards and Portuguese to sail the open seas around 1500. In his own travels to Central Asia and the Caspian Sea in 1829, he appreciated precise Arabic astronomical, geographical, and cartographic data, comparing Arabic geographical coordinates with contemporary measurements and finding them still valid (Quintern 2018). NB this was at a time when Central Asia was as yet more or less terra incognita for Europeans.

The first section of this paper focuses on the appropriation of Arabic knowledge by the old colonial powers Spain and Portugal for the purpose of world conquest. We then look at Humboldt's appreciation of Arabic science, especially geography and cartography. Finally, we discuss the potential of Humboldt's universal history of science for the Humboldt Forum. But first, let us look briefly at the historical context of Humboldt's voyage to America.

## Humboldt in the historical context of the long imperial 19th century

Humboldt's research journey to the Americas began as the old Spanish and French empires were going into obvious decline. Landing in Venezuela, Humboldt soon witnessed the effects of the Haitian Revolution (Quintern 2005). The revolutionary wave reached South America, initiating the anticolonial independence movement under Simón Bolívar, whom Humboldt met twice, in Rome and Paris in 1804 and 1805. The Haitian Revolution, conducted by self-liberated slaves and won in 1804, created the first free republic in the territories under European colonial rule, and many white French settlers and slaveholders subsequently fled to Cuba and Florida. Meanwhile, Egypt saw the French expelled in 1805. As elaborated by Edward Said (Said 2003), the so-called "civilizing mission" headed by the French had, in fact, been a failed military attempt to conquer the land on the Nile.

Humboldt was an observant witness to these historical upheavals and had to move carefully amidst them. He and his companion, the French botanist Aimé Bonpland, had initially intended to join the French imperial adventure in Tunis in November 1798 (Humboldt Chronology), but both they and Prussian diplomacy had been well advised to refrain from joining.

Unlike other European explorers before and after them, Humboldt and his companion did not have indigenous companions carry them to the places they later claimed to have discovered, though they did have them carry their equipment. European traveling researchers relied heavily on colonial infrastructures, which would pave the way for colonial conquest. One of those carried through the tropics by indigenous companions (in Central-West-Africa in the mid-1850s) was Adolf Bastian (Quintern 2014), sometimes called the father of ethnology and founder of the Ethnological Museum in Berlin, whose collections are to be partly integrated into the permanent exhibition of the Humboldt Forum.

## Alexander Humboldt as a historian of discoveries

The meticulously, scientifically planned imperial conquest of Egypt in 1798 was accompanied by acquiring Arabic knowledge, especially geographic resources essential to conquering the ancient land. How could the French army have moved in Egypt without precise knowledge of the geography of the land on the Nile? Ancient Greco-Roman sources did not offer reliability. More recent sourced were available almost exclusively in Arabic, including the historical and geographical account of Egypt and Cairo during the Mamluks by Maqrīzī (1364–1442). Maqrīzī's study, *al-Khiṭaṭ*, was translated and compiled for the *Description de l'Égypte* (Brett 2015: 245). In its earliest version, it served the French Conquest as a kind of handbook before it was later published (1809–1822).

While in Paris in 1820, Humboldt took Persian lessons from the famous orientalists Silvestre de Sacy and Andréa de Nerciain (Sundermann 2019). During these years, Humboldt wanted to go on a research journey through Central Asia and Persia to India. In the end, the journey could not be undertaken, after the British East India Company failed to grant permission. Political circumstances and other obstacles had again foiled Humboldt's intentions to explore territories little known to Europeans. His studies and exchanges especially with orientalists in Paris, however, were also important with regard to his journey to Russia, Siberia, and Central Asia, which he had also long planned and was finally able to realize in 1829.

Humboldt's Persian teacher De Sacy recognized the treasures of knowledge that lay dormant in Oriental, primarily Arabic, scientific writings. At the same time, he lamented the lack of access to them. He considered the Arabs "our [the Europeans', D.Q.] first masters in the mathematical sciences, in some of the physical sciences, such as chemistry, medicine, botany, and in various branches of philosophy"[1] (De Sacy 1810: 9).

Humboldt's "History of the Discovery of America" – the original title of the first French edition being "Examen critique de l'histoire de la géographie du nouveau continent et des progrès de l'astronomie nautique au quinzième et seizième siècle" – was published in Paris from 1834 to 1838 after his Russia-Central Asia voyage. In it, Humboldt discussed the Arabic sources already available to him in Latin. The later German edition of 1836 to 1852 deviates slightly from the original, and I will mainly refer to that edition here.

Unlike Goethe, Humboldt did not write in Arabic, instead transcribing Arabic words into Latin. It is interesting to study the contexts in which Arabic written words are used in Humboldt's oeuvre. He had a strong interest in etymology and other philological questions, drawing on sources available to him regardless of their geographical, cultural, or linguistic provenance. Ancient etymologies from Mesopotamia were just as important to him as Chinese, Persian, or Arabic sources. Exploring the etymology of "*Naphta*", he noted that the anthropogeographer

1 Original text in French: "Les Arabes, disciples des Grecs, et nos premiers maîtres dans les sciences mathématiques, dans quelques-unes des sciences physiques, comme la chimie, la médicine, la botanique, et dans diverses branches de la philosophie"

Mas'ūdī from the first half of the 10th century knew of the burning fields near Baku, unlike the later 12th century cartographer Idrīsī (Humboldt, 1858: 509). This exemplifies how closely Humboldt studied and compared Arabic sources, especially in questions of mineralogy and mining. Humboldt found "*Naphta*" to go back to old Persian, and in such cases, Humboldt would indeed include individual words in Arabic in his oeuvre.

In his "History of the Discovery of America", Humboldt wrote about Arabic sailors departing into the Atlantic from Arabic Lisbon in 1147 A.D. to meet an unknown fate. He traced the Arabic plural "Almagrurim", as those lost souls were known, albeit rendered in an incorrect transcription, to the root of the verb "Ġarra" (غرّ), which he translated as "he has deceived", suggesting "those led astray" (Humboldt, I, 1836–1852: 46). Danger resonates in the semantics of the word. Those well-documented sea journeys leave no doubt about the fate of the sailors, who never returned.

Also significant to Humboldt in the history of discovering the Americas was magnetism, including the use of the compass. The orientalist and sinologist Julius von Klaproth – founder of the Asian Society [*Société Asiatique*] in Paris in 1821 – wrote to Humboldt that the French word for compass, "boussole", could be traced back to the Arabic mouassala (بوصلة/موصلة) (Klaproth 1834: 27). This etymology remains unclear. Nautical texts from the late 15th and early 16th centuries often refer to the compass in terms of the compass needle as "âbra" (ابرة). Yet the nautical compass almost certainly reached Europe through Arabic navigation techniques in the Indian Ocean (Billig 2016: 134). Applying the compass and astronavigation was a pivotal requirement to navigate the open seas. The Portuguese and the Spanish needed to assimilate the Arabic nautical sciences and to learn to use the compass and other instruments, such as sea astrolabes, to conquer unknown lands overseas, where they suspected spices, sugar, gold, and cotton. When the Portuguese looted the North-African city Ceuta in 1415, their plunder included Arabic sea charts and nautical instruments. I have discussed the colonial robbery of Arabic science and technology elsewhere (Quintern 2020). The legendary Portuguese explorer Vasco da Gama, who circumnavigated Africa at the end of the 15th century, was guided by Arab seafarers along the East-African coast and then towards India, introducing piracy and colonial conquest to the Indian Ocean.

Humboldt even compared Arabic names translated into Latin, such as Iceland (*Lislandeh*), with the original names in Arabic geographical and cartographical works from the middle of the 12th century (Humboldt, I, 1836–1852: 371). Regional maps drawn by Idrīsī from the mid-12th century showing the Northern coasts of Germany included such fascinating details as the number of inhabitants living in the seaports. Humboldt was well aware of the scientific value of historical Arabic maps and geographical reports, including the coordinates determined with the help of trigonometry, and he received precise coordinates for his journey to Samarkand and Bukhara, computed by al-Bīrūnī in the first half of the 11th century, through the French orientalist and historian of science Louis-Amélie Sédillot (Sédillot 1859).

The archival records, along with collections of scientific instruments and historic maps, would make it well worth showing Humboldt's engagement with Arab geography and cartography in a special exhibition at the Humboldt Forum discussing alternatives to Eurocentric writings of the history of science. The maps by al-Iṣṭaḫrī (d. 951 AD), for example, discussed by Humboldt concerning the geographical shape of the Caspian Sea, classified as World Documental Heritage by UNESCO and preserved at the Research Library of Gotha (Forschungsbibliothek Gotha), would open up impressive new perspectives.

One of Humboldt's intentions in writing his history of the discovery of America may "have been [to highlight] the admirable education of men like Christopher Columbus" (Knobloch 2018, 129). But how well did this prepare Columbus for the job? Only relatively recently has he been shown to have lacked the basic scientific knowledge and skill to determine the latitude and longitude (Sezgin 2007). In fact, on the open sea, latitudes were easier to determine than longitudes, yet Columbus managed to miscalculate the latitude data for Cuba by 20 degrees (Billig 2016, 266).

As detailed by Humboldt, Columbus had compared latitude measurements he had previously taken along the West African coast on early voyages for the Portuguese in 1482–1483 with those made by the 9th-century Maʾmūn geographer and astronomer al-Farġānī (Latin *Alfraganus*) (Bucher 2006: 84). Humboldt assumed that Columbus' miscalculations were based on mistaking Arabic for Italian miles (Humboldt 1836–1852, 83–84, Sezgin 2007: 162). One degree from the equator (the length of one degree in the meridian) – a crucial distance for measuring the circumference of the Earth – had been determined to be 56 2/3 miles in the first third of the 9th century, during the reign of al-Maʾmūn in Baghdad. This corresponds almost exactly to the actual value of 111.321 km at the equator.

However, Humboldt noted the Spanish and Italian lenguas were much shorter than the Arabian miles. (83–84; 521–523). Columbus' cartographic image of the world corresponded to that of Martin Behaim and Waldseemüller, as visualized on globes and world maps at the end of the 15th century. The American continent did not appear in those early maps, even if they were more realistic than the preceding mythological and eschatological European ones. Columbus' familiar cartographic figure of the world was borrowed from the Arab cartographic worldview, depicted in the mid-12th-century by al-Idrīsī, who most probably followed the Maʾmūn geographers and their world map (Quintern 2020).

Alexander von Humboldt was aware that al-Idrisi's world map (ca. 1154) was the first to depict the triangular shape of Africa, which was also how it was to be circumnavigated. Like all Arab maps, the world map is oriented towards the south. This also applies to the European maps, which were based on or copied from Arabic maps. The

Fra Mauro World Map (ca. 1450), studied by Alexander Humboldt, is an example of the European adaption of Arabic knowledge and maps.

*Fig. 19.1: Al-Idrisi's World Map*

Nuzhat al-mushtāq fī ikhtirāq al-āfāq (c. 1250–1325), Département des manuscrits. Arabe 2221, fols. 3v-4r. Bibliothèque nationale de France.
Source: Wikipedia (https://commons.wikimedia.org/wiki/File:Al-Idrisi%27s_world_map.JPG)

*Fig. 19.2: Fra Mauro's World Map*

In Arabic tradition, the World Map of the Venetian Monk Fra Mauro (ca. 1450) is oriented towards the South and encompasses roughly 3.000 legends. Including the frame, the huge map encompasses 2.3 x 2.3 m. Many Arabic geographic and topographic names and terms are of Arabic origin. Alexander Humboldt assumed an Arabic origin for Antillia (Antilles) (Crone 1938) and for "Diab" on the southern tip of Africa.
Source: Biblioteca Nazionale Marciana, Venice. Image: Wikipedia (https://en.wikipedia.org/wiki/Fra_Mauro_map)

After his return from the Americas, Humboldt not only processed and published parts of his scientific findings, but he also worked intensively on writing the history of the discovery of America. He distinguished himself as a historian of science and discoveries, following a long-term historical, universal, and comparative historical method. Although Humboldt certainly did not question the European legend of having discovered the Americas, leaving aside the much earlier landing in Newfoundland by the Vikings, a venture not yet enabled by astronomical-mathematical methods and the mastery of nautical instruments, which does not in any way diminish the Vikings as brilliant seafarers, the questions he outlined remain relevant today to revising the Eurocentric perspective.

Humboldt studied the history of the Vikings from the book of Frähn (1823), a translation of Ibn Faḍlān's early-10th-century travel account. He was especially interested in the Vikings' settlement in Central Asia, where the Volga empties into the Caspian Sea. Arab-Persian geographers had charted the geography there since the 9th century AD. Cooperation between the ruling Sāmānids in Bukhara and the 'Abbāsids in Baghdad, both of whom followed the more enlightened and tolerant school of the Mu'tazila, initiated a long flourishing period in sciences and culture. While the language of science was ostensibly Arabic, Persian was often preferred in literature and poetry.

Trade and knowledge relations extended along the Silk Road by sea and land to China, the Baltic, and Africa. Chinese and Mongolian miniature painters illustrated fables written in Arabic as late as the 14th century (Waley and Titley 1975: 49). The Silk Road, which led via Tashkent, Samarkand, Bukhara, and Baghdad to Antioch, the Levant, and Palestine and from there to Europe, saw the migration of far fewer goods than ideas, philosophies, religions, sciences, and knowledge practices. One route led via the Volga and other river systems to Russia and the Baltic Sea.

Humboldt assumed that the wide distribution of Arabic coins to the far-off Baltic coast could be traced back to the extensive Arab trade relations during this period (Humboldt 1847: 254). In fact, Arabic coins have even been found on German islands in the North Sea. Trade relations were not infrequently preceded by scientific and cultural exchange.

Chinese physicians, for example, learned Arabic in Baghdad in the early 10th century. During this period, the envoy Ibn Faḍlān also traveled to the estuary of the Volga on the Caspian Sea; his reports contain rare knowledge about the Volga Bulgars and the Turkish-Judeo Khazars settling on the Caspian Sea, among whom Nestorians and Muslims also lived.

Humboldt refers to Ibn Faḍlān when he writes of the extensive Arab trade: "A myriad of Arab coins, all from the Abbassid khalifs and the emirs of the Samanid dynasty, are found spread by that route and buried [in] shallow depths of the earth" (Humboldt, 1844: 471). He probably brought home to Berlin some of those Arabic coins, though so far, I have yet to locate them. They would be appealing museum exhibits in the context of early Arabo-European trade relations, as well as attesting to the Vikings' long-standing role as east-west mediators.

Humboldt studied the coins by reading Joachim Frähn, who had translated the fragments of Ibn Faḍlān and published them at the St. Petersburg Academy. Frähn had systematized thousands of findings of Arabic coins before becoming director of the Asian Museum in St. Petersburg. His study was printed in St. Petersburg in 1823, entitled "Ibn Foszlan's and Other Arabs' Reports on the Russians..." (Frähn 1823).

Of special interest for Humboldt were the Idrīsī world map and the 70 regional maps of the Atlas, dating back to the mid-12th century. Humboldt underlined that Arabic maps were the first to show that Africa was circumnavigable. Contrary to the assumed world maps of Ptolemy, which misrepresented the Caspian Sea as extending from North to East, the Idrīsī maps correctly depicted the Caspian Sea as extending from North to South. The geographical figures developed on the maps of Idrīsī in Sicily lived on into the middle of the 18th century, e.g., in the maps of French cartographer Jean Baptiste Bourguignon D'Anville (1697–1782) that showed large parts of Africa in 1749. The maps show several versions of the course of the Nile, including the Nile as mapped out by Idrīsī. The Nile map by al-Ḫwārizmī is the oldest known Arabic map, dating back to 1037–1039 (Quintern 2020).

The long history of adaptation of Ma'mūnian figures and coordinates from the 9th century Abbasid period continues up to the maps of Gerardus Mercator (1512–1594). Mercator had in his library a Latin translation of al-Battānī, an astronomer and mathematical geographer from 9th century Baghdad, whose name was Latinized to Albategnius. The Ma'mūnian geographer and astronomer contributed to the further development of trigonometry and the sine theorem. The Humboldt Forum would do well to show these interconnections in the history of science along with their corresponding (nautical) instruments. At the "German Museum" [Deutsches Museum] in Munich, the permanent exhibitions integrate and visualize Arabic nautical and geographical sciences.

## The Humboldtian Cosmos: Bridging cultures, religions, and ways of living in Berlin

Moving the Humboldtian cosmos into the museum context, especially his history of sciences and discoveries, might contribute to an understanding of the history of science and discoveries beyond Eurocentric legend-building and constructions. A more universal understanding needs to enter academic curricula and schoolbooks. Museums are an alternative to two-dimensional learning methods. The aura of original, three-dimensional museum objects cannot be replaced by mere multi-media screens, hands-on electronics, or high-tech virtual realities which do not allow for the emotional perception and comprehension of how to proceed, e.g., when using actual nautical instruments. Museums are spaces for creative and communicative study and learning. The didactics of experimentation are highly motivating, especially when visitors can learn how the old instruments work, e.g., determining the latitude on land by measuring the angle of the polar star, viz., using trigonometry. This holds especially true for bridging cultures, religions, and different modes of living in multicultural, multilingual, and multireligious Berlin. A more inclusive concept that addresses the huge Arabic community in a participatory manner will bring the Humboldtian cosmos into harmony with Berlin as a cosmopolitan city.

## References


Billig, Susanne (2016) Die Karte des Piri Re'īs. Das vergessene Wissen der Araber und die Entdeckung Amerikas. C.H. Beck.

Brett, Michael (2013) Approaching African History. James Currey.

Bucher, Corina (2006) Christoph Kolumbus. Kreuzfahrer und Korsar. Primus.

Crone, Gerald Roe (1938) The Origin of the Name Antillia. The Geographical Journal 91(3) March. (London: The Royal Geographical Society, with the Institute of British Geographers) 260–262 (https://www.jstor.org/stable/1787546).

Ette, Otmar (2019) Der zweite Entdecker Amerikas. Alexander von Humboldt ist aktueller denn je. Die Zeit, September 13 (https://www.zeit.de/news/2019-09/13/alexander-von-humboldt-ist-aktueller-denn-je).

Frähn, Joachim Christian Martin (1823) Ibn Foszlan's und anderer Araber Berichte über die Russen älterer Zeit. Text und Übersetzung mit kritisch-philologischen Anmerkungen. Nebst drei Beilagen über sogenannte Russen-Stämme und Kiew, die Warenger und das Warenger-Meer, und das Land Wisu, ebenfalls nach arabischen Schriftstellern. Buchdruckerei der Akademie Saint-Petersburg.

Humboldt, Alexander von (1834–1838) Examen critique de l'histoire de la géographie du Nouveau Continent, et des progrès de l'astronomie nautique aux quinzième et seizième siècles. Librairie de Gide.

Humboldt, Alexander von (1836–1852) Kritische Untersuchungen über die historische Entwickelung der geographischen Kenntnisse von der Neuen Welt und die Fortschritte der nautischen Astronomie in dem 15ten und 16ten Jahrhundert. Aus dem Französischen von Julius Ludwig Ideler: Nicolai'sche Buchhandlung.

Humboldt, Alexander von (1847) Kosmos. Entwurf einer physischen Weltbeschreibung. Bd. 2. Cotta'scher Verlag. (http://www.deutschestextarchiv.de/humboldt_kosmos02_1847).

Humboldt, Alexander von (1858) Kosmos. Entwurf einer physischen Weltbeschreibung. Bd. 4. Cotta'scher Verlag.

Klaproth, Jullius Heinrich v. (1834) Lettre à M. A. Humboldt sur L'invention de la Bussole. Libraire Orientale de Prosper Dondey-Dupré.

Knobloch, Eberhard (2018) Wissenschaftsgeschichte. Ette, Ottmar (ed.), Alexander von Humboldt-Handbuch. Leben – Werk – Wirkung. J.B. Metzler, 127–133.

Quintern, Detlev (2017) The objects wounds. The Muzealization of Africa and the Dismembering of Colonial Violence. In: Azarin, Viviane; Gemmeke, Amber; Fink, Katharina; El Maarouf, Moulay Dris; El Nagare, Maroua; Ndogo, Samuel, Ndi Shang; Gilbert; Siegert, Nadine (eds.) Tracks and Traces of Violence. Representation and Memoralization of Violence. Views from Art, Literature, Anthropology. Münster: LIT Verlag, 299–313.

Quintern, Detlev (2018) Arabic traces in Alexander Humboldt's Kosmos and Central Asian geographies. In: Vestnik of Saint Petersburg University Asian and African Studies 10(4) 424–435 (https://doi.org/10.21638/spbu13.2018.402).

Quintern, Detlev (2019) Fuat Sezgin and The Re-writing of The History of Geography. In: ERDEM, Aralık/December 2019, Sayı (77) 1–22 (https://doi.org/10.32704/erdem.656964).

Quintern, Detlev (2020a) The Nile in Early Arabic–Islamic Maps and Sources. In: Environment and Religion in Ancient & Coptic Egypt: Sensing the Cosmos through the Eyes of the Divine: Proceedings of the 1st Egyptological Conference of the People's University of Athens (1–3 February 2017), ed. by Maravelia, Alicia/Guilhou, Nadine, Archaeopress Egyptology, 367–380.

Quintern, Detlev (2020b) From Alexander von Humboldt to Fuat Sezgin. On the discovery of America – A comparative historiography. In: F. Başar, M. Kaçar, C. Kaya & A. Z. Furat (eds.), 1st International Prof. Dr. Fuat Sezgin Symposium on History of Science in Islam Proceedings Book, 1–22. (https://iupress.istanbul.edu.tr/tr/book/1-uluslararasi-prof-dr-fuat-sezgin-islam-bilim-tarihi-sempozyumu-bildiriler-kitabi/chapter/from-alexander-von-humboldt-to-fuat-sezgin-on-the-discovery-of-america-a-comparative-historiography).

Sacy de, Silvestre (1810) Discours sur les Traductions d'Ouvrages écrits en Langues orientales, Imprimerie Impériale.

Said, Edward W. (2003) Orientalism. Western Concepts of the Orient. Penguin.

Schwarz, Ingo (ed.) Alexander von Humboldt Chronologie. Edition Humboldt Digital. Alexander von Humboldt auf Reisen – Wissenschaft aus der Bewegung. Berlin: Berlin-Brandenburgischen Akademie der Wissenschaften (https://edition-humboldt.de/chronologie/index.xql?l=de&offset=301).

Sédillot, Louis-Amélie (manuscript, before 1859): Brief von Louis-Amélie Sédillot an Alexander von Humboldt ([ante] 1859). DE-611-HS-2928881; Nachlass Alexander von Humboldt Bd. 6/2 Bl. 136–138. Biblioteka Jagiellońska, Berol. Ms. Nachlass von A. v. Humboldt, 6. Biblioteka Jagiellońska (https://jbc.bj.uj.edu.pl/dlibra/publication/361092/edition/344491/contentSchwarz).

Sezgin, Fuat (2007) Geschichte des arabischen Schrifttums. Bd. XIII: Mathematische Geographie und Kartographie im Islam und ihr Fortleben im Abendland. Autoren. Institut für Geschichte der Arabisch-Islamischen Wissenschaften an der Johann Wolfgang Goethe-Universität.

Sundermann, Werner (2018) Alexander von Humboldt und das Persische (mit einer Einführung von Christiane Reck. In: HiN – Alexander Von Humboldt Im Netz. Internationale Zeitschrift für Humboldt-Studien, 19(36) 105–109 (https://doi.org/10.18443/268).

Waley, Peter; Titley, Norah (1975) An illustrated Persian Text of Kalila and Dimna dated 707/1307-8. The British Library Journal, 1(1) 42–61.
Wood, Frances (1995) Did Marco Polo go to China? Secker and Warburg.

# 20. Ḥasan Tawfīq al-Adl (d. 1904) - Arabic Tutor and Author at the *Seminar für Orientalische Sprachen* in Berlin, 1887-1892

*Islam Dayeh*

On 10 September 1887, the twenty-five-year-old Egyptian Ḥasan Tawfīq al-ʿAdl (1862–1904), a prodigious graduate of al-Azhar and Dār al-ʿUlūm, set off for Berlin to embark on what would become a distinguished academic career. As part of an agreement between the Prussian and the Egyptian governments, he was selected to become the first native teacher of Arabic at the newly-founded *Seminar für Orientalische Sprachen* at the Berlin Friedrich-Wilhelm University (now Humboldt University). He would remain in Berlin for five years, teaching future German orientalists, diplomats, and government translators. He also engaged in the study of pedagogy, and became a prolific author and translator, researching and composing works in Arabic on a variety of themes, including child pedagogy, physical education, Arabic literary history, and the etymology of colloquial Egyptian Arabic. Ḥasan Tawfīq also composed two travelogues which provide a fascinating account of his encounter with German culture and society around the 1890s. Although these works were written primarily for an Egyptian readership and published in Cairo, many of them were either composed entirely in Berlin or had their origins during his time in Berlin.

Ḥasan Tawfīq al-ʿAdl joined numerous non-German tutors who taught their native languages and cultures at the *Seminar für Orientalische Sprachen*, and participated in research assistance and translation work. However, our understanding of their lives, activities and experiences in Berlin, and how they interacted with their German peers and amongst each other, remains limited to a few cases.[1]

1 Previous research on the lives of non-European tutors at the Seminar für Orientalische Sprachen include: Ludger Wimmelbücker, Mtoro Bin Mwinyi Bakari: Swahili Lecturer and Author in Germany (Dar al-Salam, Tanzania: Mkuki na Nyota Publishers, 2008); Katrin Bromber, 'German Colonial Administrators, Swahili Lecturers and the Promotion of Swahili at the Seminar für Orientalische Sprachen in Berlin', Sudanic Africa 15 (2004): 39–54; Astrid Brochlos, 'Das Seminar für Orientalische Sprachen an der Berliner Universität und die Japanbezogene Lehre', in Japan und Preußen (München: Iudicium-Verlag, 2002), 145–62; Holger Stoecker,

In the case of Ḥasan Tawfīq al-ʿAdl, he is generally absent from scholarly accounts of the history of orientalism in Germany. This chapter aims to shed light on this little-known figure. In particular, it will focus on the following questions: How was Ḥasan Tawfīq al-ʿAdl's work shaped by his encounter with German colonialism and scholarship? What was his experience as a native tutor of Arabic at the Berlin University? What did he teach? How was his work shaped by his time in Berlin? What impact did his work have? This chapter begins by laying out an outline of his biography, followed by an examination of his role at the *Seminar für Orientalische Sprachen* and then proceeds to give an overview of his writings, situating them in their wider historical and intellectual contexts.

***

The earliest biographical account of Ḥasan Tawfīq al-ʿAdl was written by Dār al-ʿUlūm alumnus Muḥammad ʿAbd al-Jawād (1887–1964) in his *Taqwīm Dār al-ʿUlūm* , or the Dār al-ʿUlūm almanac, a documentary history of the institution written on the occasion of its 75th anniversary (1872–1947).[2] ʿAbd al-Jawād's account draws on the information gleaned from Ḥasan Tawfīq's travel reports, documents of the Dār al-ʿUlūm (many of which are no longer extant), newspaper announcements as well as oral testimonies from people who knew Ḥasan Tawfīq. ʿAbd al-Jawād also reproduced several rare photographs of Ḥasan Tawfīq al-ʿAdl (see fig. 20.1, 20.3, and 20.4, below). A further valuable source for the reconstruction of Ḥasan Tawfīq's life, particularly in relation to his role at the *Seminar für Orientalische Sprachen*, are the diplomatic documents preserved in the German State Archives. These documents consist of correspondences between the Prussian and Egyptian governments as well as correspondences between Ḥasan Tawfīq and the director of the *Seminar für Orientalische Sprachen*, the German orientalist Eduard Sachau (1845–1930). They provide important information about the administrative and official contexts of his employment.[3]

Previous research on Ḥasan Tawfīq al-ʿAdl has focused on particular aspects of his life. Aischa Ahmed, for example, examines the modes of Arab representation and agency in Berlin around the turn of the century, and takes Ḥasan Tawfīq al-ʿAdl's

---

'Das Seminar für Orientalische Sprachen', in Kolonialmetropole Berlin: Eine Spurensuche, ed. Ulrich van der Heyden (Berlin: Berlin Edition, 2002), 118.

2 Muḥammad ʿAbd al-Jawād, Taqwīm Dār al-ʿUlūm: Al-ʿadad al-māsī yaṣdur li-murūr 75 ʿāman ʿalā al-madrasah 1872–1947 (Dār al-Maʿārif, 1952), 178–85. ʿAbd al-Jawād's 900-page work remains the most important source for the history of Dār al-ʿUlūm.

3 Many of these documents were compiled by Gerhard Höpp (d. 2003) as part of his pioneering research on the history of Arabs and Muslims in Germany. The Höpp Nachlass has been digitised and is preserved at the Leibniz-Zentrum Moderner Orient. I wish to thank the ZMO for providing me access to these documents.

work *al-Riḥla ilā Birlīn* as a case in point.[4] Hilary Kalmbach looks at certain aspects of the life of Ḥasan Tawfīq in the context of the social and cultural history of Dār al-ʿUlūm.[5] Moreover, Ḥasan Tawfīq is often credited with having a pioneering role in the development of modern Arab literary history and pedagogy, a theme which will be discussed below. However, a comprehensive biographical account that brings together the documentary sources with an overview of his works remains lacking. This article aims to provide a general sketch of his biography as well as the ways he is remembered (and forgotten) today.

***

Ḥasan Tawfīq al-ʿAdl was born in Alexandria in 1862 and moved with his family to Dimietta (Dimyāṭ) in 1874. He memorised the Qur'ān at an early age, under the tutelage of his father, who was chief judge in the court of Damietta. In 1875, he moved to Cairo and began his studies at al-Azhar, graduating in 1882/83.[6] At around that time, ʿAlī Mubārak (1824–1893), Egypt's Minister of Education, was preparing the grounds for the creation of a government teacher training college that would meet the demands created by the recent expansion of European-influenced civil schools. Dār al-ʿUlūm, as it would be called, was founded in 1882 and integrated Islamic and Arabic knowledge with European disciplines, attracting many reform-minded Azhari graduates who promoted European subjects and pedagogies. Having just graduated from al-Azhar and earned the religious title *Shaykh*, Ḥasan Tawfīq enrolled in Dār al-ʿUlūm in the year it was founded and witnessed the beginnings of this new institution. (Five years later, he would witness the beginnings of a very different kind of educational institution in Berlin). At Dār al-ʿUlūm, he continued to study the religious and philological sciences, along with some of the subjects that had no longer been taught at al-Azhar, such as geography, history, mathematics, and chemistry.[7] Among his teachers at Dār al-ʿUlūm was the prominent literary scholar Ḥusayn al-Marṣafī (1815–1890). Some of the teachers at Dār al-ʿUlūm had taught at al-Azhar before, and many of the students were, like Ḥasan Tawfīq, graduates of al-Azhar. This explains why he continued to study with some of his teachers

4 Aischa Ahmed, Arabische Präsenzen in Deutschland um 1900: Biografische Interventionen in die deutsche Geschichte (Bielefeld: transcript Verlag, 2020), 71–90.

5 Hilary Kalmbach, Islamic Knowledge and the Making of Modern Egypt (Cambridge University Press, 2020).

6 As part of the employment procedure at the *Seminar für Orientalische Sprachen*, Ḥasan Tawfīq produced a curriculum vitae, which was presented to the German consul, who then forwarded it to Eduard Sachau. See Nachlass Höpp, 07.01.

7 During his time at Dār al-ʿUlūm, the curriculum consisted of the following subjects: exegesis of the Qur'ān, Islamic law, Arabic philology, geography, mathematics, geometry, chemistry, physics, and Arabic orthography. See ʿAbd al-Jawād, Taqwīm Dār al-ʿUlūm, 19.

from al-Azhar, receiving *ijāzāt* (educational certificates) from them while he was enrolled in Dār al-ʿUlūm.[8] Moreover, Ḥasan Tawfīq began taking French lessons at the Shaykh Ṣāliḥ night school together with his close friend and colleague Muḥammad Sharīf Salīm (1861–1925).[9] In 1887, Ḥasan Tawfīq graduated from Dār al-ʿUlūm, and was the only graduate that year.

By graduating from Dār al-ʿUlūm, Shaykh Ḥasan Tawfīq also earned the civic title *effendi* (sir) and, from then on, he would often combine the two titles, *shaykh* and *effendi*, in his publications, indicating that he had joined the class of reform-minded al-Azhar graduates who were suitable for employment in Egypt's growing civil schools. Yet, as fate would have it, Ḥasan Tawfīq would never teach at any of these civil schools.

In 1887, as Ḥasan Tawfīq was preparing for his final examination at Dār al-ʿUlūm, the Prussian ministry of education and foreign ministry were jointly finalising their plans for a new educational institute in Berlin that would prepare German colonial officials for foreign service. Its emphasis was to be on practical training, with a particular focus on teaching the languages of the areas in which Germany had colonial or commercial interests. It was also envisioned that the languages in question would be taught by a native speaker. In that same year, the German foreign ministry sent an official letter to the ruler of Egypt, the Khedive Tawfīq (reigned from 1879–1892), requesting the employment of an Arabic teacher who can teach Egyptian Arabic at the recently established *Seminar für Orientalische Sprachen* in Berlin. Ḥasan Tawfīq was chosen for the task and was sent off to Berlin soon after his graduation.

It is not obvious why Ḥasan Tawfīq was selected, particularly given his young age and lack of prior teaching experience. In a 1953 essay published in the journal *al-Hilāl*, entitled "Ḥasan Tawfīq Al-ʿAdl: The Azhari who met Bismarck", the author, Aḥmad ʿAṭṭiyyatullah, comments that al-Azhar and Dār al-ʿUlūm had indeed produced many competent graduates, including prominent senior figures, such as ʿAbd

---

8 Muḥammad ʿAbd al-Jawād mentions that Ḥasan Tawfīq earned certificates from Shaykh Ibrahim al-Saqqā (d. 1289/1872) in 1297/1879, Shaykh Ḥasan al-ʿAdawī (1221–1303/1806-1886) in 1297/1879, Shaykh Muḥammad al-Inbābī (1240–1313/1824-1896) in 1298/1880, and Shaykh Muḥammad al-Shanqīṭī (1245–1322/1829-1904) in 1298/1880. See Muḥammad ʿAbd al-Jawād, 'Ḥasan Tawfīq Al-ʿAdl', al-Kitāb, no. July (1947): 1374. Al-Inbābī served as Shaykh al-Azhar from 1886 to 1895.

9 After graduating from Dār al-ʿUlūm, Muḥammad Sharīf Salīm was sent to Paris in 1888. Similar to Ḥasan Tawfīq, he composed a *Riḥla* comprising an account of his time in France. He returned to Dār al-ʿUlūm in 1894 (two years after Ḥasan Tawfīq's return to Cairo) and would also teach pedagogy. See ʿAbd al-Jawād, Taqwīm Dār al-ʿUlūm, 150–51. Other colleagues of Ḥasan Tawfīq's cohort, who were sent to Europe for further education, included Muḥammad Najīb Ḥatāta, who was sent to the University of Exeter, England, and Zaki Muḥammad al-Muhandis, who was sent to the University of Reading, England. See Taqwīm, 153–55.

al-Jawād 'Abd al-'Āl, Ḥifnī Nāṣif, Muṣṭafā Ṭuḥūm, and Sulṭān Muḥammad, but, he asserted, it was the young Ḥasan Tawfīq who was the most talented and ambitious of his generation.[10] In hindsight, this may well be true if we consider how prolific he was despite his relatively short-life (he died at the age of 42). There is no doubt that his teachers at al-Azhar and Dār al-'Ulūm saw great potential in Ḥasan Tawfīq and would have vouched for him. On the other hand, the fact that he was young and had no prior experience does not seem to have been a concern for the German officials. In fact, several other native language tutors at the *Seminar für Orientalische Sprachen* were similarly young and had no prior teaching experience.[11] It seems safe to suggest that the German officials approved of Ḥasan Tawfīq not necessarily because of his knowledge of the religious and philological sciences he had studied at al-Azhar and Dār al-'Ulūm (the point stressed in the aforementioned *Hilāl* essay) but rather because he was a "civilised" shaykh who could teach the native spoken Egyptian Arabic. This would become evident in how teaching was carried out at the *Seminar für Orientalische Sprachen*, as we shall see below.

For the twenty-five-year-old Ḥasan Tawfīq, this was an opportunity that he was eager to embrace. In addition to his teaching duties, he was also expected to study pedagogy. He would join the many Egyptians who were sent to Europe on government-sponsored study-missions since the time of Muḥammad Ali, including the reform-minded scholars Rifā'a Rāfi' al-Ṭahṭāwī (1801–73) and the aforementioned 'Alī Mubārak. In the case of al-Ṭahṭāwī, he spent five years in Paris (1826–1831), before returning to Egypt for a career as an educator, reformer, and translator. He wrote an account of his time in Paris, *Takhlīṣ al-ibrīz fī talkhīs bārīz* (1834), which encapsulated the national spirit that shaped Ḥasan Tawfīq and his generation. Ḥasan Tawfīq's path, as exemplified in his account of Berlin, was to a great extent already paved by

10 Aḥmad 'Aṭṭiyyatullah, 'Ḥasan Tawfīq al-'Adl: Al-Azharī alladhī qābal Bismārk' [Ḥasan Tawfīq Al-'Adl: The Azhari who met Bismarck], al-Hilāl, no. 6 (1953): 72.

11 Regarding the African tutors, many of whom were young when they arrived at the *Seminar für Orientalische Sprachen*, Sara Pugach writes: "The first, and most significant, of the Africans' duties involved standing next to a German coworker and mimicking difficult pronunciations .... *Lektoren* were considered invaluable but not because of their linguistic knowledge. Instead, they were prized for the purely physical ability to make certain sounds. Their worth to the developing science of phonetics in particular was assessed not on merit or personal skill but on the movement of vocal organs". See Sara Pugach, Africa in Translation: A History of Colonial Linguistics in Germany and Beyond, 1814–1945 (Ann Arbor, MI: University of Michigan Press, 2012), 148–49.

al-Ṭahṭāwī.[12] What distinguished Ḥasan Tawfīq's study-mission, however, was that it was the first of its kind to Germany.

***

When the *Seminar für Orientalische Sprachen* opened its doors on 27 October 1887, the academic study of Arabic and Islam had long existed at the Friedrich-Wilhelms-Universität in Berlin, but it was a handmaid to classical philology and Biblical studies.[13] In contrast, the *Seminar für Orientalische Sprachen* was to "teach practical knowledge for aims that lie outside the area of philology".[14] While building on the expertise already at the university, the *Seminar für Orientalische Sprachen* was by no means to be in competition with oriental studies. It was to remain independent from the existing chair of oriental studies, with its links to Biblical studies, theology, and classical philology.

Germany's entry into the ranks of the colonial powers from the mid-1880s played a major role in shaping the colonial character of the *Seminar für Orientalische Sprachen*. The lack of expertise and language knowledge of the colonised countries was increasingly felt. It was the Chancellor Otto von Bismarck himself who called for the establishment of the *Seminar für Orientalische Sprachen*, particularly following the Berlin Africa Conference in 1884–85.[15]

The *Seminar* was under the direct administration of the Prussian government and the German Empire (*Reichskanzleramt*). It was to be housed at the Friedrich-Wilhelm University but did not become part of it, reflecting the special status it had in the Prussian educational landscape and the German foreign and colonial administration.[16] It played a significant role in the German colonization of East Africa where, besides German, Swahili came to be used as an official language.[17] The *Seminar für*

12 For example, al-Ṭahṭāwī's work was so well-known that Ḥasan Tawfīq tells his readers that there is no need to provide a long description of Alexandria because al-Ṭahṭāwī had already done so in his *Riḥla*. See Ḥasan Tawfīq al-'Adl, al-Riḥla ilā Birlīn, ed. 'Abd al-Mun'im Muḥammad Sa'īd (Cairo: Maṭba'at Dār al-Kutub wa-l-Wathā'iq al-Qawmīya bi-l-Qāhira, 2008), 50, see also 38.

13 Eberhard Seraukly, 'Zur Entwicklung der Arabistik am Seminar für Orientalische Sprachen', ed. Hannelore Bernhardt (Berlin: Humboldt-Universität, 1990), 57–63.

14 From the speech of Gustav von Goßler (1832–1902), the Prussian Minister of Culture, at the opening of the *Seminar für Orientalische Sprachen*. Quoted in Bromber, 'German Colonial Administrators, Swahili Lecturers and the Promotion of Swahili at the Seminar für Orientalische Sprachen in Berlin', 41.

15 Konrad Canis, 'Bismarck als Kolonialpolitiker', in Kolonialmetropole Berlin: Eine Spurensuche, ed. Ulrich van der Heyden (Berlin: Berlin Edition, 2002), 23–28.

16 Stoecker, 'Das Seminar für Orientalische Sprachen', 116.

17 Wimmelbücker, Mtoro Bin Mwinyi Bakari: Swahili Lecturer and Author in Germany, 28.

*Orientalische Sprachen* also taught the languages of the countries with which the Reich government had (or aspired to have) commercial, diplomatic and political relations, such as Khedival Egypt. Both the Prussian colonial administration and Khedive Tawfīq, whose father Khedive Ismā'īl had been removed by the British, had a common interest in strengthening commercial, educational, and political ties, and to stop or weaken the British colonial presence on the African continent.[18] It seems that Ḥasan Tawfīq swiftly became aware of the political stakes in his mission and the role that was expected of him, and he acted accordingly.

Thus, before leaving Egypt, Ḥasan Tawfīq met Khedive Tawfīq himself, who decorated him with the Majīdī Medal of the Fifth Order (*al-Nīshān al-Majīdī al-Khāmis*) a symbol of trust and encouragement. He also met the minister of education, Yaqub Artin (1842–1919). A grand farewell ceremony was organised by the Ministry of Education, with notable attendants from the government, al-Azhar and Dār al-'Ulūm.[19] On 13 September 1887, Ḥasan Tawfīq embarked on the steam ship (vapour) from Alexandria, heading for Trieste, and from there to Vienna and then Berlin. During his brief stop in Vienna, he met the 13-year-old 'Abbās Ḥilmī and the 12-year-old Muḥammad 'Alī, Khedive Tawfīq's two sons, who had been sent to study in Vienna.[20] He would later accompany them on their visit of King Friedrich Wilhelm in Berlin.[21]

***

Ḥasan Tawfīq arrived in Berlin on 20 September 1887. Eduard Sachau, the director of the *Seminar für Orientalische Sprachen*, welcomed al-'Adl at the Berlin Train Station and brought him to his accommodation.[22] Sachau, who had been a professor at the Berlin University since 1876, was appointed as director in August 1887 and remained in this position until 1928. Ḥasan Tawfīq initially stayed at a place which he called "the mixed school" (*al-madrasa al-mukhṭalaṭa*), because it was a place where students of various foreign backgrounds lived and interacted with one another.[23] Sachau appointed a guide for him who knew some Arabic until Ḥasan Tawfīq began to learn German.

18 Canis, 'Bismarck als Kolonialpolitiker', 26–27.

19 Ḥasan Tawfīq provides a detailed account of the ceremony, including the poetry and speeches that were delivered. al-'Adl, al-Riḥla ilā Birlīn, 28–30.

20 al-'Adl, 72–73.

21 'Aṭṭiyyatullah, 'Ḥasan Tawfīq al-'Adl: Al-Azharī alladhī qābal Bismārk', 72–74.

22 al-'Adl, Al-Riḥla ilā Birlīn, 76–77.

23 Ḥasan Tawfīq would later become unhappy about this accommodation and complained about the high cost of rent. See Nachlass Höpp, 07.01.

Ḥasan Tawfīq joined a faculty of ten teachers and tutors who were appointed in 1887.[24] To facilitate language instruction, each language was taught by a German professor (deutscher Lehrer) and a native tutor (eingeborener Lektor). The German professor would teach the theory of the language, whereas the lector would teach how the language is actually used.[25] Teachers, some of whom had professor titles, had a fair knowledge of the language and the country because they had worked as missionaries or with the German colonial administration prior to joining the *Seminar für Orientalische Sprachen*.

Some lectors, especially those from Africa, were brought to the *Seminar für Orientalische Sprachen* by missionaries, while others were part of an agreement of the German foreign ministry (*Auswärtiges Amt*). Lectors usually remained for a few years and often returned home. The employment of non-Europeans as tutors contradicted the sense of moral and intellectual superiority that many Europeans claimed at the time. Nonetheless, the German teachers appreciated the linguistic competence and knowledge of the non-European tutors, without which the training in "practical knowledge" would have been inconceivable.[26] This appreciation can particularly be seen in the acknowledgements in the prefaces to their works, as we will see below. The lector was expected to teach the spoken, modern form of the language, but may occasionally also teach literature and cultural subjects.

The curriculum of the *Seminar für Orientalische Sprachen* was designed in agreement with the German foreign ministry. According to this agreement, successful graduates of the *Seminar für Orientalische Sprachen* can function as translators in the foreign ministry (*Dolmetscherdienst*). The curriculum initially encompassed the teaching of the following languages: Chinese, Japanese, Hindustani, Arabic, Persian, Turkish, and Swahili.

In addition to language instruction, the *Seminar für Orientalische Sprachen* also taught so-called classes on *Realia*, which were sometimes given by the language tutors. These included: the customs and institutions of the people who speak these

---

24 These included Friedrich Rosen, teacher of Hindustani; Rudolf Lange, teacher of Japanese; Friedrich Carl Andreas, teacher of Persian; the "Missions-inspektor Pfarrer" C. G. Büttner, Lehrer of Suaheli; "Magistrats-Büreauassistent" Amin Maarbes, lector of Arabic; the Egyptian Scheick Hasan Effendi Taufik, lector of Arabic; "Kanzler-Dragoman" Martin Hartmann, teacher of Arabic; Tetzujiro Jnouyé, lector of Japanese; "Gesandtschafts-Dolmetscher" C. Arendt, teacher of Chinese; Kwe Lin and Pan Fei Sching as lectors of Chinese. Bernhard Moritz was appointed as secretary and librarian of the SOS. He would later teach Arabic. See 'Chronik der Friedrich-Wilhelms-Universität zu Berlin, 1.1887/88' (Goslar, 1888), 64–66.

25 'Chronik der Friedrich-Wilhelms-Universität zu Berlin, 1.1887/88', 64–66.

26 There were however some instances of discrimination against some Swahili lectors. See Bromber, 'German Colonial Administrators, Swahili Lecturers and the Promotion of Swahili at the Seminar für Orientalische Sprachen in Berlin', 51–52. and Stoecker, 'Das Seminar für Orientalische Sprachen', 118.

languages, as well as instruction in tropical hygiene, colonial law, geography, statistics and contemporary history of the language area (*Sprachgebiet*). The objectives of the classes were four: 1. Knowledge of the grammar and widely used vocabulary in speech and writing. 2. Training in oral and written use of the language. 3. Familiarity with "the types of documents, both public and private, which are used most frequently in relations between Europeans and Orientals". 4. Understanding of the land and the people.[27]

For the academic year 1890–91, Eduard Sachau reported that the *Seminar für Orientalische Sprachen* consisted of eleven faculty members, three of whom taught Arabic: Martin Hartmann, as teacher, and Ḥasan Tawfīq and Amīn Maʿarbis (Amin Maarbes) as tutors. Hartmann taught the subjects "public and private documents in Arabic" ("öffentliche und private Urkunden in Arabischer Sprache") and "Laws and Customs in Arab Lands" ("Recht und Sitte in den Ländern arabischer Zunge").[28]

Ḥasan Tawfīq taught "practical exercises in modern Arabic, with a special focus on the dialect of Egypt," while his colleague Amīn Maʿarbas taught the Syrian Arabic dialect.[29] We do not know how Ḥasan Tawfīq taught the subject, but a considerable part of it must have focused on Egyptian Arabic. It is safe to say that this course was the impetus for his 1898 work on the etymology of Egyptian Arabic, which we shall discuss below. The other Arabic tutor was the Syrian Amin Maʿarbes, who taught Syrian Arabic for fifteen years. In addition to his language classes, he offered three courses on the subjects "1001 Nights," "Exercises in Reading and Explaining Arabic Script," and "Newspapers and Practice in Writing." Apparently, he chose his own texts for teaching and argued with one of the German professors over what was the best text.[30]

---

27 'Chronik der Friedrich-Wilhelms-Universität zu Berlin, 1.1887/88', 64–66.

28 "Als Docenten sind z. Z. am Seminar thätig: 1. Herr Professor C. Arendt, Lehrer des Chinesischen; 2. Herr Hsüeh Schen, Lector des Nordchinesischen; 3. Herr Au Fung Tschü, Lector des Südchinesischen; 4. Herr Professor Dr. R. Lange, Lehrer des Japanischen; 5. Herr T. Senga, Lector des Japanischen; 6. Herr Djama Chan Ghori, Lector des Hindustani und Persischen; 7. Herr Professor Dr. Hartmann, Lehrer des Arabischen; 8. Herr Hassan Taufik, Lector des Arabischen; 9. Herr Amin Maarbes, Lector des Arabischen; 10. Herr Dr. K. Foy, Lehrer des Türkischen; 11. Herr Dr. C. G. Büttner, Lehrer des Suaheli. Der Lector des Suaheli Sleman Bin Said ist verstorben. Der commissarische Director, Sachau." Eduard Sachau, Das Seminar für Orientalische Sprachen, 'Chronik der Friedrich-Wilhelms-Universität zu Berlin, 4.1890/91' (Goslar, 1891), 61–62.

29 "Praktische Übungen im Neuarabischen mit besonderer Berücksichtigung des Dialects von Ägypten, Lector Hasan Taufik, Montags, Dienstags, Mittwochs, Donnerstags, Freitags, 6–9 Uhr (6–7 ½ Uhr für den Zweiten Cursus, 7 ½-9 Uhr für den Anfängercursus), öffentlich." See Universität Berlin Friedrich-Wilhelms-Universität: Verzeichnis der Vorlesungen (Berlin: Universität Berlin, Friedrich-Wilhelms-Universität, 1888). Winter Semester, 1888–89, 29.

30 Pugach, Africa in Translation, 148.

The salary of a professor was higher than that of a lector, and the salaries of Chinese and Arabic tutors were higher than that of the African language tutors.[31] According to the agreement between the German foreign ministry and the Egyptian ministry of education, the salary of Ḥasan Tawfīq al-ʿAdl was covered by both countries and initially amounted to 3000 marks per year, paid monthly. The contribution of the Egyptian ministry of education was to be paid to the German consulate in Egypt. In December 1889, slightly more than two years after Ḥasan Tawfīq's arrival in Berlin, Sachau approved an additional 500 marks per year to be paid from the funds of the *Seminar für Orientalische Sprachen*, after Ḥasan Tawfīq al-ʿAdl had complained of financial hardship. The Egyptian government continued to pay its share, 1500 marks, as in the original 1887 agreement. The cost of travel between Cairo and Berlin was borne by both governments.[32]

***

Tutors were required to wear their native, traditional attire while they were teaching at the *Seminar für Orientalische Sprachen*. In the case of Ḥasan Tawfīq, this was even stipulated in his contract.[33] This requirement was not only to identify him as a language tutor, but also as a representation of the "orient" in the lecture halls of the *Seminar*. The "oriental attire" which he and other non-European tutors were required to wear was integral to the reification and commodification of non-European cultures and peoples which was taking place in museums and colonial "people exhibitions" in Berlin at the time.[34] From the perspective of Ḥasan Tawfīq al-ʿAdl, however, he was proud to wear his "oriental dress" (*al-malābis al-sharqiyya*), which was also his "cultural capital" as a religious scholar.[35] Until the 1920s, Egyptian graduates of al-Azhar and Dār al-ʿUlūm were expected to wear a gown and turban (*thawb*, *ʿamāma*), unlike the graduates from the Egyptian civil schools who wore a suit and tarboush. However, it was common for fin-de-siècle graduates of Dār al-ʿUlūm to engage in what Hilary Kalmbach calls "performative code-switching". She writes, "the fluid manner in which he [Ḥasan Tawfīq al-ʿAdl] deployed various aspects of his cultural capital is most visible in his switching between different styles of dress and title. For instance, he was listed as a *shaykh*in the notice announcing his induction into the Royal Asiatic Society in London and wore the dress of a religious scholar when meeting the

31 Pugach, 144–46.

32 For the diplomatic exchange and contracts, in French, see Nachlass Höpp, 07.01.

33 See Nachlass Höpp, 07.01. According to Pugach, Ḥasan Tawfīq was the only native tutor who was required to wear his native oriental attire. See Pugach, Africa in Translation, 145.

34 Ahmed, Arabische Präsenzen, 78.

35 He praises the Egyptian ministry of education for providing him with the oriental dress, Arabic books and the travel expenses. See al-ʿAdl, al-Riḥla ilā Birlīn, 29.

German Kaiser, yet he used the title *efendi*and appeared in a suit and *tarboush*in the 1895 picture of Dar al-ʿUlum's faculty."[36]

*Fig. 20.1: Ḥasan Tawfiq al-ʿAdl in the dress of a religious scholar when meeting the German Kaiser in Berlin, c.a. 1892.*

Source: Taqwīm Dār al-ʿUlūm, 41.

36 Kalmbach, Islamic Knowledge and the Making of Modern Egypt, 39–40.

***

Despite the fact that the objectives of the *Seminar für Orientalische Sprachen* were clear from the start, there was no set curriculum or textbooks to achieve these objectives in the initial years. In 1890, the first work in a series entitled *Lehrbücher des Seminars für orientalische Sprachen zu Berlin*, under the editorship of Eduard Sachau, was published. The works were prepared by a German teacher at the *Seminar für Orientalische Sprachen*, with the assistance of a native tutor. Occasionally, this assistance was acknowledged in the book's preface.[37] Some acknowledgements show clearly that German teachers needed the assistance of the native lectors, who became central to the production of colonial knowledge. As Sara Pugach argues: "*lektoren* [lectors] were not in Germany to entertain but rather to teach, and this assured a complex relationship; they may have been despised or looked down upon because of their "race," but it was difficult to deny their pedagogical importance."[38] Some acknowledgements also allude to collegial relations between the *Seminar für Orientalische Sprachen* faculty, as well as the collaboration between teachers and tutors. For example, Bernhard Moritz (1859–1939), who began working at the *Seminar für Orientalische Sprachen* in 1887 as a secretary, librarian and then professor of Arabic, thanks "Dr. Reinhardt in Zanzibar, Herrn Amin Maarbes und Herrn Hassan Taufik am Seminar".[39] Moritz later moved to Egypt and became the first director of the Khedival Library in Cairo from 1896 to 1911. Similarly, Carl Gotthilf Büttner acknowledged the important contributions of two tutors of Swahili.[40]

Ḥasan Tawfīq continued to teach at the *Seminar für Orientalische Sprachen* until the summer semester of 1892. From the winter semester 1892–93 onwards, a new Egyptian tutor assumed work at the *Seminar für Orientalische Sprachen*, Shaykh Muḥammad Naṣṣār (1863–1936).[41] The teaching of Arabic continued to grow at the

---

37 On the cooperation (or the lack thereof) between the German professors and the lectors of Swahili, see Bromber, 'German Colonial Administrators, Swahili Lecturers and the Promotion of Swahili at the *Seminar für Orientalische Sprachen* in Berlin', 41–48.

38 Pugach, Africa in Translation, 142.

39 Bernhard Moritz, ed., Sammlung arabischer Schriftstücke aus Zanzibar Und Oman, Lehrbücher des Seminars für Orientalische Sprachen Zu Berlin (Stuttgart & Berlin: W. Spemann, 1892), XIV.

40 "Einiges ist mir von den Lektoren am Seminar für Orientalische Sprachen Herrn SLEMAN BIN SAID und Herrn AMUR BIN NASUR aufgeschrieben". See Carl Gotthilf Büttner, ed., Suaheli-Schriftstücke in arabischer Schrift: Mit lateinischer Schrift umschrieben, übersetzt und erklärt (Stuttgart & Berlin: W. Spemann, 1892), Vorwort, V. The reference is to Sulaymān b. Sa'īd b. Aḥmad al-Ṣurāmī (ca. 1871–1891) and 'Amr b. Naṣr al-'Umarī (1867-after 1914). See Bromber, 43.

41 Muḥammad Naṣṣār graduated from Dār al-'Ulūm in 1891. He would spend seven years at the *Seminar für Orientalische Sprachen* as a tutor of Arabic. At the Berlin University, he studied hieroglyphics, psychology and ethics. Upon returning to Egypt in 1899, he taught at Dār

*Seminar für Orientalische Sprachen*, particularly after the establishment of diplomatic ties with Morocco. As a result, the Arabic Moroccan dialect began to be taught by the Moroccan tutor Muḥammad Bu Selham. Moreover, the Arabic of Zanzibar began to be taught by ʿAmr b. Naṣr, who also taught Swahili.[42] ʿAmr b. Naṣr arrived in Berlin in 1891 and remained until 1895. He wrote an autobiographical account of his experiences in Berlin in Kiswahili, which was translated into German by his mentor C. G. Büttner, which he published in his anthology *Lieder und Geschichten der Suaheli* in 1894, and used as teaching material. ʿAmr b. Naṣr narrates his experiences in Berlin, touching on themes such as the weather, urban life, the German language and bureaucracy, and even recounts a brief encounter with Bismarck, themes that Ḥasan Tawfīq also wrote about in his *Riḥla*.[43]

Moritz's aforementioned acknowledgment notwithstanding, it is interesting to note that none of Ḥasan Tawfīq's Arabic works were translated into German. We know that Sachau knew of his Arabic works, particularly of the *Riḥla* and the work on pedagogy, and that some of the works had already been printed.[44] Would his *Riḥla ilā Birlīn* not have served as a suitable Arabic text for the *Lehrbücher* series? There are several issues here. First, although ʿAmr b. Naṣr's autobiographical account, which was written in Swahili and translated into German by C. G. Büttner, was perhaps inspired by the work of his colleague Ḥasan Tawfīq, it was intended to be used as teaching material for the German students who planned to serve in the German East African colony. However, Ḥasan Tawfīq's *Riḥla ilā Birlīn* was written for an Egyptian, Arabic readership.

The first Arabic textbook in the series appeared only in 1897, and it was the 17th in the series. It was a translation of and introduction to the popular Shāfiʿī legal primer *Matn Abī Shujāʿ*, which Sachau prepared together with Ḥasan Tawfīq's successor Shaykh Muḥammad Naṣṣār. In the preface to the work, Sachau wrote:

"It was very helpful to me that I was able to discuss many difficult questions with Mr. Muhammed Nasṣār, who was a member of the teaching staff of the Seminar from 1892–1897, an excellent connoisseur of his mother tongue and of jurisprudence. It is my pleasant duty to express my gratitude to him at this point, as well

al-ʿUlūm and al-Madrasa al-Nāṣiriyya, before assuming the role of education inspector. See ʿAbd al-Jawād, Taqwīm Dār al-ʿUlūm, 287–89.

42 Chronik der Friedrich-Wilhelms-Universität zu Berlin, 6.1892/93 (Goslar, 1893), 31–32.

43 "Geschichte des erwähnten Knechtes des Propheten Gottes Amur bin Nasur ilOmeiri. Eigenhändig", in Büttner, Suaheli-Schriftstücke in arabischer Schrift, 178. ʿAmr b. Naṣr's account ends on 15 September 1892, shortly after Ḥasan Tawfīq left Berlin. It is highly probable that he was familiar with Ḥasan Tawfīq's *Riḥla*.

44 See *Vita* prepared in German, presumably, after 1889, listing Ḥasan Tawfīq's accomplishments before and after his arrival in Berlin. Nachlass Höpp, 07.01.

as to Dr. A. Fischer for his kind assistance in reading the corrections, especially the second half of the work."[45]

This acknowledgment suggests that Sachau had little experience with *fiqh* prior to this publication and that Muḥammad Naṣṣār did not merely assist Sachau but taught him how to read the work. *Matn Abī Shujāʿ* would have been one of the many legal texts that Naṣṣār would have studied at al-Azhar or Dār al-ʿUlūm. It is not difficult to imagine Naṣṣār actually being the teacher of Sachau and having recommended the text for study. Despite the official hierarchy established between German teachers and native tutors, the acknowledgements included in the prefaces of the publications of the *Seminar für Orientalische Sprachen* reveal some of the latent dynamics that were at play at the *Seminar für Orientalische Sprachen*. Unfortunately, we do not have academic reports or transcripts of the kind of scholarly discussions that took place at the *Seminar für Orientalische Sprachen* and in which language, but it is clear that the tutor's contributions influenced the design and content of the curriculum.

***

Ḥasan Tawfīq al-ʿAdl began writing his travelogue soon after he left Egypt in September 1887, and he would continue to write it until September 1889. The travelouge was called *Riḥlat Ḥasan Efendi Tawfīq* (The Journey of Ḥasan Efendi Tawfīq); it is also known as *al-Riḥla ilā Birlīn*. The work consists of thirteen dated, but untitled sections (*ajzāʾ*). An examination of the extant manuscript indicates that the work was serialised in the period between 1888 and 1890.[46] The sections were despatched from Berlin to the Egyptian ministry of education in Cairo. Later they would be forwarded to the Khedivial Egyptian library. This suggests that Ḥasan Tawfīq had been commissioned to write a regular report of his time in Berlin, and that he had begun doing so shortly after leaving Egypt. However, Ḥasan Tawfīq's *Riḥla* is incomplete. At the end of section thirteen, we are promised a description of the *Seminar für Orientalische Sprachen*, but we do not have this account. It seems that Ḥasan Tawfīq never got round to writing it or that it was never dispatched.

45 "Es war mir in hohem Maasse förderlich, dass ich manche schwierige Frage mit Herrn Muhammed Naṣṣār, der von 1892—1897 dem Lehrkörper des Seminars angehörte, einem ausgezeichneten Kenner seiner Muttersprache sowie der Rechtswissenschaft, besprechen konnte. Es ist mir eine angenehme Pflicht ihm an dieser Stelle meinen Dank zu bezeugen, sowie Herrn Dr. A. Fischer für freundliche Hülfe bei dem Lesen der Correcturen besonders der zweiten Helfte des Werkes." Eduard Sachau, Muhammedanisches Recht nach Schafiitischer Lehre. Lehrbücher des Seminars für Orientalische Sprachen in Berlin (Stuttgart & Berlin: W. Spemann, 1897), XXVIII–XXIX. (my translation).

46 Egyptian National Library (Dār al-Kutub), MS 113 Geography. See also copy in Nachlass Höpp, 05.13.032.

The work is a rich account of the first two years of his time in Berlin. It is written in a literary style, interspersed with poetry (sometimes his own) and curious anecdotes about his personal experiences. The serialised work sometimes reads like a report on particular historical and cultural themes, gleaned and translated directly from books he was able to read in German.

The work has an unmistakable didactic tone, which makes it clear that Ḥasan Tawfīq's main objective was to report on the pedagogical institutions and practices in Germany. His intended readers were Egyptian students and education inspectors, whom he often addresses directly. The didactic tone is softened however by humorous anecdotes reminiscent of the picaresque *maqāmāt*-like rhymed prose (*saj'*), which his readers (graduates of al-Azhar and Dār al-'Ulūm) would have appreciated.

Ḥasan Tawfīqwas conscious that his work would be the first detailed account of Germany written in Arabic. While other nineteenth-century Arab travelogue authors made Paris the centre of their work, hiswas the first to give a comprehensive account focused on the capital of the German Empire. He reported on its schools, universities, libraries and museums. He wrote about the postal service, means of transportation, the climate and the everyday life of people. He introduced various pedagogical thinkers, such as Johann Heinrich Pestalozzi (1827).[47] He gives a detailed description of the *Festtag* of the chemist August Hoffmann (1818–1892).[48] He also provided a description of gymnastics and the pedagogical importance of physical education. He provides a brief biography of the German gymnastics' educator and nationalist Friedrich Ludwig Jahn (1778–1852), commonly known as "Turnvater Jahn" (Father of Gymnastics Jahn).[49] His interest in physical education would later result in his work *al-Ḥarakāt al-Riyāḍiyya*, published in Cairo in 1895.

***

Ḥasan Tawfīqwas a keen observer and a flaneur, who enjoyed walking through the streets, squares and parks of Berlin.[50] Shortly after his arrival, Ḥasan Tawfīq went to the *Seminar für Orientalische Sprachen*, which was housed in the Alte Börse, Am Lustgarten no. 6, just across from *museum island*,[51] but finding it closed for the holiday, he

47 al-'Adl, al-Riḥla ilā Birlīn, 88.

48 al-'Adl, 143–49.

49 al-'Adl, 251.

50 Occasionally, he would introduce a topic or an anecdote with the opening sentence, "As I was walking one day, I saw…". For example, see al-'Adl, 79, 81, 156–57.

51 The building was demolished in 1893 to make room for the new construction of the Berlin Dome which began in 1894. The *Seminar für Orientalische Sprachen* moved to Am Zeughause Nr. 1 before finally moving to Dorotheenstraße 7, just behind the main building of the Berlin University. The buildings do not exist today. See Stoecker, 'Das Seminar für Orientalische Sprachen', 118.

walked to the nearby museum instead. Ḥasan Tawfīq was fascinated by the number of museums surrounding the *Seminar für Orientalische Sprachen* at the "*museum island*" (*Museumsinsel*). He frequented the museums and was asked to assist in the identification and deciphering of objects from the Islamic world. However, he was critical of the imperial and colonial agendas that shaped the Berlin museum landscape. By the 1880s, museums had become sites for the appropriation and representation of the world, and Ḥasan Tawfīq was critical of this.[52] He recorded a telling conversation he had with a museum guide at the Egyptian Museum:

"An attendant who was assigned to me asked me jokingly, '"How do you like your treasures here with us?"' I replied, '"They are beautifully displayed and indicate your efforts to present them appropriately. I am pleased that they are with you and that you remember the ancient Egyptians, even though we [the Egyptians] actually have a claim to them first."' He replied, '"Then why do they forbid export from your country? It would be better if we could increase the number [of artefacts in the Museum] to increase the memory!"' I laughed and said, '"Yes, if it were a matter of true friendship, less would have to suffice for remembrance".'[53]

Aischa Ahmed argues that Ḥasan Tawfīq articulated one of the earliest critical interventions in the debate around the provenance of artefacts in European museums.[54] His critique was not limited to Egyptian antiquities, but extended to the Spanish colonisation of Mexico: "They [the Spanish] broke the statues and destroyed the rock inscriptions and tore up what history books they could find, which, had they been preserved, would have been one of the greatest testimonies to the history of these lands."[55] Ḥasan Tawfīq even compared the Spanish colonization of Mexico with the contemporary British colonization of Egypt, an analogy that can be considered as a precursor to an anti-colonial critique:[56]

"When the Europeans came to their senses [i.e., after an age of decline], they began to search for antiquities in all lands and travelled more and more. They were led by ambition and they wanted to make a profit. They spent dirhams and dinars and set up companies in their kingdoms. How they explored in all directions! We mocked them and thought them reckless and greedy, till they took immeasurably from our and other countries. If they could, they would have even taken the pyramids. But thank God, since then we have begun registering and preserving the remaining antiquities in order to do the same [i.e., study the antiquities]."[57]

52 For an analysis of Ḥasan Tawfīq's critical views on the colonial politics of nineteenth-century European museums, see Ahmed, Arabische Präsenzen, 80–85.

53 al-ʿAdl, al-Riḥla ilā Birlīn, 288.The guide is referring to the 1835 decree of Muhammad Ali, which prohibited the export and trade of all Egyptian antiquities.

54 Ahmed, Arabische Präsenzen, 82.

55 al-ʿAdl, al-Riḥla ilā Birlīn, 276–77.

56 Ahmed, Arabische Präsenzen, 90.

57 al-ʿAdl, al-Riḥla ilā Birlīn, 276.

***

One day, as Ḥasan Tawfīq was studying German at home, he heard a loud noise coming from outside. Asking what it was, he was told that the first German Chancellor Otto von Bismarck (1815–1898) was visiting in order to attend the opening of the Parliament. Ḥasan Tawfīq immediately rushed outside to join the crowds cheering Bismarck.[58] This story then serves as a prompt for an extensive discussion about loyalty and love between leaders and the people, and a typology of nations in terms of modes of governance.[59] In fact, Bismarck appears frequently in Ḥasan Tawfīq's *Riḥla*, often depicted as the wise, exemplary prince. Ḥasan Tawfīq devotes three sections (seven to nine) of his *Riḥla* to Bismarck, in which he details the career of the first German Chancellor and at the same time provides the reader with a comprehensive overview of the historical events of his lifetime. It is the most extensive treatment of any theme in his *Riḥla*. As in the rest of the work, al-ʿAdl's framing of Bismarck's life serves a didactic purpose. Thus, most of his account of Bismarck's life is dedicated to his childhood and early education, starting with the boarding school in Berlin to which Bismarck was sent at the age of six. Ḥasan Tawfīq connects anecdotes about Bismarck's upbringing and education to his military character and leadership.[60] Furthermore, Ḥasan Tawfīq makes it clear that it was his own intention to write a biographical account of Bismarck and to study his personality, which fascinated him so much.[61] He concludes that Bismarck's leadership and success in the creation of a German nation-state should be studied and emulated by his Egyptian countrymen and all people.[62]

Ḥasan Tawfīq's extensive presentation of Bismarck's biography, probably the longest account in Arabic at the time, reached Bismarck, who was – after all – the man who was officially behind the *Seminar für Orientalische Sprachen*. He invited Ḥasan Tawfīq to attend an official gathering with him. In his oriental attire, Ḥasan Tawfīq read a poem he had composed in which he praised Bismarck, which was later translated into German, and spoke to him about Egypt.[63]

---

58 al-ʿAdl, 99–100.

59 al-ʿAdl, 101ff.

60 al-ʿAdl, 189.

61 al-ʿAdl, 235.

62 Incidentally, W. E. B. Du Bois, who was a student at the Berlin University in 1892–1894, wrote a laudatory speech on Bismarck in 1888, even before arriving in Germany. According to Kenneth D. Barkin, "the German chancellor's single-mindedness and determination to create a German nation-state impressed the twenty-year-old Du Bois." See Kenneth D. Barkin, '"Berlin Days," 1892–1894: W. E. B. Du Bois and German Political Economy', Boundary 2 27, no. 3 (2000): 80ff.

63 ʿAbd al-Jawād, Taqwīm Dār al-ʿUlūm, 41.

In the summer of 1892, before he would leave Berlin for good, Ḥasan Tawfīq was decorated with the Royal Order of the Crown, Fourth Class, in recognition of his work at the *Seminar*. This was not only a major achievement for Ḥasan Tawfīq, but was also seen as an accomplishment for the Egyptian ministry of education and affirmation of the ties between the Prussian and Egyptian governments. It was also recognition of Sachau's leadership of the *Seminar für Orientalische Sprachen*.[64] No other tutor had achieved such an award.

***

On 8 August 1889, Ḥasan Tawfīq sent a letter to Eduard Sachau seeking permission for leave. He had not been feeling well and his doctor recommended some fresh air and a tour (*Rundreise*).[65] The permission was granted and, a week later, on 16 August the twenty-seven-year-old Ḥasan Tawfīq set off on a month-long summer tour through Germany and Switzerland. The summer tour was also approved by the Egyptian ministry of education, which covered the costs. The expectation was a report on the education institutes and practices that he encountered along his journey, similar to his report on Berlin. The itinerary included the following places: Berlin, Hannover, Minden, Essen, Köln, River Rhein, Koblenz, Rüdesheim, River Nahe, Assmannshausen, Bingen, Wiesbaden, Mainz, Frankfurt (am Main), Sachsenhausen, Heidelberg, Baden Baden, Strasbourg, Bern, Thunersee, Interlaken, Giessbach, Meiringen, River Aare, Aareschlucht, Luzern, Vitznau, Rigi Hochflue, Arth, Zurich, Bodensee, München, Nuremberg, Leipzig, Dresden, Berlin. He returned to Berlin on 15 September.

Ḥasan Tawfīq kept a diary during his tour, in which he wrote down his observations on schooling, dialectical differences, the education of girls, and school curriculum, among other related topics. After returning to Berlin, he edited his notes and prepared the final version of the work, and sent it to Egypt. It was published with Bulaq in Cairo in 1891, with the title *Rasāʾil al-bushrā fī al-siyāḥa bi-almāniya wa*

64 On 30 October 1892, Sachau received the following letter: "Ew. Hochwohlgeboren benachrichtige ich mit Bezug auf den gefälligen Bericht vom 16. Juni d. Js. – No. 200 – dass Seine Majestät der Kaiser und König mittelst Allerhöchsten Erlasses vom 10. Oktober d. Js. dem bisherigen Lektor am Orientalischen Seminar Cheikh Hassan Effendi Taufik den Königlichen Kronen-Orden vierter Klasse zu verleihen geruht haben. Im Auftrage." See Nachlass Höpp, 07.01.

65 Ḥasan Tawfīq wrote: "Ew. Hochwohlgeboren: Beehre ich mich ganz ergebenst mitzutheilen, daß ich bei einem Arzt berufs Untersuchung meines körperlichen Zustand gewesen bin. Derselbe sagte mir, daß ich kein Bad zu besuchen brauche, dagegen gab er mir den Rath eine Rundreise zu unternehmen. Ihr ergebener, H. Taufik". See Nachlass Höpp, 07.01.

*siwisrā* (Letters of Glad-tiding; Being a Tour Through Germany and Switzerland).[66] The work contained diagrams and illustrations, as well as a foldout map that Ḥasan Tawfīq himself prepared, which represents the itinerary he took through Germany and Switzerland.[67]

*Fig. 20.2: Cover page, Ḥasan Tawfīq, Rasā'il al-Bushrā, Bulaq, 1891, with a dedication to al-Shanqīṭī.*

كتاب
رسائل البشرى في السياحة بالمانيا وسويسرا
في سنة ١٨٨٩ ميلاديه
لحضرة مؤلفه
حسن افندي توفيق
معلم اللغة العربية في المدرسة الشرقية
برلين
(يليه خريطة ألمانيا وجزء من سويسرا)
(تصرح من نظارة المعارف العمومية بطبعه على نفقتها)
(الطبعة الاولى)
بالمطبعة الكبرى الاميرية ببولاق مصر المحمية
سنة ١٨٩١
افرنجيه

***

Shortly after Ḥasan Tawfīq finished the final draft of his *Rasā'il al-bushrā*, he began to work intensively on a new project: a translation of the two-volume work on peda-

66 Ḥasan Tawfīq al-'Adl, Rasā'il Al-Bushrā Fī al-Siyāḥa Bi-Almāniya Wa Siwisrā (Cairo: Bulaq, 1891).

67 The 1999 edition of Ḥasan Tawfīq's Rasā'il al-Bushrā, edited by Muḥammad Ḥasan 'Abd al-Azīz, contains a reproduction of the cover page of the 1891 Bulaq edition with a dedication from Ḥasan Tawfīq to renowned philologist and editor Shaykh Muḥammad al- Shanqīṭī (d. 1322/1904), one of the teachers with whom he studied before he went to Germany. The dedication is dated Sha'bān 1318/December 1900. See Ḥasan Tawfīq al-'Adl, Rasā'il al-Bushrā fī al-Siyāḥa bi-Almāniya wa Siwisrā, ed. Muḥammad Ḥasan 'Abd al-Azīz (Kuwait: Rābiṭa al-Udabā' fī al-Kuwayt, 1999), 67.

gogy, *Lehrbuch der Pädagogik*, by Johann Christoph Gottlob Schumann (1761–1810).[68] Ḥasan Tawfīq completed the translation of the first volume in Ramadan 1308/April-May 1891, and the second volume in Rabīʿ al-Thānī 1309/November 1891.[69] As a teacher of pedagogy at Dār al-ʿUlūm in the late 1890s, Ḥasan Tawfīq would teach this work. Volumes 1 and 2 were published posthumously in Cairo in 1921.

ʿAbd al-Jawād notes that Ḥasan Tawfīq's brother, ʿAlī Jamāl Pasha, had informed him that Ḥasan Tawfīq issued a journal during his time in Germany and had called it *al-Tawfīq al-Miṣrī*, however ʿAbd al-Jawād adds that he could not find any copies of it.[70] It is not difficult to imagine that Ḥasan Tawfīq planned to do so given his ambitious character, but lacked the time or the energy to realise this. It may also be the case that he did publish one or two issues which are no longer extant. The title of the journal would have been a homage to his patron al-Khedivi Tawfiq as well as a reference to himself, Ḥasan Tawfīq.

***

Ḥasan Tawfīq completed his teaching duties at the *Seminar für Orientalische Sprachen* in the summer of 1892. He did not return to Egypt immediately, but travelled in Europe, particularly England, where he spent a few months visiting Oxford, Cambridge, Eton, Harrow School and Borough Road Training College, to learn more about public education for the Egyptian government.[71] He was one of several Dār al-ʿUlūm graduates who were sent by the Egyptian Government to study European education systems.[72]

---

68 The work consisted of two parts, theoretical and practical: 1. Einleitung in die Pädegogik und Grundlage für den Unterricht in der Geschichte der Pädagogik; 2. Zweiter Theil: die systematiche Pädagogik und die Schulkunde.

69 Ḥasan Tawfīq al-ʿAdl, Kitāb al-Bīdāghūjiyā, ay hidāyat al-aṭfāl (Cairo: Bulaq, 1921). See colophons in vol. 1, 112, and vol. 2, 378.

70 ʿAbd al-Jawād, 'Ḥasan Tawfīq al-ʿAdl', 1379.

71 In his description of the schools of London, Aḥmad Zakī Pasha (1867–1934) mentions that he met Ḥasan Tawfīq during his journey to the Ninth International Orientalist Congress, which took place in London in 1892. See Ahmad Zakī, al-Safar ilā al-mu'tamar, ed. Ayman Fu'ād al-Sayyid (Cairo: al-Dār al-Miṣriyya al-Lubnāniyya, 2000 [1893]), 134. Aḥmad Zakī's al-Safar ilā l-mu'tamar (A Journey to the Congress) is a detailed record of his six-month trip through Europe in 1892 and 1893.

72 Hilary Kalmbach, 'Training Teachers How to Teach: Transnational Exchange and the Introduction of Social-Scientific Pedagogy in 1890s Egypt', in The Long 1890s in Egypt: Colonial Quiescence, Subterranean Resistance, ed. Anthony Gorman and Marilyn Booth (Edinburgh University Press, 2014), 87–116.

*Fig. 20.3: Dār al-ʿUlūm Faculty in 1896*

Hasan Tawfīq al-ʿAdl (back row, left to right, second).
Source: Taqwīm Dār al-ʿUlūm, 24.

*Fig. 20.4: Dār al-ʿUlūm faculty 1902*

Ḥasan Tawfīq al-ʿAdl wearing a tarboush (back row, third from the left, no. 9).
Source: Taqwīm Dār al-ʿUlūm, 42.

In addition to pedagogy (*fann al-tarbiya*), Ḥasan Tawfīq taught composition (*al-inshāʾ*) and the history of Arabic literature (*tārīkh ādāb al-lugha al-ʿarabiyya*), and he invigorated research and publication in these areas. In 1894, he published a work on physical education: *al-Harakāt al-Riyāḍiyya al-Badaniyya* [*Bodily Exercise Movements*], and in 1897 he published a parental guide on child education: *Murshid al-ʿāʾilāt ilā tarbiyat al-banīn wa al-banāt, wal-tarbiya al-jismiyya mundhu al-ḥaml ʾilā sin al-bulūgh* [*The Parental Guide to Raising Boys and Girls, and to Physical Education from Pregnancy to Puberty*]. Both works were published in Bulaq, Cairo.

But the work that had the most profound impact was his *Tārīkh ādāb al-lugha al-ʿarabiyya* (A History of Arabic Literature), which he composed in 1897.[73] It is considered by many historians as the first history of Arabic literature in Arabic that is arranged chronologically, according to successive dynastic and political regimes.[74] Even before publishing this work, Ḥasan Tawfīq taught and lectured about the historicist approach to his students and colleagues at Dār al-ʿUlūm. According to the literary historian Aḥmad al-Shāyib, after Ḥasan Tawfīq returned to Cairo he began to encourage his friend, al-Azhar and Dār al-ʿUlūm graduate, Muḥammad Diyāb (1852–1921) to compose a history of Arabic literature following the methods of German literary history, and especially the work of German orientalists.[75] Ḥasan Tawfīq discussed with Diyāb how this might look.[76] And, indeed, in 1900, Muḥammad Diyāb published his *Tārīkh adāb al-lugha al-ʿarabiyya*.[77] The result was a comprehensive two-volume work on the history of the Arabic language sciences, but not a history of Arabic literature as such. Aḥmad al-Shāyib likened Diyāb's work to the compendium of knowledge, *al-Fihrist*, compiled by the tenth-century Ibn al-Nadīm.

In 1897, Ḥasan Tawfīq began to teach a course on the history of Arabic literature. The outcome was a small textbook whose circulation was limited to the students of Dār al-ʿUlūm. Ḥasan Tawfīq's divided his work into the following sections: five general introductions on 1. The human need for mutual understanding and knowledge of things; 2. on the imitation of nature; 3. on language; 4. on literature; 5. on the history of literature, followed by a section on pre-Islam (*al-adab Jāhilī*) early Islam, and

73 Ḥasan Tawfīq al-ʿAdl, Tārīkh ādāb al-lugha al-ʿarabiyya, ed. Walīd Maḥmūd Khāliṣ (Amman: Dār Usāma, 2002). This edition is based on a sole manuscript at Dār al-Kutub, MS 4221 Adab, Talʿat, copied by Muḥammad Fakhruddin, who copied it in 1322/1904, based on the author's handwritten copy, which was completed in Muḥarram 1320/April 1902. See editor's introduction, 24.

74 Abdelrashid Mahmoudi, Taha Husain's Education: From al Azhar to the Sorbonne (Routledge, 2014), 89–90; Kalmbach, Islamic Knowledge and the Making of Modern Egypt, 198–99.

75 Aḥmad al-Shāyib, Dirāsat adab al-lugha al-ʿarabiyya bi-Miṣr fī al-niṣf al-awwal min al-qarn al-ʿishrīn (Kuwait: Dār al-Ẓāhiriyya, 2018), 6–8. The work was first published in Cairo in 1952.

76 Diyab alludes to this in his preface: Muḥammad Diyāb, Tārīkh ādāb al-lugha al-ʿarabiyya (Cairo: Maṭbaʿat al-Taraqqī, 1900), ب.

77 Diyāb, Tārīkh ādāb al-lugha al-ʿarabiyya. At around the same time, Jurji Zaydan was working on his own *Tārīkh ādāb al-lugha al-ʿarabiyya*, which began to appear piecemeal in his journal *al-Hilāl* in the 1890s. Though independent of one another, they were both drawing on German philological scholarship.

the Umayyad period. It is likely that the book remained incomplete, as Ḥasan Tawfīq refers to two more periods: the Abbasid and Andalusian period, as well as the period of the subsequent dynasties. Ḥasan Tawfīq provided a short description of the historical, cultural and religious contexts of each dynasty, and then divides each period according to composers of prose (*al-nathr*) and verse (*al-shiʿr*), giving examples of the poets and prose writers of each period. He integrates the opinions of literary critics of the formative period and informs the reader whether the work is available in print. Ḥasan Tawfīq's *Tārīkh ādāb al-lugha al-ʿarabiyya* was printed posthumously in 1906.

Muḥammad ʿAbd al-Jawād reports that Ḥasan Tawfīq's small textbook was in fact a reworking of the teaching materials (*mudhakkara fī al-adab al-ʿarabī*) that he had compiled and taught at the *Seminar für Orientalische Sprachen* in Berlin.[78] The book is written in a clear didactic style, which would have made it accessible to his students in Berlin. It may have been inspired by a German work he saw in Berlin. ʿAbd al-Jawād's assertion that Ḥasan Tawfīq had already composed a draft in Berlin implies that his work was not directly influenced by *Geschichte der arabischen Litteratur* by Carl Brockelmann (1868–1956), as is sometimes assumed. It is highly probable that Ḥasan Tawfīq and Carl Brockelman may have met one another in Berlin, particularly since the latter was involved in Eduard Sachau's edition of Ibn Saʿd's multi-volume *Ṭabaqāt* in the early 1890s.[79] However, Brockelmann's *Geschichte der arabischen Litteratur* began to appear in 1898, whereas Ḥasan Tawfīq's *Tārīkh al-ādāb al-lugha al-ʿarabiyya* appeared in 1897. The suggestion by some scholars of a possible influence of Brockelman's work on Ḥasan Tawfīq's is misleading, as it ignores the fact that ideas about the periodisation of literature would have been available to Ḥasan Tawfīq through the study of German literature and European philosophy and religion more broadly. But Brockelmann's work came to represent this historical approach. Furthermore, it could be argued that Ḥasan Tawfīq's periodisation builds on the Arabic literary tradition's own sense of temporality and periodisation, as exemplified by the work of Ḥasan Tawfīq's teacher Ḥusayn al-Marṣafī, who taught him at Dār al-ʿUlūm.[80] Moreover, and more importantly, Ḥasan Tawfīq's work was a pedagogical work, not a bibliographical encyclopaedia.

Ḥasan Tawfīq's work on literary history, however modest in size and incomplete, had a significant impact on the way Arabic literary history was taught at Dar al-ʿUlūm and Egyptian secondary schools in the early decades of the twentieth-century. The teachers at Dār al-ʿUlūm emulated the design of his work and developed his periodisation. Aḥmad Ḍayf (1880–1945), a student of Ḥasan Tawfīq at

78 ʿAbd al-Jawād, 'Ḥasan Tawfīq al-ʿAdl', 1379.

79 Johann Fück, 'Nachruf: Carl Brockelmann (1868–1956)', Zeitschrift der Deutschen Morgenländischen Gesellschaft 108 (1958): 3.

80 Kalmbach, Islamic Knowledge and the Making of Modern Egypt, 151.

Dār al-'Ulūm, who then earned a doctorate in comparative literature from Paris, and later became a professor at the Egyptian University (later Cairo University), acknowledged that it was Ḥasan Tawfīq who changed the way Arabic literature was taught at Dār al-'Ulūm after he returned from Europe.[81] Similarly, the historian and author Aḥmad Amīn (1886–1954), a graduate of Dār al-'Ulūm, gives the following account:

"And al-Shaykh Muḥammad Mahdī taught us Arabic literature, and this kind of literature was new in Egypt, as people only knew literature in the form it had in the works of Kitāb al-Aghānī, al-'Iqd al-Farīd, al-Amālī, and similar works; as for a history of literature in terms of periods, and the study of the biographies of the poets in light of their epochs, that was not known until *al-Ustādh* Ḥasan Tawfīq al-'Adl, who had studied in Germany introduced this approach to Dār al-'Ulūm, where he had been teaching. He was inspired by what the Germans had done in the teaching of their literature. His student, *al-Ustādh* Muḥammad Mahdī, built on his work and prepared for us comprehensive textbooks (*mudhakkarāt wāsi'a*)".[82]

Muḥammad Mahdī (d. 1924) was a student of Ḥasan Tawfīq at Dār al-'Ulūm. He published textbooks that followed Ḥasan Tawfīq's historicist approach, and would teach at Dār al-'Ulūm and later at the Egyptian University. Through his students and publications, Ḥasan Tawfīq's influence extended beyond al-Azhar and Dār al-'Ulūm to the Egyptian University. He is credited by many scholars with advocating a historicist approach to the study of Arabic literature that examined the political and social dimensions of literary production.[83] According to the Egyptian literary critic and historian 'Abd al-'Azīz al-Dusūqī (d. 2015), Ḥasan Tawfīq "liberated [Arabic literary studies at the time] from being limited to rhetorical analysis and grammatical and morphological interest, and opened a new literary horizon that was concerned with the relation between literature and political, social and religious influences."[84]

***

Another work that was published in Egypt but had its origins during Ḥasan Tawfīq's time in Berlin was his small-sized work on the etymology of Egyptian colloquial Ara-

81 Aḥmad Ḍayf, Muqaddima Li-Dirāsat Balāghat al-'arab (Cairo: Maṭba'at al-Ṣufūr, 1921), 22–23.

82 Ahmad Amīn, Ḥayātī, 4. Edition (Cairo: Maktabat al-Nahḍa al-Miṣriyya, 1961). 74.

83 Yaseen Noorani, 'Translating World Literature into Arabic and Arabic into World Literature':, in Migrating Texts, ed. Marilyn Booth, Circulating Translations around the Ottoman Mediterranean (Edinburgh University Press, 2019), 250–51.

84 'Abd al-'Azīz al-Dusūqī, Taṭawwur al-naqd al-'arabī al-ḥadīth fī miṣr (Cairo: al-Hay'a al-Miṣriyya al-Āmma li-l-Kitāb, 1977), 221; Makkī Aḥmad al-Ṭāhir, al-Adab al-Muqāran: Uṣūluhu wa-taṭawwuruhu wa-manāhijuh (Cairo: al-Ma'ārif, 1987), 174–75.

bic: *Uṣūl al-kalimāt al-ʿāmmiyya* [An Etymology of Common Speech].[85] In the preface to the work, Ḥasan Tawfīq wrote that he began working on the Egyptian Arabic dialect (*al-lahja al-ʿarabiyya al-miṣriyya*) during his time at the *Seminar für Orientalische Sprachen* in Berlin (*al-madrasa al-sharqiyya bi-Birlīn*), where he taught "practical exercises in modern Arabic, with a special focus on the dialect of Egypt". Although what was required of him at the *Seminar für Orientalische Sprachen* was to teach the spoken dialect and to complement the "theoretical" classes offered by Sachau, Hartmann and Moritz, it seems that this motivated Ḥasan Tawfīq to think deeply and systematically about the roots of colloquial Egyptian Arabic.

The 1907 edition, published posthumously, consists of 283 alphabetically listed words. Ḥasan Tawfīq provides a phonetic Arabic transcription to show how a given word is pronounced. If the word is originally Arabic, he provides its *faṣīḥ* origin, then provides textual witnesses, extracted from the Arabic lexicographical tradition. If it is not of Arabic origin, he would indicate whether the word has a Coptic, Turkish or European root, and how it came to be used in Egyptian Arabic. Occasionally, he might provide the original spelling in Roman script. His investigation is descriptive; he does not evaluate common language use in terms of its proximity to the *fuṣha* (high register of Arabic). There are no errors, but rather morphological transformations and adaptations common to everyday speech. Yet, Ḥasan Tawfīq was not an advocate of writing in the Egyptian dialect (*al-ʿāmmiyya al-miṣriyya*). Rather, he saw an organic affinity between the *fuṣha* and the *ʿāmmiyya*, between the ideal register and the spoken register, an affinity which he sought to explore in this work. He considered his work as a contribution to the linguistic revival (*al-nahḍa al-lughawiyya*) of his time.

In 1901, Ḥasan Tawfīq published a work titled *al-Tarbiya al-Ḥadītha*, which was a translation of the French pedagogue Edmond Demolins' (1852–1907) work *L'Éducation nouvelle: L'École des Roches*.[86] And, in 1901, he completed a work on wisdom, philosophy, and poetry, entitled *Siyāsat al-fuḥūl fī tathqīf al-ʿuqūl*, which was published posthumously in 1910.[87]

***

85 Ḥasan Tawfīq al-ʿAdl, Uṣūl al-kalimāt al-ʿāmmiyya (Cairo: Maṭbaʿat Wālidat ʿAbbās al-Awwal, 1907). The first edition was published in Cairo in 1898 with Matbaʿat al-Taraqqī.

86 Ḥasan Tawfīq al-ʿAdl, al-Tarbiyah al-ḥadīthah, ta'līf Idmūn Dīmūlin (Cairo: Maṭbʿat al-Taraqqī, 1901). Incidentally, in 1899, Aḥmad Fatḥī Zaghlūl, intellectual and brother of the nationalist leader Saʿd Zaghlul, published an Arabic translation of Edmond Demolin's A quoi tient la supériorité des Anglo-Saxons?. Sirr taqaddum al-Inkiliz al-Saksuniyin (Cairo, 1899). Zaghlūl's translation included an introduction in which he criticised Egyptian society and its education system.

87 Ḥasan Tawfīq al-ʿAdl, Siyāsat al-Fuḥūl ilā tathqīf al-ʿuqūl (Cairo: Maṭbaʿat Abi al-Hul, 1910).

By the late 1890s, Ḥasan Tawfīq's impact on Dār al-ʿUlūm had been significant. Through his teaching and publications, he introduced new disciplines and approaches, and inspired students and teachers alike. It would not be an exaggeration to say that he came to embody the ideals that Dār al-ʿUlūm aimed to achieve. This was visible to all visitors to Dār al-ʿUlūm at the time. One of these visitors was the British Arabist and Persianist Edward Granville Browne (1862–1926), who met Ḥasan Tawfīq at Dār al-ʿUlūm during his visit to Egypt in 1903. Soon after, he was asked to teach Arabic at Cambridge University. Ḥasan Tawfīq accepted and arrived in Cambridge on 10 October 1903. He was to teach "future British administrators in the Egyptian government".[88] He was inducted in the Royal Asiatic Society and taught at Cambridge until his sudden death on 4 June 1904. He died while teaching, at the age of 42. E. G. Browne wrote an obituary, which was published in the *Journal of Royal Asiatic Societies*. The obituary included a biography of Ḥasan Tawfīq and a reproduction of a poem Ḥasan Tawfīq had composed and presented to his students at Cambridge on the day he died.[89] The Egyptian government arranged for his body to be transported for burial in Egypt. His untimely death, the procession, the funeral, and the obituaries and eulogies are presented in detail in *Taqwīm Dār al-ʿUlūm*.[90] The funeral was attended by heads of state and prominent figures such as Muḥammad ʿAbduh and Muṣṭafa Kāmil. He was buried on 28 June 1904.

***

Ḥasan Tawfīq al-ʿAdl is considered today as one of the founders of Arab pedagogical sciences, the historical approach to Arabic literature, and Egyptian-Arabic dialectology. His books formed part of the curriculum for decades after his death, particularly the works on pedagogy and the history of Arabic literature. A close reading of these works, which I have only briefly discussed in this study, will show how he translated and appropriated the knowledge he acquired in Berlin for the benefit of his Egyptian readers. Despite the recognition that he earned from Egyptian intellectuals in the twentieth century, there is hardly any trace of him in accounts of German colonialism or the history of German knowledge production. Ḥasan Tawfīq joined many non-European native language tutors to teach German government officials, orientalists, and missionaries in Berlin. Although the knowledge that they had to

88 'Abd al-Jawād, 'Ḥasan Tawfīq al-'Adl', 1379.

89 The poem and an English translation of it is provided in E. G. Browne, 'Obituary: Shaykh Ḥasan Tawfi'q', The Journal of the Royal Asiatic Society of Great Britain and Ireland, July 1904, 526–27.

90 'Abd al-Jawād, Taqwīm Dār al-'Ulūm, 182–84. It takes up several pages. No other funeral is covered in such detail in the biographical accounts in *Taqwīm Dār al-'Ulūm*.

offer was indispensable for the aims of the *Seminar für Orientalische Sprachen*, their status remained inferior to that of their German colleagues.

The goal of this study was to introduce Ḥasan Tawfīq al-ʿAdl and provide a basic narrative which could be the starting point for further research on the role of Arab teachers in German education and research. Although the historical circumstances are different today, there are important insights that can be drawn for our times. Ḥasan Tawfīq's case shows how he navigated through institutional hierarchies and racially-constructed boundaries in order to assert his agency and transcend the role of the "native informant". His situation was not much different from that of other tutors at *the Seminar für Orientalische Sprachen*, many of whom would later become important scholars in their home countries.[91] One important point to remember is that many of these tutors saw themselves first and foremost as students at the Berlin University. Their teaching duties were what enabled them to continue their studies. Fin-de-siècle Berlin was a major centre for the production of knowledge, and the city attracted many students from all over the world. Berlin educational institutions were key for modern theories on secularism, racism and colonial thought and practice. How did these student-tutors encounter these ideas? What sort of conversations would they have had with each other? And how did these conversations shape their respective work and later thought? While the available documentary sources are unfortunately quite limited, a close reading of their subsequent writings may reveal common themes and patterns of thought.

A further aspect in Ḥasan Tawfīq al-ʿAdl's biography worthy of reflection is the fact that he spent a great deal of his time and resources in Berlin working on scholarly projects that went largely unnoticed by his German peers. Save for the occasional acknowledgement in a preface to a publication, the idea of academic collaboration is completely absent. The colonial objectives of the *Seminar für Orientalische Sprachen* determined the sort of knowledge that was deemed relevant. The institution itself created a hierarchy not only between teachers and tutors, but also between forms of knowledge. This structural factor explains Ḥasan Tawfīq's absence from general narratives of German orientalism. There was no intention on the part of the *Seminar für Orientalische Sprachen* to seriously engage the knowledge of Ḥasan Tawfīq, except where it fulfilled the goals of training future German officials. Hasan Tawfiq's writings show a sophisticated understanding of German culture and society and the ambivalences of imperial and colonial politics. And his critique of colonial knowledge and the imperial objectives motivating the looting, collecting and order-

91 For example, Inoue Tetsujirō (1855–1944), an important twentieth-century Japanese philosopher and educator, studied philosophy in Heidelberg and Leipzig between 1884 and 1890, and taught Japanese at the *Seminar für Orientalische Sprachen* at the time Ḥasan Tawfīq was teaching Arabic there.

ing of non-European artefacts in Berlin's museums remains relevant today as it was in the 1890s.

To conclude, the study of Ḥasan Tawfīq al-ʿAdl and other tutors at the Berlin University should not remain an intellectual curiosity. This history is highly relevant today. In order to address the asymmetrical relations in academia and the colonial legacies that continue to shape our institutions and disciplines, we would do well to excavate the lives, works and legacies of the countless students, tutors and teachers who contributed to knowledge-making at Berlin's universities. And we could begin by translating their writings, integrating them into the school curriculum, and by reinscribing them into Berlin's history.[92]

## Appendix: Timeline of Ḥasan Tawfīq's Life

| | |
|---|---|
| 1862 | Born in Alexandria, Egypt |
| 1875–82 | Studies at al-Azhar |
| 1882–87 | Studies at *Dār al-ʿUlūm* |
| 1887, 20 September | Arrives in Berlin, via Alexandria, Trieste, Vienna |
| 1887, 27 October | Official opening of the *Seminar für Orientalische Sprachen* |
| 1887, winter semester | Begins teaching Arabic |
| 1889, 16 August | Summer tour through Germany and Switzerland (Itinerary: Berlin, Hannover, Minden, Essen, Köln, River Rhein, Koblenz, Rüdesheim, River Nahe, Assmannshausen, Bingen, Wiesbaden, Mainz, Frankfurt (am Main), Sachsenhausen, Heidelberg, Baden-Baden, Strasbourg, Bern, Thunersee, Interlaken, Giessbach, Meiringen, River Aare, Aareschlucht, Luzern, Vitznau, Rigi Hochflue, Arth, Zurich, Bodensee, München, Nuremberg, Leipzig, Dresden, Berlin) |
| 1889, 15 September | Returns to Berlin |
| 1890 | Completes his travel account toward the end of January |
| 1891 | The account of his summer tour is published in Cairo (Bulaq) |
| 1891 April-May/1309 Ramadan | Completed vol. 1 of his *Pedagogy* (published posthumously in Cairo in 1921) |
| 1891 November/December/ 1309 Rabīʿ al-Thānī | Completed vol. 2 of his *Pedagogy* (published posthumously in Cairo in 1921) |

92 For example, research on W. E. B. Du Bois' "Berlin days" (1892–94) has shown how constitutive his time as a student at Berlin University was for the development of his critical thought. See Barkin, '"Berlin Days," 1892–1894'; Kenneth Barkin, 'W. E. B. Du Bois' Love Affair with Imperial Germany', German Studies Review 28, no. 2 (2005): 285–302.

| | |
|---|---|
| 1892 | Receives the Royal Order of the Crown, Fourth Class, from the German Kaiser |
| 1892 | Spends several months in England visiting educational institutions |
| 1892 | Returns to Cairo and assumes work as education inspector (*mufattish*) and then lecturer at Dār al-ʿUlūm |
| 1895 | Publication of his *al-Ḥarakāt al-riyāḍiyya* (on physical education) |
| 1897 | Publication of *Kitāb Murshid al-ʿāʾilāt ilā tarbiyat al-banīn wa-al-banāt: fī al-tarbiyah al-jismiyyah mundhu al-ḥaml ilā sinn al-bulūgh* |
| 1897 | Publication of *Tārīkh ādāb al-lugha al-ʿarabiyya* |
| 1898 | Publication of *Uṣūl Al-Kalimāt al-ʿāmmiyya* |
| 1901 | Publication of his translation of *al-Tarbiyah al-ḥadīthah*, by Edmond Demolins (1852–1907) |
| 1903, October | Arrives in England and begins teaching at Cambridge University |
| 1904, 3 June | Dies in Cambridge |
| 1904, 28 June | Buried in Cairo |
| 1910 | Posthumous publication of *Tathqīf al-fuḥūl* |
| 1921 | Posthumous publication of *al-Bidagujiya* in Cairo (originally composed in Berlin in 1891) |

## References


'Abd al-Jawād, Muḥammad. 'Ḥasan Tawfīq al-'Adl'. al-Kitāb, no. July (1947): 1374–80.

'Abd al-Jawād, Muḥammad. Taqwīm Dār al-'Ulūm: Al-'Adad al-māsī yaṣdur li-murūr 75 'āman 'alā al-madrasah 1872–1947. Dār al-Ma'ārif, 1952.

'Adl, Ḥasan Tawfīq al-. Al-Riḥla Ilā Birlīn. Edited by 'Abd al-Mun'im Muḥammad Sa'īd. Cairo: Maṭba'at Dār al-Kutub wa-l-Wathā'iq al-Qawmīya bi-l-Qāhira, 2008.

———. Al-Tarbiyah al-Ḥadīthah, Ta'līf Idmūn Dīmūlin. Cairo: Maṭb'at al-Taraqqī, 1901.

———. Kitāb al-Bīdāghūjiyā, Ay hidāyat al-aṭfāl. Cairo: Bulaq, 1921.

———. Rasā'il al-Bushrā fī al-siyāḥa bi-Almāniya wa Siwisrā. Cairo: Bulaq, 1891.

———. Rasā'il al-Bushrā fī al-siyāḥa bi-Almāniya wa Siwisrā. Edited by Muḥammad Ḥasan 'Abd al-Azīz. Kuwait: Rābiṭa al-Udabā' fī al-Kuwayt, 1999.

———. Siyāsat al-fuḥūl ilā tathqīf al-'uqūl. Cairo: Maṭba'at Abi al-Hul, 1910.

———. Tārīkh ādāb al-lugha al-'arabiyya. Edited by Walīd Maḥmūd Khāliṣ. Amman: Dār Usāma, 2002.

———. Uṣūl al-kalimāt al-'āmmiyya. Cairo: Maṭba'at Wālidat 'Abbās al-Awwal, 1907.

Ahmed, Aischa. Arabische Präsenzen in Deutschland um 1900: Biografische Interventionen in die deutsche Geschichte. Bielefeld: transcript Verlag, 2020.

Amīn, Ahmad. Ḥayātī. 4. Edition. Cairo: Maktabat al-Nahḍa al-Miṣriyya, 1961.

'Aṭṭiyyatullah, Aḥmad. 'Ḥasan Tawfīq al-'Adl: al-Azharī alladhī qābal Bismārk'. Al-Hilāl, no. 6 (1953): 72–77.

Barkin, Kenneth. 'W. E. B. Du Bois' Love Affair with Imperial Germany'. German Studies Review 28, no. 2 (2005): 285–302.

Barkin, Kenneth D. '"Berlin Days," 1892–1894: W. E. B. Du Bois and German Political Economy'. Boundary 2 27, no. 3 (2000): 79–101.

Brochlos, Astrid. 'Das Seminar für Orientalische Sprachen an der Berliner Universität und die Japanbezogene Lehre'. In Japan und Preußen, 145–62. München: Iudicium-Verlag, 2002.

Bromber, Katrin. 'German Colonial Administrators, Swahili Lecturers and the Promotion of Swahili at the Seminar für Orientalische Sprachen in Berlin'. Sudanic Africa 15 (2004): 39–54.

Browne, E. G. 'Obituary: Shaykh Ḥasan Tawfi'q'. The Journal of the Royal Asiatic Society of Great Britain and Ireland, July 1904, 523–29.

Büttner, Carl Gotthilf, ed. Suaheli-Schriftstücke in arabischer Schrift: Mit lateinischer Schrift umschrieben, übersetzt und erklärt. Stuttgart & Berlin: W. Spemann, 1892.

Canis, Konrad. 'Bismarck als Kolonialpolitiker'. In Kolonialmetropole Berlin: Eine Spurensuche, edited by Ulrich van der Heyden, 23–28. Berlin: Berlin Edition, 2002.

Chronik der Friedrich-Wilhelms-Universität zu Berlin, 1.1887/88. Goslar, 1888.

Chronik der Friedrich-Wilhelms-Universität zu Berlin, 4.1890/91. Goslar, 1891.

Chronik der Friedrich-Wilhelms-Universität zu Berlin, 6.1892/93. Goslar, 1893.

Ḍayf, Aḥmad. Muqaddima li-dirāsat balāghat al-ʿarab. Cairo: Maṭbaʿat al-Ṣufūr, 1921.

Diyāb, Muhammad. Tārīkh ādāb al-lugha al-ʿarabiyya. Cairo: Maṭbaʿat al-Taraqqī, 1900.

Dusūqī, ʿAbd al-ʿAzīz al-. Taṭawwur al-Naqd al-ʿarabī al-ḥadīth fī miṣr. Cairo: al-Hayʾa al-Miṣriyya al-Āmma li-l-Kitāb, 1977.

Fück, Johann. 'Nachruf: Carl Brockelmann (1868–1956)'. Zeitschrift der Deutschen Morgenländischen Gesellschaft (1958): 1–13.

Kalmbach, Hilary. Islamic Knowledge and the Making of Modern Egypt. Cambridge University Press, 2020.

———. 'Training Teachers How to Teach: Transnational Exchange and the Introduction of Social-Scientific Pedagogy in 1890s Egypt'. In The Long 1890s in Egypt: Colonial Quiescence, Subterranean Resistance, edited by Anthony Gorman and Marilyn Booth, 87–116. Edinburgh University Press, 2014.

Mahmoudi, Abdelrashid. Taha Husain's Education: From al Azhar to the Sorbonne. Routledge, 2014.

Moritz, Bernhard, ed. Sammlung arabischer Schriftstücke aus Zanzibar und Oman. Lehrbücher Des Seminars für Orientalische Sprachen Zu Berlin. Stuttgart & Berlin: W. Spemann, 1892.

Noorani, Yaseen. 'Translating World Literature into Arabic and Arabic into World Literature': In Migrating Texts, edited by Marilyn Booth, 236–65. Circulating Translations around the Ottoman Mediterranean. Edinburgh University Press, 2019.

Pugach, Sara. Africa in Translation: A History of Colonial Linguistics in Germany and Beyond, 1814–1945. Ann Arbor, MI: University of Michigan Press, 2012.

Sachau, Eduard. Muhammedanisches Recht nach Schafiitischer Lehre. Stuttgart & Berlin: W. Spemann, 1897.

Seraukly, Eberhard. 'Zur Entwicklung der Arabistik am Seminar für Orientalische Sprachen'. edited by Hannelore Bernhardt, 57–63. Berlin: Humboldt-Universität, 1990.

Shāyib, Aḥmad al-. Dirāsat adab al-lugha al-ʿarabiyya bi-miṣr fī al-niṣf al-awwal min al-qarn al-ʿishrīn. Kuwait: Dār al-Ẓāhiriyya, 2018.

Stoecker, Holger. 'Das Seminar für Orientalische Sprachen'. In Kolonialmetropole Berlin: Eine Spurensuche, edited by Ulrich van der Heyden, 115–21. Berlin: Berlin Edition, 2002.

Ṭāhir, Makkī Aḥmad al-. al-Adab al-Muqāran: Uṣūluhu wa-taṭawwuruhu wa-manāhijuh. Cairo: al-Ma'ārif, 1987.

Universität Berlin Friedrich-Wilhelms-Universität: Verzeichnis der Vorlesungen. Berlin: Universität Berlin, Friedrich-Wilhelms-Universität, 1888.

Wimmelbücker, Ludger. Mtoro Bin Mwinyi Bakari: Swahili Lecturer and Author in Germany. Dar al-Salam, Tanzania: Mkuki na Nyota Publishers, 2008.

Zakī, Ahmad. al-Safar ilā al-mu'tamar. Edited by Ayman Fu'ād Al-Sayyid. Cairo: al-Dār al-Miṣriyya al-Lubnāniyya, 2000 [1893].

# 21. "In Berlin, I feel free – but COVID-19 made the city feel like a giant prison"

*Julia Gerlach with Nadine Abdalla*

**Julia Gerlach:** Nadine Abdallah, you are a frequent traveler between Berlin in Cairo. Nice to meet you!

**Nadine Abdalla:** Exactly, I am a frequent traveler. At the moment, I am living in Cairo. If not for COVID-19, I would be in Berlin in the summer in addition to two to four visits a year. I previously lived in Berlin for three-and-a-half years intermittently. I was in Berlin for the last year-and-a-half of my PhD in 2012–13 and a postdoc year at Freie Universität Berlin in 2015/16. I also spent the summer of 2019 in Berlin, thanks to an AGYA fellowship at Freie Universität Berlin.

**J.G.:** Tell us a little more about yourself. Who are you?

**N.A.:** I am an Assistant Professor of Sociology at the American University in Cairo. I finished my Ph.D. in Political Sociology in 2014 from Sciences Po Grenoble after completing my master's at Sciences Po Paris in 2006. My research field is social movements, especially workers and youth movements in the MENA region, with a focus on Egypt. I am also a columnist at the Egyptian daily, Al Masry Al-Youm. Even though I did my Ph.D. in Grenoble, I received a fellowship from SWP (*Stiftung Wissenschaft und Politik*) in Berlin. So, I spent the last year of my Ph.D. writing in Berlin. That was a very special year, 2012/13, with many things happening in Egypt, and at the same time, me having to finish the thesis. That last year of writing the Ph.D. is always very tough. Being far from Egypt was also challenging, with all the exciting political developments happening there. Being in Berlin softened the experience for me.

**J.G.:** What do you mean?

**N.A.:** I met very interesting people. At SWP, I learned a lot from my colleagues and from the highly interesting debates there. In Berlin, there was a great interest in what was happening in Egypt and many debates. I felt I could participate and give something back to the city. I met many people from the Arab World and Germany.

On a personal level, it was a great year. Berlin is very open and easy to live in. I believe no other city would have been as nice for me at this time.

**J.G.:** Sounds fantastic. No downsides?

**N.A.:** There were downsides, as well. For example, it is not always so easy to communicate my point of view and analysis of the political situation in Egypt to European colleagues. Quite often, I realized that the perception, assessment, and focus of the research were different.

**J.G.:** What do you mean?

**N.A.:** Let me find a good example. Western researchers often get information on the situation in Egypt from English sources. This means they have information on only selective parts of reality but not the whole picture. This is not always helpful in a debate.It often leads to formulating conclusions and beliefs that might be very different from what we actually want to highlight. The Western academic sphere is very focused on publication and research production. So the feelings and the experiences of the people actually living in the turbulent situation they are working on are often not considered.

**J.G.:** You spent the period from the summer of 2012 to the summer of 2013 in Berlin. That was a very interesting year, with many events in Berlin related to the uprising in Egypt and the other countries in the region.

**N.A.:** Yes, I missed Mohammed Mursi's year in power and returned to Egypt right after Abdelfattah al-Sisi had come to power. The most significant difference between the debates in Berlin and Cairo was that the people in Cairo were in the middle of it all. They lived the events, with all the ups and downs. In Berlin, most academics focused more on writing and publishing. That's understandable, in a way. However, I think it would have been good to avoid the kind of academic tourism where people go very briefly to Egypt, talk to a few people, and come back with simplistic conclusions to write down in their papers.

**J.G.:** Interesting! For me, it was the other way around. I lived in Cairo then, working there as a correspondent for German Media. I sometimes came to Berlin to participate in panel discussions on what was happening in Egypt. I found the discourse in Berlin much more rigid and even more polarized than the already very tough debates in Cairo. At a time when people in Cairo still had some doubts or would admit what to believe and what not to believe, people in Berlin were very straightforward in their conclusions and judgments.

**N.A.:** Then you understand what I was trying to describe! Formulating a clear point of view is easier if you are not part of what is happening. But the problem is that this clarity reflects a very simplistic analysis that neglects the situation's complexity.

**J.G.:** You mentioned Berlin as a city that softened this experience for you. What is it that you like about Berlin?

**N.A.:** Berlin is a city that is easy to connect to. I like the many events and small concerts where you don't have to pay much, and everybody can be there and participate. In Kreuzberg and Neukölln, for instance, I attended concerts performed by Turkish bands, others by a band with Palestinian and Lebanese performers, and others with Egyptians and Germans. Once, I attended a film in Kreuzberg by a Palestinian filmmaker about the situation in Palestine. After the film, there was a discussion with an audience of both Arabs and Germans. It was extremely interesting. You can find many events like this. It's intellectually and culturally rich. Many of the events are based in the Arab community. But – and this is the nice part – there are also many others who go there. Many Germans find it exciting and cool to attend these events. I also like the many green spaces in Berlin. You have the feeling that you can breathe. The urban landscape is designed in a way that lets you feel freedom.

**J.G.:** Do you mean that Berlin is greener than other European cities?

**N.A.:** Yes. In many other cities, you typically have narrow streets. That's also nice, but you find this extraordinary atmosphere in Berlin. There is a unique energy in this city. I do yoga, meditation, and energy healing. So, I am very sensitive to the energies surrounding me. Even if many parts of the city were destroyed, unlike other beautiful European cities, you can enjoy Berlin's freedom through its green spaces, broad streets, and vibrant nightlife.

**J.G.:** At the same time, you have enough people from the Arab World not to feel like a stranger, right?

**N.A.:** Yes. There is another big difference compared to other European cities. In Berlin, you will find many Arabs, but still, people mingle. German Berliners still find it interesting to go to Arab events and migrant neighborhoods, and vice versa. This doesn't mean Arab migrants don't encounter difficulties and racism, but integration has great potential if the right policies are pursued. I hope this mixing will continue despite the rise of populist currents in Germany and Europe. It would be a pity if there were more segregation and separation of the cultures.

**J.G.:** Some people talk about Berlin as the new cultural capital of the Arab World. Is that an exaggeration?

**N.A.:** I think it is an exaggeration. Berlin is a great city, but we shouldn't romanticize it. Yes, you have many artists and intellectuals coming to Berlin. But at the same time, it's not a wealthy city, and it's challenging to find jobs and flats and meet basic needs in this city. This pushes migrants to other German cities where job opportunities are more readily available.

**J.G.:** You wrote an article about how Berlin has changed during COVID-19.

**N.A.:** Yes, it was after a trip to Berlin in December 2021. Honestly, I would like to forget what I saw. I don't want to return to Berlin under COVID. It's a different city, and it reminded me of a giant prison. When I arrived at the airport, I realized the energy had changed. People in the street had changed their level of energy. They were so slow. And you were constantly asked to show your vaccination record and get yourself tested. People were not going out anymore. They were afraid to meet in groups, so they only met one-to-one. If people are afraid to meet, it is no fun to meet them. The best part about Berlin is the vibrant social life; people go out, and you can meet new people at these friendly small events. But they didn't exist anymore. I understand why the government is introducing these rules to protect the population, but at the same time, it destroys the city's atmosphere.

**J.G.:** Sometimes people have different personalities depending on where they are.

**N.A.:** Yes, same here. In Berlin, I feel freedom. I mean, in general, not now under COVID-19. I like the feeling that you can move freely in public spaces. I can't do that in Cairo simply because of the absence of public spaces. Everybody can enjoy public spaces in Berlin, while those spaces are very limited and increasingly privatized in Cairo. I hope that Berlin can keep this spirit.

# 22. "We help international academics who have found their way to Germany"

*Julia Gerlach with Florian Kohstall*[1]

**Julia Gerlach:** Florian Kohstall, you are one of the few non-Arabs portrayed in this book. Who are you, and how are you linked to Arab Berlin?

**Florian Kohstall:** Thank you, I'm delighted to be part of this project, although I'm not of Arab origin and originally not even from Berlin. I was born in Rosenheim, a small town in the southeast of Germany, and I came to Berlin for my studies in Political Science. I guess I am honored to be part of this book because of my doctoral studies and decades of living and working in Morocco and Egypt. In addition, my previous role as head of the Freie Universität Berlin Cairo Office and later the Welcome@FUBerlin Program for refugee students, and my current role leading the program "Academics in Solidarity" all involve working with students and scholars of Arab origin.

**J.G.:** Why did you start to study Arabic in the first place?

**F.K.:** It was by coincidence. During my studies in Political Science, I wanted to do a semester abroad and applied to universities in Spain. I found the University of Granada quite interesting and read on the website that the university sees itself as a bridge between the Christian, Jewish, and Islamic civilizations. In my application letter, I referred to that, and when I started my studies there, I did several seminars on the topic. That's how I got interested in the Arab region, and I subsequently shifted my studies to Middle Eastern Studies. That was in 1997 when I was 23. That's how it all started. And I've spent many years in Morocco and Egypt since then and traveled to most of the countries on both shores of the Mediterranean.

**J.G.:** Interesting, and please say a little more. What exactly made you interested in the Arab world? Other people who go to Spain for a year abroad study the history of the Spanish Civil War or other similar topics.

---

1 Translated from German by Julia Gerlach.

**F.K.:** Yes, you're right. Let me think about what got me interested...

**J.G.:** Well, while you're thinking, let me tell you how it was for me. We may have had similar experiences. I went to France as an exchange student and met many fellow students originally from Algeria. I had a professor, Bruno Etienne, who studied Islam in France. He would always insult us students, telling us that we were too stupid to understand the world, especially the relationship between the Arab world and Europe. The students of Algerian origin also told me that I would never be able to understand what really mattered to them. That's when I decided to learn Arabic.

**F.K.:** Bruno Etienne? I know him. He was my professor later when I did my Master's in Aix-en-Provence. My experience was similar, indeed! In Granada, it was also a professor who got me interested in the region. He didn't tell us that we were stupid, but he provoked us in other ways and made me curious to explore and learn for myself. He was part of the old tradition of orientalism, and this encouraged me to challenge his views.

J.G.:

And your first visit to the Arab world was Morocco?

**F.K.:** Yes, I traveled to Morocco with friends, and we had a good time exploring. Later on, I did an internship with the Friedrich-Ebert-Stiftung. I loved it. I lived in Rabat city, and every day was an adventure. From the moment I left the house, I could be sure that it would be anything but boring. At first, everybody in the neighborhood came up and asked where I was from. After a few days they got used to me and I became part of everyday life there. The office was in a very modern part of the city. So every day I moved between these very different worlds. I enjoyed the contrast between the different communities.

**J.G.:** And from there you moved to Cairo?

**F.K.:** Yes, about four years later. Originally, I went to Cairo because I was looking for a country of reference: I wanted to compare my scientific findings from Morocco to another country in the region – I was working on education reform back then. I went to Egypt, and my plan was to stay for one month. In the end, I stayed for nearly ten years.

**J.G.:** How was your experience of Cairo when you first got there?

**F.K.:** Cairo was very different from Rabat and Casablanca. Life there was much tougher. In Morocco, you can constantly dive into the flair of the old towns and Kasbahs and breathe the past. Cairo is very different. If you are not in places like Khan Al Khalili you won't find this flair.

**J.G.:** Still, you decided to stay in Cairo...

**F.K.:** Yes, I quickly found a job there at the German Academic Exchange Service (DAAD) office and soon got a scholarship. It was easy to connect to a network of researchers there and it was good for my career, and I stayed for – on and off – ten years. I didn't make a conscious decision to do so; it just happened and was very good. Cairo is a very interesting, vibrant, and also a very tiring city.

**J.G.:** I know two types of people: The first type comes to Cairo and finds the city awful – loud and polluted – and they leave as soon as possible. The other type falls in love with all the different aspects of this city immediately. I know very few people who remain indifferent, and hardly any change their opinion later.

**F.K.:** Hmm, so I might be an exception. When I first arrived, I was sure I wouldn't like to stay more than a week at most. But then I got along very well, and I liked living there. There are ups and downs, and I still go there a lot to visit our family.

**J.G.:** When and why did you decide to leave Cairo?

**F.K.:** Between 2013 and 2015, I felt I needed to get out of there. I felt like I was losing touch with life in Germany and starting to get *verbuscht*. It took me two years to find the right perspective to return to Germany. It's not easy. Many people I met in Cairo really struggled to move back to Germany. It's challenging to find a job or develop a perspective or some sort of plan.

**J.G.:** You used the ugly German word "verbuscht". Can you describe what it means?

**F.K.:** Do you think it's ugly? I would say it is a phenomenon that many expats in Arab countries experience: We have this saying, "*Im Ausland ein Fürstchen und in Deutschland ein Würstchen*" – a princeling abroad and a nobody (a sausage!) in Germany. As an expat in countries like Egypt, you have many privileges you don't have at home. That's something you get used to. You lose contact with reality.

No matter how much you try to integrate into the Arab host society, you will always experience living in a bubble – even though I must admit that my bubble here in Berlin is even smaller than my bubble in Cairo was! The people I meet these days in Berlin are even less diverse than those I was meeting back in Cairo. This is not only because of the pandemic and because I have a family now, though these things do play a role.

**J.G.:** When you came to Berlin in 2015, many people from Cairo – ex-pats and Egyptians – also moved to Berlin. So, I guess parts of your old bubble migrated with you, right?

**F.K.:** Right. I found many of my Cairo friends in Berlin.

**J.G.:** You came back to Berlin after a long time abroad. How was it to come back?

**F.K.:** I studied in Berlin from 1997 to 2002, and then I left first for France and then for the Arab World. I came back in 2015. I was always in touch with people in Berlin and came here often over the years. But Berlin has also changed a lot, especially in terms of Arab Berlin. After 2015, you started hearing people speaking Arabic everywhere you went. Arabic became a part of the city's soundscape. That has changed the atmosphere in the city.

**J.G.:** And the cultural sphere has also changed, with all the artists and intellectuals coming from Syria and the other post-Arab Spring countries, right?

**F.K.:** Hmm, you're reminding me of the concerts and events I used to attend. It seems so long ago. Before the pandemic. Yes, that was a very vibrant time that started in 2011.

**J.G.:** You started the Welcome@FUBerlin program to welcome students from Syria and other countries to the region.

**F.K.:** Yes, that seems so long ago! We are now receiving the seventh cohort of refugee students; in many ways, things are similar to 2015. There is this enormous wave of volunteer work and initiatives to support and welcome the refugees from Ukraine. Especially in the beginning, it was very similar to Syrian refugees back in 2015. Many people wanted to meet Syrians and host them. There was a lot of solidarity and sympathy. Of course, in hindsight, this sentiment didn't last long, and nobody can predict how long the current wave of solidarity will last. It is our task now to build on past experiences and institutionalize support programs for refugees, regardless of which region they are coming from.

**J.G.:** Still, things are different now, right? How is your program different compared to that of 2015/16?

**F.K.:** We have much more experience with students from abroad without the typical framework of scholarships and exchange programs. It makes a big difference whether someone comes here with a scholarship from the DAAD, for example, or whether they come as refugees. The DAAD-sponsored students come with a complete support package, and everything they need is provided. Refugee students, by contrast, need funding and housing and often much more help to settle their residency status. We've learned a lot in this respect, but there is still much to do.

Back then, we also had some incidents and problems. For example, we had language classes with a very low percentage of female students. There were cases of homophobic and antisemitic incidents among students. The university is very sensitive to these cases. Still, it is important not to blame all problems on where the students are from. We try to solve some problems by getting a good mixture of students. But that's not always easy. In 2015, we had classes with 90 percent of male students of Arab origin. I'm sure we will see classes with many female students from Ukraine. We try to connect newcomers with regular students through our Buddy Program. At the moment, we have 100 students who are in our one-year preparation program.

**J.G.:** And is the program successful?

**F.K.:** We have quite a few students who entered the faculties. It's not easy, but it is possible. Some even got scholarships from the *Studienstiftung des Deutschen Volkes*. Others changed their faculties or even stopped. This is also sometimes due to their family situation or problems getting settled. Despite good counseling, you can't always plan trajectories from beginning to end.

**J.G.:** And how has your work changed over the years?

**F.K.:** Now I'm more involved with coordinating our Global Responsibility program, and I've started other programs, such as *Academics in Solidarity*. This program was born out of an AGYA idea competition, and it aims to match newly arrived researchers with established researchers all over Germany. Unlike other programs, we help those academics who already live in Germany. Many faculties are enriched through these researchers, especially concerning regional studies. At the same time, the number of applicants for academic positions in Germany is so high that it's challenging to get one. We try to identify niches within the system and work on changing it from within through this transnational network of solidarity and its unique expertise in the academic systems in our members' home and host countries. We currently have 130 mentees from Arab countries, Turkey, Iran, and Afghanistan, as well as Sub-Saharan Africa and Latin America.

**J.G.:** What impact does all of this have on regular German students? Would you think that interest in Arab society and civilization is growing? I remember when I started learning Arabic in FU in 1992, we were seven students in the Islamic Sciences course.

**F.K.:** Ok, that's really a long time ago. We've seen some changes since then. The first big increase in the popularity of the course and the topic, in general, was in 2001 when we had over 100 students, and there was another wave in 2011. For these students, it has become complicated: When they were ready to start their fieldwork and research abroad, it became increasingly difficult to travel to certain countries.

**J.G.:** For you, the Arab World is not only a region you work on. For you, it is also part of your daily life, as you have family in Egypt.

**F.K.:** Yes, I think family visits changed my relationship to Cairo . I used to live in the quarters where foreigners typically live: Zamalek, Mounira, and Downtown. When I travel to Egypt now, I mostly come to see our family, and we spend a lot of time in New Cairo. Our flat is in a gated community the size of a mid-sized town in Germany. I think there must be something like 200.000 inhabitants. It's primarily Egyptian upper middle class, and many Syrians live there now. Some people might argue that this is not the real Cairo, but it is part of it, just as we are now part of Arab Berlin because in our household, we speak both Arabic and German.

I'm sure this also has an impact on my professional work. I have become known as someone who prefers to sustain the dialogue and continue cooperation even in difficult times. Others may have a different point of view in that regard. My experience from living and working in Egypt and my connection to Egypt through my family have shaped my perspective. It gives me valuable knowledge, insight, empathy, and understanding of life and the people there.

# 23. On the Egyptian-German transfer of medical knowledge

## On cooperation, mobility, and similarities

*Ehab El Refaee*

This chapter reflects on the century-long education cooperation between Germany and Egypt, focusing on medicine. Taking global structural challenges, like the health care providers, the Covid-19 pandemic, and the global flow of migration into account, the chapter chronicles how a triangle of cooperation between Berlin, Cairo, and Greifswald engages with those challenges and what possible future lies ahead. This chapter lays the background for the medical collaboration between Egypt and Germany, particularly emphasizing the challenges and the future.

### The long history of German-Egyptian academic exchange and mobility

Throughout the past 200 years, there has been ongoing scientific mobility between Egypt and Germany in many fields. During the era of Khedive Ismail, about 100,000 foreigners settled in Cairo and Alexandria. The majority were Germans, among them archaeologists, with German interest in Egyptology playing an essential role in creating the academic bridge. (Yehia 2015). As a long-term result, German scientists disseminated knowledge about ancient Egyptian civilization. Despite the numerous benefits, this era left us with an ongoing conflict regarding the Egyptian treasures excavated and exhibited in European museums. Berlin takes pride in the beautiful bust of Nefertiti at "Neues Museum", which for an Egyptian, always triggers the question, "How did that get here?" – unfortunately, without receiving convincing explanations. Nefertiti can be said to have migrated to Germany many years ago and is now fully integrated as the most beautiful "Berliner." Meanwhile, newly migrated, highly skilled Egyptians settling in Berlin are still searching for new life prospects.

These activities laid the foundations for bridging knowledge between the two countries (Schneider & Raulwing 2012). The 19th century also saw the start of mobility in the other direction. A famous example is the Arabic-language documentation of the travels of Hassan Tawfiq Al-Adl[1] to Berlin as a scholar sent to the University in Berlin to teach Arabic (Arab 2008). Tawfiq's journey is described in great detail: how he reached Berlin, including the details of his travels, what the streets of Berlin looked like, how the people of Berlin treated him, what amused him about the local hospitality, and how impressed he was with German culture. He wrote a masterpiece that can serve as a roadmap for integration and understanding others to reach a common ground for cooperation and innovation.

Additionally, he spent much time describing how to fit the insights he had won into Egyptian society, always summarizing "take home" messages (Arab 2008). Unfortunately, Tawfiq died young, and his work did not become as popular as the works of his colleagues. Having discovered this diary accidentally at the annual Cairo book fair in 2019, I can attest that a German translation of this book is warranted.

Jumping again to recent history, we find a progression in the bilateral academic cooperation in education which is, in many instances, supported by the German Academic Exchange Service (DAAD). Funded mainly by the German Federal Foreign Office, with a settled establishment in Zamalek in Cairo, the DAAD office has offered numerous opportunities for Egyptian academics to travel to study in the German higher education landscape. One example: the German Egyptian Research Long-term Scholarships (GERLS) supported many Egyptian medical and paramedical researchers until 2013, helping them to get part of their academic and professional training in Germany. These scholars are afterward included in the DAAD Alumni Society in Egypt, representing one of the most prestigious networks for both countries.

## Egyptian and German medical education: Different yet similar?

Analyzing the main highlights of medical education in Germany and Egypt helps us understand the cooperation initiatives that would be intensive and fruitful. In Germany, medical education is offered mainly in public universities, with a few private universities conducting similar programs. Nearly 80,000 students are enrolled in faculties of medicine, where about 10,000 students start medical education every year and 6,000 graduate annually. The learning and evaluation process takes six years (two years of preclinical, four years of clinical studies) before the students graduate after the successful completion of the board exams, the *Staatsexamen* (Zavlin et al., 2017).

Both countries have structural similarities: The undergraduate medical education in Egypt does not differ in the amount of required study time from that in Ger-

1 Editors' note: See Chapter 20 by Islam Dayeh. The chapter documents the scholarly contributions by Hassan Tawfiq Al-Adl at the Seminar für Orientalische Sprachen 1887–1892.

many. Most medical faculties are public medical schools, with only a few private institutes. Nearly 10,000 students graduate annually (Abdelaziz et al., 2018). The young graduates then choose their specialty and begin a residency program which includes their postgraduate studies. In Egypt, the opportunity to enroll in a competent residency program with a properly organized training program is limited to university hospitals and only selected educational institutes. It is not easy to get into residency programs. Given limited resources and financial obstacles, many graduates look for places in residency programs abroad. (Schumann et al., 2019). There is an ongoing and fierce discussion on how to upgrade the healthcare system in Egypt: not only to stop the profound loss of young doctors, the most important resource to build the system but also to improve the quality of health services offered to Egyptian patients. The World Health Organization (WHO) announced a global shortage of 7.2 million healthcare providers in 2013. This shortage is expected to reach 15 million by 2030 (Liu et al., 2017).

Although thousands of Egyptian medical students graduate annually, Egypt reports a shortage of physicians in certain areas. Between 2019 and 2020, 11,500 Egyptian medical graduates left the Egyptian health sector for the United Kingdom (Mahfouz, 2023). In 2016, the density of physicians stood at one physician for every 12,285 inhabitants. Physicians congregate in Cairo and surrounding areas or move abroad, intensifying physician shortages in other areas of Egypt. New recruitment cannot replace this loss. Although it supplies the world with significant numbers of immigrant medical graduates, physician migration follows highly random, nearly untraceable patterns. (Kabbash 2021).

In Germany, postgraduate medical education has a well-established system that offers places for young residents to work, earn money, and complete their clinical training and postgraduate studies. As in Egypt, there is a growing shortage of medical professionals and physicians in Germany, which increases the demand for more students to study medicine and enroll in the healthcare system to serve patients. Thinking about the needs of each side would help grow the potential to build a steady, durable healthcare convention between the two countries to fulfill mutual demands.

During the last decade, and especially after the Arab uprisings and the instabilities experienced in Egypt, the immigration of healthcare professionals to Germany played a significant role in Egyptian-German medical collaboration. On the upside, several medical and surgical professionals started a career in Germany with high achievements in several clinical and research engagements. Their mobility adds visibility in the international literature, where we can find several Egyptian medical professionals involved in highly cited paramount studies (Mueller et al.; Pfaff et al.; Schiering et al.; West et al.) On the other hand, the migration of Egyptian doctors to Europe harms the healthcare system in the country of origin. In a recently published survey, the lack of resources, weak infrastructure, and financial stress were the most common motives for immigration from Egypt to Western countries (Schumann et al., 2019). In another recent study, the ineffective communication among physicians, between physicians and patients, and between physicians and nurse staff was a push factor for medical professionals (Kabbash 2021).

Therefore, the healthcare system in the home country urgently needs to implement a transformation project. This could induce Egyptian healthcare professionals to return and reintegrate into the Egyptian healthcare profession. In parallel, the integration of medical professionals from the Arab region, including Egypt, directly impacted the progression of medical tourism, as Arabic-speaking patients would mostly need clear communication about the procedures and the expected outcomes. There are substantial medical establishments, as in Berlin, with a long experience with medical tourism and evolving experience with Arabic medical professionals. However, the time taken for professional integration and the communication obstacles that might happen along the working career, as these with language problems, would slow down and sometimes stop the expected progression.

Therefore, initial collaborative efforts in medical education on the undergraduate level reaching the postgraduate training and research would be a well-defined objective to start with in order to find afterward the needed human resources for both communities in Egypt and Germany.

## The neurosurgical collaboration between Egypt and Germany: from regional to the Capital

Berlin has long been an attractive destination for Egyptians wanting to study medicine and work as medical professionals. History remembers Dr. Mohamed Helmy, who moved to Berlin in 1922 to study medicine and continued living there with a memorable struggle to treat his patients, who included Jews, and an additional struggle against the racism towards him during the Nazi regime (Finkel 2017).

Berlin annually receives a vast number of immigrant medical professionals seeking language courses that qualify them to apply for jobs nationwide. Another group of Egyptian medical professionals enrolled in various academic and clinical jobs in Berlin.With its numerous clinics, including Charité, Berlin has absorbed numerous Egyptian doctors and has gradually integrated them into the German health sector.

In addition, the longstanding collaboration between Cairo and Greifswald Universities stands on solid ground. The neurosurgical collaboration started between Cairo University and Greifswald University with individual fellowships supported by the DAAD aiming for surgical training in neuroendoscopy. Appointing the first Egyptian fellow to Greifswald to work as a coordinator between both university hospitals was an unprecedented step. This unique activity provided new intercultural experiences that put such coordinators in confrontation with the working conditions in both healthcare systems, which would offer tremendous experience that helps to make collaborations succeed. The collaboration started at the research and postgraduate education level and has now reached the point of teaching a bi-institutional curriculum for medical postgraduates in both countries (El Refaee et al., 2021). This innovative experience is an initiative to build a fully integrated undergraduate and postgraduate medical education program. Such a program would not only support an upgrade of the health service in Egypt but also represents an outstanding opportunity for exposure to expand the scope of accredited medical education needed for the maintenance and growth of the German healthcare system, which in turn creates significant brainstorming for improvement of the current education and training standards. No one can deny that Berlin played a role in the success story of this collaboration. From our experience, Berlin played a central role in preparing medical professionals before they started working in Greifswald, as they needed to learn the German language and integrate gradually in the German culture, and this happened in Berlin. In addition, the strong ties between the departments of Neurosurgery in Berlin and Greifswald led to the joining of neurosurgical academics from Charité to the committee of lecturers of the Cairo-Greifswald collaboration. Critical concepts for future development are more technology integration, intensified practical teaching, and obligatory knowledge exchange through meetings abroad or training. In the future, strong ties between the German University in Cairo and University Greifswald would give a strong potential to the GUC branch in Berlin to activate mutual training programs and be a central meeting point for a for promising collaboration that would strongly push both health care sectors towards the expected edge of excellence.

## COVID pandemic and the transformation of medical education worldwide

The impact of the COVID-19 pandemic on the practice of medicine worldwide is expected to have long-lasting effects (McKee & Stuckler, 2020). Since the start of the COVID-19 pandemic, online educational activities have increased, both for previously established online courses and new online events. A large turnout encourages the widening of the scope of such activities. For example, the 2020 annual meeting of the American Association of Neurological Surgery was made available exclusively as an online event for the first time. The impact this will have on the future of medical and neurosurgical education is unclear (Rasouli et al., 2020; Dedeilia et al., 2020; Teton et al., 2020; Tomlinson et al., 2020; Planchard et al., 2020). Medical students and faculty alike have found online learning platforms enticing. Virtual platforms were extended to patient care and clinical teaching during the COVID-19 pandemic, when telemedicine played an increasing role, given the mobility restrictions enforced (Speidel et al., 2021; Gachabayov et al., 2021). The shift towards the increased incorporation of digital learning platforms encouraged the development of organized teaching modules on using such platforms in formal medical education to enable a systematic optimal usage of online medical curricula (Poncette et al., 2020). Virtual reality was integrated into medical curricula and used as a substitute for traditional cadaver labs in undergraduate anatomy classes. More advanced virtual reality modules were developed for neurosurgical resident training.(Nakai et al.; Roh et al.) These advances can undoubtedly enrich the learning experience when integrated into existing medical curricula and offer alternative teaching methods that might be of value in situations where face-to-face learning is impossible. However, online courses carry the disadvantages of distance learning and poor communication. Therefore, online learning platforms require evaluation, interaction, and communication tools for a better learning atmosphere.

On the other hand, a large part of medical education, especially surgical education, depends on acquiring technical skills best imparted through face-to-face interaction with hands-on experience in cadaver labs, on the wards, and in operating rooms. The use of technology to simulate such experience could be helpful at times where face to face learning is not possible such as during the pandemic, or for facilitating international exposure with a minimal financial burden; however, it would be erroneous to assume that traditional hands-on in medicine could be replaced by technology (Dohle et al., 2021).

In the Cairo Greifswald neurosurgical experience, a blended learning experience merged online and hands-on training. Online modules were enriched with interactive discussions, assignments, and two examinations after the first and the final module. For hands-on training, the candidates had to travel to Germany to get outstanding technical training after accomplishing the theoretical learning objectives in the online courses.

The German Egyptian cooperation, Cairo-Greifswald, which slowed with the start of the COVID-19 pandemic, the collaborative work has started to gain intense experience in the new trends needed in medical education, not only to overcome the mobility and long-distance restrictions but also to upgrade the curriculum and implement new teaching methodologies. The learning program was named "Fellowship of Neuroendoscopy" and organized between Greifswald and Cairo Universities. This fellowship has several modules that are coping with the new trends in education, such as the training-the-trainer module, which started and will be upgraded to increase engagement with the trainers before interacting with the trainees. The skills they acquire will lead to more efficient learning and reduce burnout scores during the learning program (Olm et al., 2021).

## Future Prospects and Outlook

Using virtual reality to create atmospheres similar to surgical theatres and anatomical laboratories is one of the current innovative projects. Widening the collaboration to reach newly developed upgradable curricula for the undergraduate and postgraduate medical studies that are accredited by both countries, together with improving the health information system in Egypt all these together might serve for the inauguration of a collaborative Egyptian-German Health Foundation that offers balanced medical education, young medical professionals that are capable of doing their duties in any of the two countries, and an efficient healthcare system on both sides. With the global rise of interest in health care and the rising need for more medical and paramedical personnel, such an initiative can be a substantial move to encounter great demand soon. In the medical world, Charité is the largest university hospital in Europe, and Kasr Al-Ainy is the largest in the Middle East. Creating a medical collaboration between both university hospitals would strengthen the cooperation between the two capitals. One example of potential cooperation in the medical profession is a possible Berlin-Cairo collaboration to treat Hydrocephalus (water in the brain): Cairo University Children's Hospital currently accepts more than 1,000 children annually suffering from that disease. In Berlin, Charité endorses a well-established pediatric neurosurgery unit concerned with the same disease. It secures a binational fund to support an international medical program towards better management and treatment by bringing together two top medical university hospitals, Charité in Berlin and Kasr Al-Ainy in Cairo. That dream guarantees to reach better worldwide guidelines to offer healthier futures for these children across Arab-German borders.

## References


Abdelaziz, Adel, et al. (2018) Medical Education in Egypt: Historical Background, Current Status, and Challenges Health Professions Education 4(4) 236–44 (https://doi.org/10.1016/j.hpe.2017.12.007).

Arab, Mohammed Saber (2008) The journey of Hassan Effend Tawfik ElAdl 1887–1892: The journey to Berlin – Messages of Hope in Travelling Germany and Switzerland (in Arabic). رحلة حسن أفندي توفيق العدل 1887–1892: الرحلة إلى برلين رسائل البشرى في السياحة بألمانيا وسويسرا Cairo: Supreme Council for Culture.

Blanchard, Ryan, et al. (2020) Telemedicine and Remote Medical Education within Neurosurgery. Journal of Neurosurgery, Spine, May 1–4 (https://doi.org/10.3171/2020.5.SPINE20786)

Crisp, Nigel; Chen, Lincoln (2014) Global supply of health professionals. N Engl J Med. June 5, 370(23) 2247–8 (https://www.nejm.org/doi/10.1056/NEJMra111161 0 ).

Dedeilia, Aikaterini, et al. (2020) Medical and Surgical Education Challenges and Innovations in the COVID-19 Era: A Systematic Review. In Vivo 34(3) suppl. 1603–11 (https://doi.org/10.21873/invivo.11950).

Dohle, Niklas Julian, et al. (2021) Peer Teaching under Pandemic Conditions: Options and Challenges of Online Tutorials on Practical Skills. GMS Journal for Medical Education 38(1) Jan. 28 Doc7 (https://doi.org/10.3205/zma001403).

El Refaee, Ehab, et al. (2021) Letter: A New Trend of Blended Learning in Neurosurgical Training: Fellowship of Neuroendoscopy. Neurosurgery 89(1) June E89–90 (https://doi.org/10.1093/neuros/nyab134).

Finkel, Taliya (2017) Mohamed and Anna – In Plain Sight. Film directed by Taliya Finkel.

Gachabayov, Mahir, et al. (2021) The Role of Telemedicine in Surgical Specialties During the COVID-19 Pandemic: A Scoping Review. World Journal of Surgery Nov. (https://doi.org/10.1007/s00268-021-06348-1).

Kabbash, Ibrahim (2021) The brain drain: Why medical students and young physicians want to leave Egypt. East Mediterr. Health Journal 21 WHO (https://doi.or g/10.26719/emhj.19.049).

Liu, Jenny X., et al. (2017) Global health workforce labor market projections for 2030. Human Resources for Health, 15(11) (https://doi.org/10.1186/s12960-017-0187-2).

Mahfouz, Heba (2023): Young doctors are leaving Egypt in droves for better jobs abroad. The Washington Post, February 26. (https://www.washingtonpost.com /world/2023/02/26/egypt-doctors-economic-crisis/).

McKee, Martin; Stuckler, David (2020) If the world fails to protect the economy, COVID-19 will damage health not just now but also in the future. Nature Medicine 26(5) 640–42 (https://doi.org/10.1038/s41591-020-0863-y).

Mueller, Daniel, et al. (2015) Plasma Levels of Trimethylamine-N-Oxide Are Confounded by Impaired Kidney Function and Poor Metabolic Control. In: Atherosclerosis 243(2) Dec. 638–44 (https://doi.org/10.1016/j.atherosclerosis.20 15.10.091).

Nakai, Kohga, et al. (2021) Anatomy Education for Medical Students in a Virtual Reality Workspace: A Pilot Study. Clinical Anatomy (https://doi.org/10.1002/ca.23 783).

Olm, Michaela, et al. (2021) Increased Professionalization and Lower Burnout Scores Were Associated with Structured Residency Training Program: Results of a Cross-Sectional Survey. In: Medical Education Online 26(1) Dec. 1959284. (http s://www.tandfonline.com/doi/full/10.1080/10872981.2021.1959284)

Pfaff, Elke, et al. (2019) Brainstem Biopsy in Pediatric Diffuse Intrinsic Pontine Glioma in the Era of Precision Medicine: The INFORM Study Experience. European Journal of Cancer 114 (June) 27–35 (https://doi.org/10.1016/j.ejca.2019.03.019).

Poncette, Akira-Sebastian, et al. (2020) Undergraduate Medical Competencies in Digital Health and Curricular Module Development: Mixed Methods Study. Journal of Medical Internet Research 22(10) e22161 (https://doi.org/10.2196/22161).

Rasouli, Jonathan J., et al. (2020) Virtual Spine: A Novel, International Teleconferencing Program Developed to Increase the Accessibility of Spine Education During the COVID-19 Pandemic. World Neurosurgery 140 (Aug) e367–72 (https://doi.org/10.1016/j.wneu.2020.05.191).

Roh, Tae Hoon, et al. (2021) Virtual Dissection of the Real Brain: Integration of Photographic 3D Models into Virtual Reality and Its Effect on Neurosurgical Resident Education." In: Neurosurgical Focus 51(2) Aug. E16. (https://doi.org/10.3171/2021.5.FOCUS21193).

Schiering, Chris, et al. (2014) The Alarmin IL-33 Promotes Regulatory T-Cell Function in the Intestine. Nature 513(7519) Sept. 564–68. (https://doi.org/10.1038/nature13577).

Schneider, Thomas; Raulwing, Peter (2012) Egyptology from the First World War to the Third Reich: Ideology, Scholarship, and Individual Biographies. BRILL.

Schumann, Marwa, et al. (2019) Doctors on the Move: A Qualitative Study on the Driving Factors in a Group of Egyptian Physicians Migrating to Germany. Globalization and Health 15(1) (https://doi.org/10.1186/s12992-018-0434-x).

Speidel, Robert, et al. (2021) Did Video Kill the XR Star? Digital Trends in Medical Education Before and after the COVID-19 Outbreak from the Perspective of Students and Lecturers from the Faculty of Medicine at the University of Ulm. GMS Journal for Medical Education 38(6) Sept. 15 Doc101 (https://doi.org/10.3205/zma001497).

Teton, Zoe E., et al. (2020) The Neurosurgical Atlas: Advancing Neurosurgical Education in the Digital Age. Neurosurgical Focus 48(3) E17 (https://doi.org/10.3171/2019.12.FOCUS19820).

Tomlinson, Samuel B., et al. (2020) Editorial. Innovations in Neurosurgical Education during the COVID-19 Pandemic: Is It Time to Reexamine Our Neurosurgical Training Models? Journal of Neurosurgery (Apr.) 1–2 (https://doi.org/10.3171/2020.4.JNS201012).

West, Nathaniel R., et al. (2017) Erratum: Oncostatin M Drives Intestinal Inflammation and Predicts Response to Tumor Necrosis Factor-Neutralizing Therapy in Patients with Inflammatory Bowel Disease. Nature Medicine 23(6) 788 (https://doi.org/10.1038/nm0617-788d).

Yehia, Enas Fares (2015) The German Archeological Missions in Egypt during the

Era of Khedive Ismail 1863 – 1879. Journal of Association of Arab Universities for Tourism and Hospitality 12(2) 1–14 (https://doi.org/10.21608/jaauth.2015.61502).
Zavlin, Dmitry, et al. (2017) A Comparison of Medical Education in Germany and the United States: From Applying to Medical School to the Beginnings of Residency. German Medical Science GMS E-Journal 15 (Sept.) Doc15. (https://doi.org/10.3205/000256)

# Part 6: Outlook

# 24. Beyond Berlin

## Why the rest of Germany also matters

*Jan Claudius Völkel*[1]

## Introduction

Since being designated the capital of unified Germany in 1991, Berlin has gained tremendous national and international standing. Riding on its particular image as "poor but sexy", a frame famously bestowed upon it in 2003 by the mayor at the time, Klaus Wowereit (Ewert 2016), Berlin has become a "capital of cool" (Frary 2018). Concurrently, Berlin has steadily improved its score in the Global Power City Index, bringing it to rank eight in the 2022 edition, a slight slip from rank seven occupied in the two previous 2020 and 2021 editions.[2] Berlin has attracted a growing number of people from all over the world as new temporary or permanent inhabitants. This includes expatriates from the Middle East and North Africa (MENA), whose number has significantly risen among Berlin's population over the last decade. Especially Syrians, who had to leave their home country in great numbers and moved to Germany due to the civil war back home (Streitwieser et al. 2017: 231), have made the city

1 The author wishes to thank Rabia Ergen and Korbinian Ferstl for their invaluable help in the conduct of this research.

2 (Berlin's positive ranking is mainly due to its good achievements in the categories "Livability" (rank 7), "Cultural Interaction" (8) and "Environment" (9), whereas evaluations for "Economy" (26), "R&D" (16) and "Accessibility" (23) were less favorable (https://www.mori-m-foundation.or.jp/pdf/GPCI2022_summary.pdf).

a favorite host for Arabs.[3] Most of the chapters in this book provide plentiful insights into their lives and realities in today's Berlin.

Berlin offers an unmatched fabric of history weaving together threads from Germany's Prussian, Weimarian, Fascist, and Socialist past, as well as its democratic present. It is a city that constantly redefines itself and charms visitors with its creativity, flexibility and, sometimes annoyingly for its permanent residents, unpredictability. As a result, the editors of this book assert that Berlin symbolizes a location where transformation processes begin and new activities, possibilities, lifestyles, and experimental spaces open up. This dynamic is, for one, rooted in Berlin's unique history of glory, devastation, division, and resurrection; but it also results from very mundane circumstances, such as affordable rents and decent living costs, especially when compared to London, Paris, New York, Toronto and other metropolises that have become leading centers of immigration.

This mix of vibrancy and affordability, plus the underlying political liberalism and economic potential the Federal Republic of Germany offers, has made Berlin a prime destination not least for persons under political persecution. Irrespective of frequent, and probably legitimate, criticism of cumbersome bureaucracy, lengthy asylum processes, and decade-long lives in limbo for foreigners seeking refuge (Tize 2021), Germany has become a preferred destination for gagged opponents of illiberal regimes, and its capital exerts a unique attraction: It is where top Turkish journalist Can Dündar escaped to after being convicted for espionage in his home country in 2016. Kremlin critic Alexei Navalny was brought to Berlin after suffering severe poisoning in Russia. Chinese artist and regime detractor Ai Weiwei lived in Berlin from 2015, before moving to the UK four years later after criticizing that Germany was "not an open society" (Ponzanesi 2020: 233).

Australian-Egyptian sociologist Amro Ali (2019) has argued that Berlin has developed a transformative power that cannot be found in any other city, be it in Germany or elsewhere. All other cities "appear to have a relative absence of ingredients that lead to the blossoming of a full-fledged political exile community like we are witnessing in Berlin". He concludes this has made Berlin the most important host city for the "exiled Arab body politic".

3 As of December 31, 2020, 1,344,612 inhabitants of Berlin had a "migration background", with almost 500,000 coming from other European countries (incl. the Russian Federation). 789,076 of the total 3,769,962 registered inhabitants had a foreign passport. From the MENA region, the by far most dominant Berlin group were Syrians (41,418), followed by Iraqis (9,472), Iranians (9,124), Lebanese (8,279), Egyptians (5,279), Israelis (5,239), Tunisians (2,984), Libyans (2,858), Moroccans (1,943), Jordanians (1,527), Yemenis (1,174), Algerians (1,118), Saudis (698), Kuwaitis (107), Bahrainis (95), Emiratis (59), Qataris (32), and Omanis (16) (https://download.statistik-berlin-brandenburg.de/fa93e3bd19a2e885/a5ecfb2fff6a/SB_A01-05-00_2020h02_BE.pdf).

This chapter here argues that while Berlin has undoubtedly gained largely unparalleled importance for politically woke citizens with roots or interests in the MENA region, other regions beyond Berlin should be brought to their notice, as well as these can generate transformative energy too. If, as stipulated by Amro Ali, a new "Berlin school of thought" is required among Arab thinkers that goes beyond philosophical ideas about a better political future in the Arab world and this school of thought should be stimulated by the environment they actually live in, then members of the Arab body politic need to leave Berlin to expand their horizons to explore other German regions. There they will detect features of today's Germany that deserve consideration. These are not only shining and positive examples; many are more worrying than encouraging. But given the benefits of learning from failure over learning from success, negative aspects deserve as much study as the positive ones do. They can send important signals back into the societies across the MENA region that suffer from authoritarianism, outright dictatorship, a lack of security, insufficient human rights protection, and economic perspectives (Völkel 2022). So while Arab body politic members might prefer to meet in hip Berlin, venturing out beyond the capital bears true promise.

Before we venture out on a tour of the German regions, however, let's look briefly at some specific German characteristics that are important for the theme of this chapter.

## The Nazi past in Germany's DNA

2021 marked Germany's 150th birthday after the founding of the German Empire in 1871. Yet hardly any Germans took note of this anniversary, let alone celebrated it. This might in part have been due to the COVID-19 pandemic, but no major commemoration events had been planned even before. Where they did occur, they were reflective and educational – museum exhibitions, lectures and discussions among historians and social scientists, intellectual analyses in newspapers, radio features and academic publications, and official commemoration sessions in parliaments and other places of public relevance. There were, however, no mass festivities, no music festivals, no military parades or pompous galas on TV celebrating "Germany at 150" (Matthies 2021).

This absence of national self-celebration is connected to Germany's broken national pride (Blank/Schmidt 2003: 298), resulting from its difficult history, most obviously the devastating Nazi era. The twelve years under Adolf Hitler's fascist regime from 1933 to 1945 left a lasting mark on Germany that can still be sensed almost everywhere.

This broken national pride is only one aspect particular to modern Germany; another is a broad consensus on the need for power diffusion. In the former German

Democratic Republic (GDR) communism had dominated politics from a centralist perspective, with the SED (*Sozialistische Einheitspartei Deutschlands*, Socialist Unity Party of Germany) and its omnipresent state security organization *Stasi* ruling the country under Soviet guidance from East Berlin. By contrast, the Federal Republic of Germany (FRG) began as a decentralized political system. This meant that in Bonn, an intentionally chosen modest capital (Campbell 2003: 13), the executive had to be firmly rooted in the parliamentary majority, and the president, as the state's highest representative, had only strictly limited powers. Power was also dispersed geographically among the eleven and later sixteen federal states, or *Länder,* which have enjoyed a remarkable level of independence, albeit under the pretext of far-reaching symmetry – the claim that living conditions everywhere should be "equivalent" (note: not equal!), as expressed in Germany's Basic Law (Article 72.2). This means that the *Länder* were to provide all citizens with comparable living conditions: access to education, health, and public services, but also jobs, public transportation, and overall security.

One surprising result of this decentralized system is that Germany's two highest courts, the constitutional court (*Bundesverfassungsgericht*) and the federal court of justice (*Bundesgerichtshof*), are both located in Karlsruhe, a medium size city in southwest Germany, some 675 km away from Berlin (and 280 km from Bonn). This has historical roots, but even after unification in 1990, both courts were not moved (back) to the capital – a telltale that power was meant to remain distributed as an overarching principle in the reunified, "new" Germany. The Federal Administration Court (*Bundesverwaltungsgericht*) moved from its two former seats, West Berlin and Munich to Leipzig in 1997, occupying the historic building of the German Reich's supreme court.

Likewise, to this day, half of the federal ministries have kept their main seat in Bonn and have only secondary seats in Berlin. Berlin is thus one of the world's few capitals that does not host all relevant state institutions. It has even ceded Germany's leading airport (Frankfurt, Munich), leading industries (the Ruhr area, Munich, Stuttgart, or Wolfsburg), leading media outlets (Cologne, Hamburg, Mainz), and leading football clubs (Dortmund, Munich) to other cities. And while Berlin's universities have found their way back into the country's scholarly elite, students receive excellent higher education in other German university towns such as Göttingen, Greifswald, Jena, Siegen or Tübingen – towns and cities that many people might need to search for on a map.

Egyptians would probably disagree if asked to relocate their supreme court to, say, Minya or Luxor, and Tunisians would certainly not consider opening their constitutional court in Kasserine or Gabes. Jordan's leading universities are in and around Amman, Algeria's leading airport is in Algiers and Lebanon's financial district is in Beirut. By contrast, Germany proves that national capitals do not need to be the undisputed center of power per se and that comprehensive regional development is a goal worth striving for. Morocco is the only MENA country with similar features, where the capital, Rabat, is economically less powerful than Casablanca and historically less important than Marrakech or Fez. Israel (Tel Aviv versus West Jerusalem) and Palestine (Ramallah versus East Jerusalem) are obviously special cases. So is Türkiye, with its break from the Ottoman Empire and the resulting choice of Ankara over Istanbul as the republic's capital. In all other MENA countries, the capitals are the largely undisputed national centers. Regional development meanwhile has remained insufficient, and citizens outside the capital often lack access to health, education, and other fundamental state services. This is not so in Germany.

## Places of transformative relevance outside Berlin

In the following, some places across Germany are presented that bear a transformative relevance for certain aspects of democratization, such how minorities and outcasts are treated, borders and boundaries are managed, citizens are involved in state activities, and economic and social needs are met. These cases afford insights which stand for themselves and that cannot, or can only in limited terms, be gleaned in Berlin itself. This list is not meant to be exhaustive, but only to illustrate a variety of inspirational and possibly revolutionary impulses outside the German capital.

### Minorities and outcasts

Just 200 kilometers to the south of Berlin, the Lusatia region would be a worthwhile area for members of the Arab body politic to learn from. Home of the Sorbs, a West Slavic ethnic group who have gone through decades of assimilation at the risk of extinction (Magris 2018: 105–115), they have nevertheless kept their cultural traditions, including their own language. State authorities started in the 1950s to massively expand the exploitation of the major lignite reserves. Industrializing the region, they brought in workers from all over the GDR, who in time outnumbered the native Sorbs and gradually marginalized them. Apart from the Danish minority in Southern Schleswig (northern Germany), the Frisians in the coastal regions, and the Romani people, the Sorbs are the only legally recognized and formally protected ethnic minority in Germany that run their own schools and cultural centers and keep their distinct language and culture alive. For that purpose, Leipzig University features an Institute for Sorbian Studies, going back to the "Societas Lusatorum Sorabica" founded in 1716, and the city of Bautzen features a Sorbian museum to keep this specific part of German history alive. Lessons to be learned here might include impulses for how a marginalized minority has been involved in developing institutions to cultivate cultural identity, under both dictatorial and democratic conditions.

Bautzen is also worth exploring for its distinct history of imprisonment. Originally founded in 1906, the "Bautzen II" prison became an important site for the Weimar Republic's efforts to reform incarceration from pure punishment to crime prevention through the rehabilitation and "moral advancement" of offenders (Wachsmann 2014: 118). A miserable place of torture and degradation during the Nazi era, Bautzen II then gained sad prominence by becoming one of the leading *Stasi* penitentiaries for political prisoners. Inmates were kept there without giving reasons or providing proper legal assistance, and imprisonment destroyed future prospects. The *Stasi* aimed at breaking the prisoners rather than rehabilitating them, seeing their value only in the ransom they could generate if sold to the Federal Republic for Western currency (Horster 2004). A visit to the Bautzen II complex, now an official commemorative site, provokes questions about inviolable rights for jail inmates, the relation between state authorities and citizens, and the function of punishment.

## Borders and boundaries

Not far from Bautzen lies the city of Görlitz, one of the very few German cities that suffered no major destruction during the second world war. It also survived the following period of post-war reconstruction largely unchanged, when many German cities lost additional historic buildings to "modernization" – primarily because cars were given unconditional priority over public transportation, bicycles, and pedestrians. Görlitz, however, kept its medieval character, and thanks to the quick response of the fire brigade on November 9, 1938, even their synagogue survived the *Night of Broken Glass* largely undamaged. Yet Görlitz's historic city center stood to face imminent destruction in the 1980s due to decade-long negligence. Only after German unification were such plans scrapped, and Görlitz was admitted to the exclusive consortium of historic cities, the *Arbeitsgemeinschaft historischer Städte,* then numbering only three in Western Germany – Bamberg, Lübeck, and Regensburg. Meißen and Stralsund have since joined as additional Eastern German cities. Today, Görlitz's old town is comprehensively renovated, albeit at the price of gentrification.

Historically, Görlitz struggled with a challenge related to its sudden location on the periphery. Though it had enjoyed a central location, lying between Dresden and Wrocław (*Breslau* at the time) in the German Empire and the Weimar Republic, it now found itself divided at the Polish-German border, with its eastern boroughs beyond the Neiße river forming the Polish city of Zgorzelec. Former German citizens were expelled, and the city found itself in a militarized border zone with more and more Poles settling in. The end of the Cold War brought a remarkable healing effect: in 1998, Görlitz and Zgorzelec declared their collaboration under the joint label *Europastadt* (Europe city).

It would be similarly informative to visit one of the former German-German border crossings, such as the *Grenzübergangsstelle* (GÜST) Marienborn–Helmstedt. At the time Europe's largest border point, this well-preserved checkpoint is now a museum and memorial of the Stasi-controlled migration management. While the apparent aim was to prevent escape from the East to the West, visitors to the GDR and even transit travelers from West Germany to West Berlin were thoroughly checked and investigated. This included psychological pressure, recalled by Germans on both sides of the border – although Western memories might overrule Eastern perspectives in retrospectives today (Knischewski/Spittler 2010). A visit to this remarkable spot not only reveals lessons about authoritarian state security, border control, and the general mistrust of one state towards its (and other) citizens; considering the arbitrary acts of massive state power and the way it has been dealt with since 1990 also speaks to questions of transitional justice, oral history, and conciliation.

## Citizens in uniform

Munich and Hamburg host two universities of the German armed forces (*Universität der Bundeswehr*), Münster hosts the German Police University (*Deutsche Hochschule der Polizei*). These special institutions of higher education are not simply military or police academies that serve the primary purpose of turning out professional soldiers or police officers; they were created to make civil education available to them while on duty, following the concept of military personnel as "citizens in uniform" (*Staatsbürger in Uniform*), born in the 1950s to discuss the rearmament of the Federal Republic and the eventual foundation of the *Bundeswehr* in 1955. According to this concept, soldiers and police officers remain citizens of the democratic polity with all of their rights and responsibilities. They are entitled to exercise their democratic rights and to strive for political education. The populace being protected by fundamental democratic ethics places limits on military orders, which soldiers are encouraged to disregard should they deem them illegal. Finally, the "citizens in uniform" concept emphasizes that both the armed force and the police force are not homogenously comprised of cadre elites but reflect Germany's pluralistic society (Koltermann 2012: 113). For all these safeguards, the security forces have a persistent problem, namely racism and the non-discriminatory performance of their duties. Globally, and not least in the MENA region, relations between the armed forces, the citizens, and the state are contested and problematic. Interviewing staff and students at these German universities could provide interesting insights for transformative thinking.

## Economic and social transformation

Arab body politic members could also visit the Rhine-Ruhr area between Dortmund, Duisburg, and Cologne, Europe's largest urban agglomeration (Zimmermann 2013:

104). This was the prime destination for Arab migrants in Germany between 2007 and 2017 (Heider et al. 2020: 9–10). Its former rich coal mines made the region Germany's traditional industrial powerhouse. The population here will remember the exorbitant levels of air pollution along with decent neighborhoods in the early decades of the young Federal Republic. Many lost their jobs in the ongoing transformation of the former steel mills into more sustainable enterprises. Millions of "guest workers" (*Gastarbeiter*) who were initially supposed to stay for a limited time eventually stayed indefinitely, giving rise to diversified restaurant menus, shopping opportunities, lifestyles, and arts. Second and third-generation migrants have grown up in a Germany that is both home and hostile to them. The changing needs of both locally born and immigrant citizens have grown from purely economic to include cultural and social expectations (Akmir 2015: 148). They have been exposed to xenophobia, racism, exclusion, prejudices, and suspicion. Economists explain how unavoidable change has destroyed formerly prestigious specialized professions like mining. Politicians have struggled to decide whether mines and steel mills should be closed, and city planners have been obliged to make their cities keep pace with staggering social, economic, and political changes. Migrants from the MENA region have been an integral part of those changes with their ups and downs. No wonder the DOMiD, the Documentation Centre and Museum of Migration in Germany, is located not in Berlin but in Cologne, which also hosts Germany's most prominent mosque since 2018.

## Conclusion

For multiple reasons, Berlin is an attractive city for Arab expatriates who have had to escape their countries or have chosen to live outside the MENA region. But it is not the only place in Germany that holds relevance for those who try to understand social phenomena and political and economic relations under changing conditions – aspects that we commonly associate with transformation.

Germany with its unique history has a lot to offer regarding safeguarding the indispensable dignity of humankind vis-à-vis the state, and of citizens within their society. That is not to deny massive breaches through racist and disrespectful behavior. It contains impressive examples of changing living conditions in cities and the countryside, where socioeconomic and demographic change challenges have required political and economic responses encouraging the "winners" of transformation and cushioning the "losers". Germany has not succeeded in all these challenges, as attested by the growing tensions between progressive Germans and those who have lost their trust in political institutions and now support anti-democratic, even fascist deputies in the federal *Bundestag*, the 16 *Länder* parliaments, and the many city councils. But Germany's failures and ongoing socioeconomic struggles do hold lessons for Arab aspirations for reform and transformation and be it to show how things should *not* be handled.

Ultimately, looking beyond the Berlin horizon offers great transformative insights. Germany's federal system, first and foremost, aspires to ensure comparable living conditions all over the country. Could it be that life outside capitals such as Amman, Cairo and Tunis would improve if only they were no longer idealized over other parts of the country? Then, focusing on the specifics that its various regions and municipalities offer, Germany narrates stories steeped in the challenges of overcoming its nationalist past that may help to generate ideas for contemporary transformation processes as well.

Last but not least: revolutions might happen in cities (Lévesque, 2019: 21), but people in their majority live outside such metropols. Germany's 14 cities with more than 500,000 inhabitants each host not more than 15 of the country's total 82 million inhabitants. Most Germans rather live in mid- to small-size cities or outright villages. Questions of how to provide them with sufficient childcare and quality education, comprehensive medical care, efficient transportation solutions, attractive jobs and affordable housing are crucial for the overall social transformation in Germany; and they are not less crucial for the transformation trajectories in Arab societies. Neglecting the daily realities of these non-metropolitans bears the potential risk of neglecting the majority of Arab citizens as well. Missing their empathy and support, however, would likely mean that no transformation can ever take societal roots and consequently take off. Neither here nor there.

## References

Akmir, Abdelouahed (2015) European Arabs: Identity, education and citizenship. *Contemporary Arab Affairs* 8(2) 147–162 (https://doi.org/10.1080/17550912.2015.1016762).

Ali, Amro (2019) On the need to shape the Arab exile body in Berlin. Open Democracy, February 18 (https://www.opendemocracy.net/en/north-africa-west-asia/on-need-to-shape-arab-exile-body-in-berlin/).

Blank, Thomas; Schmidt, Peter (2003) National identity in a united Germany: Nationalism or patriotism? An empirical test with representative data. Political Psychology 24(2) 289–312.

Campbell, Scott (2003) The enduring importance of national capital cities in the global era. Urban and Regional Research Collaborative Working Paper 03–08 (Ann Arbor: University of Michigan).

Ewert, Benjamin (2016) Poor but sexy? Berlin as a context for social innovation. In: Brandsen, Taco; Cattacin, Sandro; Evers, Adalbert; Zimmer, Annette (eds.): Social innovations in the urban context (Cham: Springer) 143–158.

Frary, Mark (2018) How Berlin became the capital of cool. The Times, April 14 (https://www.thetimes.co.uk/static/how-berlin-became-capital-of-cool).

Heider, Bastian; Stroms, Peter; Koch, Jannik; Siedentop, Stefan (2020) Where do immigrants move in Germany? The role of international migration in regional disparities in population development. Population, Place and Space 26(8) e2363 (https://doi.org/10.1002/psp.2363).

Horster, Maximilian (2004) The trade in political prisoners between the two German states, 1962–89. Journal of Contemporary History 39(3) 403–424.

Knischewski, Gerd/Spittler, Ulla (2010) Memorialization of the German-German border in the context of constructions of Heimat. In: Niven, Bill; Paver, Chloe (eds.): Memorialization in Germany since 1945 (London: Palgrave Macmillan) 318–327.

Koltermann, Jens O. (2012) Citizen in uniform: Democratic Germany and the changing Bundeswehr. Parameters 42(2) 108–126.

Lévesque, Carole (2019) Finding room in Beirut. Places of the everyday (Goleta: Punctum Books).

Magris, Claudio (2018): Journeying (New Haven: Yale University Press).

Matthies, Bernd (2021) Heute vor 150 Jahren war Berlin erstmals Hauptstadt. Der Tagesspiegel, January 18, https://www.tagesspiegel.de/berlin/jubilaeum-ohne-jubel-heute-vor-150-jahren-war-berlin-erstmals-hauptstadt/26825656.html.

Ponzanesi, Sandra (2020) The art of dissent: Ai Weiwei, rebel with a cause. In: Buikema, Rosemarie; Buyse, Antoine; Robben, Antonius (eds.): Culture, citizenship and human rights (Abingdon: Routledge) 215–236.

Streitwieser, Bernhard; Brueck, Lukas; Moody, Rachel; Taylor, Margaret (2017) The potential and reality of new refugees entering German Higher Education: The case of Berlin institutions, European Education 49(4) 231–252.

Tize, Carola (2021) Living in permanent temporariness: The multigenerational ordeal of living under Germany's toleration status, Journal of Refugee Studies 34(3) 3024–3043.

Völkel, Jan Claudius (2022) A disastrous decade. Regional Report Middle East and North Africa, Bertelsmann Transformation Index 2022 (Gütersloh: Bertelsmann Stiftung) (https://bti-project.org/fileadmin/api/content/en/downloads/reports/global/BTI_2022_Regional_Report_MENA.pdf).

Wachsmann, Nikolaus (2014) Between reform and repression: imprisonment in Weimar Germany. In Wetzell, Richard F. (ed.) Crime and criminal justice in modern Germany (New York: Berghahn) 115–136.

Zimmermann, Horst (2013) Berlin: An almost symmetrical case. In: Nagel, Klaus-Jürgen (ed.): The problem of the capital city: New research on federal capitals and their territory (Barcelona: Institut d'Estudis Autonòmics) 103–121.

# 25. "I've seen them grow up. They're almost like my children."

Salah Yousif, a poet from Sudan, came to Berlin in the 1970s by accident. For over thirty years, he has run his store for antiques, vinyl, and African design on Urbanstraße. From his store, he observes Berlin and processes his impressions in poems. He has watched generation after generation of Arab migrants pass by in Berlin. Julia Gerlach visited him.

**Julia Gerlach:** How did you come to Berlin?

**Salah Yousif:** I wound up in Berlin by chance. Actually, I was just passing through. I came here and then lost my passport in the first few days. It took me a year to get a new one, but by then, I had developed a taste for life here, so I stayed. It was a beautiful time, the seventies in Berlin. Music, politics, and people came together, with lots and lots of discussions. That was great.

**J.G.:** How old were you?

**S.Y.:** Oh, age doesn't play such a role with us. I was twenty, twenty-two. Very young.

**J.G.:** And you've been writing ever since, right?

**S.Y.:** I've been writing poetry since I was a child, and when I came to Berlin, I took a little break. In the '80s, I started again. When you arrive someplace new, you first have to find your bearings before you can write. Once you begin to participate in local life, you begin to understand.

When I came here, of course, I had no means and needed to find work. That was exhausting. I began working in construction. I remember arriving in a suit. An academic going into construction. That was something! I had studied pharmacy and social sciences.

**J.G.:** And now you have this store.

**S.Y.:** Yes, I'd initially opened a grocery store, but that was very tiring. And then my neighbor here recommended that – like him – I could sell antiques instead. That's what I've been doing ever since. I used to restore things myself, but now I sell what others restore. I also sell records. I love music. In the beginning, I just sold off parts of my record collection. Now that business is doing well again. Many young people buy records from me. Lately I also offer these African things in the store. I sell them for a niece of mine. That's nice because it makes the store a little warmer.

**J.G.:** How has Berlin changed over the years?

**S.Y.:** So much! Berlin has changed, and so have the people who live here. It's become colder. The atmosphere was more humane back then. In the beginning, people helped me out an incredible amount. If you didn't have a place to sleep, they would take you home. If you went out, you would split the bill. The concept of "this is mine and that is yours" wasn't as strong back then as it is now. It was more humane then. People showed more solidarity and were friendlier. Maybe that had something to do with the Wall. People were packed more closely together back then.

You can still feel some of that in Berlin today: if you go to a café, it's easy to meet new people.

**J.G.:** Over the years, Berlin has also become much more Arab.

**S.Y.:** Yes, that's true. First the Palestinians and then the Lebanese. Always after a war, many people would come here. The arrival of the Syrians has changed a lot because overall, the level of culture is very high in Syria. They have changed the art scene here in Berlin. But I myself don't notice much of that. I've been here for so long and settled into my life. I live with influences from many different directions. I am not your typical Arab.

**J.G.:** What do you write about?

**S.Y.:** These days I do readings of my poetry more often. I read in German and in Arabic. I have five books out. I have an inner urge to write. There's something inside that wants out. I also write so that people understand that there are many voices in the culture. I write a lot about Berlin. I feel good here and write about people and places. For example, I've got a poem about *Urbanstraße* and about *Tempelhofer Feld*.

**J.G.:** Sitting here like this in your store and looking out of the shop window onto the street is a little like being in the cinema. You see people passing by, and cyclists. Berlin is passing by out there.

**S.Y.:** Yes, it's a beautiful view.

**J.G.:** When people Google you, the first thing they find is an article about how your store was completely destroyed by rioters in March 2022.

**S.Y.:** Really, is that the first thing you find about me? It was horrible. A gang. A clan. From around here. They wanted my store for themselves. They said they wanted to buy the store from me, but I wouldn't give in. So, they smashed everything to pieces.

**J.G.:** Do you know them?

**S.Y.:** Not that well, but I know who they are. They're gone now. That's good.

**J.G.:** The gangs are also part of Arab Berlin, right?

**S.Y.:** Yes, among the Arabs, there is also a share of criminals, of course. That's normal. There are artists, and there are criminals.

Just put yourself in the position of those people: They came here as refugees from countries at war and found themselves in a situation where everything was walled off. They could not work; they had no chance to build something for themselves. Today things are different. Today, newcomers receivelanguage and integration courses. I've seen this, and I know the different generations of refugees. I have seen them grow up. They're almost like my children.

**J.G.:** But it's not nice when the children come in and destroy your place.

**S.Y.:** They were so angry. They broke everything, and I had to clean up afterward for three weeks straight. Now they're gone. That's a good thing.

**J.G.:** You said: People living in Berlin have changed. What do you mean?

**S.Y.:** Life is getting harder and harder. People all have a lot of problems and are getting more anxious. That liberal flair that Berlin had is getting lost. You have to be a little more reserved in voicing your opinions. That development is not good. And the new militarism is not good, either.

There were so many terrible wars in Europe, and finally, peace. Now the war is coming back[1]. And there is not even the necessary space to question militarism.

1 Editors note: The war refers to the Ukraine war.

What people forget is that there used to be a lot of older people here. Now only young people remain. There are also hardly any children – only Arab children. And then there are the hipsters.

**J.G.:** You'd think that if more Arabs lived here now, it would be warmer and more communal.

**S.Y.:** What is an Arab? We have certain ideas about that. But what is an Arab, actually? What does he or she do? Does he or she have to fulfill specific criteria? What unites the Arabs? I think a lot is changing right now. I have the feeling that something has been destroyed inside many of them.

**J.G.:** Is that perhaps because after 2011, many people feel that they first have to find out which side the other person is on – for example, whether someone is for the regime or the revolution? Have people come to distrust each other because of that?

**S.Y.:** Yes, solidarity and self-confidence within the Arab world have taken a big hit. There are so many problems... and that is reflected in people's attitudes. They are becoming distrustful and losing solidarity. In addition, it's not easy for newcomers to come here and find a place. We are looked at with suspicion. That's not nice. The rug has been pulled out from under people's feet. It's easier for the children.

**J.G.:** But when the children integrate, it's easy to feel like you're losing them.

**S.Y.:** That's a complicated thing. On the one hand, you wish them lots of success, but on the other hand, you don't want to lose them. Because then they're no longer really part of the family. It's not at all easy to be an Arab in Berlin.

# Appendix

# Contributors' Biographies

## Book Editors

**Dr. Hanan Badr** (Dr. phil. Universität Erfurt) is Professor and Chair for Public Spheres and Inequalities at the Department of Communication, University of Salzburg, Austria. Her work focuses on the interactions between journalism, media, power, and transformation processes, focusing on digitization and globalization. She held positions at Freie Universität Berlin, Cairo University, Gulf University for Sciences and Technology, and Orient-Institut Beirut/Max Weber Foundation. Her work has been published in Digital Journalism, International Communication Gazette, Media and Communication, and Media, War & Conflict. She is an Associate Editor of the Journal of Communication. She serves on the editorial boards of the International Journal of Communication, Digital Journalism, and the Middle East Journal of Culture and Communication. Her awards include the Kluge Fellowship at the Library of Congress and the DAAD Scholarship Award. She is elected Chair for Activism, Communication and Social Change at the International Communication Association.

**Dr. Nahed Samour** is a postdoctoral researcher and Core Emerging Investigator at the Integrative Research Institute Law & Society in the Faculty of Law at Humboldt University Berlin. She studied law and Islamic studies at the universities of Bonn, Birzeit/Ramallah, London (SOAS), Berlin (HU), Harvard, and Damascus. She was a doctoral fellow at the Max Planck Institute for European Legal History in Frankfurt/Main. She clerked at the Court of Appeals in Berlin, held a postdoc position at the Eric Castrén Institute of International Law and Human Rights, Helsinki University, Finland, and was an Early Career Fellow at the Lichtenberg-Kolleg, Göttingen Institute for Advance Study. She also taught as Junior Faculty at the Harvard Law School Institute for Global Law and Policy from 2014–2018. Her current work focuses on religion, race and gender in law.

## Authors

**Iskandar Abdalla** is a researcher, educator, and film curator. He was born in Alexandria, Egypt, and is now based in Berlin. He studied history and Islamic Studies at Ludwig-Maximilians-Universität in Munich and Freie Universität Berlin, and is currently a doctoral fellow at the Berlin Graduate School Muslim Cultures and Societies. His research interests encompass Islam and migration in Europe, film and cultural production in modern Egypt, and feminist and queer research methods. Apart from his academic pursuits, Iskandar has been working in the field of political and cultural education in Germany for several years, conceptualizing workshops on topics like racism, gender and sexuality, and empowerment through artistic and cultural practices. Iskandar is also a program curator at the Arab Film Festival in Berlin.

**Fadi Abdelnour** was born in Jerusalem and studied archaeology, linguistics, and cultural studies at Birzeit University in Palestine, where he was socially and culturally active in the student movement. He graduated in Visual Communication/Communication Design from the art school Burg Giebichenstein in Halle in 2010. Since then, he has been working as a freelance designer in Berlin. Fadi Abdelnour co-founded the ALFILM – Arab Film Festival Berlin in 2009 and was its artistic director until 2019. In 2020, he co-founded Khan Aljanub, an Arabic bookshop and publishing house in Berlin. He lectures on Critical Design and Creative Thinking at the design university, Hochschule für Medien, Kommunikation und Wirtschaft in Berlin. He was a member of Berlin's Art Council (Rat für die Künste) between 2014 and 2016 and has also served on various juries, including the Stuttgart International Festival of Animated Film.

**Hashem Al-Ghaili** is a producer, filmmaker, and science communicator based in Berlin, Germany (and soon Dubai, UAE). Originally from Yemen, Hashem Al-Ghaili graduated from Jacobs University Bremen and earned his master's degree in molecular biology. He uses his knowledge and passion for science to educate the public through social media and video content. His flagship page, Science Nature, has garnered over 33 million followers on Facebook, with his hundreds of original videos viewed over 17 billion times. His sci-fi film short, Simulation, received multiple international awards at film festivals, with his first sci-fi novel, Simulation: The Great Escape, appearing in 2023. He is currently completing his first sci-fi feature film, Orbital. Hashem Al-Ghaili uses his background in science and technology to develop brand-new concepts, including the Sky Cruise Flying Hotel, and the world's first artificial womb facility, EctoLife.

**Amro Ali** is a member of the Arab-German Young Academy of Sciences and Humanities (AGYA), a researcher, and a visiting fellow at Hassan II University of Casablanca. In his work, Amro Ali focuses on Arab public spheres, Mediterranean studies, intellectual history, cities, citizenship, exile, technological modernity, and political philosophy. He received his Ph.D. in political sociology and political philosophy from the University of Sydney. Currently, he is co-writing a book on the Arab exile and intellectual phenomenon in Berlin. His writings can be found at http://www.amroali.com.

**Dr. Mohamed Alwahaib** is a faculty member at the Department of Philosophy at Kuwait University and a member of the Arab-German Young Academy of Sciences and Humanities (AGYA), a facultuy member. He completed his Bachelor of Arts at Kuwait University and his Master of Arts in philosophy at Boston College, earning his Ph.D. in political philosophy at Florida State University. His doctoral dissertation explored the thought of Hannah Arendt.

**Mahmoud Dabdoub** is a photographer known for his emotionally charged, black-and-white photography that explores themes of displacement, hope, and human dignity. Born in Lebanon to Palestinian parents, Mahmoud Dabdoub assisted at the Palestinian Cultural Office in Beirut before going to the GDR in 1981 to study photography at the Academy of Fine Arts, carrying with him nothing but a Praktica LLC. After graduating in 1987, he stayed in Leipzig as a freelance photographer, observing everyday situations. Documenting the hopeless life in the Palestinian refugee camps in Lebanon and Syria for over 20 years was also a matter close to his heart. Since then, his photographic work has been published in magazines and books, including An Archive of Love, as well as in exhibitions in Jerusalem, Berlin, Beirut, and elsewhere. His numerous books include: Alltag in der DDR (Everyday life in the GDR), Wie fern ist Palästina? (How far is Palestine?) and Neue Heimat Leipzig (New home Leipzig). Mahmoud Dabdoub has been recognized through several awards, including silver and bronze medals from Ogoniok magazine and the International Journalists Organization competition in Baghdad.

**Dr. Islam Dayeh** is Assistant professor of Arabic and Islamic studies at Freie Universität Berlin. He received his PhD from FU Berlin in Arabic studies, MA degrees from the University of Leiden (Islamic studies) and the University of Oxford (Jewish studies), as well as a BA from the University of Jordan in Amman. He is the director of the transregional research programme "Zukunftsphilologie: Revisiting the Canons of Textual Scholarship" (2010-), and the founding editor of the journal and monograph series *Philological Encounters* (2016-). In 2022, he was awarded a European Research Council Consolidator-Grant for his project "Polymathy and Interdisciplinarity in Premodern Islamic Epistemic Cultures". He has held visiting professorships and fellowships at Columbia University, the Doha Institute for Graduate Studies, the American University in Cairo, the Library of Congress, the Luxembourg School for Religion & Society and the Maria Sibylla Merian Centre (Mecila) in São Paulo.

**Dr. Ehab El Refaee** (MD, MSc, Dr. med.) is a professor of and consultant for Pediatric Neurosurgery at Cairo University. He also works as the coordinator for the long-standing collaboration between the Greifswald and Cairo universities. After completing his specialized surgical training, he was accredited as a German-certified neurosurgeon in 2015. Ehab El Refaee's outstanding scientific work on nervous system diseases has been complemented by his extraordinary focus on promoting intercultural medical education. He and his colleagues have developed and published unique approaches to modernizing neurosurgical research in postgraduate and undergraduate medical programs. He has received several grants from the DAAD to support his work.

**Julia Gerlach** is a Berlin-based journalist and author. In 2016, she and her sister founded Amal, a local news platform with news reporting in Arabic, Farsi, and since 2022 Ukrainian. Amal started in Berlin and now has branches in Hamburg and Frankfurt. Julia Gerlach was based in Cairo from 2008–15, working as a correspondent for the Arab World, and worked for ZDF heute Journal before that. She earned her degree in political science from Freie Universität Berlin and Aix-en-Provence and trained as a journalist at Berliner Journalistenschule. She has written several books on Arab Uprisings and Young Muslims in Germany.

**Dr. Sonja Hegasy** is Vice Director of the Leibniz-Zentrum Moderner Orient (ZMO) in Berlin. She studied Arabic and Islamic Studies at the American University in Cairo, and the Universities of Witten/Herdecke and Bochum, graduating from Columbia University in 1990 with a thesis on Violent Narratives – Narrative Violence. Her Ph.D. on State, Public Sphere and Civil Society in Morocco was published in German in 1996. Her research and publications focus on modern Arab intellectual thought, civil society, social mobilization, and the politics of memory in post-conflict societies (including Germany). Recent work was published in Memory Studies, Arab Studies Journal, and polylog. Forum für interkulturelles Philosophieren. In 2016 she was a Fulbright Fellow at the City University of New York. From 2019 to 2021 she was the guest professor for Postcolonial Studies at the Barenboim-Said Akademie in Berlin.

In 2023 she was a Fellow at the International Centre of Advanced Studies 'Metamorphoses of the Political' (ICAS:MP) in Delhi.

**Eman Helal** is an Egyptian photographer based in Germany, with experience in breaking news coverage and documentary projects in the Middle East, Africa, and the US focusing on women´s rights and religious minorities. She studied photography at the Danish School of Media and Journalism in 2018 and is currently a master's student at Fachhochschule Bielefeld. She was a Human Rights Fellow at Magnum Foundation between 2013 and 2016. Eman Helal has won several awards, including the Portenier Human Rights Bursary in 2016 and the Egypt Press Photo Award in 2014. Her photographic work has been published worldwide in The New York Times, The Times, Stern, Polka, The Guardian, CNN, and AP. She has had exhibitions in New York, Amsterdam, Barcelona, Seoul, Addis Ababa, New Delhi, Hannover, and Berlin. She served on the TPS, Egypt Press, and Shawkan Photo Awards juries. She is co-author in the books "Our women on the ground" and "Balas para todos".

**Tal Hever-Chybowski** is a historian, editor, and translator who resides in Paris and Berlin. He has been the director of the Paris Yiddish Center—Medem Library (Maison de la culture yiddish—Bibliothèque Medem) since 2014, where he teaches Yiddish literature and Jewish history and culture. In 2016 he founded *Mikan Ve'eylakh: Journal for Diasporic Hebrew* (Berlin & Paris), of which he is editor-in-chief. He is founder and coordinator of "Yiddish in Berlin: Summer Program for Yiddish Language and Literature" at the Free University, Berlin. Recently, he directed the apocalyptic tragicomedy *Jacob Jacobson*, written in Yiddish in 1930 by Aaron Zeitlin, which premiered at Paris' Theater of the Oppressed (Théâtre de l'Opprimé) in October 2021. Currently, he is pursuing a PhD in history at the Georg-August University in Göttingen.

**Abir Kopty** is a journalist and writer, based in Berlin. Abir Kopty completed her BA at Haifa University in economics and accountancy. She then moved to work in the media and communication field in Palestinian civil society organizations. In 2006–2007 she was a Chevening Scholar of the British Council and completed her MA in Political Communication at the City University of London. Currently, she is a PhD candidate in the Institute for Media and Communication Studies, Freie Universität Berlin. Her research interest includes power dynamics in online communities.

**Abdolrahman Omaren**, a journalist and writer of Syrian origin. He worked in several Arab newspapers and magazines, and moved to work on Arab television, but he was forced to leave his country because of the conflict after the Arab Uprisings. Today, he is the editor-in-chief of the Arabic section of the Amal, Berlin! platform. He has many articles published in German newspapers and magazines.

**Dr. Detlev Quintern** (Dr. phil. University Bremen) is Assistant Professor at Turkish German University in Istanbul where he teaches History, Heritage and Museum Studies. His work focusses on universalist history of knowledge, science, ideas and culture, and its musealization. He conceptionalized museum exhibitions in Germany and Turkey. Detlev Quintern is on the editorial board of the "Islamic Philosophy and Occidental Phenomenology in Dialog (IPOP)" series. His latest collectively edited book is "From Marx to Global Marxism: Eurocentrism, Resistance, Postcolonial Criticism" (2020).

**Nazeeha Saeed** is a Bahraini Journalist based in Germany, with more than 23 years' experience in journalism and human rights issues in the Gulf region and the SWANA in general. Nazeeha focus work is on Human rights, politics and gender. She studied English Literature & Psychology in University of Bahrain 2006. Liveing in Exile since 2016 because of her journalist work. Saeed won several awards like Johann-Philipp-Palm- Award for Freedom of Speech and Press 2014, Heikal award for Arab journalism. She is also Journalist Security & Safety, Gender journalism Trainer. Saeed's work could be found on Raseef22, Awmaj.media, Muwatin.net. and other independent platforms. She served on the jury of Interfilm Berlin 36th International Short Film Festival Berlin 2020. She co-wrote "We Shall Bear Witness" and "Kein Land, nirgends".

**Dr. Miriam Stock** (Dr. phil. Europa Universität Viadrina Frankfurt O.) is Professor of Cultural Studies and head of the master's programme "Interculturalism and Integration" at the University of Education Schwäbisch Gmünd. In her research, she focuses on migration and societal transformation between the Middle East and Europe. She has conducted research about urban consumer landscapes, about transnational families, as well as about school participation and interaction of newly migrated families. She has been the head of two EU Erasmus Plus Project "Enable-Tamkin" (2017–2019) as well as "Parentable" (2019–2021) which were both honored as "good practice". Her work is published as monograph at transcript (Der Geschmack der Gentrifizierung, 2013) and diverse journals such as City, Culture and Society and the German Journal for Forced Migration and Refugee Studies. She also co-edits a series at Springer "Migration – Gesellschaft – Schule".

**Dr. Jan Claudius Völkel** (Dr. rer pol. Universität Freiburg) is DAAD Seconded Professor in German Studies and International Relations at the School of Political Studies and the Graduate School of Public and International Affairs, University of Ottawa, Canada. His work focuses on Euro-Mediterranean relations and the contemporary Middle East and North Africa (MENA). Before coming to Ottawa, he was Academic Dean at the Institute for the International Education of Students (IES Abroad) in Freiburg and held positions at Vrije Universiteit Brussel, Cairo University, the European University Institute in Florence, Universität Salzburg and Universität Freiburg. Besides, he is the MENA regional coordinator at the Transformation Index of Bertelsmann-Stiftung (BTI). His articles have been published in European Foreign Affairs Review, the Journal of North African Studies, Mediterranean Politics, Middle East Critique, Middle East Law and Governance, and others. He was awarded the European Union's prestigious Marie Skłodowska-Curie Fellowship in 2017 and is an alumnus of the Arab-German Young Academy of Sciences and Humanities (AGYA).

## Interviewees

**Dr. Nadine Abdalla** is an Assistant Professor of Sociology at the American University in Cairo (AUC), Department of Sociology, Egyptology, and Anthropology (SEA) and AGYA alumna. In 2014, she received her Ph.D. in Political Science from Sciences-Po Grenoble with the highest honors, and in 2006, her MA from Sciences-Po Paris in France. Her research interests include contentious politics, social movements (labor and youth movements), state-society relations, local politics, and bottom-up approaches to democracy in the MENA region, focusing on Egypt and Euro-Med relations. Nadine Abdalla's research papers and articles have been published by distinguished academic journals such as Mediterranean Politics and renowned policy outlets such as the Middle East Institute (MEI) in Washington and the German Institute for International and Security Affairs (SWP) in Berlin. She is working on her book, Labor against the State in Egypt: Workers Mobilizations Post-2004, to be published by Syracuse University Press. She is also a columnist at the Egyptian Daily, Al-Masry al-Youm.

**Younes Al-Amayra** is a comedian, political scientist, and teacher. He co-founded "Datteltäter", a group that produces satiric videos on life in Germany from a Muslim perspective. These videos are part of the FUNK video-on-demand service operated by the German public TV broadcasting service ZDF. In 2019 the group set up Datteltäter Academy, offering social media training to encourage POC talents to succeed in social media. Younes Al-Amayra has trained in deradicalization programs and taught as a schoolteacher.

**Christoph Dinkelaker** is a co-founder of Alsharq Travels. At 16, Christoph Dinkelaker learned about the Middle East during a concert trip to Syria and Lebanon. After this formative experience, he volunteered at a Lebanese orphanage for one year. During that time, he started to guide tours in Lebanon. Having traveled to most MENA countries and focused on the region during his university studies, he combines academic knowledge, language skills, and first-hand experiences there. With Alsharq Travels, he has designed and guided numerous study trips to countries such as Turkey, Iran, Oman, Lebanon, Jordan, Israel, Palestine, Syria, and Northern Iraq.

**Dr. Florian Kohstall** heads the Global Responsibility Unit at the Center for International Cooperation at Freie Universität Berlin. In 2016, he founded Academics in Solidarity, a transnational peer-to-peer mentoring program for displaced scholars. Since 2020, he is responsible for the Berlin Center for Global Engagement, the platform of the Berlin University Alliance. From 2010 to 2015 he directed Freie Universität Berlin's Cairo Office. His research focuses on varieties of internationalization and the politics of higher education reform in the Middle East and North Africa. He has taught political science in Aix-en-Provence, Cairo and Lyon. He is a former research fellow of CEDEJ, the French research center in Cairo, and an alumnus of AGYA, the Arab-German Young Academy of Sciences and Humanities. His recent publications include: "Academics in Exile: Networks, Knowledge Exchange and New Forms of Internationalization", co-edited with Vera Axyonova and Carola Richter, transcript 2022.

**Mahmoud Salem** is blogger and cybersecurity activist. He was in his late twenties when the revolution in Egypt started. He had been blogging anonymously for several years, publishing the "Rantings of a Sandmonkey," and had accumulated 35,000 Twitter followers by February 2011. He described himself on Twitter as a "micro-celebrity, blogger, activist, new media douchebag, pain in the ass!" After what happened, he specialized in cybersecurity and now lives in Berlin.

**Salah Yousif** is a poet and owner of an antique shop. He came to Berlin when the city was at its best: In the Seventies, Berlin was still an Island that attracted interesting people, revolutionaries, and hippies from all over. He came for a stopover and stayed. He started writing when he was thirteen and wrote about his life in Khartoum. Now he is writing about Berlin and its streets and people. He owns a shop in Urban Strasse, selling old cupboards, African handicrafts, and records from his collection.

GPSR Authorized Representative: Easy Access System Europe, Mustamäe tee 50, 10621 Tallinn, Estonia, gpsr.requests@easproject.com

www.ingramcontent.com/pod-product-compliance
Lightning Source LLC
Chambersburg PA
CBHW070054030426
42335CB00016B/1882
* 9 7 8 3 8 3 7 6 6 2 6 3 4 *